always someone to kill the doves

always someone to kill the doves
A LIFE OF SHEILA WATSON

F. T. FLAHIFF

Library and Archives Canada Cataloguing in Publication
Flahiff, F. T. (Frederick Thomas), 1933-
Always someone to kill the doves : a life of Sheila Watson / F.T. Flahiff.

Includes bibliographical references and index.
ISBN 1-896300-83-9

1. Watson, Sheila, 1909-1998. 2. Authors, Canadian (English)--
20th century--Biography. 3. Canada, Western--Biography. I. Title.

PS8545.A88Z63 2005   C813'.54   C2004-907181-5

Editor for the Press: Smaro Kamboureli
Cover and interior design: Ruth Linka
Cover image: Photographer unknown; Digital processing: Matthew Bronson

NeWest Press acknowledges the support of the Canada Council for the Arts and the Alberta Foundation for the
Arts for our publishing program. We also acknowledge the financial support of the Government of Canada
through the Book Publishing Industry Development Program (BPIDP) for our publishing activities.

NeWest Press
201-8540-109 Street
Edmonton, Alberta T6G 1E6
t: (780) 432-9427 / f: (780) 433-3179
www.newestpress.com

1   2   3   4   5   08   07   06   05

PRINTED AND BOUND IN CANADA

Matisse is dead and Utrillo is dead and last month
Picasso had one of his caretakers jailed for destroying
his doves. . . .
Today when I thought how hard it is for an artist to live
at all my heart was filled with compassion. There is
always someone to kill the doves—sometimes merely
a clumsy hand—sometimes, as Simone Weil points out,
pain turned to destruction—or as Iago: 'He has a certain
beauty in his life'.

Sheila Watson,
Paris, 8 November 1955

Table of Contents

Preface

WHEN I INTERVIEWED ONE OF SHEILA WATSON'S FORMER STUDENTS while I was preparing to write this book, she said that she did not envy me the task of writing the life of a saint. When I spoke with a librarian about the possibility of depositing Sheila's papers with her library, she showed no particular enthusiasm for the remains of someone she described as hardly a household name. While I recognized some truth in both these responses, I have remained disinclined to take on the role of hagiographer, or to attempt to market Sheila as a Warhol icon. In writing what I have called "a life" of Sheila Watson, I have assumed rather than argued for her importance. More immediately, I have tried to honour a wish she made to me late in her life when she said, "I want my story told." She did not ask me to undertake this task, but only to ensure that it be performed.

I have taken on this task-not-laid-on-me with the caution of an old friend uncertain of my capacity to distance myself sufficiently to tell Sheila's story. We had been friends for more than forty years, and we had both come from the same small provincial world perched on the western edge of the European legacy: "Western as West can be," in a phrase of Emily Carr from her autobiographical *Growing Pains*, "before earth's gentle rounding pulls West east again." Twenty-four years separated us, but a network made up of family connections, of schools and universities attended, of religion and names and local lore had linked us even before we met. From the beginning, ours was the intimacy of cousins.

What follows is in a double sense partial. My friendship with Sheila and my indebtedness to her have made impartiality impossible. I could have no place on a jury expected to pass an unbiased judgement on her life. I am a witness, rather, attesting to the authenticity, to the genuineness of my subject. My narrative is partial in another sense as well. Because some materials of her life, letters and journals, for example, have been lost or destroyed by her, I have chosen to present what remains rather than to conjecture about what has not survived. I have not had in mind any theoretical framework or precedent for telling her story, only the desire to remain true to what can be known of her. As has happened so often during my life, Sheila herself provided me with a gloss on what I was attempting. In the early fifties in Calgary, she had come upon a two-volume set of lectures given by the French philosopher and playwright Gabriel Marcel entitled *The Mystery of Being*. As I read these to gain some sense of their importance for her, I came upon the following passage in which Marcel reflected on a person's relationship to his or her own past. It seems to me now as applicable to one like myself who has attempted to write of another's past, as it would be to one who would write his or her own life:

> The past cannot be recaptured except in fragments made luminous by a lightning flash, a sudden glare, of memory, for which the fragments are present rather than past; and here, of course, we touch on the central experience around which Proust's great novel was planned and built up. For, though we are given certain such luminous fragments out of the past, the mind, all the same, has to work hard to rebuild the rest of the past around them; and in fact this rebuilding of the past is really a new building, a fresh construction on an old site, modelled more or less on the former edifice there, but not identical with it. What I mean is that it would be an illusion to claim that my life as I turn it into a story corresponds at all completely with my life as I have actually lived it.

If my narrative appears at points fragmentary, it is because I have hesitated to propose connections—what Marcel termed "ready-made developments"—to fabricate an edifice, or to pave over gaps with illusory or, at best, unsubstantiated continuity. This is the main reason I have called this *a life* rather than *a biography*. The roots of *biography* lie in the word's first letters: "Gk *bios* (course of) life." The note of continuity in the word *course*, with the hint of a life sharing the visibility and inevitability of a river, lends to the name *biography* overtones of completeness, or at least of a systematic representation of a life. The term *life*, on the other hand, suggests greater intimacy between what has been led and what is being recorded. My use of the indefinite article is an acknowledgement of the provisional nature of what I have written.

I make no claims to impartiality, then, and I make no claims to completeness. Still, I have attempted to see Sheila Watson whole.

What follows is as much the story of a marriage as it is the story of an artist. That both Sheila and her husband, Wilfred Watson, were writers is simply the first fact in the history of a long, sometimes tortured and always tortuous, relationship. To what extent this relationship inspired or inhibited them as writers is for their readers to decide.

Archives, interviews, and my own memory included, the most important source for this work was contained in banker's boxes of papers Sheila sent me during the years just before her death. She said to me then, "I am sending you my life."

Epilogue as Prologue

ON THE 24 OCTOBER 1998, A CEREMONY OF SORTS TOOK PLACE in central Toronto. The day would have been Sheila Watson's 89th birthday. She had died on the 1st of the previous February, and this ceremony was the final stage in her interment.

Sheila had indicated that she should be cremated. Her niece and confidante Barbara Mitchell, who had been with her when she died, saw to it that this decision was respected. But the question of the disposal of her ashes became complicated when a friend, Sherrill Grace, told Barbara that Sheila had asked that she and her husband scatter her ashes at Dog Creek, the settlement in the Cariboo country of west central British Columbia where Sheila had gone to teach in the mid-thirties, and where her two novels had their origins. Barbara and her mother, Sheila's only sister, Norah, and other members of their family had already decided to scatter her ashes in the Fraser River, near its mouth, at New Westminster, where Sheila was born.

Barbara asked me what I knew of Sheila's wishes. These had been as various as her moods and her interlocutors. Years earlier she had entrusted to me responsibility for her burial, a requiem mass to be followed by interment of a more traditional sort. But later she told me of the arrangement she had made about Dog Creek, and, more recently still, she had said that she supposed she would return to the "salmon people," a comment I took to refer to the Fraser River.

Determined to honour her aunt's wishes, Barbara had Sheila's ashes divided: one portion to go to Dog Creek with Sherrill and John Grace, one portion to be scattered by members of her family in the Fraser River, and a third portion to be given to me to deposit in Toronto.

There was a time when Toronto would have been the last place to which Sheila might have bequeathed anything, much less a part of herself. "Only the most deliberate exercise of caritas would unite me with Toronto in any way," she had written to her husband in the fall of 1956. But time was kind to Toronto and to Sheila's view of it. After her aunt's death, Barbara wrote to me enclosing a final letter she felt compelled to write to her. Because she did not know the area code for heaven, she told me, she had decided to write "care of" Toronto, because Sheila had come to view this city as the next best place to heaven. This is how a third of Sheila's ashes came to rest on my desk for some months while I considered what to do with them.

I did not witness the scattering of Sheila's ashes by water or by wind. Barbara has told me of going out in a small boat with her brothers and sisters, of travelling down river past the now deserted Provincial Hospital for the Insane, where Sheila had spent the first eleven years of her life, of reading aloud her story of that place, "Antigone," which begins: "My father ruled a kingdom on the right bank of the river," while their portion of the ashes—contained in a handsome clay pot made by a friend and used by Sheila as a cookie jar—was committed to the Fraser's currents. The pot was then broken, its shards sharing the fate of its final contents.

Sherrill and John Grace have told me of driving to Dog Creek from their cabin-retreat near Bridge Lake, east of the Cariboo Highway. They inquired at the Post Office/General Store where they might find the site of the school Sheila had taught in. No traces of it remain, but on a low bluff overlooking a declivity where poor ranches lay like discarded beads, they found in the midst of the prickly-pear a solitary tree, likely a white spruce, from which a bird, as if expecting them, shrilly insisted that this was the place. They opened the box containing their share of Sheila's ashes, inviting the breezes to scatter them.

Central Toronto does not lend itself to the type of ritual gesture that the ranch country of central British Columbia or the Fraser River do. I thought of places here that had special significance for Sheila—the University of Toronto, St. Michael's College, Bloor Street—places where she had lived: on Spadina Avenue, Admiral Road, Willcocks Street, Sussex Avenue. I thought of ravines and parks and lakefront spaces. It is a difficult thing to dispose of a third of a friend, especially in a city—where the elements have been subdued or licensed or paved over. I had thought of my own place, but its postage-stamp lot seemed so much less grand than a place of mountains and valleys or the delta of a great river. The ashes remained on my desk until the spring of 1998, when a tree trimmer provided an answer, to at least my question of "where?"

Aside from two Manitoba maples and a mulberry, whose berries are a source of late summer liquorish delight to birds and to squirrels, there stands behind my house what another tree trimmer had identified as an ailanthus. In wet weather it can be, as T. S. Eliot described its kind in "Dry Salvages," "rank." When the May 1998 trimmer gave me his itemized bill for that spring's pruning, he listed the trees as I have described them—all, that is, except the ailanthus. This he listed by its other name: "tree of heaven." I have since learned that such trees once grew in the gardens of the Heavenly City in Peking. They grow tall and straight—even the one behind my house—would-be Jacob's ladders.

A tree of heaven located in the next best place to heaven settled where the ceremony that took place, on what would have been Sheila Watson's 89th birthday, occurred. Three friends joined me. One read the closing passage from the last of Eliot's *Four Quartets* and dug the final resting place for what remained of Sheila's ashes. The others read from Sheila's works: one her "Antigone," and one "Be Fruitful and Multiply" (her translation of Madeline Ferron's "Le peuplement de la terre"), and I read the brief "In Paradisum" from the end of the Mass for the Dead, and we all joined in the burial. Then we drank Irish whisky and ate birthday cake, satisfied that the only third of Sheila not scattered by wind or water rested in Toronto, behind a mid-town house, at the foot of a tree of heaven.

This was not the only observance of Sheila Watson's death in Toronto. On the night after she had died, on the second of February 1998, a group gathered in the small chapel in Elmsley Hall at St. Michael's College to attend a mass concelebrated by her cousin, Father Frank Mallon, and an old friend, Father Charles Leland. This was in fulfilment of a promise I had made to Sheila years before that I would have a mass said for her as soon after her death as possible. Old friends, former students, and a godson were among those present. Her godson Peter Brückmann read the lesson, and Father Leland took as subject for his brief eulogy Christ's Sermon on the Mount and the embodiment in Sheila of the Beatitudes there proclaimed. Afterwards, we toasted her with champagne her friend Corinne McLuhan had brought for the occasion.

Sheila had died, as I have said, on Sunday, 1 February 1998. She had been taken to hospital on the previous Wednesday as the result of a fall and a broken hip. Because she was talking on the telephone when she fell, it is very likely that the fall was occasioned by her hip breaking and not the break by a fall. Her husband, Wilfred, had been in hospital for some days because he too had fallen, although with less painful consequences. His confinement had provided Sheila with something of a respite from caring for him. Sleeping and smoking, she told me, were her recovered pleasures. She had not visited Wilfred, in part because her own difficulty with walking—occasioned by earlier falls—would require the use of a wheelchair at the hospital, which her determination and her vanity balked at. Finally, her doctor, who also attended Wilfred, persuaded her to visit him. After she had been brought home from this visit, their all-but-last meeting, we spoke on the telephone. Not knowing why Wilfred had fallen, I asked if he had had a stroke. "No," she said with uncharacteristic curtness, "he has given up."

And then she said that he had asked her why they had had no children.

I suggested that I come out to Nanaimo, where they lived. "No," she said, and the telephone went dead. I assumed that she had hung up, and took this unexpected gesture as a measure of her agitation. It was some hours later when Barbara Mitchell phoned to tell me that Sheila had in fact fallen, taking the telephone with her. Telephone still in hand, she had been able to contact Wilfred's sister and her husband, who lived close by. They came and called for an ambulance, and took her to hospital.

Because of Sheila's frailty, and because of instructions she had earlier given to him, the doctor did not attempt to set her hip. She was sedated against the pain and soon fell into a coma. Barbara went to Nanaimo from Vancouver, where she lives, and we spoke often during the next few days. On Sunday, the first of February, she telephoned to tell me that Sheila had died. Barbara had been with her, and at the end Sheila had awakened from her coma. With a ghost of a smile, she raised her arms and shook her fists, but said nothing. Then she died. Gestures of defiance? of despair? of celebration? God alone knows.

Wilfred died within two months of Sheila. His wish to be released from hospital was granted when a nurse was found who would stay at the house with him. He died one midnight, attended by the nurse and by his and Sheila's friend Linda Shannon, just as a startled and, for that time of night, a startling flight of birds rose clamorously from the lagoon at the foot of their property. It was, as Linda Shannon remembers it, a serene death, accompanied by no gestures of triumph or despair or defiance.

~ I ~

SHEILA WATSON WAS BORN SHEILA MARTIN DOHERTY IN NEW Westminster, British Columbia, on the Sunday of the Thanksgiving weekend in 1909. Thanksgiving was later in those days—25 October that year—not as now the second Monday of the month. Being a Sunday, there were no newspapers on the day of her birth. On Saturday the 23rd there were headlines in the *Vancouver Province* that told something of the world she was about to be born into, something of its familiarity and something of its strangeness. GREATEST CHANCE FOR HOME RULE one headline declared—Irish optimism then, as now, as familiar as Irish grudges. CZAR NICHOLAS IS WELCOMED TO ITALY—just eight years before the revolution that would see him deposed and with his family assassinated. Closer to home, JEALOUSY CAUSES TRAGEDY IN NORTH introduced a story timeless in its essence, although time-bound in what it could not communicate to its readers about its outcome.

> Enraged by the fancy that Jack Stewart had been paying too much attention to his wife while she was outward bound from Dawson, a man named Boardman shot Stewart in the neck at Skagway on the night of October 15 and then turned his revolver on himself, putting a bullet through his temple on the right side and blowing his left eye clean out of its socket. Both men were Klondike pioneers and both may by this time be dead in hospital in Skagway. News of the tragedy was brought south by the steamer Princess May, which reached port yesterday afternoon from the north.

News and its carriers were provisional and serial then, not identical and instantaneous as they have become.

In the next week, on the first of November, the *Vancouver Province* and the New Westminster *Daily Columbian* reported events that tell of the times. Under the headline ASHES THROWN INTO RIVER, the *Province* carried the following story from Kansas City, Missouri:

> In accordance with his dying request, the ashes of Dr. E. H. Osborne, who died here last week, were thrown into the Missouri river from the Hannibal rail-road bridge here yesterday. His request that all who attended his strange funeral be given a drink was not complied with, as the Sunday liquor laws here forbid it.

The *Daily Columbian*'s story was closer to home. In fact, it was about the home to which Sheila had already come. It was one of a monthly series entitled ASYLUM REPORT.

> The report for the month from the Public Hospital for the Insane at New Westminster shows a decrease in the number of patients by 25. During October a large number have been discharged. There are at present a total of 554 undergoing treatment at the asylum, including 389 males and 165 females. At the beginning of October there were in the asylum 551 patients. 21 were admitted during the month, one returned from probation, one returned from having escaped, 36 were discharged, without probation, 5 were discharged on probation, 14 discharged at the expiry of probation, one was transferred to Vernon, 4 died, and 2 escaped.

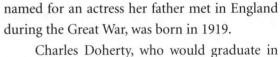

Sheila was the second of four children of Dr. Charles Edward Doherty, who had been born in Toronto in 1873, and of Mary Ida Elwena Martin, born in New Westminster in 1882. Their first child, William Charles (Bill), had been born in 1908; their third child, Charles Edward (Kelly), in 1912. Their fourth child, Norah, said to have been named for an actress her father met in England during the Great War, was born in 1919.

Dr. Charles Edward Doherty

Charles Doherty, who would graduate in medicine from the University of Toronto in 1899, had come to British Columbia in 1898 to serve his internship as assistant medical officer of the Crow's Nest Pass Coal Company in Nelson. He then joined the staff of the Kootenay General Hospital in the same city until, in 1905, at the age of thirty-two, he was appointed medical superintendent of the Public Hospital for the Insane in New Westminster. Shortly after this, a younger brother, Frederick, assumed an equivalent position in a similar hospital nearby, in Cedro Wooley, Washington, a position which had at first been offered to his brother Charles.

Their great grandfather, Bernard Doherty

(the original Celtic spelling was O'Dochartaigh, which has been anglicised as Docharty, Dogherty, Doherty, Dougherty, and O'Dogherty), had, with his wife and six sons, emigrated from Donegal, Ireland, in about 1812 to what is now southern Ontario. He rejected, "scornfully" it is said, as "too low and wet to be suitable for agricultural purposes," a grant of land which today forms a significant part of downtown Toronto: bounded on the south by Queen Street, on the east by Yonge Street, on the west by University Avenue, and on the north by College Street. Instead, Bernard Doherty settled on five hundred acres at Dixie in Peel County, where he farmed with some success. He was recently in the news when, in 2000–2001, he and his co-habitants in the old 5th-line Catholic cemetery, that long lay under what is now Toronto's Pearson International Airport, were removed to a quieter resting place.

Bernard's son Charles Frederick Doherty succeeded to his father's farm and oversaw the building of a stone house in 1844 to replace the log cabin that had originally stood on the property. Before this, however, Charles Frederick had gained a niche in Canadian history by driving William Lyon Mackenzie, who was fleeing to the border after the collapse of his cause in Toronto, "from Willcock's Farm at Dixie on Dundas Street, as far west as the Sixteen Mile Creek." It was a brave or a reckless act—or a bit of both.

Bernard's son William Frederick, Sheila's grandfather, maintained the family farm, and he is believed to have established an organ and piano factory. His marriage to Maria Henley saw the birth of seven children, three sons and four daughters, of whom Charles Edward was the eldest. A sister and a brother, Agatha and Frederick, like him, took degrees in medicine from the University of Toronto. Another sister, Marguerite, became a nurse, and in the 1920s presided over the infirmary at St. Michael's College in the same university. His brother William Manning Doherty, who was next in age to Charles Edward, lectured at the Ontario Agricultural College before becoming a stockbroker and founding partner in the firm of Doherty, Roadhouse. For a time, Manning, as he was called, was Minister of Agriculture in the provincial government formed by the United Farmers of Ontario. When this government was defeated in 1924, he became, for a time, Leader of the Opposition in the Ontario legislature.

Sheila and her sister and brothers knew more of the history of their mother's family than of their father's. The nature of what they knew of their Martin ancestors was, however, a mixture of verifiable fact and splendid perhapses. Samuel Barclay Martin, their grandfather, had come with a cousin from northern California to British Columbia in 1877. According to family lore, he had been banished by his father, whose full name he bore, because father and son were vying for the attentions of the same actress.

The cousin with whom young Martin came north, Marshall Martin English, appears to have been the more enterprising of the two young men. Shortly after their arrival, he built a fish cannery across the Fraser River from New Westminster, and established a "fish camp" nearer the mouth of the river, where native fishermen caught what he then canned. This was perhaps the first cannery on the Fraser. A few years later, in 1882, he moved his operations closer to his fish camp, building what was certainly the first cannery in what soon became known as Steveston. A family taste for mythology was reflected in the name they chose for the cannery: the Phoenix. Samuel Barclay, junior, was his partner in this venture, as it was his father's money that had financed these undertakings.

The Martin money had come originally from cotton. Samuel Barclay, senior, had owned a large plantation in North Carolina before he moved to Demopolis, Alabama, where his son was born in 1853, and then with his family to the San Francisco area of California after the Civil War. Lore hangs like Spanish moss on young Sam Barclay's early life, hardly distinguishable from what it feeds upon. His mother, Eliza Kearns, is believed to have helped slaves on their plantation escape to Nova Scotia by means of the underground railway. Her descendants have long believed this, and that somewhere in the South a statue was erected to commemorate her actions. Her son, and Sheila's grandfather, Samuel Barclay, junior, as a boy is said to have witnessed one of the battles of the Civil War from his perch on a fence. He is also said to have been in the audience at the Ford Theatre in Washington on Friday, 14 April 1866, the night that President Lincoln was assassinated. He would just have turned thirteen on 21 March of that year. In the next year, 1867, he is said to have been sent abroad—to take the Grand Tour, according to one family member, or, according to another, to attend the University of Heidelberg. Either he went alone or with his sister, Elwena, his only sibling. Sheila maintained that his sister attended school in Paris while he studied in Germany. All, including Sheila's sister and at least two of her daughters, agree, however, that Samuel, alone or with Elwena, crossed the Atlantic in the company of Samuel Clemens/Mark Twain, who documented this journey in *Innocents Abroad*.

The rest of Samuel Barclay Martin's life is less eventful, perhaps because it is more easily documented. He married Ida Theresa Macaulay, daughter of an Ontario timber baron, who had come west to stay with relatives in Victoria. They had five children, of whom Sheila's mother was the eldest. Both his and his cousin Marshall

English's families settled on Lulu Island (named for yet another actress, and now known as Richmond), near their cannery and fishing camp. As they had thirteen children between them, the provincial government permitted the cousins to establish a school—what became known as the English School—to accommodate them and the few children of other Caucasian settlers on an island in the delta of the Fraser which was largely inhabited by native and Japanese fishermen. The school's first teacher was English's eldest child, Anna Virginia.

In time, bad feelings developed between the cousins, and they and their families went their separate ways—the English family to New Westminster and the Martins to Victoria, where Sam took a modest position with the provincial government. It was here that Sheila's mother

Ida Mary Elwena Martin

grew up and received her education. This was at the hands of the Sisters of St. Ann, at what was then the only private girls school in Victoria, St. Ann's Academy.

Ida Mary Elwena Martin, or Ween as she came to be called, received an education suited to her family's standing and to their somewhat reduced circumstances. Aside from traditional academic subjects (including Latin and French), she received training in what were recognized as the womanly subjects of music and drawing and, more surprisingly perhaps, in such "commercial" subjects as typing, shorthand, and bookkeeping. Even at the time of the school's founding, in 1858, the program of studies listed the two branches of arithmetic as "practical and rational."

If Ween Martin was not the witness to earth-shaking events that her father had been, she did remember having her face tickled by the whiskers of Rudyard Kipling when he visited their home and sat her on his knee. And she did know Emily Carr and was, in her own words, "great friends" with her nieces. Moreover, in her own right, the fact that she was a whiz at typing (68 WPM) and shorthand (120 WPM) is a part of her family's lore. But perhaps the most intriguing evidence of the effectiveness of her early education comes from the nuns themselves. Many years later, in the mid-1930s, when Ween (now Doherty and a widow) was living in New Westminster, a certain priest in Vancouver—who was enormously popular and very bright, and who had, incidentally, baptized Sheila—left the priesthood to marry. As he had received no dispensation from his priestly vows, he was subject to excommunication, and canon law required that public notice be given of this. The popularity of the priest and the nature of his circumstances aroused great curiosity, which was scarcely satisfied by the fact that the detailing of these circumstances in the diocesan newspaper was in Latin. Ween hurried to St. Ann's Academy in New Westminster—which had been attended by her daughters—newspaper in hand, in order to translate the notice for those nuns whose Latin was not up to hers. She was, in the words of a nun who was witness to this, and who told me of it, "a smart lady."

Near the end of her life, in a letter to Sheila, Ween looked back on "those good old days in Victoria." Despite its distance from England and its rough, colonial status, Victoria then sounds more like Jane Austen's Meryton than like a remote outpost of the Empire—Meryton with sailors rather than with soldiers. The Martins lived in the nearby municipality of Esquimalt, headquarters of the British Fleet in the Pacific, and Ween and her sisters enjoyed the attentions of young midshipmen, who were deemed appropriate companions for them. Her father, for all his fecklessness, seems at first glance to have been more discerning than Austen's Mr. Bennet; when Ween appeared to have become too attached to one young man, he sent her off for a year to stay with an aunt and uncle who lived near San Francisco. Her aunt, a sickly woman, was her father's sister, the same who had possibly studied in Paris while her brother possibly studied in Heidelberg. Her husband, Thomas Phelps, was an Admiral in the United States Navy, and they lived at the Mare Island Naval Yard, north of San Francisco. According to Ween's daughter Norah, "There were young men everywhere, [her uncle] was very often overseas, and [her aunt] was an invalid."

By the time Ween returned from California, her father had reconciled with his cousin and had moved his family to New Westminster. It was here that she met Charlie Doherty, and they were married on April Fool's Day, 1907.

⤚

Sheila's father, as well she knew, was the stuff of myth. In 1910, when she was just a year old, an article about him and his stewardship of the New Westminster hospital appeared in a journal formerly named *Westward Ho!* though by then called *Man to Man: An Index to Opportunity*. The article was written by an obviously transplanted Englishman named H. Sheridan-Bickers, and it was entitled "The Treatment of the Insane: Farming as a cure for madness—British Columbia's novel experiment." The centrepiece of the article is an interview with Dr. Doherty, who is described in suitably heroic terms:

> Dr. Charles E. Doherty is a young man with the courage, enthusiasm and virility of youth, combined with the keen perception, sagacity and self-reliance of experience. A man of the world in the best sense, he strikes one at once with a suggestion of a dominant individuality—intensely alive and full of peculiar magnetism and reserve power. Big-framed, blue-eyed and fresh-complexioned, he is a living advertisement of his views on health, preservation and mind development.

Those views, at least where the treatment of mental illness was concerned, were revolutionary. The article allows Doherty to speak of them in his own words:

> Repressive measures such as confinement and punishment are, to my mind, as ineffective as they are unjust. They are morally an outrage to helpless sufferers, medically unsound, and at times fatal. Since I became superintendent in 1905 I have endeavored to adopt the methods of the general hospital rather than [those] of an asylum.
>
> I have removed the eighteen-foot fence that formerly surrounded the hospital and the gates are unlocked during the day, leaving the patients, except, of course, the acute cases, to come and go more or less as they pleased. . . .
>
> I am willing, indeed proud, to admit that I am now putting in vogue a system where not a door of a single room or dormitory is closed at night, and every patient can use the toilet rooms, drinking water, etc., as in the day time. Throughout my regime I have attempted to prove the feasibility and wisdom of handling acute maniacal cases by hydro-therapeutic measures and to abolish mechanical restraint.

His approach was "to adopt the methods of the general hospital rather than [those] of an asylum"—or, for that matter, of a prison. Patients had formerly been locked up at night and left without access to toilets or drinking water—only to be punished for and humiliated by what such confinement resulted in. Ten years before his arrival, such devices as "handcuffs, leather mitts, pinion straps, camisoles, and straight jackets, with the cruel rope called 'the Martingale' that could be used as a strangulation device, were in almost daily use." Dr. Doherty's moral outrage, combined with his energy, his practicality, the clarity with which he perceived the situation, led to reforms that saw him hailed at the time of his death, only ten years after this interview, as "one of the foremost alienists of America," and his hospital as "one of the greatest mental institutions on the continent."

Aside from removing locks and disposing of strait-jackets, Dr. Doherty started an orchestra in the hospital and, in what Sheridan-Bickers exuberantly described as "the biggest adventure in mental therapeutics that has been heard of since the days of the Apostles," he established the Colony Farm, a dairy farm run by inmates of the hospital.

> We have hitherto prided ourselves in Canada that it was the sanity of our agriculturists that made farming so profitable. [Sheridan-Bickers declared:] Now we are to test the theory that it is *the* agricultural work that accounts for the sanity of our farmers.

If this was not precisely what Doherty intended, contact with the soil and livestock, of which he had had experience in his youth, was to provide a type of occupational therapy which would help to heal the patients minds as it prepared them to find work once they had been released. The *Farmer's Advocate* for December 1912 described the farm as possessing "the best equipped barns, stables, dairy equipment, and yards in Canada, if not the continent," and a dairy herd which was among the most prized on the continent.

From New Westminster, Sheridan-Bickers invoked the old Westminster in his praise and justification of Doherty's methods:

> Treat a man as a responsible citizen and he will endeavor to justify that confidence. . . . Home Rule is the secret of the success of British administration throughout the world. Mutual trust and self-reliance are the bedrock on which the British Empire stands— supreme, united and invincible. So do we see that the dignity of labor and the proud spirit of individual responsibility which work begets are the hall-marks of the colonist. Self-expression is the father of self-reliance, and self-reliance is the mark of the man.

What Charles Edward Doherty thought of the way his methods were contextualized is impossible to know. He spoke of moral outrage at the treatment of helpless sufferers as occasioning his reforms. Others, Sheridan-Bickers and even Sheila in her "Antigone," viewed what he accomplished in imperial terms as well.

After their marriage and a wedding trip to the East, Charlie and Ween settled in the superintendent's quarters, in an ivy-covered tower at the hospital, where they lived until his death in 1920. It was a manor house set in a lunatic estate. The furnishings were the last word in fashion: mission oak crafted according to William Morris designs. There was a Chinese cook, Hong, and, when the babies came, a Scottish nurse as well. The gardens were cared for by patients who did not require confinement. Charlie bought Ween a horse and carriage, and there was a groom to take care of these. When there were automobiles, there was a chauffeur. Qualities that Sheridan-Bickers recognized in him—"intensely alive and full of peculiar magnetism and reserve power"—made Charlie an exciting but not always an easy person to live with.

He was a man comfortable in the company of men. He loved sports, and in 1912 he was on the board of the local hockey team, the New Westminster Royals, when they won their Pacific Coast League championship. His position and his lobbying for his projects required him to become familiar with all levels of government. He worked closely with the provincial Minister of Health, Dr. Henry Esson Young, in building the farm and a new hospital. Among his friends was the Premier of British Columbia, Richard McBride, later Sir Richard McBride, whose home was also in New Westminster. McBride was as energetic and as enterprising as Doherty, and he supported the innovations the latter was set on making. He was three years older than Charlie and had become premier at thirty-two, Charlie's age when he became superintendent of the hospital. They died, the premier in 1917 and Charlie in 1920, both at the age of forty-seven.

In biographical notes she wrote for McClelland & Stewart at the time of the publication of *The Double Hook,* Sheila recalled her father and her childhood in his domain:

> I admired my father because he was always busy and could not be disturbed. He was, I knew even then, engaged in some sort of revolution . . .
>
> The hospital was built on a hill looking down on the Fraser river. Here we watched the trains, the men fishing for oolichans and the great booms of logs headed for the sawmill. Here, too, we peered over the walls into the outer grounds of the penitentiary, for the grounds of the hospital and the penitentiary were separated only by

a fence. On the high walls of the inner enclosure we could see the guards keeping watch with their guns.

Sometimes we went with our nurse for walks in the cemetery, which like Chinese cemeteries was placed on the hill. When we were bored we escaped into the earth-smelling greenhouse to talk to Mr. Booth, the gardener, or even farther off to steal rhubarb out of the vegetable gardens and to watch the men working in the cobbler's and the carpenter's shop. Every night our mother read to us.

In an interview with George Melnyk, in Edmonton in the early 1970s, Sheila elaborated on her reference to their excursions to the cemetery, which had become a staple of their outings with their Scottish nurse. "This went on for several years," she recalled,

until my younger brother wrote to Santa Claus asking for a grave with a chain around it. Then our walks changed. So we were taken to the Fraser River Bridge instead. . . . The bridge had a swing span and my brothers hoped that we'd get there just as the span began to open up. I was terrified. I was always afraid I'd fall through cracks in the bridge.

Perhaps the most suggestive of her memories of this time and this place, and especially of her father, was recorded by Bruce Meyer and Brian O'Riordan in a 1984 interview with Sheila:

I remember when I was small we had a pony which one of the patients named Jack looked after. I remember my father called me in to his office and said, "What did you say to Jack?" And I must have had a bad conscience about it and admitted, "I said 'You're crazy Jack.'" But I just meant it in a general sense, without thinking. And my father just looked at me and said, "It is not what you mean, it is what you say."

"I can still hear him now," she recalled. "It is not what you mean, it is what you say. For people can only interpret what you *say* to them. That was the most fundamental single influence on my attitude to language."

One of Sheila's earliest memories—according to the notes she wrote for McClelland & Stewart—was of "the dark night [in 1914] when my father left from Coquitlam with the first New Westminster contingent for France." She was five then, her brother Bill was six, and her brother Kelly, two. The "contingent" was the 104th

14

Westminster Fusiliers of Canada, later known as The Westminster Regiment, and Charlie Doherty joined it with the rank of Major. He and his fellow Fusiliers were, in the words of his daughter Norah, "loyal to the King and would do anything to preserve the Empire. They had all come from a long royalist tradition and were prepared to die if necessary."

Dr. C. E. Doherty (on the right), in France, with the Canadian Medical Corps during World War I.

His medical experience and his administrative skills qualified him for his new duties: he was appointed to supervise the setting up and running of Canadian tent hospitals in France. Some sense of the good-humoured esteem in which he was held in this post by his staff is suggested by a photograph of him in uniform. The photo has been touched up—a green shamrock has been added to a lapel, and green and gold ribbons to his jacket. An inscription reads: "Presented to Major C. E. Doherty, ADMS / March 17, 1917 / On the occasion of the UNOFFICIAL report that he had settled the IRISH QUESTION. (See tomorrow's "JOHN BULL") / 'Leave Ulster to me!' (CED)." At the same time as his work overseas, he remained titular head of the mental hospital, now named Essondale for Dr. Esson Young. With a base in London and responsibilities to Ottawa and in New Westminster, Major Doherty made at least seven trans-Atlantic and trans-continental crossings in the course of the war. Early in 1918, before the war's end, he was called back to British Columbia to become Director of Medical Services for the province. By this time he had been promoted to the rank of Lieutenant Colonel, and he had been mentioned in dispatches to the King. But all this was at a price. Little more than a year and a half after his return, he was dead, at the age of forty-seven, of what was then called interstitial nephritis, or Bright's disease.

He died on 12 August 1920, and his funeral took place on 18 August. It was a military funeral with elements of a state funeral: a lying-in-state, a gun carriage for his casket, and a riderless horse. The Vancouver and the New Westminster newspapers mourned his passing by chronicling his achievements. His methods of treating his patients, in the words of the *Vancouver Province* (Monday, 20 August 1920),

have now been largely adopted throughout the world. At the recent

Canadian medical convention in Vancouver, the chairman of the Dominion committee on mental hygiene declared that Dr. Doherty was without a peer in the Dominion or probably in America in his chosen field.

The *Vancouver Sun* on the same day struck a more personal note:

> The members of his staff and employees worshipped him and his death has cast a shadow of gloom over the entire establishment. Among returned veterans he was considered a man in every respect and one and all realize that they have lost a staunch comrade and friend.

The respect and the affection of his staff at the hospital resulted in a remarkable gesture. They raised money to buy a large granite headstone for Dr. Doherty's grave, in that same cemetery where the children's nurse used to take them for walks, "high on the hill" as Sheila described it, overlooking the Fraser River. But Ween was troubled by the stone—not by the circumstances of its purchase, but by its size. She was afraid it would be too heavy for Charlie to bear.

⤸

Sheila was ten when her father died. Like her mother and her brothers, she had lived with his absences during the war, but they had lived in this place of his making—where he remained even when absent—in their privileged status and in the evidence of his jurisdiction. Readers of "Antigone," which has its roots in this place, and which was to her mind the most fully realized of her fictions, might wonder about the relationship between the convivial and humane revolutionary who was her father and the martinet who is the story's father-king. Suffice it to say that through the latter's veins runs the blood of Sophocles' Creon as well as the blood of Charles Edward Doherty.

Sheila came to associate her father's last illness with her own earliest writing:

> The year my father was ill I was sent to stay with my cousins [the family of her Uncle Henry and Aunt Fan Doyle, a daughter of her great uncle Marshall English and Sheila's godmother] at Chewasin. It was at this time I began to write as most children. I wrote, I remember, a story of a man who died in a swamp for reasons which I have now forgotten. We all wrote. One cousin, a boy younger than I was by a year, was engaged with a typewriter and the *Encyclopaedia*

Britannica in compiling a history of the Mamelukes. Another cousin and I wrote a story about a mouse. My cousins' father had a large library. He let us read anything we wanted to read.

At another time, she recalled them all writing there, reclining on tree branches.

⸜⸝

When Charlie Doherty died, his widow was left with four children and very little else. There was no pension, either from the provincial government or from the Canadian military. He had bought an insurance policy, which paid $85 a month, but this did not go far in providing for five people. What is more, Ween was given six months to vacate their quarters in the hospital—for a life without cook and nurse and gardener and groom. The acumen she had shown in the commerce program in her youth in Victoria did not signal a practical nature. And what is more, since her marriage thirteen years earlier, she had led a very sheltered life. To paraphrase her daughter Norah, Ween before Charlie's final illness and her early widowhood, had had babies and she had had fun. And she had been taken care of.

Ween had family and she had friends, and with their assistance she moved with her children to a house on 5th Avenue in New Westminster, where they lived for a year before moving to a larger and more convenient house at 56 Merrivale Street, where they lived for the next fifteen years. At the time of their father's death, Sheila and her older brother, Bill, were in school at St. Ann's Academy. Charlie had not approved of children starting school too early. He had believed they must be given time to develop their own natures, their own sense of themselves, before being subjected to the inevitable manipulations of any educational system. Accordingly, Sheila was seven (ten in the biographical notes she wrote for McClelland & Stewart) and her brother eight when they went as day students to be taught by the same order of nuns that had taught their mother in Victoria. Sheila was to remain at St. Ann's Academy through high school, but her brother moved to a boys school, St. Louis College, which was located directly behind their Merrivale street house. Her younger brother, Kelly, was educated largely in public schools, perhaps because more tuition was out of the question. Norah, the youngest, started in grade one at the Academy in 1926, the year before Sheila graduated. Norah doubted that her tuition was ever paid.

Memories of their mother and of their home life during those years vary with the recollections of the sisters, the principal witnesses to that time. Aside from a

Sheila with her brothers, Bill (left) and Charles Edward (Kelly),
at Crescent Beach, south of Vancouver.

general sense that her mother had gone to bed for a year after her father's death, leaving her largely responsible for the care of her siblings, Sheila remembered specific incidents: starting a fire in her bed one night when she attempted to read by candle light under the covers; having scalding tea poured on her back by a distraught mother when she—Sheila—had to tell her that a colleague of her late husband who had become attentive to Ween had, like Charlie, died young. Sheila's memories of this double abandonment—in death in her father's case and into grief in her mother's—combined with her sense of responsibility for her brothers and her very young sister to form a sense of a childhood cut short which she never lost.

Norah was not yet two years old when their father died. Her memories are less complex than those of her eleven-year-old sister. She remembers attentions paid to their mother, but with less dreadful consequences than Sheila had experienced (who did bear the mark of the scalding tea for the rest of her life). Norah recalls a man named Dan who, although married, came to call and sent Ween a dozen red roses every Christmas for many years. Photographs—except an early one (p. 9)—give little sense of what must have been her charms. She was not a beautiful woman, nor was she a woman of means, and she did have four children.

Norah's earliest memory was from the year they lived on 5th Avenue: "I recall sitting on the bottom step of a long staircase watching mum wash clothes in the bathroom across the hall. She was on her knees beside the bathtub sloshing the clothes around . . . I had never seen her do such a thing before." Norah believed that her mother "lived on an emotional roller-coaster": "there were many tears and some-times a lot of fury. I think we were kind of scared as well as sorry for her at the same time. I know that none of us ever felt very secure especially when we saw the bills pil-ing up in the front hall. There was always a sense of impending doom." Still, their mother "was always there for all of us."

One of the nuns from St. Ann's Academy, Sister Mary Patricia, came for a time to help with the cooking and the washing. And then a Mrs. Crick was found to do the ironing, and a Chinese gentleman to mow the grass, wash the kitchen floor, and occasionally cook. Ween and her brood made do.

~ II ~

THE ST. ANN'S ACADEMY SHEILA ATTENDED WAS AS SIMILAR TO and different from the Academy attended by her mother as New Westminster was both like and unlike Victoria. New Westminster, or the Royal City as it liked to be called, had been named by Queen Victoria and had been the first capital of the colony of British Columbia. When the Crown Colony of Vancouver Island joined with the mainland in 1866, its seat of government, Victoria, became the capital of the new province of British Columbia. Both cities were ports, and this was their only resemblance. Victoria retained the air and the customs of an English garrison town. It had developed from a fort of the Hudson's Bay Company into the centre of operations for the British Pacific fleet. Rank was of great importance there—of greater importance, even, than money.

New Westminster's connections with the Old Country were more distant: more populist and more festive. They had to do with maypoles and May Queens rather than with an actual British presence. The city derived its identity and livelihood from the river and its commerce. Sawmills and canneries lined the Fraser, as well as docks and, increasingly, factories. One made money in New Westminster, and one retired to Victoria.

St. Ann's Victoria was the parent school: it had been established in 1858. St. Ann's New Westminster was opened in 1865 by two nuns who had come from Victoria. They were members of an order which had been founded in 1850 in Quebec. Details from the first prospectus they drew up for their Victoria school are worth noting:

> Reading, Writing, Arithmetic, practical and rational, Book Keeping, Geography, Grammar, Rhetoric, History, Natural History, English, French, plain and ornamental Needle and Net Work in all their different shapes, will form the course of studies in this institution. [Music and Drawing were to be included "ere long."]
>
> The disciplinary government will be mild, yet sufficiently energetic to preserve that good order so essential to the well-being of the Institution.
>
> Parents may rest assured that every necessary attention will be paid to the comfort of Pupils, whilst the utmost care will be taken to nourish in their minds those principles of virtue and morality which alone can make education profitable.

The Sisters are also prepared to attend to the sick at any time their services are needed.

Difference of Religion is no obstacle to admission into the Institution, but whilst pupils are left, without interference, to follow their own profession, good order requires that they should conform to the general regulations of the establishment. . . .

Destitute Orphans will be received GRATIS as Day Schollars; and parents actually not able to pay are requested to call at the Establishment.

If a prospectus drawn up in 1858 seems remote from the schooling of Ween, and especially of her daughters, the extent to which it defined the ethos in which Sheila received her early education is reflected in a document which appeared during her time at the New Westminster Academy. In 1924, the order published at its mother house in Lachine, Quebec, *Rules of Christian Pedagogy for the Sisters of St. Ann.* It was addressed to the nuns engaged in teaching, rather than to the parents of prospective students. Like the 1858 prospectus, it is very much of its time, while remaining free of some, although certainly not all, of the prejudices of those times. It contains the following "mission" statement:

> The aim of this mission is to train good scholars and true Christians. In the case of girls, teach them to be satisfied with little, to live within their means, to like manual work; make them realize that a woman should be able to sacrifice her inclinations for the happiness of others; in short, bring them to understand the seriousness of life's duties. . . . In mixed schools of boys and girls, rewards or penalties based on difference of sex are more detrimental than helpful. They are more apt to wound than correct.

The *Rules* propose as the "first great principle of education: 'Example is better than precept.'" and then glosses this rather intriguingly in visual terms. "This is especially true with children," it maintains: "What they see strikes them more than what they hear." They "are both sharp observers and ready imitators." Teachers are encouraged to "speak a great deal to the eyes of the children." One consequence of this emphasis was the importance the nuns attached to the visual arts. They had introduced the first art classes on Vancouver Island. The extent to which painting was a part of the *lingua communis* shared by those educated by the Sisters of St. Ann is suggested in a brief, two-paragraph essay Sheila wrote in 1932 for a volume honouring the New Westminster Academy. She had graduated five years earlier and was then attending the University of British Columbia in Vancouver. Her first publication, it is entitled "Memories of Our Alma Mater," and it begins thus:

> It is impossible to forget your childhood—vivid memories— crimson streaks, purple-grey—a picture in the cubist style, if you will. I remember clearly my first day at school. My last day there is not stamped more clearly in my mind. All our memories indeed are much the same. We lived together for some ten years— why shouldn't they be? It is the emphasis only which varies. You may have a splotch of gold where I have only a yellow shadow, that is all.

The 1924 *Rules of Pedagogy* proposed a holistic approach to education which involved "the harmonious development of the child's faculties: memory, imagination, sensitiveness, taste." Of these faculties, imagination was deemed a sort of double hook: capable of magnifying and distorting, it was at the same time essential to the discovery of "the great educational factor, beauty." Literature shared in imagination's ambiguous nature. It could tend to "sensualism, materialism, and rationalism," as the document judged that the literature of the times did, but to neglect its study was to starve the soul.

Music and dance were also parts of the curriculum, the latter under the designation "Physical Culture." A lay woman, Grace Goddard, a devotee who had perhaps even been a student of Isadora Duncan, led the bare-footed and be-togaed girls in exploring the freedom of movement championed by her mentor. Sheila recalled her own efforts in this area with a kind of zany fondness—loving to strike poses that confirmed her own sense of herself as a daughter of her time. Her relations with her piano teacher were, according to an account she gave to a friend years later, less happy:

> when I was young and struggling to master the piano, I longed to play Beethoven's bagatelles. . . . Miss Ethel Homer, who looked like a sparrow and had a hand like a sledge hammer, kept me playing Schumann. I hated Schumann and his beastly "impromptus" and didn't have sense enough to master him out of the way so to speak.

Sheila entered the Academy in 1917 and graduated in 1927, satisfying the normally twelve-year program in ten years. The curriculum was as prescribed by the provincial Department of Education, supplemented by such subjects as Christian

Doctrine and Church History. She was a good student, standing always near the top of her class, although occasionally Latin Grammar and Arithmetic nearly undid her. She was seldom absent or late. She consistently won prizes. In her second-to-last year, for example, in an essay contest which included the Catholic schools of Greater Vancouver, she won second prize. In that same year, at commencement exercises, she was awarded a gold cross "for Liturgy of the Mass," which appears to have been a part of her Church History course. In most respects, her education by the nuns was very traditional.

The school was a short walk from Merrivale Street. It was majestically located on Albert Crescent, looking down on the river and its bridges. It was, as she was later to write in "Antigone," close by the entrance to her father's kingdom. Above it was the cemetery, and below, in a square of grass, stood a statue of Simon Fraser surveying his river.

Where St. Ann's New Westminster differed from its parent school in Victoria was in its relationship to the life of its city. Despite being something of a Catholic island in a Protestant sea, it very early took its place in the Royal City's affairs. Between 1871 and 1935, twelve of its students were chosen May Queens, which, in the eyes of many, was the highest honour the city could bestow. And one of its first boarders figured in an episode which in the history of New Westminster holds a place reminiscent of the abduction of Helen in the history of Troy.

On Sunday, 19 March 1877, amid the cries of Sister Mary Praxiletes, sixteen-year-old Emma Keary bolted from a crocodile of St. Ann's boarders making its way across the Crescent into a waiting carriage and the arms of her twenty-seven-year-old—and Protestant—abductor, George Ward de Beck. They hastened to the river, where de Beck had arranged for a tug, the Leonora, to take them to the south bank. They continued their journey until they crossed the border into Washington state and reached Port Townsend, where de Beck had made arrangements for their marriage. Leaving nothing to chance, he had bribed two loggers with a bottle of liquor to cut the telegraph lines connecting New Westminster with the United States so that Emma's family could not reach American authorities and spoil his plan. The bribe worked, for some say that two miles of telegraph wires lay upon the ground between the river and the border.

The couple was married on that same day and shortly after returned to New Westminster, where they were forgiven—for what else was there to do? There was no call for "burning towers and Agamemnon dead." In 1937, Emma and George de Beck celebrated their sixtieth wedding anniversary.

The abduction of Emma was a part of St. Ann's Academy lore when Sheila was a student there. Although it had happened forty years before she started school, it was made more immediate to her by the fact that the Keary family lived two doors from the Dohertys when they moved to Merrivale Street. That the narrator of "Antigone" should find "Helen who'd been hatched from an egg" walking naked among the chestnut trees of his father's kingdom seems somehow less surprising, less aberrant, when one considers New Westminster as a place of her abduction.

Less romantic, although no less surprising as evidence of the Academy's relationship to this place, is an article in *The Daily Columbian* dated 5 March 1926. It tells of a program undertaken by the school whereby students were to visit local industries. They were to tour plants, a gypsum plant and Westminster Paper Mills, for example, in order to gain first-hand experience of manufacturing processes—the better to understand economic and social conditions presumably—as well as the processes themselves. At this point, Sheila was in her second last year at St. Ann's. There is no evidence of her participating—or not participating—in any of these excursions. Regardless, the program itself was symptomatic of the Academy's—and the nuns'—sense of what every young woman should know.

⌒

When Sheila graduated from St. Ann's Academy, instead of going on to the University of British Columbia, she attended the Convent of the Sacred Heart in Vancouver, which offered the equivalent of the first two years of undergraduate Arts in a less secular setting than that afforded by the University. According to Sheila, she was a boarder during these two years, although her sister, Norah, remembered her going daily by tram from New Westminster—an exhausting even if a more economical solution to the family's continuing state of insolvency. The memory of a student at the Convent during these years—of Sheila Doherty falling asleep in classrooms, in hallways, in the grounds—lends credibility to Norah's version.

Mesdames du Sacré Coeur, or the Mothers as they were called, was a French order of nuns which had been expelled from France in the nineteenth century, which, in time, relocated its Mother House in Rome, where it still stands at the top of the Spanish Steps. Its members came originally from aristocratic families, and its mission remained the education of Christian gentlewomen. They would have been less inclined than the Sisters of St. Ann to encourage commercial courses, or visits to factories. In Canada they had schools in Halifax, Montreal (where they had two schools), Winnipeg, and in Vancouver. They had schools and colleges throughout the United States, in Britain and on the continent, in South America (it is in the gardens of their convent in Buenos Aires that nightingales sing to Eliot's Sweeney), and even in Egypt and Japan. In short, they were as cosmopolitan as the Sisters of St. Ann were regional. In Sheila's day, every member of the order went to Rome to make her final vows.

The Mothers were thought, and even thought of themselves, as female Jesuits, although not in the dissembling sense of the name. Like the Jesuits, they possessed the intellectual and the social qualifications necessary to educate an elite wherever they taught. The parish church adjoining their convent in Vancouver was Jesuit-run. It had been built close by Point Grey on the west side of the city so that a planned college would be proximate to the campus of the University of British Columbia, with which the two orders, as well as the local Roman Catholic hierarchy, hoped to establish some form of affiliation. The fact of the convent offering the first two years of an undergraduate Arts program was the beginning of a plan which soon after Sheila's time came to naught.

The cosmopolitan nature of the order and the scope of its mission seem strangely at odds with the fact that Mesdames du Sacré Coeur was a semi-cloistered order. Only under extraordinary circumstances did any of the nuns leave their convent grounds. In fact, the grounds in Vancouver even contained their cemetery.

These grounds were extensive, and with the exception of lawns and drives and playing areas, they were heavily wooded. Moreover, they were adjacent to a forest which extended to the University's as-yet-undeveloped endowment lands—half a mile or so west. And after this there is the delta, where the Fraser meets and mixes with the Gulf of Georgia. Amidst the tall trees at the world's end stood a grey granite and crenellated outpost of Catholic Europe. Many of the nuns were Canadian, but their *lingua communis* was French—Parisian French, mind you, not patois—and, as I have noted, they had all visited Rome. Some, however, had come from the continent. The sacristan, who tended to the chapel and to the boys who served on its altar, was one of those. Born in Lisieux, France, she had been a school friend of Teresa, later, St. Teresa of Lisieux, sometimes referred to as the Little Flower. The Sisters of St. Ann had a school for girls in Vancouver named for the Little Flower, but the Mothers had one of her playmates among their number.

The routines and rituals of the convent remained with Sheila—the feast days, the examinations of conscience, the gloves, the ribbons and the medals. "All Sacred Heart convent schools are the same," wrote the famed American novelist and essayist

Mary McCarthy in *Memories of a Catholic Girlhood*. McCarthy was attending one such convent just a few hundred miles south of Vancouver, in Seattle, at the same time Sheila was at Point Grey:

> the same blue serge dresses, usually, with white collars and cuffs, the same blue and green and pink moire ribbons awarded for good conduct, the same books given as prizes on Prize Day . . . the same congés, or holidays, announced by the Mère Supérieure, the same cache-cache, or hide-and-seek, played on these traditional feast days, the same goûter, or tea, the same retreats and sermons, the same curtsies dipped in the hall, the same early-morning chapel with processions of girls, like widowed queens, in sad black-net veils, the same prie-dieu, the same French hymns ("Oui, je le crois"), the same glorious white-net veils and flowers and gold vessels on Easter and Holy Thursday and on feasts peculiar to the order.

Sheila's journals record, and with some wryness, memories of the gentility of the nuns and of their attempts at frankness ("Smoking leads to drinking, and drinking leads to—you know what!"). But here, as Mary McCarthy knew, there was also valuing of the intellectual life—by women and for women. When, years later, Sheila visited and was asked by one of the Mothers if she still "believed," and she responded, "Like Pascal, groaningly," she was merely recalling the nature of past discourse. McCarthy remembered first hearing of Voltaire and first reading Baudelaire in her convent school, and thinking of the nuns as "cool and learned, with their noses in heretical books."

Among the friends from those days at the Sacred Heart Convent were Ellen Wright, who was to be Sheila's attendant when she married, and Marjorie Reynolds (Bunny) Pound, a cousin of Ezra Pound.

In their *Rules of Christian Pedagogy*, the Sisters of St. Ann emphasized the importance of students learning about the place where they lived. "The native land must be thoroughly taught in all its parts," the *Rules* declared: "first, the locality, then the country, the province, and the whole country." For the Mothers, there was their community and then there was the world. To attend their convent was to enter their convent. For some, this could be an expansive as well as a confining experience, as expansive and confining as some readers' experience of Joyce's Dublin, or even of Eliot's waste land.

↩

Sheila entered third year at the University of British Columbia in the fall of 1929. Because the Sacred Heart Convent was not the only school in the province to offer "junior college" preparation in the form of the first two years' courses, departments at the University arranged their programs so that majoring and honouring in a subject began in a student's third year after two years of general education. Sheila enrolled in the Honours program in English.

Meanwhile, her older brother, Bill, had graduated from public high school and had taken a job as a bank teller in Edmonton. Her younger brother, Kelly, had established himself as something of a maverick and a prodigy. He was famed for having built his own bicycle and, when he was in grade twelve, he signed as a cabin boy on one of the Empress liners that sailed from Vancouver to China. His mother's and his teachers' concerns that he would jeopardize his chances to matriculate from high school proved groundless. On his return from this trip, he successfully wrote his examinations, standing second among all matriculating students in the province. But the fact of the Depression made attendance at university difficult. This, plus his own maverick nature, led Kelly to train as a telegrapher at a commercial school, and then to take a job in this capacity on a rum-running ship, which plied between Seattle and Chewasin as long as Prohibition lasted.

Norah had continued at St. Ann's Academy. She started in grade one at seven and a half, and by the time she was eleven she was qualified to enter grade eight. She had been encouraged by the nuns to proceed at this rate, but they now judged her too young to advance further immediately. What she perceived to be the injustice of the situation—"They did not keep their promise," she continued to maintain— began her separation from the church of her childhood and of her family.

Their mother continued to be sustained by friends and by family. Her sister-in-law, Charlie's sister Agatha Myatt, who like her brother had graduated in medicine from the University of Toronto (one of the first women to do so), had gone on to become head of pediatrics at Guys Hospital in London, and had then married and moved to where her husband practiced his craft as a silversmith, outside Birmingham. With her husband, Agatha visited her brother's widow and family in New Westminster. The couple was childless, and they appear to have taken a particular interest in Sheila, to the extent that they contributed generously towards her education. Closer to home, Henry Doyle and his wife, Fan, made sure that the children had holiday time with their own children at Chewasin Beach. With the help of someone to do the ironing and someone else to wash the floors and mow the grass, Ween, in spite of her concerns and responsibilities, was able to enjoy a round of teas and bridge parties and even the occasional dance. Her continuing love for Charlie did not call for public shows of grief, and her circumstances did not stand in the way of her daughter attending university.

⌒

During four years at the University of British Columbia, Sheila completed her Bachelor of Arts degree and an MA in English, and she qualified to teach high school. She "lived at a furious pitch," as years later she recalled, quoting Thoreau, "life had no margin." She commuted daily from New Westminster for the first couple of years, until she came to live with Henry and Anne Angus and their family as an au pair. Henry Angus was a Professor of Economics at UBC and, later, Dean of Graduate Studies; his wife was a sometime poet and sometime chair of the Vancouver School Board. Anne Angus had been born in Persia, the daughter of an American missionary and a Scottish soldier. Very soon after this, her family moved to the Okanagan district of British Columbia, where she grew up. She was nine years older than Sheila, and she was to become, at certain crucial moments in Sheila's life, her principal confidante. The Anguses and their two children, Michael and Anne, remained parts of her life.

In 1929, the staff and student body of UBC were small. The English Department consisted only of six or seven members. The setting of the university, however, was vast and spectacular—hundreds of acres of forest on the western edge of the city, far from the downtown, located on the Point Grey peninsula that juts into the Strait of Georgia. There were clearings for barns and pastures, which served the Agricultural school, and, in time, for an eighteen-hole golf course which served the public. The main campus, including the library, an administration building, and classroom and office buildings for the arts and sciences, was strung along a mall whose north end on clear days provided, and still provides, a breathtaking view of water and mountains. Even on cloudy and foggy days the sea is always present in the smell and taste of salt, in the sound of fog horns.

The yearbook, *The Totem*, encapsulated Sheila's undergraduate career at the time she took her BA, in 1931.

Sheila Martin Doherty
We were joined in our third year by this trim little miss from New Westminster. She quickly showed herself to be a brilliant student whom English Honours was proud to claim. Ability to make

marvellous marks in the most abstruse subjects would be sufficient reason for anyone to be just a wee bit conceited—but not Sheila. Clearness in thinking, steadiness in acting and a saving sense of humour place her far on the path towards success.

The Chair of the English Department was Dr. G. G. Sedgewick, a teacher and scholar whom Sheila and others remembered as having "built his hurdles high." In her first (i.e., her third) year, he taught courses on Shakespeare and Chaucer, and to these he added a course entitled "Narrative Writing" in the next year. He became a legendary figure—and not only in Sheila's mind—for the quality and the rigor of the program that he was largely responsible for putting in place. But Sheila remembered him especially for having included contemporary literature in this program. At a time when English departments in Canadian universities tended to follow the Oxbridge model of ending English studies with Matthew Arnold, Sedgewick insisted that students read the literature of their time. Accordingly, Hunter Lewis, once a student of Sedgewick and by now a colleague, offered a course entitled "Contemporary Literature" which included works by Eliot, Joyce, Pound, Lawrence, and Woolf, among others, even when key texts were banned in Canada. In later years, Sheila liked to point out to students that she had studied Lawrence and Woolf as they were being published, and to those struggling with the complexities of *Ulysses* or *Finnegans Wake*, that Joyce, as well as Woolf and Gertrude Stein and Wyndham Lewis, were all born in the same year—1882— as her mother. Hunter Lewis, incidentally, in the words of the painter Jack Shadbolt, at this time also "galvanized art life on the campus" by lobbying for an art gallery and arranging the university's first ever art shows, which featured the work of Emily Carr.

Half a century after this, in the summer of 1981, on a panel discussing "Criticism and BC Writing" at Simon Fraser University, Sheila responded to a question about literary

Sheila about the time she graduated with her BA from UBC, in 1931.

studies at UBC during her student days. She spoke of reading bootleg copies of *Lady Chatterly's Lover* and *Ulysses*, and observed, "part of my experience in BC was reading Pound when he was just writing the *Cantos*, reading Eliot before he wrote the *Four Quartets*, reading Faulkner, reading Dos Passos, reading Hemingway." Then she added, "[t]hat was as much a part of my life in BC as encountering a bufflehead in one of the lagoons on Vancouver Island."

Emphasis on the moderns and on contemporary art was also reflected in subjects that members of the undergraduate Letters Club chose to talk about during the twenties and thirties. This was an organization "formed," according to its announcement in the 1930–31 yearbook, "for the purpose of encouraging 'the study of English as a joy.'" Meetings consisted of students reading papers on subjects of their own choosing. In its first year, 1920, for example, there were papers on John Masefield and Yeats and Conrad and Synge and Amy Lowell. "English," however, really meant world literature as, over the next few years, there were papers on Ibsen, Maeterlinck, Anatole France, and, in Sheila's final year, 1933, one entitled "Movements in Germany and France."

Membership in the Letters Club was originally limited to undergraduates, but as more students took master's degrees rather than face the workless world of the early thirties, a graduate branch of the club was formed. The first joint meeting of graduate and undergraduate members of the clubs was held on 14 March 1933. It was addressed by Sheila, now a graduate student, who spoke on Robert Browning "from a modern's stand-point," as the student newspaper reported a few days later. At this same meeting, the last of that academic year, prizes were given to the year's two best papers by undergraduates, with an added "special prize," a copy of Robert Bridges's edition of Hopkins's poetry, for that evening's speaker. This was presented to her by Anne Angus, who had been an early member of the club. Sheila's paper has since been lost. The student reporter who commented on it, however, wrote of its "finished skill."

Sheila had completed her BA in 1931, satisfied the requirements for her Academic Teaching Certificate in 1932, and took her MA in 1933. This last degree had as one of its requirements a thesis. Under the supervision of Professor W. L. MacDonald, she wrote on the eighteenth-century essayists Joseph Addison and Richard Steele, "an evaluation of the periodical essay as a medium for ethical instruction." Her conclusion, that "their works are witty, amusing and brilliant but a reform based on wit and a morality founded on decorum and sentiment could make no obvious impression on the moral tone of the day," revealed her greater sympathy

Sheila (second from the left in the front row) with fellow graduate students in the spring of 1933. At this time she was completing her MA at UBC.

for the tradition of "practical reformers" that included Daniel Defoe and Jonathan Swift. She credited MacDonald with her discovery of Swift, whom she was to claim as one of the two most influential writers on her own development as a writer. The other was Laurence Sterne.

Sheila's years at UBC, incidentally, coincided with some remarkable advances in the status of the visual arts in Vancouver. I have already mentioned Hunter Lewis's work on behalf of British Columbia painters at the University. In October 1931 the Vancouver Art Gallery was formally opened. In that same year, the painter, and later friend to Sheila and Wilfred, Jack Shadbolt, at the age of twenty-one, moved from Victoria to Vancouver, where he taught in a local public high school. A few years earlier, in 1926, the photographer John Vanderpant, who had come from Holland by way of New Westminster, opened the Vanderpant Galleries in downtown Vancouver. He was a part of the fine-art movement in photography that sought, according to Helga Pakasaar, to "prove that photography had a soul," that photographs were "made" and not merely "taken." Vanderpant's gallery became a focal point for Vancouver's artists and intellectuals, a venue for lectures and poetry readings as well as for exhibits of photography. Frederick Varley, "Jock" Macdonald and, upon occasion, Emily Carr were familiars there during these years.

~ III ~

THE WORLD INTO WHICH SHEILA DOHERTY GRADUATED IN 1933 WITH A teaching certificate and an MA had no place for her skills or her services. Being a woman and a Roman Catholic, she was even less in demand than many who had fewer qualifications. But her sense of her responsibilities for her family remained, although the prospects of satisfying these were bleak. There were her mother, now in her early fifties, and her sister, Norah, who was still in school, to be provided for. Sheila appears to have cast herself, rather than have been cast, in the role of provider: she must do for others what others had done for her. She had prepared herself to teach, and she would assume her father's role in maintaining the family, or that part of it that required her assistance. She had done her part, but the world was now letting her down.

Years later she was to speak of the Depression as "a fortunate fall, after a time without work, I went to teach in the Cariboo." It is an odd reading of history, this celebration of her own forging of virtue from necessity. It is odd because of the phrase "after a time without work." The year after leaving UBC she spent in New Westminster, living with her mother and sister and teaching boys in a parochial grade school. She was not "without work," even if she was often without pay. Father Murphy, the pastor of St. Peter's, the church affiliated with the school, whose short and compassionate homilies she remembered with affection, had to appeal regularly to his parishoners for money to pay the only teacher in the school who was not a nun. Her salary was $50 a month, and when he could not raise so much he would give Sheila a packet of cigarettes to tide her over.

These were the depths of the Depression. Despite its growing industrial base, New Westminster remained vulnerable because the natural resources that a large part of its work force depended upon—fish and timber in particular—even in the best of times led only to seasonal employment. And these were not the best of times. A strike of dock workers left the homes of many of her students impoverished. She remembered a boy fainting in class from hunger. She remembered, too, a ritual the boys had worked out among themselves, taking turns walking her home from school, knowing that her mother would have something for them to eat.

Norah recalls Ween's own make-work program: "She dreamed up things they [the hungry and unemployed who begged from door to door] could do just so that they could retain their dignity." She had them rake or chop wood or sweep, and then she would feed them on her back steps. And those who had been reduced to begging, like their children, created rituals that reinforced their brotherhood. In a striking variation upon blood on the lintels of a chosen people, as a sign to their fellows, they put chalk marks on the gates or fences or steps of those houses that had not turned them away.

The federal government had set up work camps, primarily for single unemployed men. These camps were remote from urban centres so as to relieve cities and towns of the financial and social burden of providing relief for a growing number of unemployed. The camps existed as much to contain the consequences of the situation as to deal with the situation itself. When conditions in these camps deteriorated, however, another kind of fellowship emerged. In April 1935, seventeen hundred men from the work camps, in the words of British Columbia historian Margaret Ormsby, "occupied" Vancouver, organizing "a march on the warehouses of grocery wholesalers, and then to the Hudson's Bay Company store." When they were driven from this store by the police, the men marched to Victory Square, where the city's Cenotaph still stands. They sent a delegation to City Hall to interview the mayor, who in turn had some of them arrested for organizing an attempt "to capitalize on, for revolutionary purposes, the conditions of depression which now exist." The mayor, "Gerry" McGeer, then went to Victory Square and read the Riot Act to those assembled there. In the name of "Our Sovereign Lord and King," the Act entitled him to order the demonstrators to disperse under threat of "imprisonment for life."

Sheila's memories of those times are like images in a cinematic montage. There are the hungry boys in New Westminster. There is the Roman Catholic cleric—who was to appear later in her life in a more benign light—declaring at this time that Sheila Doherty—undoubtedly because she had attended what many Catholics in the city considered a godless University and supported the leftist League for Social Reconstruction—cut her hair with a "hammer and sickle!" There is the spectacle of police on horseback with whips and truncheons beating down demonstrators. There is the mayor reading the Riot Act. There is the post office filled with straw and the unemployed. All these became the memories of Stella, the protagonist of Sheila's first-written novel, *Deep Hollow Creek*:

> No, no, she didn't want to see it—a man on a horse raising a whip,
> letting the great bull tongue of it lick and fleer and sear the flesh of
> an old greybeard in the street—the mayor in all his pomp of tweed
> and hair lotion and shaving lotion and devotion standing on the
> cenotaph reading the riot act—men rifling the counters—men

hurling bricks through the windows—men sitting in the sun—sitting in the post office waiting for the mail from nowhere—tear bombs and jeer bombs.

It is unlikely Sheila witnessed the episode of the Riot Act, which occurred while she was teaching in Dog Creek, but these events and their causes radicalized her politically; they also introduced her to the kinds of community that can develop in response to need, injustice, and social chaos.

༑

Sheila prefaced her first public reading from *The Double Hook*, in 1973 in Edmonton at Grant MacEwan Community College, with comments on the novel and on circumstances that gave rise to it. It was here that she spoke most succinctly about going to Dog Creek in the Cariboo district of central British Columbia:

> I didn't go there because I thought, I'm going to write about this part of the country. I went there to teach, and that's where I happened to be. I didn't choose, it chose me. It was the only place in 1934 that said, "Come, and teach our children." I had no idea where it was when I left by train in Vancouver, except somewhere else.

When she got off the train, she was some 350 kilometres east of Vancouver, in a village called Ashcroft. It was here she was to be met and from here that she was to be driven to Dog Creek. Not too many years before, the drive took three days in a stage with four horses. The automobile shortened the trip to a matter of ten hours or so, but it did not lessen the hazards along the way.

Very likely, Sheila spent the night at the "Old Ashcroft" hotel, across from the railway station. It is gone now, destroyed by fire, so there are no registers to verify this. Evidence of her stay—either at first or later—remains in the figure of a parrot—"Paddy's parrot," as it is referred to in the fourth section of *The Double Hook*. Sheila insisted that the only character in that novel for whom there was a source in her experience was the parrot. "I knew the parrot," she said years later in response to a question of Daphne Marlatt. "He didn't live in Dog Creek, but in a beer parlour of the Ashcroft Hotel." As his owner in the novel, Paddy the bartender, observes, "He gets his way because he's unique. Men don't often have their own way. It's not many have the rights of a dumb beast and a speaking man at the same time." Sheila's story of the parrot continued. Some years later, when she was teaching in Edmonton at the

Cariboo landscape, with the Fraser River. A scene close by Dog Creek.
PHOTO BY GLENN WILLMOTT

university, a young man appeared one day through her open office door. He had a message for her: "The parrot is dead." She claimed not to know who the young man was, preferring, I suspect, to leave the anecdote mysterious.

The parrot may have been dead, but it was not—nor is it—forgotten, at least not in Ashcroft. It was indeed owned by the bartender at the Ashcroft Hotel, whose name was Paddy—Paddy O'Sullivan or Paddy Sullivan, depending on your source. The parrot was famous, as it is in Sheila's novel, for its taste for beer. But according to one account, the parrot's was not just a taste: "it used to grace the bar in a cage, where it used to squawk quite a lot, but didn't talk much. He was an alcoholic, and if he didn't get his ration of beer, he wouldn't let up until he was supplied with [it]." The parrot's name was Bob, and it is unlikely he would have been found in the bar in the summer heat of James Potter's meeting with his counterpart in the novel. In summer he was accustomed to perch in the branches of maple trees that lined the street, and from here he would whistle at the young girls who were seasonal workers in the district produce canneries. The girls at first accused old men sitting on the hotel's verandah of Bob's sauciness. Bob survived the fire that destroyed the Ashcroft Hotel, only to perish in a hotel fire in Blackie, Alberta. A son of the owners of one or other of these hotels was studying pharmacy at the University of Alberta at the time of Bob's death. It was he, presumably, who announced the event to Sheila.

"When I went to the Cariboo in the early thirties," Sheila said, "I thought this is it. This is where God has flung me." It would be difficult to imagine landscape more dramatically different from the rain forests and inlets and mountains of the coast than the landscape of Ashcroft and the country north of it. This is desert country— a northern reach of the Mojave Desert to be precise. Bunchgrass grows naturally here, and sagebrush and flowering cactus. The lowlands appear barren and the hills around have the look of something once molten that has been baked and hardened over the ages. The hills are not craggy, but tawny and sinuous, like crouching animals with muscles tensed. It is no wonder camels were imported as beasts of burden when the railroad was being built through this part of the continent. North of Ashcroft had been Gold Rush country in the nineteenth century. It was now given over to ranching.

Dog Creek lies about 150 kilometres north and somewhat west of Ashcroft, and 4 kilometres east of the Fraser River. The river from here runs south to Lytton, where it joins the Thompson River (by which Ashcroft is situated) for its final journey down the Fraser canyon and through the Fraser valley and New Westminster, then by Point Grey to the Strait of Georgia. In the Cariboo, the land on the east side of the Fraser was the traditional home of the Shuswap Indians, whose friendliness to white settlers was reflected in the number of ranches located east of the river. To the west of the Fraser, and at a distance from the river, was the land of the Chilcotins, a less friendly tribe because they discouraged white settlement on their land. On the west side of the Fraser, opposite the road to Dog Creek, lay (indeed still lies), however, the Gang Ranch, the largest in the province and one of the largest ranches in the world.

Even today the drive from Ashcroft to Dog Creek is arduous—for vehicle as well as for driver and passengers. After Clinton, about forty kilometres north of Ashcroft, pavement gives way to a gravel and dirt logging road, and in time this road narrows to allow no passing at all. The growth is largely jack pine and sagebrush, but after some miles of scrub land you turn into views of the valley through which the Fraser flows, and on the far side (the west side of the river), views of the vast table lands that provide pasture for the Gang Ranch. You are high above the river, as if riding the spine of a mountain range. And then you reach a point where, on your left, the land falls off into a deep valley, which is as verdant as the hills around are brown and barren. It is a steep road down into the valley where you come upon the creek and grass and deciduous trees, and a junction where three roads meet, including the one you have come on. If you take the road on your left, you proceed into what remains of the settlement of Dog Creek.

Dog Creek—at the place where three roads meet.
PHOTO BY FRED FLAHIFF

No one is certain how the creek got its name. Some say it was named for the number of dogs belonging to the Shuswap people at the local reserve; others, that it was for a famous chief whose name, Skaha, means dog. Its origins seem unimportant or else too obvious in a country which includes Antler Creek and Goose Creek, and a town called Horsefly and even one called Likely. Originally an Indian village, in the wake of the Gold Rush the town became a station for trains of pack animals that hauled provisions and commodities to the new settlements to the north. It provided good winter forage for the animals and so became a favourite wintering spot for these pack trains. In 1856, a Mexican named Raphael Valenzuela built Dog Creek House as wintering quarters for the packers. In his *Dog Creek: A Place in the Cariboo*, Hilary Place records that by the time his grandfather had come from England and had settled there in the early 1880s, Dog Creek was "a thriving settlement of several hundred people. There were three large stores, four hotels, a dance hall, two houses of ill repute, and cabins all over the place."

The population of Dog Creek in the late nineteenth century testified to the universality of gold fever. Prospectors and adventurers had come from other parts of Canada, from the United States and Mexico, from as far afield as England and France and Scandinavia. There was a time, according to Robin Skelton in *They Call it the* CARIBOO, when Dog Creek "must have been one of the few places in Cariboo where French was more usually spoken than English." The first sawmill was contrived by Le Conte Gaspar de Versepeuch. And about one hundred Chinese panned for gold close by on the banks of the Fraser, and some owned businesses in the town. And there was and is the Native presence—before and during and after the floruit of Dog Creek.

The school at Dog Creek where Sheila taught.

There was no schoolhouse until January 1926. Like the Martin and the English families in Steveston in the 1880s, the parents of ten children, ranging in age from five to sixteen, petitioned the provincial government to build a school and provide a teacher. The school was to include eight grades in one room, and it would remain open only so long as a specified minimum number of students was enrolled. Graduates who were not sent away did their high school by correspondence courses through the provincial Department of Education.

In a note which she wrote in the early 1990s, at the time *Deep Hollow Creek* was being prepared for publication, Sheila described the circumstances of the school:

Unless there were nine children in a rural district there was no school. If the original number fell below nine the school was automatically closed. During the thirties at least the BC provincial government paid the salary of the teacher (at that time six hundred dollars or less for a school year paid in twelve monthly instalments of about fifty dollars a month). This money . . . was the only sure cash in a community which depended for its income on the price of beef (about one and a half cents a pound on the hoof), if the beef could be sold at all, or on the operation of bars, stores, or by securing government contracts to haul mail or other goods.

Despite the presence of Indian children in the community, if so it could be called, these children were not enrolled in the public school but were sent at a very early age to the residential schools. The one referred to indirectly in the text [*Deep Hollow Creek*] was opened in 1891 under the direction of Father J. M. Le Jacq, OMI. In it the children were brought up by the Sisters of the Child Jesus. Fifty-seven children were enrolled in the school in 1935. . . . As far as I know the residential schools, although apparently their "quota grants" were paid by the federal, not the provincial government, were not inspected. Their management was entrusted to the Catholic clergy and they were usually staffed by Catholic nuns.

In response to a question about the name "the Rock" that she had given to the town north of Deep Hollow in her novel, she was more specific about the residential school attended by the Native children from Dog Creek:

> The Indian mission school at Williams Lake . . . seemed like a penal colony out of which children were released, finally into a starving and decimated community in which language and culture—religious and social—had been destroyed—but not obliterated—not completely.

According to her sister, Norah, Sheila received none of her $600 salary. This is hard to imagine, as she did return to teach a second year at Dog Creek.

Sheila claimed to have kept journals during her two years there, and then to have burned these, leaving us with no access to her immediate experience of Dog Creek. What we have are recollections occasioned by interviews, and published conversations and publishers' queries about her novels. It was as the author of *The Double Hook* that she recalled the place that had given rise to it. In biographical notes she wrote for McClelland & Stewart in 1959, she observed, "I went to teach in the Cariboo where I sank roots which I've never really been able to disentangle."

> For the better part of two years I lived by myself in a log cabin. I thought I would probably have to live there for the rest of my life. During the time I lived there I had a horse called Fiddle and a Labrador retriever called Juno. I also raised two litters of pups: Chilco and Chezacut; then Silk and Dinah. One night when I bent down and offered a match to Juno as I lit my own cigarette after dinner, I decided I'd better cut my way out of the bush, or perhaps it would be better to say out of the jack-pine and the sage-brush. Although I had all sorts of time I wrote nothing. I only felt and looked. I had nothing to say.

There is no reference to the journals she claimed to have kept, no reference to her first-written novel, *Deep Hollow Creek*, which ends with an episode derived from her experience of the match and the dog. And there is no reference to her teaching.

In a conversation with Daphne Marlatt, Roy Kiyooka, and Pierre Coupey, which took place in a Vancouver hotel room and was published in 1975, Sheila spoke of the broader, vaster conversation that "creates the country." It is a conversation made up of voices and of the voices that speak through those voices. "It's like Emily Carr," she said:

> Emily Carr did certain things. If I go to the Island now—although I've looked at trees, not just noticed them—I do see them through Emily Carr's eyes. She created part of British Columbia just the way the School of Seven, for good or for ill, created Northern Ontario. It's a question of whether these images are viable as a part of history— not because they are representational, but because they have created a way of seeing which then becomes part of the history of seeing in Canada. It is something which goes beyond reference—beyond access to archives.

Presumably one does not go to the forests of Vancouver Island to find Emily Carr, but to Carr's paintings and drawings to learn how to see these forests. By the same token, one does not go to Dog Creek to find Sheila or the landscape or the characters of her first-published, although second-written, novel, *The Double Hook*. "It wasn't an act of reconstruction," she observed of this novel in this same conversation, "like going back and saying I remember this—no one I ever knew did or said the things which are done and said. The people and the country and the animals and the plants gave me images for what I wanted to say."

Only a beer-drinking parrot and a bartender named Paddy lie outside the limits of Sheila's disclaimer. But *Deep Hollow Creek* was different. Little in this novel was consistent with such a disclaimer—as little as impinged upon it in her second novel. She did offer a match to her dog, and it was a Labrador bitch named Juno. Someone did bring her as a gift the heart of a slaughtered steer, as Sam Flower does to Stella. She did bring a friend back with her from the coast—although not at Christmas time as in the novel, but at the beginning of her second year—and the friend did barter with the Native people for a "moose-hide jacket" as Miriam in the novel does. Catherine Moss (this was the friend's name) did indeed find herself riding unwittingly, like Miriam, at the head of a Native funeral procession.

Like Stella, in the course of her first year Sheila chose to move from the house where she boarded to live alone, except for her horse and dogs, and except for the time Catherine spent with her. It was a maverick gesture, an isolating move, but one which brought her into more immediate contact with the place and its people than her "guest" status could ever have allowed. She prided herself, as only one from the city might, in her attempts to achieve a kind of self-sufficiency. She rode well and became a good shot. Once she bagged two small game birds and, when she was returning in triumph to her cabin, she saw in the distance a Mountie/Game Warden approaching. Because she had acted out of season, or because she had shot the birds on Native land, she attempted to conceal her crime by stuffing her plunder in her shirt. It was only after they had passed, and she had absorbed the strange look the Mountie had given her, that she realized a feathered neck was sticking out from between buttons on her shirt. Natives from the reservation visited her, selling their handiwork or doing odd jobs in

Sheila with Juno.

return for cash. As the school teacher, and assuming that she was paid, she was one of the very few in the district to operate by a cash, as distinct from a barter, economy.

When her first-written novel was finally published in 1992, Sheila sent a copy to Catherine Moss, now Catherine Hanson, whom she had not seen in more than fifty years. She kept her friend's reply in her own copy of *Deep Hollow Creek*. It plays Catherine's response to the novel ("I did enjoy the book and had many laughs at the expense of 'our story'") off against her account of a visit to Dog Creek with her husband, who had not been there before. When Hanson searched in vain for evidence of what she had known of the town, her husband remarked, "'didn't I think it might all [be] a figment of my imagination?' There just was nothing familiar." Not so with the novel: "Reading it was almost like a game for me—each new page I turned left me figuring just 'who' everyone was—but I am sure I was able to attach the correct names—it is a novel experience for me to read of my feature[s] in your novel—I was happy to see you remembered 'Juno' by name."

Years later, in that hotel room in Vancouver, as the author of *The Double Hook* and of an as-yet-unpublished and unacknowledged *Deep Hollow Creek*, Sheila observed, "I've always had a resistance to—almost a dread—of using experience which involves people I know as if somehow or other you robbed them." She was persuaded that representation in any narrow, naturalistic sense could have no place in any attempt "to create a total fiction out of experience which was concrete—which defied clichés imposed on it. . . . I wanted to create a language from what I had learned." And this remained her aim after the writing and the rejection of her first novel.

The accounts of the writing, the rejection, and the publication of this novel will be told in time. Before it and Miriam, however, there were Dog Creek and Catherine. Her response to the novel suggests that very little distance separated them. We know from Sherrill Grace that Deep Hollow Creek was another name for Dog Creek, and it appears that Miriam was another name for Catherine. She did recognize her own features in her counterpart, including her red hair. Whether she recognized herself in Miriam's well-intentioned officiousness, or in her capacity to fill any space she occupied, it is impossible to say. Whether she occasioned the uneasiness that Miriam occasions in Stella need not be known:

> As Miriam reached up to move the lamp Stella noticed the curve of her hip under the gold-haired brown wool of her Harris tweed skirt and the light bathing her braided hair as water bathes pebbles in the creek.
>
> Nor "in things extreme and scattering bright"—no "not in nothing"—certainly not in nothing. Why, Stella thought, slipping from the literacy of the past into the literacy of the present, must the immediacy of the moment act itself out in the klieg light of a thousand dead candles.
>
> She rose quickly from the end of the camp cot on which she was sitting and, going to the bucket, poured a dipper of water into the white enamelled hand-basin.
>
> Is supper ready? she asked. (142)

Catherine's family had lived across the street from the Dohertys in New Westminster, and she had attended St. Ann's Academy with Sheila. Their paths did not cross again, however, until she wrote to Sheila at the time of Ween Doherty's death in 1980. Catherine had become a nurse, had married a Norwegian fisherman, and they had two children. She wrote from Chewasin, where they lived in their retirement. In the letter occasioned by Deep Hollow Creek, she credited Sheila with having led her into "an interesting and different life from Westminster. . . . Your influence on my life has been lasting."

Sheila's novel and the photographs she took at the time provide us with a sense of this place and this time. Snapshots with her dogs, or riding Fiddle, of her cabin and of the landscape—sometimes populated by ranch hands or by friends up from the coast—give a sense of the moment that, but for her first novel, would have been lost to us when she chose to burn her journals written at Dog Creek.

Her departure after two years there had both its mythic as well as its prosaic sides. There was the episode with Juno and the match, and according to Sheila, Stella's response to it recalled her own: "It is time for us to get out of here," Stella says to Juno. For all her sense of sinking roots in the Cariboo, Sheila realized that this was not ground from which she could not be separated. But her decision to leave had a more obvious source as well, in the fact that the school was to be closed because its student body was about to fall below the required minimum of nine students.

Sheila with Fiddle.

Hilary Place, with whose family Sheila had boarded when she first went to Dog Creek, and who was a student of hers for one year, recalls her simply as having "introduced me to Keats, Browning, and Shelley," and as having received a good report from the school inspector. Her impact on the place appears to have been rather less than its impact on her.

⁓

In October 1934, shortly after she had gone to Dog Creek, Sheila's first professional publication appeared. It is a poem entitled "The Barren Lands," which was published in *The Canadian Forum* above the mistranscribed name Theila Martin Doherty. It is interesting not only because it was her first creative work—and only poem—to be published, but also because it is her only work written before Dog Creek to have survived.

Awake, spring is at hand
And the low-voiced laughter of the ptarmigan breaks
The cold grey silence of the earth which lies
Yet stark and dead beneath the leaden sky.

The stunted trees, bush-high, are leafless yet;
Who knows what time they will unfold their damp green leaves?

Awake, the waters move,
Uncoil like grey-skinned snakes,
Move sinuous folds,
Begin to flow.

Awake, spring too awakes though slowly
In the heart grown cold beneath the finger touch of chilling fears
And laughter shatters with its silver spears
The vast grey voiceless silence born of hate.

The young writer seemed determined to make both traditional matter and traditional form her own. Sonnet forms lurk beneath the poem's surface, but they did not inhibit Sheila's manipulations of rhymes and the lengths and the groupings of lines. It is an Eliotic spring, as its title suggests, but like Browning too in "Childe Roland to the Dark Tower Came," she represents nature—with its "leaden sky" and "stunted trees" and snake-like waters—as itself menacing. It is highly rhetorical and skillful—and very, very literary. It might provide a clue to the modern approach she had taken in her talk on Browning to the UBC Letters Club in the previous year.

THE PLACE WHERE SHEILA BEGAN TO FIND A VOICE, AND VOICES
for the images and the language she had absorbed during her two years in the
Cariboo, was near New Westminster, on the south side of the Fraser River. After the
closing of the school at Dog Creek, she found another job in the public system, in
the Langley Prairie High School, where for four years—1936 to 1940—she taught
English, German, and Agricultural Economics. By her own account, it was here that
she began to write.

Langley Prairie is located in the Fraser Valley, south and somewhat east of New
Westminster. The site of a Hudson's Bay fort, preserved as a heritage site, Langley is
now, as it was in Sheila's day, an agricultural centre.

By 1936, the year Sheila returned to the coast, Norah was entering her last year
of high school. In the previous year, her mother had decided to have her move from
St. Ann's Academy to the local public high school, Duke of Connaught, so that she
might graduate from a public school. This had less to do with Norah's own earlier
crisis of faith than with what Ween perceived to be the practical problems of finding work in a Protestant world. Norah spent two years at Connaught, completing
both her junior and her senior matriculation. This entitled her to enter UBC in her
second year.

Norah's education was a concern of Sheila as well as of her mother. It was, after
all, still the Depression, and while Bill and Kelly were self-sufficient, neither was in a
position to lend much by way of assistance. Sheila and her mother decided to combine their households. Accordingly, after her first year in Langley, Sheila rented a
large house close by, in Murrayville, and Ween gave up the house on Merrivale Street
where they had lived for fifteen years to move in with her. When Norah started university in 1937, she spent her weekends and holidays with them, but she boarded
near the campus during term.

It was, as Norah recalls, "a very happy household" in Murrayville. The property
was located on a hill, and it was large enough to support Sheila's horse, Fiddle, which
she could now arrange to have brought down from Dog Creek, and two of Juno's offspring, Dinah and Silk. Norah remembers the dogs meeting Sheila each day on her
return from school, and playing hide-and-seek with her in the long grasses that grew
along the irrigation ditches. Fiddle, like so many others, appears to have been capti-
vated by Ween. According to Norah, he would not let her out of his sight, peering in

the windows along the side and back of the house where he was pastured. Both Norah and Sheila rode Fiddle, although gently, as his legs had been injured in transit from the Cariboo.

The nature of the property and the need to economize led Sheila to add chickens to their menagerie, to provide them with fresh eggs. This gave rise to an episode which she recounted at her own expense. When the chickens grew large enough to be the stuff of good meals, Sheila was faced with the prospect of wringing their necks or chopping off their heads. She could do neither, but during her years in Dog Creek she had become a good shot, as the episode of the game birds has revealed. She decided, then, to bring out her .22 calibre rifle, and with it in hand she advanced upon the chicken run. She lined one up in her sights, but the designated victim turned on her what she described as "a baleful glare," and she lost heart and nerve. A neighbour performed with an axe what she could not perform with hands or axe or rifle.

This then was the place where Sheila began to write out of her experience of the Cariboo. Years later, she was very precise about the dates of the action of the novel and of its writing:

> The time of the events of the novel would be from September 1935 to the end of June 1936—in BC the nadir of what was known as the great depression—and in Europe and its various colonies the beginnings of the Second World War.
>
> The novel, if so it can be called, was written in 1938 just before the beginning of the Second World War.

The time of the novel's action was the time of Sheila's second year at Dog Creek. She illustrated this from references in the novel. Her interlocutor was Ellen Seligman, the editor of her first-written novel when it was finally accepted for publication in 1991. Seligman had noted—simply in passing—that *Deep Hollow Creek* contained no reference to the years of its action. Sheila's very detailed reaction to this observation reveals a recovered sense of the present in which the action of the novel occurred and in which it was written, as well as her passion for documentation, which would lead her to admit that her only hobby was reading footnotes, and to confess, "I'm hopelessly academic:"

> you are right when you say no specific year is mentioned in the novel. It is by specific references, however, like the reference to the reading of the riot act by Mayor G. G. McGeer in Van[couver] that the date is established.

i.e. also (p. 139) Clintock called his fee-pup "Selassie"—Current news from the outer world sometimes seeped into the Cariboo district of British Columbia. Mussolini, who declared that he saw a great future for Italy in developing Abyssinia with Italian labour in 1935 attacked Abyssinia and drove out the negus Haile Selassie. His chief of staff Badaglio used gas to demoralize Selassie's armies. On May 8, 1936, Mussolini proclaimed the foundation of a new Roman empire. The Japanese had invaded Manchuria (see p. 126) and in 1932 it was declared an independent state by Japan and renamed Manchuko. In Spain in Oct. 1936 Franco became the leader of the nationalist forces—the military uprising against the republican government [resulting] in the Spanish Civil War.

Historical time was as carefully worked out and as important in Sheila's first novel as the "times" of Shuswap myths, of Old Testament prophets, of the Latin Mass and the *Oresteia* were to be in *The Double Hook*.

When *Deep Hollow Creek* was finally published, in 1992, she commented in an interview with Philip Marchand of *The Toronto Star*:

> It's dated by these things [contemporary references], . . . it's dated by
> the events. It's not retrospective—it is written out of the blindness
> of the moment. It's not going back and recreating the Depression—
> it's not, in that sense, a documentary at all. It's a book, a text, which
> emerges from the conditions of the times.

Her sense of the time-bound nature of her novel—"the blindness of the moment," "the conditions of the times"—expressed itself in an apology in the fullest, most contradictory sense of the word. She regretted what she had or had not done; at the same time she felt the rightness of what she had done. For example, she was clearly uneasy about possible responses in the 1990s to a Jewish character who comes into the district of her novel to buy hair. "The mention of him," she insisted to Marchand, "was part of the thinking of the times. It was what happened. I wouldn't take it out now."

Sheila's quarrel with her first-written novel remained a quarrel with its very premise, the encounter between an urban and urbane consciousness and a small, remote, and heterogeneous community. Or perhaps it might be more accurate to say that her quarrel was with her working out of this premise by means of a narrator who was not the protagonist but who, like narrators in certain of Jane Austen's novels, privileges the main character by moving easily and approvingly into her consciousness. In *Deep Hollow Creek*, natives of the district into which an alien Stella comes remain alien in the ground of her consciousness. Sheila was determined to keep such an alien and alienating presence out of her next novel. Accordingly, as she told Marchand, she would attempt "to get the narrator out of it" by " kill[ing] the schoolteacher."

Her failure to find a publisher for her first novel seems to have confirmed her conviction that the fault was hers. Even before she started work on her second novel, she experimented with problems of consciousness in narrative—more specifically, in two stories she wrote during her time in Langley.

Her first published work of fiction, as with her first poem, appeared in *The Canadian Forum*, in September 1938. A fellow UBC graduate and former member of its Letters Club, Earle Birney, who twenty years later would recommend against the publication of *The Double Hook*, was the *Forum's* Literary Editor and was likely responsible for the acceptance of Sheila's first short story. Entitled "Rough Answer," like *Deep Hollow Creek* it has its roots in her experience of Dog Creek. In fact, it has strong affinities with the novel's first section. The story involves three characters, a husband and wife, Joe and Margaret, and a young and unnamed teacher who has come to live with them. The setting is rural: yellow hills and coyotes recall Sheila's Cariboo. The story hinges on the undeclared attraction that develops between Joe and the teacher. Central to the story is the patience of the witnessing wife. She and her husband are, in Sheila's later phrase, "figures in a ground, from which they could not be separated." "He's life," Margaret thinks to herself. "Like rain for plants or hay for critters." They are just such similes as these that constitute the rough answer of the story's title, delivered by Joe to the teacher when she would exploit the seductive possibilities of her loneliness. She is appalled by what she perceives to be his crudeness. "I'm not made your way," she declares to Margaret and leaves their house and the district immediately.

The strength of the story lies in its spareness and in the seemingly casual way it moves among, and is made up of the perceptions of, the characters. There is no privileging the consciousness of the teacher here. Her namelessness, her petulance, and the very short duration of her stay combine to alienate her from the reader's interest as surely as from the household of Margaret and Joe. But to such an extent are the reader's sympathies engaged on behalf of this household that its locale loses much of the strangeness, the foreignness that would characterize the place to which the teacher has journeyed. There is no want of strangeness, however, in a second story Sheila likely wrote at this time. It was originally entitled "The Black Dogs," but it was finally published under the name "And the Four Animals."

What she said in 1975 in the Hotel Georgia of her failure in *Deep Hollow Creek* provides a context for her shortest, and strangest, story:

> I realized that I was writing about something which was not experi-
> ence[,] necessarily[,] although I had lived in the place I was writing
> about, the Cariboo. I was really an outsider, and I had introduced an
> alien consciousness into a situation which had still not manifested
> itself in any meaningful way to that consciousness. I had lived there,
> as I said, because in a sense I had been thrown there.

There is a narrator in "And the Four Animals"—or at least a spinner of words—who
observes at once three black dogs, "Labrador retrievers," and a man observing them,
a man who has "whistled up from his depths" a fourth black dog, as presumably he
has already "whistled up" its companions. The narrator is a creature of this place.
The dogs—things of the man—are not, or at least are no longer, of this place:

> They were in the land but not of it. They were of Coyote's house, but
> became aristocrats in time which had now yielded them up to the
> timeless hills. They, too, were gods, but civil gods made tractable by
> use and useless by custom. Here in the hills they would starve or
> [lose] themselves in wandering. They were aliens in this spot or
> exiles returned as if they had never been.

To save them from starvation, the man then feeds them to themselves, saving a last
tooth for "his own belly."
   Sheila, who raised Labrador retrievers, found in the cultivation of dogs their
loss of place—in their obedience and the dependence it spawns a type of self-anni-
hilation which is ritualized in this bleak, dazzling, witty and mysterious fable. The
story is no less rooted in Sheila's own experiences as breeder and outsider than it is
in the nature of dogs and the landscape of the Cariboo.

&

Murrayville provided Sheila with a place and time to absorb and to explore her
experience of the Cariboo. What she wrote during these years shows her working
and reworking that experience and the image-hoard she had amassed during her
two years at Dog Creek. Years later, at the time of the publication of *The Double
Hook*, she looked back to these as years when "I still hadn't found a way to do what
I wanted to do. . . . I wanted the things I knew to create their own space." Despite

her continued reservations about what she had accomplished during this time, she had found a voice very different from the Eliotic and Browningesque voice of "The Barren Land." It could accommodate a character's consciousness, as it often does Stella's in *Deep Hollow Creek*; at its most neutral, the narrator's voice registers a more complex nature than her early poem acknowledged.

Twice during the Murrayville years Sheila spent extended time away. In the summer of 1938, she attended a summer program offered by the University of California at Berkeley. It was intended to qualify her to teach and coach her students in athletics, and particularly in basketball. This was her first lengthy experience of the United States. She was unprepared for the extent to which she had to attune her ear to the rhythms of speech and types of elision that made simple elements into incomprehensible compounds at first. "Wawitman" became her code word for this experience.

She had been awarded a scholarship to undertake this unlikely expedition. She had developed into a good horsewoman in the Cariboo, and a good shot. She was always a good walker, but at "five-foot nothing" she did not have the physique for basketball. In fact, bartenders in San Francisco refused to serve her—although she was twenty-nine years old—because of her diminutive size. And this was more of a hardship than it might at first appear. Sheila's scholarship was modest, and she and some of her fellow students discovered that among the most easily available sources of free food were bars, with their bowls of nuts or pretzels. Her career as a cadger died with her career on the basketball floor—and for the same reason.

Her second trip occurred during the next summer, 1939, and was again to the United States. With Henry and Anne Angus and their two children, she visited Massachusetts. Angus was attending a conference near Tyringham, in the Berkshires. It was just months before the outbreak of the Second World War, and Sheila remembered an encampment of physical cultists in the hills nearby who reminded her of what she had seen in newsreels and photos of German youth in gymnasia and stadia and on parade. The trip also provided her with the opportunity for her first visit to New York City. She went alone, and she visited galleries and went at least once to the theatre. She attended a performance of *Pins and Needles*, the famed Depression musical revue produced by the International Ladies' Garment Workers' Union, and she saw for the first time El Greco's *Night Scene of Toledo*, which was to remain with her always.

Sheila's last year teaching in Langley Prairie was 1939–40. The staff of the high school, which was being paid the floor salary of $1200 per annum, agreed to provide a test case for all schools negotiating with the local school board. In response to their request for a small increment, the board dismissed the entire staff of the high school. In time, it was forced to reinstate them, but by then Sheila had found a job teaching in Duncan, on Vancouver Island. This meant the breakup of the family home in Murrayville. Accordingly, Norah and her mother moved into Vancouver, to a house on Beach Avenue in the city's west end near English Bay. The house had been left to Ween before her marriage, and rent from it had to this point supplemented her income.

During her last year teaching in Langley, Sheila had staked a claim to a property in the Cariboo. According to her own account, it consisted of "a house, a barn, and eighty acres of land in the hills near Hihume [HiHiume] lake." Presumably the land had not been surveyed, for attached to her tax assessment bill and her subsequent agreement to sell is a copy of a provincial brochure entitled "Purchase and Lease of Crown Lands," with the section on acquiring leases of unsurveyed lands marked. This brochure is a reminder of the literal origins of a process which has become for many now merely figurative. It is dated 1939, and the would-be landowner

> will place securely in the ground or in a stone mound at one corner or angle a legal post—a post at least 4 inches square and standing at least 4 feet above the ground—and upon this inscribe his name and the angle or corner it marks, thus: "A.B.'s N.E. corner," or as the case may be. . . .

When she sold it in 1944, for $1500, Sheila's property was described as

> the South Half of the North-east quarter of Section Twenty-four (24), of Township Twenty-three (23), Range Twenty-five (25), West of the Sixth Meridian, and containing Eighty-one and fifty hundredths (81.50) acres more or less.

It is located in the assessment district of Ashcroft and, according to a recent account of the lake, it is a great place for fly fishers who are warned that only single barbless hooks are permitted.

"I went back to the hills . . . whenever I could," she wrote some years later. She confided to a friend that she had hoped to retire to this property to write. Her family appears to have known nothing of her purchase or of her plans.

$$\sim V \sim$$

SHEILA'S MOVE TO DUNCAN IN 1940 WAS NOT HER FIRST EXPERIENCE of this part of Vancouver Island. For two summers during her years at UBC she had worked at a camp for crippled children, the Mill Bay Solarium, north of Victoria. Little is known of this time except for her comments years later to the *Western Catholic Reporter* of Edmonton that it was a "fantastic experience" which "had a lot to do in determining my view of life." According to this same article, what she termed a "bothersome bureaucracy" prevented her from teaching for more than one year in Duncan. That year, 1940–41, was time enough, however, for her to meet Wilfred Watson and to fall in love with him.

We know as little of the circumstances of their meeting as we do of the details of Sheila's time at Dog Creek, and for the same reason. Years later, when they were preparing to move from Edmonton to their last home, near Nanaimo on Vancouver Island, Wilfred complained to friends that Sheila had undertaken wholesale destruction of her personal papers, including, presumably, letters written and received at the time of their courtship. What we do know is that they were married on 29 December 1941, and we know something of the consequences of that event.

In fact, it is not clear whether they met in Duncan, where Wilfred lived with his family, or in Vancouver, where by 1940 he was attending UBC. He had come late to university—he was twenty-eight when he started—after years of working in a sawmill situated north of Duncan, at Chemainus, where his father also worked. Wilfred had been born in 1911 in England, near Rochester, and when he was fourteen, his family—consisting of himself, his parents, and two sisters—emigrated to Canada, settling finally in Chemainus. This was in 1925. But there was no school in Chemainus, and so the family eventually moved the few miles south to Duncan. Years later, in a letter to T. S. Eliot following Faber & Faber's acceptance of Wilfred's first volume of poetry for publication, Sheila summed up his life before he left the Island: "As far as I can gather, he read poetry and wrote it, while he stripped bark from the great logs." It is tempting to sketch for him a Laurentian youth and young manhood—Wilfred as a west-coast Paul Morel, reading and writing amid the sawdust and wood chips of the mill. But by the time they met they were both in their early thirties, and Wilfred's days in the mill had given way to a life with which Sheila was familiar. He was studying and writing poetry. He was intelligent and gifted, and Sheila never lost sight of his gifts or of his intelligence. Nor did she ever lose sight of his having been taken from a good grammar school at Malden in England and set down at the green-chain of a sawmill in Chemainus, where for eleven years he worked to support the writerly life he always felt was his destiny.

A one-time mill hand who had set for himself the goal of rewriting Shakespeare, Wilfred's claims—if not the first upon Sheila's heart—were nonetheless formidable. And Sheila's reputation in Duncan, as the school teacher who could ride like a rancher, proved no less intriguing to Wilfred. A fellow student at UBC and later at the University of Toronto, William Blissett, who was ten years his junior, recalls Wilfred the undergraduate in 1943 as tall and broad-shouldered and sandy haired, with the sidling gait of one who had often found himself in spaces too small for his frame. He recalls his mildness of manner and his English accent—with *saw-mill* become *sore-mill*. He remembers his early interest in eighteenth-century literature. He was not aware then that Wilfred wrote poetry, or that he was married. He did know, however, that he went on weekends to Mission City, where Sheila was then teaching, always carrying a stuffed briefcase.

We catch only glimpses of this time in memories she set down in journal entries written as many as fifty years after the events. In the early 1990s, a newspaper article about walking the seawall round Vancouver's Stanley Park evoked one such memory:

> just after the beginning of the war or into it (the fall of 1941 to be exact) . . . late in the evening a soldier armed with a rifle popped out of the underbrush bellowing "Halt!" as W and I were walking around that self-same perimeter; then, after what might be called a visual inspection, in peremptory tones called out "Advance one! (Pause) Advance two." At that point we looked at one another and dissolved into laughter—unseemly laughter as he disappeared into what was left of the forest.

Other memories were more reflective than anecdotal. In Paris in 1956, at a time which was particularly painful for her, she confided in her journal: "I take it now as an axiom that one should never enter into a relationship or perform an act which needs justification—I mean justification against a conviction, justification argumentative." What did she mean by "justification against a conviction"? Had she felt the need to justify her marriage, and if so, against what conviction? Like Joyce's Stephen Dedalus, against family, church, and nation? Perhaps. They did come from very different backgrounds. Or to justify it as an act—like offering a match to Juno? Perhaps.

Within days of formulating this axiom, Sheila had reason to think back to 29 December 1941, and their wedding. It had been a civil rather than a religious ceremony:

> I remember thinking on the steps of the Courthouse in Vancouver—without more than natural grace—This is for always—whatever I have thought since this thought has never been in question.
>
> There is no comparison with other contracts which are in their nature material and temporal. What I think about contracts, terms of tenure, wages has no relevance. There is marriage and there is a marriage contract—the contract is material and temporal—Marriage itself is an act of faith and consequently an act of perfect love—or inversely and perhaps more truly an act of perfect love consequently an act of faith. Only a belief such as this would have made and did make the first years of our marriage possible. When a parent has a child he knows that at a certain age the child should leave him except under unusual circumstances. Even these circumstances are a violation in a sense—as the parent realized—as mother for instance realized. . . .
>
> There is no analogy between the relationship of parent and the relationship of husband and wife. . . .
>
> The law does not make marriage—It protects or rather tries to protect often bunglingly and inadequately in a temporal world something which is not temporal, although rooted in beginning as human life—and, I suppose, even the soul is—though one does not think of soul as temporal. . . .
>
> All human social wisdom to the contrary—

Sheila's attempts to understand their marriage and to accommodate to less than a perfect symbiosis of faith and love are central—although hardly unique—to her story.

Wilfred's family learned of his plans to marry only days before the event. He had gone to Duncan for Christmas in that December 1941, and when he was leaving to return to Vancouver he announced his plans. Although Sheila had lived and taught in Duncan during the previous year, Wilfred's sister Doreen had known nothing of her. There seems to have been something of Dickens's Wemmick about his determination to keep his worlds apart—even about the abruptness with which he announced his impending wedding. Sheila's mother and sister, on the other hand, knew of her plans. Ween had announcements engraved, and there was, according to Norah, a large influx of gifts—all of which, as she recalls, Sheila returned, exchanging them with what they really wanted or needed. All, that is, except lingerie that her friend from convent days and attendant at the courthouse in Vancouver, Ellen Wright, had made for her.

Ween and Norah did not attend the wedding, but after it, and after Sheila's reflections on the courthouse steps, the bridal party came to their house on Beach Avenue for a modest celebration. This was followed by a wedding trip to Victoria.

Sheila was not living in Vancouver at this time. After her year in Duncan, she had found a position teaching in Mission City, about 30 kilometres up the Fraser Valley from Langley, about 70 kilometres from Vancouver. "From the hill at Mission," she wrote years later, "I could see the Cheam Mountains which cut off the valley from the interior"—and the Cariboo, her magnetic north. She had come there in September 1941 and remained until the spring of 1945. Wilfred was still in Vancouver, where he did not complete his undergraduate degree until 1943. This meant that from the very beginning of their marriage physical separation was a factor. This was further aggravated by the War.

Their wedding had taken place in the wake of Pearl Harbour. The effects on the Canadian west coast of Japan's attack on American territory have been considered almost exclusively in light of the internment of Japanese Canadians living on or near the coast. A precedent for this inhuman move, however, already existed in the work camps to which unemployed men had been sent in the thirties, and from which the men of 1935 had emerged to be met by truncheons and the Riot Act. The same man who had read that act, G. G. McGeer, was still mayor of Vancouver at the outbreak of the War and was soon to earn the nickname "Two-gun Gerry" for measures he took on behalf of the defense of the city; most notably, the installation of two anti-aircraft guns—one in Stanley Park and one on the property of UBC—that had the effect of preventing citizens access to what became restricted parts of these sites. Sheila and Wilfred being challenged by a soldier in Stanley Park recalls those days, as their sense of the comic incongruity of that encounter reflects a fairly widespread attitude among the citizenry.

Rationing, of course, was countrywide, as were Registration cards, which were introduced in August 1940 and were required of all over the age of sixteen, with the exception of "cloistered nuns, armed service personnel on active duty, and patients of mental hospitals." Coastal cities and communities had as an added reminder of world events—blackouts—that were enforced in Vancouver within days of the attack on Pearl Harbour. They were a fact of life until the end of the War. Black-out curtains and street lights whose tops had been painted to ensure that no light escaped to the sky—with the dividend that the stars could be more easily seen—and white-helmeted ARP wardens patrolling the streets with flashlights: these were parts of the landscape of the coast during the Second World War. Less apparent were the mines that were said to have been laid in the waters between Vancouver Island and the mainland to prevent enemy submarines from penetrating local defenses. And yet another kind of protection for some took the form of badges that read "I am Chinese."

Conscription came late in Canada, but Wilfred had not been of a mind to volunteer his services to the War effort. Hatred of violence, a refusal to countenance the taking of human life, perhaps even a sense of the complexity, the ambiguity, and the absurdity of it all, confirmed him as a conscientious objector. When he was called up, the mechanical know-how he had acquired during his years in the mill at Chemainus and, more casually, from boating in the straits of Georgia, fitted him for life below deck in the navy. This is how and where he fulfilled his war service.

⌒

The month of her wedding and the influx of exchangeable gifts had seen a gift of another sort. That Christmas of 1941, someone had sent Sheila a copy of Emily Carr's first publication, *Klee Wyck*. The following February, Sheila wrote Carr asking if her interest in and experience of Native arts and lore and customs extended beyond the coast tribes she described in her book. "I wondered if at any time you had found any material of interest in the interior of BC," she asked, and then she went on: "I am sure that this will seem a peculiar request but I am so intensely interested in this particular field that I thought you might be able to tell me what work you had done or what contacts you had been able to make with the Shuswaps."

There is no evidence that Sheila knew that many years earlier Carr had spent some time in Shuswap country. Returning to the West in 1904, after five years in England, Carr had left the train at Ashcroft and had proceeded by coach up the Cariboo Road to 150 Mile House, somewhat farther north and east of Dog Creek, where she stayed with friends for two months. It was an exhilarating time for Carr. "I can never love Cariboo enough for all she gave to me," she wrote in her account of this time, a vignette entitled "Cariboo Gold" which appeared in her autobiography, *Growing Pains*, that was not published until 1946, the year after her death. "In

Cariboo I did not paint," she would write, but she did barter with the Shuswaps—her clothing for their baskets. And she met a coyote, "face to face in a field once," and recorded an old miners' tale that the coyote is a ventriloquist who "from a far ridge . . . can throw his voice right beside you, while from close he can make himself sound very far." "Their cries," she observed, "expressed woe, cruelty, anger, utter despair!"

Oblivious to all this, Sheila concluded her 1942 letter to Carr: "I enjoyed *Klee Wyck*. I am glad you allowed it to be published. Too little is known and too much is being lost of the spirit which is native to British Columbia." Her use of "allowed" is puzzling, and she made no mention of her mother having known Carr and having been friends with her nieces during the Victoria years. Nor did she comment on the fact that one of those nieces, Emily Nicholson, had married into the English family, forming a connection between them. There is no evidence that Carr replied to her inquiry. No letter from her survives among Sheila's papers, and she made no notation on Sheila's letter that she had answered it—a practice of hers. What does remain, however, is Sheila's statement of continuing intense interest in the Native world of the Cariboo, and her conviction—even perhaps her need to express—that she and Carr shared in "the spirit which is native to British Columbia."

Norah Doherty had graduated from UBC in the spring of 1940, just at the time of the breakup of the Murrayville household. She took a year of teacher's training, but her prospects when she had completed this were little different from those that had confronted Sheila seven or eight years earlier. She could have gone off as her sister had to teach in a remote part of the province but, by her own admission, she was not as adventuresome as Sheila; moreover, she was reluctant to leave her mother alone in Vancouver. She stayed in the city and worked for a while with a creation of the times, the Censorship Office, and then with the Unemployment Insurance Commission, before her marriage in 1946 to David Mitchell.

After working for a time with a bank in Edmonton in the early thirties, Sheila's older brother, Bill, had returned to New Westminster and had taken a position as sports reporter with the local newspaper, *The Daily Columbian,* and had married Dorothy Taylor, daughter of its editor and owner, Senator J. D. Taylor. When war broke out, Bill joined a motorcycle unit of the Canadian army. He sustained a head injury in the course of his duties, and his family traced many of his subsequent trials to this accident.

Sheila's younger brother, Kelly, after his careers as cabin boy and rum-running telegrapher, became an attendant at the hospital that their father had presided over. He shared, as well as his father's name, and to an uncanny extent his father's build and appearance, his father's fate of a short life. On his thirtieth birthday, in 1942, he died of leukemia, caused, it was believed, by radiation burns he had suffered during treatment for a "truck elbow." Kelly had married but, like all in his family save Norah, he left no children.

Ween Doherty remained in Vancouver. In 1942 she and Norah had bought a house in the Kerrisdale district, in what was to become her "village," where she lived until age—great age—and attendant frailties required the resources of a nursing home.

ꙮ

The distractions of war and lengthy separations, including a year Wilfred spent in Halifax, made the Mission years very difficult. It appears that Sheila did no writing to speak of during this time—or at least none that has survived—and that she did little or nothing about trying to publish the novel she had already written. By "writing" I mean "creative" writing (a distinction, incidentally, which Sheila would have deplored), for she did publish one essay during this period. Entitled "Remedial Reading," it appeared in *The BC Teacher* in January 1945.

This is an important statement by Sheila of her attitude—then and ever after—towards English studies and the place of literature in education. As the title of her essay indicates, her first concern was with reading: "To master a page the child must be provided with tools for the work and since the problem which he faces will vary he must be provided not with a single tool but with a box of tools from which he can choose at need." She questioned the accepted wisdom that it was the responsibility of the English teacher to provide these tools as well as instruction in their use. "By what special training is he qualified for [this] task?" she asked. Different subjects, she insisted, demanded different tools and different skills. After Babel, presumably, "teachers of Mathematics, Social Studies, Science, and other subjects must accept responsibility for providing practice [in] the language skills peculiar to their field."

The differing natures of the language requirements of different subjects were in her eyes only part of the problem that faced teachers whose training had been in language and literature. If the English teacher's time is to be devoted primarily to preparing students to study all subjects, then, in her words, "who is to take upon himself the function of providing the child with the common body of Literature which is his heritage and the critical judgment to appreciate and estimate the writings of today?" Students must learn to read literature as something distinct from history or physics or grammar or literature will become marginalized and its lessons lost:

> A mastery of some common body of knowledge—"the all in each of all men" as Coleridge called it—is an essential tool in the process of communication. The writer presupposes [this] knowledge on the part of the reader. He does not supply the complete context. The understanding of the reader depends on his ability to bridge gaps, to grasp implications, to understand references, to relate his experience, which is often acquired only through previous reading, to the subject which the writer is discussing. Herein lies the value of English studies in any reading program.

Sheila believed then and continued to believe that English studies consisted of more than communication skills; their nature deriving from that "common body of knowledge" called literature, which requires of a reader, at the same time that it instils, tentativeness, openness and suppleness of mind, willingness to make what Coleridge called an act of "poetic faith," to "hover" (his verb) free of perches offered by other modes of knowledge. Literature was not just a canon of works for Sheila: it represented ways of reading necessary for the student who would gain access to new modes of knowledge and of experience. What she wrote of its cryptic nature—with "gaps," "implications," and "references"—recalls Eliot, Pound, and Joyce, and the demands of High Modernism, while anticipating *The Double Hook.*

WHEN, TEN YEARS LATER, SHEILA THOUGHT BACK TO HER FLAT
IN Mission City, and to the time when she heard on the radio that the War had
ended, she remembered thinking, "W and I would be together as we had never
been." Given their ages at that time, Sheila was thirty-six and Wilfred thirty-four,
and given prospects of a more stable domestic situation, the matter of children
must have entered their considerings. Much later they both spoke of sharing with
many at the time the view that the world as it was unfolding had no place for children. Sheila became more specific, however, when she spoke of Wilfred's fears that
a mental condition which had required the institutionalizing of one of his sisters
might be hereditary.

They were indeed to be together soon, although not in Mission but in Toronto,
where they settled in 1945 so that Wilfred might continue his studies in the graduate program in English at the University of Toronto. They moved into a house at 151
Admiral Road, in the Annex district of the city, close by the university. Their landlady, a Miss Hopewell, was an absentee, and so the house was divided into two flats
with a shared kitchen. In their last year there, 1948–49, fellow student from UBC days
William Blissett and his mother shared the house with them. Blissett recalls Wilfred
and Sheila living by some mysteriously reached consensus that was expressed in such
dicta as "We never touch soft fruit" and "We call them DOVES" and "Sheila's uncle
who really knows coffee . . ." Outside their second-floor rooms were the eaves, under
which pigeons (see DOVES) nested and cooed to such an extent that Wilfred, with
Sheila's assistance, took measures to be rid of them. Looking back in 1955 to this
time and to her cooperation in this enterprise, Sheila concluded that Venus, the
pigeons' patroness, "has served me ill because of it."

They lived in Toronto for four years, until the summer of 1949. Because they
were together there were no letters exchanged that might have provided access to this
time, as their letters do during Sheila's second stay in Toronto (1956–61). Nor did
Sheila keep a journal, as she was to do later. Consequently, this time in Toronto
reveals itself in biographical fragments rather than in a sustained narrative. And
these, for the most part, are based upon recollections, rather than on records of the
moment. Without question, what we do know of this time we know from what it
resulted in: within a few years, Wilfred's doctoral thesis on Laurence Sterne's
Tristram Shandy, and, then, Sheila's second novel.

We also know that Sheila taught. She had already been teaching for a dozen years, and the school inspector at Dog Creek was not alone in recognizing her gifts and effectiveness in the classroom. She was to be the breadwinner during these Toronto years, for within a year of their arrival she took up a position at Moulton Ladies College, a preparatory school for girls, housed in its foundress' former mansion-home located on the north side of Bloor Street, just east of Yonge Street. A plaque in the building complex that now occupies this location honours the memory of the school.

Moulton College was an academic department of McMaster University, and it operated under the direction of its Board of Governors. Like the parent university, its religious affiliation was Baptist, and according to their original agreement (dated 1889), no one who was "not a member in good standing of an Evangelical Christian Church" was permitted to teach in the school. But much had changed by 1946. Under Marjorie Trotter, who was its Principal from 1930 to 1952, Moulton became one of the most progressive private schools in the country—and not at the price of secularization. Like the convent schools Sheila had attended in the west, Moulton balanced moral and religious commitment (granted, of a more moderate sort than its original agreement with McMaster spelled out) with an equally strong commitment to academic excellence, and in a setting in which women were aware as women.

Sheila taught English at Moulton from 1946 to 1949, but she is also described in the 1948 yearbook (*The Heliconian*) as "our dramatics teacher." In that year, she had been responsible for productions of Shaw's *Arms and the Man* and Goldsmith's *She Stoops to Conquer*. Earlier she had supervised productions of *A Midsummer Night's Dream* and *Twelfth Night* as well as Synge's *Riders to the Sea*. The exquisite "Cariboo-ing" of *Macbeth* by the school children in *Deep Hollow Creek* suggests something of the theatrical experience she brought to her position at Moulton.

The distance from their flat to her school was about eight blocks, which she walked daily. Looking back to this time years later, she recalled, "I had a lot of time to think during those walks. . . . The walk was the one time I had to myself. . . ." There were domestic routines to be established, something that their separate lives to this point had made unnecessary or impossible, and aside from these and her responsibilities at the school, Sheila also completed three graduate courses during these years in Toronto.

It was on one of her walks from Admiral Road to Moulton College that, according to accounts she has left in talks and interviews, Sheila experienced what was to become *The Double Hook*. In the fullest and most suggestive of these accounts, a conversation with Bruce Meyer and Brian O'Riordan in 1984, she described the episode as follows:

> We lived on Admiral Road and I remember walking down past the Park Plaza Hotel along Bloor Street. The school was just opposite where the subway station is now—just off Yonge Street . . . and I remember thinking on the corner just opposite the Anglican Church [the Church of the Redeemer stands at the corner of Bloor and Avenue Road], "I know what I am going to do—I can hear the voices beginning." Yes, that was the moment—far from the West Coast, under completely alien circumstances. I had wanted to get away from any idea of setting. Here the voices came from somewhere else. Place was important only in its relationship to them as ground. . . . It was just as if I had caught the sound of voices coming and trying to say something and I was concerned.

"Concerned"—like some urban Joan of Arc? Not very likely. Earlier in this same conversation, thinking back to what she considered the failure of *Deep Hollow Creek*, she had remarked:

> I realized . . . that there was something wrong with it and felt that somehow or other I had to get the authorial voice out of the novel for it to say what I wanted it to say. I didn't want a voice talking about something. I wanted voices.

She agreed with her interviewers that the characters named on the opening page of *The Double Hook* were the sources of these voices:

> Yes, I was thinking rather of a cry of voices—a *vox clamantis*—voices crying out in the wilderness. Something like the voices one hears in early litanies—voices reaching beyond themselves. I was thinking of a group of bodies that were virtually inarticulate and I had to make them articulate without making them faux-semblants so to speak.

At the time of her first public reading from the novel, in 1973, she had described its characters as "figures in a ground, from which they could not be separated," not as characters in a play; "I didn't think of them as people in a place, in a stage set, in a place which had to be described for itself, as it existed outside the inter-action of the people with the objects, with the things, with the other existences with which they came in contact." When, shortly after its publication in 1959, a friend attempted a dramatic adaptation of it, Sheila wrote to Wilfred: "I rather think things shouldn't be translated from one form to another—at least not from the novel into the dramatic form—the dramatic medium is too exacting—at least it has its own necessities."

Aspiring to the condition of drama is not necessarily the same as wanting to write a play, however. Sheila liked to preface her account of the voices on Bloor Street with T. S. Eliot's claim that a poem can originate in a rhythm as well as in an image, an incident, or an idea. Her journals, as we shall see, provide evidence of the extent to which—and especially in *Four Quartets*—Eliot gave her words and rhythms, a language suited to her pains and uncertainties. But he also provided a precedent for what she would do as she moved from her first to her second novel. Drama was not just a literary form whose possibilities he explored and with which he experimented as he grew older; it also came to represent for him a moral condition, an escape from a limited and limiting sense of self into a state of, in his words, "Knowing myself yet being someone other":

> So I assumed a double part, and cried
> And heard another's cry. . . .

Much earlier than the last of his *Quartets*, from which these lines are taken, Eliot had already conceived of "figures in a ground, from which they could not be separated," in a poem he originally entitled "He Do The Police In Different Voices," but which he renamed *The Waste Land*. Sheila's later insistence that the characters in *The Double Hook* "are entwined in, they're interacting with the landscape, and the landscape is interacting with them . . . not the landscape, the things about them, the other things which exist," also suggests the plays and novels of Samuel Beckett.

Her second novel was not the only fiction spawned by Sheila's experience on Bloor Street. Years later, she wrote of this Toronto period, "At this time I first began to write about the Cariboo." Had she forgotten about Murrayville and *Deep Hollow Creek* and the stories she had written in the late thirties? That is hardly likely. For a time her literary autobiography became co-extensive with the history of the writing and publication of *The Double Hook*. So intense was her reaction against an as yet unpublished *Deep Hollow Creek* that she attempted not just to repudiate it, but to bury it. We are confronted then by two chronologies, the one we have been tracing, and one that for a time Sheila herself was to promote. According to her own some-time accounts, her literary identity came into being on Bloor Street—"far from the West Coast, under completely alien circumstances." Toronto became a place of beginnings. And, as we shall see, the rewriting of her own history and of the history of *The Double Hook* did not end here.

⌇

One of Sheila's friends at Moulton was the school's librarian, Betty Endicott. Her husband, Norman, was a professor in the Department of English at the University of Toronto. His two great literary passions were the seventeenth century of John Donne and Sir Thomas Browne, and "minor" poets of the early twentieth century. He had an interest in the writings, paintings, and drawings of Percy Wyndham Lewis, who would in time become the subject of Sheila's own doctoral work. She took a graduate course with him during this period, as she did with Wilfred's thesis supervisor, Kenneth MacLean. Endicott became a mentor when Sheila returned to Toronto in the mid-fifties, and with MacLean she came to share a square of sense, recognized by both and occupied by none but themselves. She also took a course taught jointly by the head of the graduate English program, doyen of the old historicism and self-appointed spokesperson for English studies in Canada, A. S. P. Woodhouse, and his lieutenant F. E. L. Priestley.

Someone whom she did not mention during these years was Marshall McLuhan, who had joined the University of Toronto English Department in the fall of 1946, a year after Sheila and Wilfred had come. Paul Tiessen has discovered among Wilfred's papers at the University of Alberta that Wilfred had met McLuhan by chance in 1947, after a performance of *The Silver Cord* at Hart House Theatre. They crossed the campus together exchanging small talk, including their responses to the play. Wilfred made no mention of Sheila being present on this occasion, nor did she leave any record of such a meeting. Years later, in a letter to Sheila, Marshall looked back with Miltonic gusto, and something of Milton's tendency to be self-serving, to the "ghastly crew the Eng. dept. had been or become just before my arrival 18 yrs ago!"

⌇

From Toronto we went back to the University of British Columbia where I taught for two years and studied Greek and wrote the first of a series of short stories, one of which Malcolm Ross published in *Queen's Quarterly*. The story was "Brother Oedipus."

Thus Sheila, in the biographical notes she wrote for McClelland & Stewart, described the two years, 1949–51, she and Wilfred lived and taught in Vancouver. It had been sixteen years since she had left UBC, and the university she returned to differed significantly from the one she had left. The post-war influx of veterans both doubled the enrolment and changed for a time the complexion of the student body as well as of the campus itself. There were now much larger numbers of mature students, who were taught, and where necessary housed, in a type of pre-fabricated tar-papered huts which had become familiar on military bases during the war. It was very likely this association that led to the naming of one such campus residential complex, Fort Camp. Like many new faculty, including the musician–composers Frances and Harry Adaskin, their next-door neighbours, Sheila and Wilfred lived in Fort Camp. In Vancouver, the almost universal post-war housing shortage was aggravated by the numbers of veterans from other parts of the country, and especially from the prairie provinces, who chose to re-enter civilian life there.

Sheila returned to a post-Sedgewick world at UBC. The Chairman of the English Department now was Roy Daniells, who had been a year ahead of her as a student in the thirties. A protégé of Sedgewick, he had gone to Toronto to take his doctorate, and he had taught at the University of Manitoba before returning to his alma mater. His background was an interesting variation on both Sheila's and Wilfred's backgrounds. He had been born in England, of Plymouth Brethren stock, and his family, like Wilfred's, had emigrated to Vancouver Island. His father was a carpenter, who settled with his family in Victoria. In her biography of Daniells, *Professing English*, Sandra Djwa has detailed his early life, and in particular his struggles with his evangelical upbringing. Daniells grew for a time into a too scrupulous observer, and too impressionable an adherent, of the fundamentalism and the millenarianism that characterized the branch of the Brethren to which his parents belonged. Like Sheila in her youth, he experienced for a time in his adolescence an indelible kind of isolation, not in a hospital for the insane, but at the only leper colony in Canada, on D'Arcy Island, close by Victoria. Here he lived and worked with a family of Plymouth Brethren whose mission it was to care for the three lepers, all Chinese, who were quarantined there. What Sheila was to write years later in her journal remains as true for him as for herself: "The accidents of one's place of birth or upbringing one simply has to include—since exclusion makes one a cut not a picked flower."

Daniells grew into an original who was determined so to be. He became a brilliant teacher who combined the old historicism with a magnetic personality, whose touchstones for an understanding of Milton included Bernini's sculptures as well as

Puritan theology. He came to believe that the ways of Milton's God, or of anyone's God for that matter, could not be justified. He became very much a man of his place and of his times, ultimately reluctant to be tagged where matters of the soul were concerned, still admitting to being rather pleased when a British immigration officer entered "C. of E." in a space on his landing card too small for his by then preferred "Non-denominational." The tolerance he demonstrated in his love for Milton's poetry extended to a rather puzzled and uncomfortable respect he showed those whose beliefs deviated from his own secular Humanism.

Sheila was fond of Daniells, and she admired his poetry, as Wilfred did, who subsequently was to see more of him than she would. After a meeting with him in Toronto in 1952, when among other things they talked at length about Quebec and the place of the Catholic Church there, Wilfred wrote to Sheila that he found Daniells "trenchantly anti-Catholic." This was another facet of this strange, prismatic man, and of this place and these times. G. K. Chesterton's observation about John Ruskin, that he had valued everything about a Gothic cathedral except the altar, might be adapted to Daniells and his relationship with Milton, whose poetic gifts he cherished while remaining uneasy with his religious beliefs. Since the mid-thirties, Sheila had also distanced herself from the religion of her birth and her upbringing, and her marriage to Wilfred "outside the Church" ("without more than natural grace," as she phrased it) was a mark of her position. She was to observe in Paris in 1955 that she had not attended mass in twenty years. After her return to the Church in the mid-sixties she spoke almost casually of this matter. "I lost my attachment to an institution for what I now consider an irrelevant reason," she said to an interviewer with the *Western Catholic Reporter* in the mid-seventies: "As you get older the details seem to matter less; when one is younger, it's the details that are upsetting." We can only guess at the intellectual or social or political details she was referring to.

The UBC to which she and Wilfred returned in 1949 was a place where she was not alone in having been upset by "the details"—Daniells himself embodying this condition. Among Sheila's papers at the time of her death was a long fragment of a novel (about seventy pages) which she had begun working on in the fifties, as she was making her final revisions to *The Double Hook*. She refers to it in her journals simply as "Landscape," but its full title was to be "Landscape of the Moon." Its setting is a university, fairly obviously the UBC of this time when she and Wilfred were teaching there. The story was to hinge on the theft by a faculty member of a painting by an English painter whose work had long interested Sheila, Paul Nash, whose

Landscape of the Moon's Last Phase was to give the novel its title. His *Solstice of a Sunflower*, which hangs in the National Gallery in Ottawa, was to form part of a show visiting the city of the novel. It was to be stolen by one faculty member on behalf of another. All this is only anticipated in what she left.

I am introducing this work now because the nature of the details that had caused Sheila to separate herself from the Catholic Church—and their place and the place of her decision in the world to which she returned in 1949—are suggested in an exchange between this fragment's two major characters: the sometime thief, Donato Bolas (a biologist with a passion for spiders), and Niki Ehrler, (a member of the English Department whose commitment to teaching has isolated her from her students as well as from her colleagues). Bolas speaks first:

> "My life has been spent in dissecting. Once I felt I could pass on a vision of truth to my students. Now I believe only in the poetry of existence, the illusion if you will. I want to live and the young can find what truth they can. I have no faith, Miss Ehrler, in my ability to find truth for myself and no faith in my ability to transmit truth to others. But the habit is there when term begins."
>
> . . . .
>
> "What," she said, "do you intend to do? How can one teach when truth is unavailable? I have lived through a series of myths— God the Father in his Majesty crying out 'This is my beloved son,' the son asserting 'I am the resurrection and the life'; Zeus, the Great Trumpeter, white and soft and heavy with feathers, and the women crying by the river for Adonis. Then I fastened my eyes on earth and took your myth for truth."

Where Sheila differed from her characters—even from the sometime-Catholic Niki Ehrler—and, indeed, from Daniells, was in her acceptance of incoherence and inequity. She understood and sympathized with searches for order and pursuits of justice, but at the same time her response to "It isn't fair" or "right" or "just" was inevitably to ask: "Who ever said it would be?" In 1975, she would observe to an interviewer: "You see, I first went to Mass . . . with mentally-deranged Catholics. . . . It made the absurdity of life seem normal." She could not have been surprised by an event which occurred during their time at UBC, when some members of the faculty—including Roy Daniells—demonstrated outside a lecture given by the distinguished French philosopher and historian Etienne Gilson. What occasioned this demonstration was not the fact of the presence of a Catholic intellectual on the campus, for the student Newman Club had sponsored many such. It was the fact that Gilson had been invited by the university.

⌒

The English Department in which Sheila and Wilfred became sessional lecturers included some, like Hunter Lewis, who had taught her, and some, like Daniells and Bill Robbins, who had been students with her. It also included Earle Birney, and Ruth Humphrey, a colleague, a confidante, and a friend when Sheila was most in need of the kind of support she would generously provide. Humphrey had come from Victoria where she had taught at Victoria College, which like the Convent of the Sacred Heart had offered the first two years of an Arts program, and where, incidentally, she had been a friend to Emily Carr until the painter's death in 1945.

When they returned to Vancouver, Sheila was approaching forty, and she had been teaching for sixteen years. As she wrote to Daniells a few years later from Paris, "I have too many years experience . . . to be a good economic investment for any board." With the exception of a year she would teach at Powell River immediately after they left UBC, however, the rest of her teaching career was spent in universities. Aside from (or perhaps because of) her age and the classroom experience she brought to this, her first academic appointment, she also brought a satirist's eye—and ear—to her accounts of the business of a university. Such a perspective, which was to infuriate colleagues, also underlies "Landscape of the Moon." From that fragment, an account of an English Department meeting echoes her own accounts of such meetings—at UBC and elsewhere. The point of view is that of the chairman:

> The meeting, like all other department meetings, had left him dejected. But knowing that human nature was as it was he had no compensating fury to take off the misery in flame and smoke. Niki Ehrler had not answered his note and she had not come to the meeting. Bray had complained about his time table because his schedule cut up the time he wanted to spend on a new novel. Miss Simmons had sent word that she had to meet a committee from the residences. She had asked that her time table be sent to her office. Jones had objected to the length and number of essays to be assigned in the freshman classes. He was not, he said, paid—nor

were the others—to do the work the high schools had left undone. There was no more reason now than there had been ten years ago to set and mark more essays—less, indeed, since the rising cost of living had not been met by comparable increments in salary. He had, he said, taken upon himself the thankless task of drawing up a slate of essay topics. If everyone set the same subjects there would be a degree of uniformity.

He unfolded a piece of paper and read slowly so that everyone could make notes:

(a) Why I came to college

(b) The function of *The Tumbleweed,* our college paper, in college life

(c) The folly of prejudice

(d) How to make (variation allowed here to instructors and students in choice of object)

(e) The democratic way of life.

With a gesture he implied that the choice permitted ample scope for individual variation, while it insured [sic] maximum uniformity.

"I move," he said, "that we penalize all essays equally for the following gross errors:

(1) Sentence fragments

(2) Dangling modifiers

(3) Vague pronoun reference . . ."

He went on consulting his paper from time to time.

There is in the voice of Jones the voice of the administrator of Freshman English at UBC during the two years Sheila taught sections of the course. It is a voice which speaks of "a degree of uniformity" as if it meant harmony and consensus, when what it really means is "conformity"—a voice like voices Sheila would hear in Edmonton near the end of her own teaching career.

⌐

Very particular memories of these two years remained with Sheila. Buying small oeufs paté d'amande in a Paris market at Easter time in 1956, she remembered "buying egg dyes when we were in the Camp at UBC—then putting them away" admitting,

"I keep wanting to do the traditional family things." Or again in Paris, when she received word that Faber & Faber was not interested in publishing *The Double Hook*:

> I went to bed and slept and dreamed that I was going up and down the Dunbar hill in a bus. The bus finally went in through the *University* gates and along the road, through the farm into an area of factories, which seemed to have sprung up on the skull brow hill.

The "skull brow hill" recurs in her dreams and memories, and in "Landscape of the Moon." "Last night I began to write The Landscape again," she recorded in Paris in the winter of 1955, followed by, "I think of UBC and the cliffs crumbling down to the beaches, the skull brow hill in the field beyond the cows and the pig pen." At least one of the associations of the hill is with her decision to study Greek when they returned to UBC. She said later that she was prompted mainly by a desire to declaim in their original the opening lines of Aeschylus' *Prometheus Bound* from atop this same hill. In a later journal entry, partially excised by her, she records having done just this—in the company of Wilfred.

Aeschylus' tragedy, incidentally, is present in "Landscape," as Sophocles' Theban trilogy is present in a bolder fashion in four of her stories, and the *Oresteia* in *The Double Hook*. A later assertion that she had written "Brother Oedipus" and had begun to write of the Cariboo (ignoring Murrayville and Toronto) during these years at UBC give added significance to the course in "Beginners Greek" she took with Mr. Guthrie (and in which she earned 91%) in her first year back in Vancouver.

⟿

"Brother Oedipus," which Sheila said she began during these Vancouver years, was the first of four stories ("The Black Farm," "Antigone," and "The Rumble Seat" are the others) in which names from Sophocles' Theban trilogy recur. Oedipus is the only character in this first story to have a name. The others—his brother, his mother, and his wife—derive their identities from him, and from the resonance of his name: "Perhaps our father, who was a doctor, chose the name in some moment of illumination as he snipped and sewed together fragments of human life. Perhaps he chose it during his long hours of consultation. He did not say." In Sophocles, of course, mother and wife are one, and brother is also son. But they are not the mad configurations of family relations in the plays that engaged Sheila, although these are certainly present ("Of all of us Oedipus was most attached to our mother," the narrator observes). Other kinds of reality also lurk behind a name. Years later, she spoke of her use of Oedipus as a means of avoiding "experience which involves people I know." It is not always clear whether it was alternative experience she was looking to find in these materials, or masks to conceal and to transform people and situations she knew. But there was certainly something she knew—and from her earliest days—which was cunningly served by her use of myth in these stories.

Oedipus' wife, exasperated, addresses his brother, Creon, the narrator of "Brother Oedipus":

> "You sound like Oedipus," she said. "Perhaps you aren't normal like me, but mad like Oedipus. Your mother is wrong. She thinks it's alcohol. That is merely a symptom—a symptom of a greater disorder. He has never grown up. Like her he refuses to face facts. He looks at the tree as a child would. The tree has an intrinsic value, but he thinks nothing of that."

The third-written of these stories, "Antigone," contains a passage which recalls this. It involves both the narrator, a son of Creon now, not a brother of Oedipus, and one of his father's subjects, named Kallisto:

> I look at the tree. If I could see with Kallisto's eyes I wouldn't be afraid of death, or punishment, or the penitentiary guards. I wouldn't be afraid of my father's belt or his honing strap or his bedroom slipper. I wouldn't be afraid of falling into the river through a knot-hole in the bridge.

Oedipus is looking at a willow tree, in his wife's eyes as a mad man or a child would. According to Haemon, the narrator of "Antigone," Kallisto is looking at a magnolia, clear-eyed and fearless, unhampered by premonition or significance.

Sheila achieved something of the quality of vision that Oedipus' wife believed was madness in her husband, and Haemon coveted in Kallisto, precisely by her use both of these names and of the unselfconsciousness of those who bear them. They wear them like their skin, oblivious to their significance for others, aware of them only as theirs and not others' names. Witnesses to such innocence are, however, rarely innocent themselves. To be innocent in Sheila's eyes was, like her Oedipus and Kallisto, to have no sense of analogy, to see persons and things as "being" and not as "being like—." "Ha? here's three on's are sophisticated," Shakespeare's Lear admits, confronted by what he takes to be a "natural": "Thou art the thing itself."

But Lear's aspiring to the condition of a "natural" is very different from Haemon's recognition of the otherness of Kallisto. For Kallisto, Helen and Pan and the other subjects in the kingdom of Haemon's father are not present as embodying modes of existence, like poor Tom's, to be idealized and imitated. They remain remote and mysterious in the world they share with the sophisticated.

⤶

These two years in Vancouver, 1949–1951, represented the middle of Sheila's life. She entered her forties shortly after their arrival, and she also reached the mid-point in her teaching career. She appears to have crossed a shadow line which separated her early writing—her first novel and her first published story—from the mythically charged "Brother Oedipus" and her similarly charged second novel. It is tempting to speculate about factors that might explain this movement. The world into which she had been born provided evidence that the distance between naturalism and what myth can embody was sometimes no distance at all. Myth could be a mode of realism, and not merely an alternative to it. It could provide ways of seeing that approximated Kallisto's vision—and which could also explain the presence of Kallisto—and of Antigone, Oedipus, Coyote, Jonah, and others in the world in which she lived. And that was not solely an intellectual and a literary discovery. It ran deeper than this. It underlay her impatience with the non-naturalized colonialist ignoring the authenticity of what is at hand. It underlay her religion's insistence that one is never removed from the extremities of human experience—that in the eucharist, Calvary is always present. Oedipus' roots may be in Thebes and Jonah's fate might be associated with Nineveh, but they increasingly became the stuff of Sheila's fiction because of their fabulous presence, and not because of their remoteness.

⤶

In the November before Sheila and Wilfred had moved from Toronto to Vancouver, Norah gave birth to the first of her five children. This was Ween's first grandchild and Sheila's first niece. Sheila and Wilfred marked the occasion by going west that Christmas. There is a photograph—taken presumably by Norah—which shows five adults wearing paper hats such as one finds in Christmas crackers—five adults and one baby. The baby—hatless—is in the middle of the picture, held by her paternal grandmother, who is seated on a chesterfield, flanked by Ween and by Sheila, who are in turn flanked by the baby's father—David Mitchell—and Wilfred, sitting on either arm of the chesterfield. Over David Mitchell's shoulder, there is the unmistakable thin, vertical glitter of tinsel on a Christmas tree. There are glasses, and cigarettes in the hands of Wilfred and his brother-in-law. There are good-humoured looks being exchanged by the men, as Ween smiles indulgently on the baby, and on the obvious bliss of the baby's other grandmother. Sheila sits between the viewer and the baby, by the baby's head, seeming to touch or at least to tend towards it. We see her and her paper hat in profile. The mitre-like hat seems twice the size of her head. With its polka dots set against a light background, it dominates the picture. It insists upon its own centrality—the hat, that is, not its wearer—as it vies with the intended focus of the picture.

The baby is Barbara Jane, beloved of Sheila and Wilfred, witness to Sheila's final gesture. The carnivalesque air of the photograph, with just a hint of a mock-baptism being administered by Sheila, transforms a tender domestic moment into something surreal, rather like a scene in a play by Genet.

Sheila must have liked the photograph. She was made uneasy by sentimentality, and not merely as a sign of foolishness or weakness. "I've always been afraid of sentimentality—the two kinds—the—the second as frightening as the first—the sentimentality of the naturalistic novel, the sentimentality of violence, the ash-can world and the prostitutes and so on." "Afraid" and "frightening" are strong words in this context. Daphne Marlatt, one of her interlocutors on the occasion of this statement, in the hotel room in Vancouver in 1975, grasped the significance of her words:

> The not-falling between the two sentimentalities makes for a very
> spare form of writing which recognizes the simple facts of existence,
> both of oneself and others, as well as what may happen between
> them. They happen, they *happen*, and nothing is made of them
> internally in the stream of consciousness way. That allows for a kind
> of phenomenal quality.

Sheila responded, "I'd like to think so"—for this is to see as Kallisto saw. Then she would have no fear—of death, of her father's belt, or "of falling into the river through a knot-hole in the bridge."

∼ VII ∼

BY 1951, THE HUGE INCREASE IN UNDERGRADUATE REGISTRATIONS
following the Second World War had come to an end, and universities had entered
a period of smaller enrolments, which would last until the baby-boom of the early
sixties. With the prospect that their sessional appointments would not be renewed,
and with Wilfred in the final stages of preparing his thesis, which he would present
for its defense in October 1951, Sheila decided that the bird-in-the-hand principle
required her to return to high-school teaching. She applied for, and was appointed
to a position in the public high school in Powell River, a coastal lumbering town,
six hours and two ferry rides north of Vancouver. But in the meantime, Wilfred
received an offer from a satellite college of the University of Alberta located in
Calgary. He accepted it on the understanding that he would be eligible for an
appointment to the English department at the main campus in Edmonton when one
became available.

He asked Sheila to break the contract she had signed and go to Calgary with
him. But it was not in her nature to break contracts. Wilfred came to believe that
her refusal to go with him led to their subsequent domestic trials. Even Sheila came
to repeat this as accounting for what followed, as if there had been a decisive
moment in their relationship, and it was she who had made the wrong decision. It
is likely that it was Sheila who made the decision, but it is unlikely that the issue to
be decided was ever as clear as their memories made it. A passage in a letter Wilfred
wrote to her from Calgary that December 1951 gives a more accurate sense of what
had confronted her: "I had not intended to give you the impression that I accepted
your decision with a bad grace—but I didn't feel I cd. decide against it—and yet I
felt I shd.—and wd. hate you to think that I didn't want to decide against it—for I
did—but still couldn't."

Sheila spoke only glancingly of her year in Powell River, the school year
1951–52. She spoke of the place and the time as not figuring in her history or in the
history of her writing as her two years at Dog Creek had. It was potentially a rhyming
situation which simply did not rhyme. "I knew I was only going to teach there for a
year," she replied to a question of Daphne Marlatt about the impact of this time and
place on the novel conceived in Toronto. "When I went to the Cariboo in the early
thirties, I thought this is it. This is where God has flung me. The Powell River experience was quite different."

What she remembered in particular of that year were "the damp trees, and the sea, and the weekends of talk" with the art teacher at her school, Vito Cianci, and his wife, Erol. They lived at the edge of town, and Sheila often spent weekends with them, sitting for a head sculpted by Erol and talking with Vito about Dante, who had been read to him by his mother when he was a child. Cianci had studied at the then newly established Vancouver School of Applied and Decorative Art in the late twenties when Frederick Varley was teaching there, and he had accompanied Varley on at least one of his sketching treks into Garibaldi Park. He had written of this while he was still a student, and of "the boundless sweep of sky and country away from man's depressing influence," and of "a feeling of absolute unity with all the gorgeous manifestations of the surroundings." His conversations with Sheila, however amiable, must have been a study in contrasts: this son of Wordsworth as well as of Dante and this daughter of Swift.

Although she lived and taught in Powell River for only the one year, she was remembered. In July 1989, her senior matriculation class invited her to attend their first-ever reunion. Sheila and Wilfred were living on Vancouver Island, in Nanaimo by this time, but that spring Sheila had the first of a series of falls that marked and marred the final decade of her life. One of those who attended the reunion reported on it to her and sent her copies of pages from their yearbook that included pictures of the staff and of the class. There are two photographs of Sheila, one with photos of the staff that is captioned "Mrs. Watson/English" and one with photos of the matriculants of 1952. This is captioned "Sheila Watson" and is accompanied by a verse:

> Explains to Bernie
> Discusses with Allan
> Coaches Bill
> Encourages Bruce
> Reasons with Stan
> Laughs with Fred
> Understands Art
> Defends Muriel and Angella
> Likes us all in spite of our ways
> . . . Forgets herself.

It was the Muriel of this litany who had written to her, telling her of the lives of her one-time students, and of their memories of "the warm and gentle way you taught English."

In the spring of 1952, when the academic term in Calgary had ended and Sheila was finishing her year in Powell River, Wilfred travelled to Toronto to a conference of university teachers of English. He gave a paper on the "New Romantics" (Edith Sitwell, Dylan Thomas, et al.), and met, as he wrote Sheila, "most of the English professors across Canada." Many of these he knew from his days at UBC, at Toronto, and now at Calgary. The chairman of the University of Alberta's Department of English, F. M. Salter, was there, and he judged Wilfred's the best paper of the conference, although he took exception to his delivery. "Endicott squirmed once, but said nothing" while "Ned Pratt came over and spoke warmly of it." Robbins of UBC "gave a passionate defence of the teaching of composition as an education in itself." Woodhouse of Toronto "declared that what was wrong with freshmen was that they needed to be told that they were illiterates." Also present, "Frye gave an incomprehensible harangue on the archetypes."

The time in Toronto gave Wilfred an opportunity to visit with Roy Daniells. They were staying in the same student residence, at Victoria College, and for some days shared over coffee, beer, Jewish rolls, Swiss cheese, their poetry and thoughts. At lunch one day, Daniells showed Wilfred a poem he had recently written entitled "Quebec." It was this occasion that evoked from Wilfred the judgement that Daniells was "trenchantly anti-Catholic."

It was also during this time that he came upon Marshall McLuhan's first-published book, *The Mechanical Bride*, at Britnells Bookstore. He sent a copy to Sheila so that she and the Ciancis might read it together. His mentioning the book before she had received it elicited from Sheila the question, "What is this *Mechanical Bride*?"—and from Wilfred, a blurb-like response: "an investigation into modern attitudes via the comic strips, advertisements, etc."

Wilfred went on to Boston, which they had visited together when they were living in Toronto, for three weeks of work in the libraries at Harvard. He was revising his recently-defended doctoral thesis with an eye to its publication. Meanwhile, Sheila was making preparations to leave Powell River and to join him in Edmonton, where he was to teach summer school. And then they were to proceed to Calgary.

The two years they were together in Calgary—1952–54—were, according to her own accounts, her most productive years as a writer. They would also prove to be among the most painful years in her relationship with Wilfred. In Sheila's mind, Calgary became synonymous with the writing of *The Double Hook* as well as with her memory of the pain of those years: "conceived in Toronto and written in Calgary," she declared in 1984. Earlier, in 1975, she provided a chronology of the novel's gestation, which she elaborated upon, but from which she never deviated:

> One day on Bloor Street, when we were living in Toronto just after the war, I knew what I was going to do. And then we came away and worked at UBC, as you know. And then I went to Powell River for a year and then to Calgary, and it was then that I started writing *The Double Hook*.

She could be even more precise: "I wrote the book in Calgary, you know, the second year I was in Calgary." That she was working on it then is clear from a letter which Wilfred wrote to her in April of that second year (1954) from Edmonton, where he had gone to mark final examinations. He refers both to "Brother Oe[dipus] and the Double Hook" as preoccupying her. But two years earlier, in January 1952, when she was teaching in Powell River and before she had moved to Calgary, Wilfred wrote of the Christmas they had just spent together: "What talk we did have, we did have— And this is a saying from the Double Hook or might well be." A few months later, in April 1952, he wrote that he had bought her a painting by A. Y. Jackson entitled "Cariboo Spring" (for $60), as a companion to "your Cariboo work." Wilfred might have been referring to *Deep Hollow Creek*, which the previous November he had urged her to send to Macmillan's, but he might also have had in mind her second Cariboo novel.

Wilfred's January letter suggests that Sheila had at least started to work on this in Powell River, if not earlier. She spoke later of both Toronto and Vancouver as places where she first wrote out of her experience of the Cariboo, consigning to oblivion what she had written earlier, in Murrayville. In 1948, when they were living in Toronto, and before she had consigned it to oblivion, she had sent the manuscript of *Deep Hollow Creek* to McClelland & Stewart, together with what the editor described as "the excerpt of the new novel." The editor, Sybil Hutchinson, passed this last on to Robert Weaver of the CBC, who found the excerpt "a little insubstantial" to be read on the network.

Sheila's insistence upon associating the writing of *The Double Hook* with their time in Calgary was rooted in her memories of those years. These memories, like a disease of the retina, transformed everything that occasioned them. Bach came to remind her of a Christmas Eve in Calgary, when "the music was like a noose." She wrote of that time as well, "I remember bringing home G[abriel] M[arcel]'s lectures from the Calgary Public Library—then having them used as the ground of my own destruction." In Paris, she would observe Wilfred turning "his face to Calgary and to his vision," and later, in Vancouver, imagine him "getting off the train at Calgary bird-dog eager." Because her stories of those years became entwined with her accounts of the writing of the novel, those who heard the stories assumed some connection—some broadly causal rather than narrowly autobiographical connection—between them. She had coped by writing. She had tried to distance herself from the emotional ground on which she found herself. And this was not the first time she used writing as a means of coping with pain. She had started to write as a child during the time of her father's fatal illness.

Years later, Sheila observed, "It seems curious to record that I have been defended and consoled by a horse and three dogs." A dog named Doto was one of the latter, providing her with a hedge against loneliness during these Calgary years as Juno had done in Dog Creek. Wilfred had bought Doto, a pointer who acted as conscientiously upon the dictates of her own nature as Sheila did upon the dictates of her conscience. Doto persisted in pointing long after the game whose scent had aroused her had disappeared. She was Sheila's companion for walks in the hills and by the river. She provided a gauge for her loneliness, as Juno had, although not in a smoking way. Sheila confessed to talking to Doto about T. S. Eliot's criticism and quoting his poetry to her.

Sheila's seemingly unambiguous accounts of the time and the place of the writing of her second novel were hardly intended to deceive Wilfred—or herself. She appears to have exaggerated the importance of her time in Calgary in the writing of *The Double Hook*—as some writers have endowed their works with false sources and, consequently, with false genealogies. For most of her readers, it makes little difference if it was begun in one place and finished in another. But for Wilfred, the prospect of its being an "objective correlative" for their time in Calgary must have been indeed disturbing. It is small wonder that he would attempt to trivialize her second novel, and that, as he admitted much later to me, he preferred *Deep Hollow Creek* to it.

During the year of their separation—not really a year, as they were together for Christmas and Easter and perhaps at other times—Wilfred had begun a relationship with a student which was to haunt their marriage for years to come, and all but destroy it. This was not to be his only liaison, and perhaps it was not even the first since their marriage, but it did mark a point that once passed admitted of no return.

78

Before they married, Sheila had told Wilfred that he was not the first man she had loved. "In the torment of the winter . . . in Calgary," as she referred to that period later, she decided to tell him what that earlier relationship had meant to her. She believed that Wilfred's new alliance required her honesty. In an agonized variation on the confession of Gretta to Gabriel in Joyce's "The Dead," her action betrayed her intention. In consequence, "Now when I have hurt him . . . and he wants to hurt back he says something to remind me." "He reminds me often," she continued, "that when I wrote *The Double Hook* in its first drafts, I believed that complete communication between two people was not possible. This belief he says had contorted all my writing: perhaps—and perhaps—."

The memory from her two years in Calgary that remained most vividly with Sheila was of sitting on the landing in the house where she and Wilfred had an apartment, alone and abandoned after he and his young friend had, in a painful interview of their arranging, told her what her own Felix Prosper could only imagine telling an unwelcome guest, to "keep-moving, scatter, get-the-hell-out." During this same time, she had reason to believe that she might have breast cancer. Before she learned that her fears were groundless, she had to acknowledge to herself that the only person she could talk with about her condition—Wilfred—was the one person she could not talk with now. Her correspondence with Anne Angus in Vancouver during this time was a life-line, in Sheila's words, "a guy-rope that I steady the load with when it seems in danger of toppling." "I can really quite understand why even in the very private act of dying," she wrote to her friend in November 1953, "a person wants the assurance of some steadying hand—a mere standing by." Their bond was a thing of gender, education and class, of place, and creative sympathy (Anne Angus wrote poetry), and temperament. "Both you and I belong to the type of emotional beings who can best help ourselves," Mrs. Angus wrote to Sheila in January 1954:

> Perhaps we are each too intelligent to accept attempts at "straightening out" from less intelligent beings? Perhaps, too, we are each too delicately balanced to risk that so fine adjustment in the hands of the less sensitive, the less perceptive. . . . Reticence is a necessity with both of us, but more so for you—I am eight years older! Perhaps always more should be implicit than explicit between us?

Each respected and understood the reticence of the other: there were shared interests, affection, and discretion.

Sheila read Anne Angus's poetry with care and interest, and wrote more openly to her than to anyone about her own work. In November and December 1953, during her second year in Calgary, she gave her an account of the writing of what would become the first draft of "Antigone": "I have just finished a short story—an impulse in the midst of *The Double Hook*. I started it one evening when W was out and have finished it in about a week—not bad time for me. Now I must concentrate on James Potter." A few weeks later she continued: "I will try to type a copy of the story and send it to you. I had called it 'The Funeral' (Trust me) since the central theme and the situation suggested the title—but it might better be called 'The Magnolia Tree.' It is a slight story but I enjoyed writing it. I am convinced that one must write as one can—under discipline." Then she commented on a reaction against the modernists which she knew would have implications for her own work:

> There is a tremendous voice rising in Canada (echoed from England and the USA) crying out for clarity. John Sutherland quotes from *Poetry Chicago*: "By now James, Pound, Eliot, Joyce are dowds, jades and trulls of Parnassus." This reminds me of the anti-Tennysonians of my youth. God rest James, Pound, Eliot and Joyce. They did and wrote as they could. Why must fury be used to drive out fury? I have little hope for *The Double Hook* even in its expanded form.

Sheila's final comment suggests that, in her second year in Calgary, she reworked rather than wrote *The Double Hook*.

In this same autumn of 1953, at the suggestion of Professor F. M. Salter of Edmonton, Sheila sent "Brother Oedipus" to *Queen's Quarterly*, whose editor then was Malcolm Ross. Years later, Ross recalled his response to it: "Well do I remember the day when 'Brother Oedipus' came to my office at Queen's—and the excitement I felt as I read the story. I felt like 'stout Cortez' and knew that something unique and great had come to pass." At the time, his language—to Sheila at least—was more measured. He suggested that she reconsider what seemed to him certain "over-literary" and "self-conscious" references early in the story. She complied, and the story appeared in the summer number of 1954.

A part of Sheila's own re-working of her literary life, which saw it begin with voices on Bloor Street and not with "The Barren Lands" and "Rough Answer" and the years at Murrayville, took the form of crediting Ross with being her first publisher. It was an acknowledgment fondly intended. In the spring of 1954, while she was still in Calgary, she sent him the second of the four stories in which Oedipus and his family figure, the story entitled "The Black Farm." Ross was prepared to publish it, but he suggested that she send it to *Hudson Review*, believing publication there "would do a lot for you in the US." When this strategy failed, he proposed a joint venture with the CBC, with *Queen's Quarterly* publishing the story and its being read on radio. Sheila was in Paris when she heard that the CBC was hesitant about such an arrangement. The story did, however, appear in *Queen's Quarterly* in the summer of 1956.

⌐

It is not clear when or under what circumstances Sheila first met Frederick M. Salter. He was Chairman of the English Department at the University of Alberta at Edmonton when Wilfred was hired to teach at Calgary College. He had done distinguished work in the field of medieval drama, more specifically on the York Cycle of plays, and he taught Shakespearean drama as well. More important in the present context, he taught a creative writing course, which numbered among its alumni W. O. Mitchell.

In early December 1951, with Sheila in Powell River and Wilfred in Calgary, Wilfred wrote concerning plans for Christmas, which they were to spend in Edmonton, that the Salters had invited them to a party. This is perhaps when she and Salter first met. By autumn 1953, when she sent "Brother Oedipus" to Ross at Salter's suggestion, she had obviously had discussions with him about her work. In autumn 1954, after Wilfred had been promoted to Edmonton and they had moved there from Calgary, she gave Salter a typescript of *The Double Hook*. She had already had it returned by the publisher Rupert Hart-Davis of London, with his judgement that it had "too many characters and themes, all insufficiently explored, too much motion and dust," and by the editor of MacMillans in Canada, Kildare Dobbs, who has since admitted that his first response to Sheila's novel had been conditioned by his recent reading of *Cold Comfort Farm*. In this same autumn, in November 1954, Sheila also sent a collection of Wilfred's poems, gathered under the title *Friday's Child*, to Faber & Faber in London for their consideration.

The novel that Salter received from Sheila, already read and returned by two publishers, differed from the novel that was finally published in seemingly small, though significant, ways, many of which are traceable both to Salter's editorial suggestions and to his formulation of what it was he saw in *The Double Hook*. His final comment in a letter to Sheila, dated 12 December 1954, remained his estimate of her accomplishment: "Of the quality, artistry, moving power of your book there isn't, and cannot be, the slightest question. It is an amazing performance." Earlier in this same letter, he had referred to it as "a perfect work."

In prefatory comments to her first public reading from the novel, in Edmonton in 1973, Sheila spoke of Salter and of his first response to it:

> He used to lecture me every once in a while and say, "The way you write a novel, the way you put a novel together is the way you put together a pigpen—you do it with craft and skill, and in an orderly fashion." He read the manuscript and he combed it through trying to find that the roads didn't go in the right direction or the people had on the wrong clothes or the clock was telling the wrong time of day, because he thought, well somehow this must happen in a novel that was written in this way, there must be some slip.

"I have even gone to the trouble of mapping the countryside," he had written to Sheila, "and your references to it never slip." He did, however, discover other slips— in syntax, in detail, in taste. "I don't like the word *bugger*," he wrote of an expletive used by James Potter, and of Theophil's *bullshit*, he insisted: "You can't use this word. It seems in character for Theophil, but you can't use it." The offending words disappeared from the novel.

Salter showed an eye for detail which matched Sheila's own. He responded to the phrase "as they that take off the yoke on their jaws" with "Yokes lie on the neck, not in the jaws." At James's reference to a "stud book" he demurred: "does not the stud book belong to show-horse or pedigreed stock? I should expect all their [the Potters's] stock to be scrub." At the prospect of a prostitute named Lilly unbuttoning James's shirt pocket to steal his wallet, he observed, "You make Lilly a far more skillful pick-pocket than she needs to be. I should say nothing about the button."

His main concern was with the novel's ending. It did not satisfy him because it seemed too calculatingly right. As he wrote,

> I suppose it could be justified as a happy ending, the baby being a promise of the future. Some readers would take it so. And, after all, you have got rid of some poisonous intrusions into your little Eden, and no dread consequences are to be expected from the death[s] of Greta and the old lady. Even Kip has forgiven James, and seems content with things as they are.

In the draft of the novel he was reading, the last words were Lenchen's, spoken upon the return of her lover, the father of her child: "I see James in his plaid shirt. He's lifting up the baby in his own two hands." Salter commented: "I feel the need of a hint or suggestion of some kind that you have been dealing with things eternal and not transitory." Accordingly, he proposed a coda which would include references to Coyote, the double hook, glory and pain and fear, all ending with the traditional acknowledgement of endlessness, "*per omnia saecula saeculorum.*" Sheila herself was to achieve something of the effect he desired by reordering the last lines of this draft and adding only one detail—Lenchen's "His name is Felix."

Salter was determined to see the novel published, and he brought to his determination the experience of a teacher who had had success placing the work of student-writers. He believed that "a campaign" had to be mounted. He knew that "in the ordinary way, no publisher will take it"; "No editor will publish what he does not understand." Central to this campaign, therefore, was an "explanation" of the novel:

> I have . . . roughed out a Foreword. It would, of course, be best done
> by yourself—provided you did not get off into the cloudy abstract
> and unintelligible symbolic. Such an explanation would not only
> show the publisher and editor what sort of goods he was dealing
> with, but it would give readers a necessary leg-up for the ride.

His gibe at Sheila's taste for "the cloudy abstract and unintelligible symbolic" was occasioned by a statement she had already written about her novel and its origins, which had earlier evoked from Salter a bemused response: "What amazes me is that you should do such a perfect work and not be able to explain it."

His campaign took the form of writing to the editor of *The Atlantic Monthly*, enclosing a copy of his foreword; this on 17 December 1954. "If you should be interested in *Double Hook* as an 'Atlantic Serial,' or for separate publication, we can send on the novel itself; but if you are dismayed by the difficulties which are described in the Foreword , we shall both save time by keeping the novel home." He had chosen *The Atlantic* because two of his protégés—W. O. Mitchell and R. H. Blackburn—had been launched there, and because, as he had observed to Sheila, its tie-in with Little Brown meant two birds with one stone, or at least two publishers with one foreword.

The foreword served its purpose. *The Atlantic* sent for the novel, and considered it as part of a competition. In early May 1955, however, the Director, Dudley Cloud, wrote to Sheila to tell her that they did not think they "could make a success of the book." "The jury divided quite sharply," he reported, and those who "doubted that enough readers would understand it" prevailed. Cloud ended his account of these deliberations with what was to prove a prescient observation: "This novel will never be accepted by a committee, but it might achieve publication wherever the decision depends on the judgement of one man." Before she found that "one man"—in the person of Jack McClelland—Sheila had Paris ahead of her and the final revisions to her novel.

The statement about her second novel, which Sheila had written before it had reached its final form and that evoked Salter's gibe about her taste for the abstract and the unintelligible, provides an interesting gloss upon Wilfred's claim that when she wrote "its first drafts" she "believed that complete communication between two people was not possible." Sheila confirmed that the loneliness and the sense of isolation she had experienced when she had gone to Dog Creek were where the novel had begun:

> Here for perhaps the first time in my life I was alone for hours of the day and night and often for days in succession. I was alone physically I mean except for the dog at hand and the horse in the stable. Yet round me and in myself too I became actively conscious of another kind of loneliness, the kind Angel speaks of when she says to Felix: "Take a man and a woman. There's no word to tell that when they get together in bed they're still anything but two people." Man is born with this loneliness or he becomes aware of it at least with his first consciousness. The human heart cries out not to be freed from spatial separation, but from the isolation of which spatial separation is a symbol, the isolation of mind from mind, the intolerable burden of I-ness.
>
> . . . .
>
> The theme of the book is simply this: A man thrown back on the resources of his own nature alone responds to life with violence or inertia. If men are thrown back on their own nature alone and on the contemplation of natural or mechanical forces, if they have neither an image of church or state or even of tribal unity, if they are cut off from a rooted pattern of behaviour whatever that pattern may be, they respond to life with violence or apathy, because overwhelmed with a sense of isolation they attempt to wrench themselves away from human contact, to force themselves into conjunction with it, or to retreat further into themselves to seek protection in their loneliness. They want to bear witness to the

curious power which they feel in themselves and yet to shrink from the hostile attention of others.

This had been Sheila's first account of the origins of *The Double Hook*, and her first reading of it, written while she was still in the time and place of its writing and before she had undertaken her final revisions to it. It is uncertain if Wilfred read this statement, and whether his claim (recorded by her) that she did not believe "that complete communication between two people" was possible arose in response to this passage, to the novel, or to their own deteriorating relationship. Common to all three was Sheila's experience of isolation.

⌣

Meanwhile, Sheila's efforts on behalf of Wilfred's poetry met with greater success than Salter's efforts on behalf of her novel. Faber & Faber, in the person of T. S. Eliot, wrote to "Miss Sheila Watson" on 5 January 1955: "I and one of my colleagues and a third critic have all read FRIDAY'S CHILD, and we are very positively of the opinion that Faber & Faber should publish these very remarkable poems." A few years later, a senior editor with Faber provided Sheila with a first-hand account of Eliot's response to Wilfred's manuscript: "how 'Tom' had read steadily for two hours and came in wonder at the discovery—the first real Canadian poetry—that is the first real poetry written in Canada."

Eliot had asked for information about the author, and to be put "into direct communication with him in relation to a contract." It was Sheila, however, not Wilfred who replied to his letter. "I have given your letter to my husband. He has authorized me to accept Faber and Faber's offer of publication." On a more personal note, she admitted to Eliot that his letter "was the answer to an act of faith," and she ended the requested brief account of Wilfred's life with a declaration: "His complete and consuming passion is poetry. His whole life is turned to it as to the sun." To Anne Angus she wrote, "I feel now that W will be able to fend for himself. As far as I am concerned now . . . I could sing my 'Nunc dimittis.'"

∼ VIII ∼

WITHIN TWO MONTHS OF THE EXCITEMENT AND GRATIFICATION OF Eliot's letter, their domestic situation had reached a breaking point. On 14 March 1955, Wilfred received a special delivery letter from his young friend, which, as Sheila wrote to Anne Angus, "apparently . . . forced the issue." It was in response to this letter and these times that Sheila started the journals that she kept until 1995.

"Since the 14 & the s[pecial] d[elivery] letter, time stretched tight," is her opening comment in the first of her surviving journals. The entry is dated 25 March [1955]—as any convent alumna would know, the Feast of the Annunciation, or as the English have it, Lady Day—in the Middle Ages, the first day of a new year:

> Last night I dreamed that W took me into a room where [his young friend] was sleeping. "See," he said, "how beautiful she is and weep." Today all day except for a moment when I walked with Doto through the sunlight over the snow, I whirled on the circumference—I can't bear to be the cause of hurt. Yet it is the very incarnation of this moment. If W goes tomorrow I shall say nothing at all. Already I break from the moment. Yet all winter I have said to my soul "be still, and wait without hope / For hope would be hope for the wrong thing."

A few weeks later, on 6 April, another special delivery letter arrived for Wilfred—"at a little after eight," Sheila noted in her journal. "This is the unwitting cruelty of the child surely—dramatic and urgent—comment on the 'misery and torment' of another is meaningless in the clear light of action—not meaningless in intent." In this same month, she left Edmonton, first for Calgary, and then for Vancouver.

Within days of her departure, Wilfred wrote her in Calgary:

> You said if I called you, you'd come. I do call you now—and please, if you love me, come soon—immediately—I want you to come back to me completely—perhaps I have killed all your affection for me— if some remains—please don't—I don't know what I mean—please come right away. Bless you—

He added as a post-script: "If only the French thing could happen—it would give us both a chance." The reference is to a fellowship "for study in France, Holland or Italy which [had] been established to use up 'blocked funds' and which [were] administered by the Royal Society of Canada." This passage is from a letter which Henry Angus had written to Sheila in the fall of 1954, encouraging her to apply for such a fellowship, whose value was $4000. It was very likely at her suggestion that Wilfred—and not she—applied.

On the third of May, Wilfred wrote her to Vancouver, where she was staying with her friend and former colleague Ruth Humphrey.

> Because there is now an absolute and irrevocable end to that, there is also the possibility of the beginning again which you said I'd never given a chance. It has all the chances now—if you wish it—the possibility of the summer's change of climate and scenery—at once. I know about "giving comfort root room." But your coming quickly would be the real answer, decision, forgiveness.
>
> Beyond that, I think it would be better to discuss nothing. The hurt is more in the words than the act. And the healing is in the act not in the words.

Before she had left Edmonton, Sheila had recorded in her journal some of those "words":

> W has said: "You have no rights except the right of support (financial)—you are like a harpooner with your rope on the whale—your morals are the morals of a pharisee. Your tragedy is the tragedy of Othello—you would upbraid any one who acted as you are acting . . . you say you will not divorce me merely to torture me—to make me feel the way you want me to feel—"
>
> These things I record to remind me, although I don't think I shall forget. He said: "You use everything even Doto to torment me."
>
> He said: "You can do what you did before you married me—get a job."

She concluded this entry, "This part of him speaking against the other part, I have no defence—the intolerable shirt of fire—."

Wilfred had no grounds for suing Sheila for a divorce, and she had no heart to sue him. At the time in Canada, only adultery could provide reason for divorce—as distinct from annulment—and Wilfred was as reluctant to provide evidence of his own actions as Sheila would have been to act upon such evidence. Both Anne and Henry Angus counselled her during this time, as did Salter, whose "in situ" advice she had sought. She also consulted a lawyer recommended to Salter by the Dean of the Faculty of Law.

She agreed to apply for a legal separation, but complications obscured even this step. She was advised that Alberta courts seldom granted separations unless both parties appeared. This meant that Sheila would have had to remain in Edmonton, staying "in a room somewhere," as she wrote to Anne Angus, a prospect she found "intolerable." She was also advised that she should "make a claim for support whether I enforce it or not." "My whole inclination is to ask for nothing," she responded.

On 16 April, while still in Edmonton, she had written:

> I try to understand. W said tonight "I stopped loving you when there was a stronger bond between me and some one else—" Whatever I try to think I cannot help feeling the malicious time element. How is it that I suddenly become cruel, lacking in under-standing, pusillanimous? I can understand the falling in love but not the endless hours—the cabin outside Calgary—turning things over like fallen leaves—.

Eight days earlier, on Good Friday, she had recalled another Good Friday three years earlier when she had travelled to Calgary from Powell River for the Easter break. "I did not know then why our world had turned to granite but it had. I remember W sitting in the front bedroom of the Goetts's—where he had put up a table—the sudden wild furies without any objective correlative—the unutterable days again in the cabins—."

On the day before this, Maundy Thursday of 1955, her thoughts had been driv-en by the season. "The water rises—it covers the face of the earth but there is no ark." Wilfred read to her from one of his poems. "The waves abate for a moment—the heart responds to the slightest vibration of the voice—the flash of a glance—I say to my heart be still—." The day before this, the day on which the second special deliv-ery letter from Wilfred's friend had arrived, Sheila indulged in a kind of emotional bookkeeping. Again, she had moved out from the Old Testament: "I remember the torment of reading the Book of Job last winter—W becomes Bildad et al.—bar-barous divorce laws—legal fictions—until the mind whirls like one of the little whirligigs we loved so as children." And then she had tallied:

Yesterday my thoughts again walked through the past years—the indecision about the army—the year in Halifax—Rupert—the going to Toronto—pressure brought to help with work resignation from Moulton—the year [sic] at UBC—W's going back to Toronto—the year at Powell River and the cold horror of the year at the Goetts' with its miserable denouement in the squalor of the Stockdale cabin—.

Yet balanced by a thousand still moments—the platform at Jasper—the meeting in Toronto—the rocks at Cape Cod—music and books and pictures—the letter from E[liot] about *Friday's Child*—other moments molded into the perfect chrysolite that I would hold as something not to be set down for Helen, or Heloise, or Eve—or Stella [of Swift's *Journal to Stella*].

"So one joins the furious tribe," she concluded her tallying, a tribe which presumably included Medea.

When Wilfred was awarded the fellowship that would take him to Paris, he asked Sheila to accompany him. Why? Because she was his audience and his better self, because she mediated between him and the world. What is more, his young friend—for all her apparent eagerness—declined his invitation to go with him, and Wilfred never relished the prospect of a bachelor existence. But why did Sheila accept his invitation? The "slightest vibration," "the flash of a glance," perhaps, and "the perfect chrysolite that [she] would hold as something not to be set down."

◠

Of the four places to which by will or by circumstance she became especially attached, the only one that did not receive a share of Sheila's ashes, was Paris. Here she made her final revisions to *The Double Hook*, and all but completed what she considered her most fully realized work, "Antigone." Here she also kept a journal.

She was to write in 1958, in Toronto, "One writes in a note book, I suppose to keep the darkness pushed back." And she added, "It seems a foolish occupation—like drawing arabesques in the dust." Dog Creek occasioned notebooks that Sheila chose to destroy and fiction that has survived. In Paris, she revised and completed what had originated elsewhere—in Dog Creek and New Westminster—but she also wrote and sketched to the moment, and she saw to it that her "pen and pencil sketches" were not lost. A brief attempt to fictionalize her life here as she lived it is the only evidence we have of an impulse to transform, not simply to record her experience in and of Paris. On the cover of the "cahier" that contains this fragment, she had written, "Defenser d'ouvrir./ aussi./ Defenser d'afficher/ loi Mardi 30 aout 1955."

"Keeping a journal," Sheila observed during this year, "is a sort of private correspondence." But with whom? When I discovered the Paris notebooks among papers she sent me in the nineties, and told her that they along with her other journals must be published, although only after Wilfred had died, there was silence at the other end of the telephone line, and then: "I want my story told."

And that is what I am about. My first instinct was to let her tell her own story, to publish the journals, along with such materials as would fill gaps and furnish contexts. Some, including Ellen Seligman of McClelland & Stewart who had worked with Sheila when *Deep Hollow Creek* was being prepared for publication, felt my proposal would result in something ungainly, and that a biography was a necessary prologue to a reading of the journals. I am still persuaded that the journals were not left for a friend or a biographer to peruse or plunder, but for a wider audience. Montaigne observed of his essays, "Many things that I would not tell anyone, I tell the public. . . ." Marshall McLuhan was intrigued by this passage: "The man of letters as engaged in self-expression is meaningless without his public," he wrote to a friend. "He can, as it were, carry on an inner dialogue between himself and his public."

To provide the reader with some experience of such "an inner dialogue," I intend for a time to withdraw into the role of editor, to function in ellipses, and to speak in occasional square brackets, and in notes that I have appended to the text of this book. What follows is all-but-all of the journals Sheila kept during the year, 1955–1956, she and Wilfred spent in Paris. Ellipses do not signify concealment but more often than not repetition. Occasionally, her reflections on what she was reading are more extensive than this account of her life warrants. I have not hesitated to correct French as well as English misspellings. In assuming the role of editor, then, I have taken my responsibilities to my reader into account as well as my responsibility to my subject.

~ IX ~

[1955]

Friday Aug 19

Today we left New York on the Liberté. I thought of a new novel. Venus Pigeons. Do you remember the time you wired up the corner of 151 Admiral so that the cooing of the pigeons would not wake you?

I did it for you because you didn't like the mess they made and Venus has served me ill because of it.

Aug 19–23

Still at sea. A small bird flew to the next deck chair. Its feathers were matted with spray—its eyes half shut with fatigue and fear.

A sailor took it away cupped in his hands. He kept saying, 'J'en trouve.'

In all the men caught seven birds which they put in a box with a ping pong net over it. All but two were dead by yesterday.

August 25

Came into Plymouth early this morning. We were taken out of NY harbour by the *Michael Moran* and the *Maria Moran*. Here we were met by the *Sir Richard Greville* and the *Sir John Hawkins*. At Le Havre by the *Minotaure*—a fine tug—and the *Titan*. From Le Havre to Paris rich rolling country—blue tiled roofs—apple trees—fields of spinach and hay—

Aug 26

We spent the night at the hotel Helios on la rue Victoire then came by taxi to 28 rue Vignon. Madame Gouzien had expected us the night before. She had put a bowl of red zinnias on the dining room table. I met my first Parisien cat—Jean. He wears a red leather collar about his fat black neck. We went to the Embassy and walked back along the Avenue des Champs Élysées and by devious routes to the Boulevard Haussmann. W and I stopped for bread, butter, cheese, wine, coffee. Then I went out with Madame Gouzien—bought a string bag—soap—tea, potatoes, salt, four eggs.

[See Appendix A—note 1]

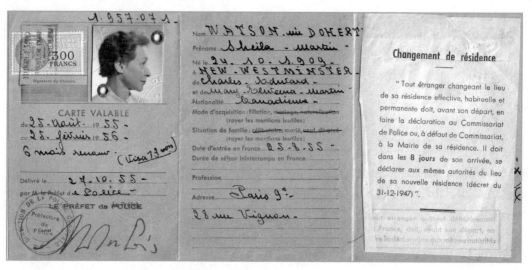

Sheila's temporary residence permit.

Today is September 4

I have been thinking a great deal. This morning I went to eleven o'clock mass at the Madeleine.

When I came back W said it was the 14th Sunday after Pentecost. This is the first time I have been to mass for more than twenty years.

The gospel for the Sunday, Matthew 6: At that time Jesus said to his disciples: No man can serve two masters; for either he will hate the one and love the other, or he will sustain the one and despise the other. You cannot serve God and Mammon. Therefore I say to you, be not solicitous for your life, what you shall eat, nor for your body, what you shall put on. Is not life more than meat, and the body more than raiment? Behold the birds of the air—a sea of faces—old women and men in Toulouse-Lautrec clothing—young women—a few children—a Spaniard next to me sang the credo in a loud voice—very old priests in ugly vestments—a great disturbance collecting the cinq francs—the offering: "Bénissez"—an old crooked woman in black collecting for "les pauvres"—then the priest in the pulpit reading the gospel. Yet the church was full of people turning towards God—curious tourists too no doubt, but people from everywhere telling their beads and bowing their heads when the priest elevated the host—people crossing their foreheads, their lips and their hearts—people bowing quietly to the priest as he passed during the "Asperges." W said he thought the sign "piétons" indicated a pilgrim's way—Chaucer would agree. Man the eternal pedestrian.

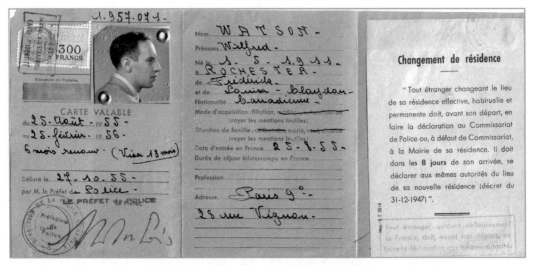

Wilfred's temporary residence permit.

The "ascenseur" here is like a bird cage suspended between the cobbled court and the 5ème étage. Every time I get into it I think how the frail cord moves in space. Yet one trusts that it will reach the fifth floor. The other day as I was carried slowly past the 3ème a man lifted his hat as he passed in the hall.

In the afternoon we walked down the rue Royale, through the Place de la Concorde and through the gardens of the Petit Palace and the Grand Palace. The trees are turning in the parks. Children were riding donkeys, but the black goat harnessed in a little cart stood idle and inquiring.

At the door of the Museum of Modern Art we were greeted by the monstrous rolling nude of Malliol. In a whole gallery there is always so little at a time—today the Utrillos—two Braques—the Modigliani sketch for a caryatid—Miró's lion— Henry Moore's figure on the stairs going down to the salle de sculpture.

Between the ave. Montaigne and the Champs Élysées is an attractive street, rue Jean Goujon—on the east side of ave. Fr. D. Roosevelt it becomes the av. de Selves. On it there is an Armenian chapel and a small Church of Our Lady of Consolation. We sat at the Eiffel Tower and drank coffee. A woman with a dog sat at the table next to us. The dog wanted sugar from our table. It sat in its chair politely staring at the sugar until she asked for a piece.

It is a quarter to two and the baby across the court is coughing and whimpering a little in its sleep. The images of Matisse and Picasso and Braque and Utrillo . . . are everywhere—the blue black sky and the moving clouds above the chimney pots—windows and people in windows. Tomorrow the laundress comes with the "demi souple" shirts.

Somehow tonight I can't sleep—W's misery cuts across my heart. It is the night of last year.

Sept 6

Today a day of black melancholy—a Simone Weil day.

I bought a handful of zinnias from a woman in la Place de la Madeleine. When I put them in a pewter jug I found that each flower was stiffened by a wire. They look brave and gay—a fan of colour above the dark wood of the table. In the bureau de poste I stood next to a young girl with dark circles under her eyes who stood clutching a letter a M etc.—Across the corner ran the urgent message "Faire suivre s.v.p."

In the Métro I noticed the amusing advertisement: "Donnez les petites poitrines le galbe de les poitrines américans." Went in search of stamps for the Hogarth Press—down the rue Drouot. Pomps funèbres—the can-can—then the stamp shops.

The Boulevard Haussmann was alive with people—shopping in front of the Printemps and in the stalls on the other side.

Sept 7

Today we went to see an exhibition of Renoir at the Galerie Durand-Rull (37 avenue de Friedland). W got a reproduction of a red-haired woman in a hat nursing her child. Renoir noticed not only the way the skin takes the light but also the way hair takes it. There were a number of pictures of children. This morning W said he walked down the quais but all the book stalls were closed. They were open when I came home on the bus. This morning too the Seine was green—soapy jade as W calls it. I had an extra bus ticket so I rode in the bus to the Havre-Caumartin stop—a great luxury not to tangle with the noon hour traffic in the Place de l' Opéra. Mme Tomasilli told an amusing and pointed story this morning. "Un fou" hung from the ceiling. Someone told him to come down. He said: "I am the light. If I come down how will the rest of the world see?"

Last night Mme Gouzien spoke of Mme Tolstoy. She said as if telling me a truth: "The life of an artist's wife is not easy—especially if she has children. If she has none then it is her duty to be compliant in all things—if she can." I had taken Jean some fish. We talked until after eleven. She told me that both Victor Hugo and Alphonse Daudet had often been in these rooms. They came to visit her grandfather. She had gone just the other day to see Charles Daudet and had asked him about Gabriel Marcel. He had confirmed her belief that [Marcel] had no influence in France. Then she told me about Colette whom she knew intimately—about the way she had begun to write when her husband locked her in a room with "un petit cahier d'enfant."

Sept 8
This afternoon I walked down the rue des Capucines to the Place Vendôme to settle my affairs with the Westminster Bank. Sometimes I think that the best thing I could do would be to go. Today W had letters. . . . What excuse have I for staying when my being is simply a cause for anger or vexation? Until January there seemed reason— some support for what my heart said so violently.

How can one say to one's heart "Be still"?

Sept 10
The same thoughts pursue me through the streets. Yesterday W brought home a grinder, a coffee pot and a bunch of red carnations. Today he must have had reassurances of some kind because he is gay and beginning to work at the trio of short stories which he began in Vancouver.

This morning the concierge rang about nine. Later I saw her cleaning the long circular stair with an "aspirateur." Her husband was polishing the windows and flicking about with a great feather duster.

When I use the word "home" I think of the American woman on the bus who kept saying "Back home we do this and that . . ." and the haricot-vert of an English guide who smiled the vacuous smile of one who thinks he can measure another person's depth with his thumb-nail.

The fish stall in the Madeleine Market was spread with crabs and lobsters and prawns—other shellfish of all kinds. Yesterday I saw some "canards" trussed up peacefully, their yellow webbed feet against their breasts—their eyes and feathered heads quiet in death; but the rabbits fierce and defiant—naked except for their soft furred feet—heads and all, their eyes still with anguish. The sun sinks yellow into the walls. As if in sympathy, the woman with the croupy baby has hung a yellow blouse in the window. The tin attics are grey blue as a pigeon's back.

From time to time now—especially at night—I am shaken with cold desolation as I was the morning W flew to Calgary—not symbolically but physically.

I want to walk in the sun—simply to sit in the sun. I remember shivering through the hot day Aug. 10—in a thick tweed suit—everywhere women in thin cotton dresses—

Sept 12

Yesterday I walked with Mme Gouzien. We were going to read but the sun shone so mildly that it seemed ridiculous to stay indoors. First we went to the Louvre where we saw only the Victory of Samothrace and a gallery of David and Courbet's paintings. There is nothing that I would have wanted to see less than the Davids. Then we went to Notre Dame, and the Church of St. Julien-le-Pauvre and St. Séverin. It was a grand tour with glimpses of the rue de la Huchette, le chat qui pêche, or Arab boys and sisters of St. Vincent de Paul in their white butterfly head dresses collecting for the poor at the doors of Notre Dame, of the gargoyles peering across the street at a working man's "bal"—the rose windows, a child being baptised in a side chapel, a turn through the Palais Royal and a stroll along the quais on the Left Bank—a glance at the three flats in which Colette had lived and a vague gesture towards Jean Cocteau's windows. I pray to be kept from saying: "I have known and lived with artists and writers." I saw a dictionary of "argot," but Mme G. laid a warning hand on my shoulder. Sometime I shall go back for it.

This morning in the Métro station I saw a curé in a black shovel hat standing under the sign 1ere Classe Direction—

September 18

There are things I have wanted to note but I haven't the heart to write—an old man dressed like Van Gogh's le Facteur Roulin singing in front of the Hotel Vignon—a girl on the rue Castellane waiting between the café-tabac and les halles of the Madeleine who said "bête" every time a man passed her without turning—the four Arabs in their white gowns and yellow leather slippers somewhere between rue Caumartin and rue Drouot on the Boulevard Haussmann—the warm sunlight and going to T. Champion 13 r. Drouot to get stamps for sending mss. off to John Lehmann—the concierge's little girl playing in the cobbled court—a small dark girl with gold rings in her ears—Monsieur la concierge's husband fat and smiling with the pleasure of her return.

On Wednesday Mme Gouzien took me to Les Invalides. We walked down the rue Royale and across the bridge. It was an autumn with drifts of light rain. The trees on either side of the Champs Élysées are turning red. The Seine was grey—several small boats were tied up to the quais. One or two people were fishing. At first we wandered in the court belonging to the national guard. Here we saw carrier pigeons and bundles of rusted barbed wire. Then we went into the Museum— much to excite and much to horrify—the paintings, as Mme G. said with feeling, "effroyables." The first thing I really noticed was how small the coats belonging to Napoleon's soldiers were—the coats of mere boys; Napoleon's grey coat—the buttons almost worn away on one side and his monstrous black hat.

Words ring out curiously in a foreign tongue—"la peau véritable" of Napoleon's white horse stuffed by a taxidermist and splitting with time—"la peau véritable" of the white hound still in tact.

The armour unbelievably beautiful—the lion armour of Francis I—a cuirass scaled like a fish—intaglio—two-handed swords and arquebus—short knives and long—

A view from 28 rue Vignon.

We walked back past the Petit Palace through the rond-point of the Champs Élysées—"embouteillage" of cars because of the strike—the Métro moving feebly, the autobuses not at all—a few days ago the poinconneurs sat with their arms folded and let everyone travel "gratuit."

I bought some "bifteck" from the boy in the market—then went through the triple "au revoir." Today I saw a woman on the other side of rue Vignon—another 5ème étager plucking her eyebrows at the window while she carried on a vigorous conversation with a man who was drinking beer at the table behind her.

The new chimneys are white against the sky—at night they glow in the moonlight—the other chimneys are black against the clouds. The drop from the ledge—on which I stand to watch the comings and goings in the street or simply to feel the warmth of the sun—to the street below doesn't frighten me at all—perhaps it is the closeness of the buildings on the opposite side. Perhaps one outgrows vertigo—the fear of high places. Since part of me died on August 10 I don't feel anything much at all—except the unexpected kindness of strangers and the soft warmth of the sun. [See Appendix A—note 2] The coral-coloured Etruscan dances on the wall in his blue chiton—the stems of the carnations remind me of their bright blossoms. I can hear the rain falling on the roofs above—I look at the reproduction of Klee's "Sacrifice barbare." It is gay and witty and wise.

Sitting here with my arms on the old wooden table I am terribly afraid—not of what will happen but of myself—

Sept 19

Today I stayed here because of the Métro strike. . . . This morning was a clear autumn morning. I went to the kiosk to look for the *Times Literary Supplement* and the *New Statesman*. W's poetry is announced in the *Times* (16). I took the papers up to the garden on Boulevard Haussmann. W says that the notice only marks something which is already accomplished but I felt strangely happy. The sun was bright in the garden, the leaves green in the light. I sat on one of the little chairs outside the monument built to house "les dernières dépouilles" of Louis XVI and Marie Antoinette. Some old men were sitting on the benches and a woman knitting.

This afternoon I went to the Petit Palace to see the Giradin collection. Mme Gouzien told me the other day that Dr. Giradin had been her dentist from the time she was a little girl. Modigliani's woman with blue eyes is in the collection—a good showing of Dufy—but it was the Rouault sketches which really spoke to me. I noticed a curious and lovely Pietà by Marcelo Gromarie dated 1933, and, in another lot of pictures altogether, Monet's "Coucher de Soleil à Lavacourt" painted in 1880.

W and I had had a discussion of Renoir's dates, which I find are 1841–1919. Rouault was born in 1871. I saw too the paintings of Bernard Buffet which Plaskett spoke about [Joe Plaskett is a BC painter whom Sheila and Wilfred came to know when they taught at UBC]: Artist and his model—Le Filet—and picture of a drinker sitting—or some such title. Question: Why is it that the only strong nudes are those painted in the late 20s and early 30s? Perhaps the question could be proved pointless by example. W would say: What of Renoir—whose women fascinate him now—In one of the rooms I particularly noticed one of Durer's sketches . . . the Knight with his helmet open and a fox tail on his lance—the horned beast and death with his glass.

On the way back I sat in the park long enough to smoke a cigarette, to watch the children play and the lovers kiss. At the far end of the Champs Élysées I picked up a pocketful of chestnuts. They felt cold and smooth in my pocket and shone brown when I pulled them out into the sunlight. . . .

I met a woman in the Petit Palace who asked me a question about the catalogue, which I didn't have. She asked me if I were an artist then she told me she worked in enamel. She said: "Paris is the one city where a person can be completely alone yet not lonely." For the moment I felt inclined to agree with her.

Sept 20

This morning W asked me to call Gabriel Marcel on the telephone to make an appointment for him. He is to go to the rue Turin tomorrow at six. M. Garneau had written to G. M.

G. M. spoke English in the high voice of an old man. I remember bringing home G. M.'s lectures from the Calgary Public Library—then having them used as the ground of my own destruction. [See Appendix A—note 3]

This morning the market was crowded with people. The sun was a warm summer sun. Today W forgot his keys. When he came back from having his hair cut the flat was locked. He drank blonde beer at the café tabac and waited for me to come back with my keys. Then he took me out with him again to sample the blonde beer. The past two weeks dissolved in the warm autumn sun. . . .

Sept 21

Today W had a letter . . . [t]o say that Faber itself had arranged for publication in the States with Farrar, Straus & Cudahy . . . Robert Giroux . . . was formerly with Harcourt Brace and has looked after the American publications of T. S. Eliot. The concierge gave him the letter as he was going out to rue Turin. I had gone out with him to show him where to get the Métro at the Madeleine. I would have gone with him to Odéon but his determination to lead his life quite apart from mine inhibits anything I might do. He reads his work to me at intervals during the day if I am in, but that is all.

This morning we talked of Henry Miller at breakfast. W says Henry Miller is a perfect example of the damned soul—that is of someone who has estranged himself and built a private world of hate. This, W says, is his concept of hell, which does not exist but subsists. Redemption comes through love—

I suspect he defines love in his own terms. There are a thousand questions I would ask—Why W came back to me at all when the clear break had been made. He would, I suppose, say that no clear break had been made since he had to find grounds himself for divorce. I told him before we were married that he was not the first person I had loved—and in the torment of the winter at Rae's in Calgary I thought in honesty and because of [his young friend] I must tell him what those years had meant. Now when I have hurt him . . . and he wants to hurt back he says something to remind me. He doesn't know and won't understand how much I have loved him. If he thought without defence he might. All intimacy between us is gone. As I told him the other day: I define love as the feeling of complete intimacy in which one walks naked before another. This is not physical nakedness only, which itself is the symbol of the naked spirit. Perhaps this was not possible for us though I would have had it so. He reminds me often that when I wrote *The Double Hook* in its first drafts, I believed that complete communication between two people was not possible. This belief he says had contorted all my writing: perhaps—and perhaps—

I have forgotten what I was going to say. W came in and for some reason—the strain of the last weeks—I asked him just what he intended to do—if we were to go on living this way—at least that is what I intended to say—then everything again with the inevitable recriminations. W pointed out again that I had made it impossible for him to act otherwise than he has done. Now he asks for what I asked for last year—a legal separation.

I didn't say truly what I wanted to say which was this: Did he go back to [his young friend] because he wanted to tell me that he wanted me to go—or had he gone as I thought he possibly might have gone. But the question is as foolish a question as his reply, that I said I wanted to go. He wants [his young friend] and the possibility of beginning again in the confidence of her love. Indeed, his argument seems most reasonable. What he says Macbeth might have said before the forest came to Dunsinane. Only it is another play—Hamlet married to Lady Macbeth—"Madam, s'il vous plaît." But the play *Macbeth* begins when there is no longer the intimacy of a first name— surely we began somewhere before the ringing up of the curtain on the letter—

Sept 26
It is very early in the morning—probably the 27th. It is still quite dark although the darkness begins to ebb. I woke feeling that I was somewhere else—then I thought of the Place Vendôme—the buildings with their chimneys and Napoleon looking down from his triumphal column—and heard the cars in the rue de Rivoli and the children in the Gardens of the Tuileries. Then I must have slept and woke again, this time in the Place Vendôme, which was quite empty and deserted—a great enclosed space with the light just breaking.

Last night Mme Gouzien told me about the actor Dullin—the actor who trained Jean-Louis Barrault. She saw him first, she told me, at the Vieux-Columbier when she was thirteen. It was with Mme Dullin that she was having dinner the other night—Saturday when I gave Jean his supper. We had gone to Montmartre, which is really a place of horror now. The Métro strike had just finished and two women had a fight in the elevator about the strikers. I could follow nothing but their anger—and hear nothing but the references to communism.

We went up to the top of the hill on the funicular—and saw Paris spread flat before us. In the Sacré Coeur nuns were chanting their office. Then Mme G. took me to show me what was left of the old Montmartre: the Lapin Agile, some of the old streets, the theatre of the Enfants Pulbots, men and curious looking girls and young boys, some of them children, everywhere drawing and painting in the Utrillo mode—as if someone went into a forest to make a copy of Emily Carr when they could have done it from a canvas deep in their own basement.

I spend most of my day away from rue Vignon. In the morning I shop in the market, then after lunch I go out until nearly six. I can't write so I walk and think.

Yesterday I went to the Passage de Choiseul. It is a narrow passageway lined on both sides with tiny shops: the Papeterie du Bon Marché, the Lemerre, shoe shops and dress shops. As soon as I went in from the street I heard a great cry of birds. I thought there must be a bird market and looked about for one—but the great cry came from the sparrows clustered under the glass roof. Some sat together—others flew from girder to girder. How they come in and how they go out I could not guess. Just as I was turning out of the avenue de l'Opéra I saw Jean Coulthard Adams [a composer who taught at UBC] with her little girl. I could not bring myself to speak to her so I let her walk on into the early afternoon crowd. Then I thought: perhaps this is the beginning of a pattern.

Then I made a great circuit through the Palais Royal into the Louvre and through the Gardens of the Tuileries, across the Place de la Concorde and down the rue Gabrielle under the trees of the Théâtre Marigny. The air was fragrant with the scent of leaves burning in one of the embassy gardens—everything brown and green and grey under the slate blue sky.

A[gnes Hammond] wrote to say that the *Hudson Review* had sent back "The Black Farm" and today Louise [Riley] writes of disaster stalking—and Cornwall becoming a thin dream. W turns his face to Calgary and to his vision. There is nothing more to say—and I write his name here for the last time. I have died without grace and would forget the agony. The present is the time of waiting, between the death and the burial and the arrangements lawyers make to set the world right again so that the living may get about their loving and house building and begetting, and the dead about their subterranean affairs—or like the grain lie waiting for the sun.

Today I saw two Chirico horses—a Utrillo—a nude by Suzanne Valdon—some inconsequential Laurenciens—and a grey church by Buffet.

The days grow colder. Tonight I can't sleep.

. . . .

If Doto were here now she would come to the door—still with sleep—but anxious because the house was not at peace. Will she too think I have forsaken her for some vanity or pride of my own? for some ambition, for some assertion of my private will, some hysterical desire to be unkind to her because I am unhappy myself?

Colette noticed too how dogs lie like frogs, close to the ground—

C'est propre, la tragédie. C'est reposant, c'est sur—

October 1

This morning I went through the streets before eight—no cars, no people—except rag pickers among the garbage cans and street sweepers with their twig brooms. The fishermen, too, were at their fishing along the Seine—a chill morning—autumn mist and the smell of leaves dying. Mgr. Nasrallah, the curé of Saint-Julien-le-Pauvre, was officiating at a mass according to the Byzantine rites at Notre Dame. The whole a curious experience—Mgr. Nasrallah in a black veil like a nun's—the French cardinal fat in his red robe and cap speaking of devotion to the rosary—the choir voicing the cry of the world: "Seigneur ayez pitié"—the procession of the offerings—a priest in a green vestment carrying the cross—the young men in white and gold carrying the bread and wine—their heads bent above the patens and chalice.

Someone behind the altar taking pictures with flash bulbs. Before the lights are turned on the church seems like a narrow valley in which people crowd together to see the reflection of light on the high peaks—only the sense that behind the stained glass window there is light.

The Sainte-Chapelle is quite different. It is alive with light—and the blue sky and the wonder of flame rising from the earth—the light falling on the patterned floor and picking out the details under the mouldings.

On Thursday Mme Gouzien and I went up and down the Seine "bateaux-mouches." It was an afternoon of lone shadows and cool sunlight—light playing under the arches of the bridges and on the climbing figures of Notre Dame. We sat on deck with the people having tea around us. I noticed for the first time the brick towers of the Conciergerie—"les tours [enfumées]." Workers in the Renault factory leant out of the windows to watch the boat go by and to wave to the children. In the evening we (not Mme G.) went to the Palais de Chaillot to hear the Brahms 1st symphony (Cantelli and the Scala Orchestra of Milan).

We were, thanks to my stupidity and the man at Durands, in most uncomfortable and badly placed seats. I hope the seats for Jean-Louis Barrault's *Aeschylus* are better. Back by the Métro from Iena. No wonder Pound noticed the faces in the

Métro—but it is strange that they were to him as like one another as leaves.

Tonight Mme G. met me in the hall just as I was about to come in—the door half open. Tant pis!

The cat went out by the open window as punishment.

There are things I would write, but can't. Could one write a history of love systematically destroyed—

Oct 3

Grey light everywhere, a white mist half concealing the Arc de Triomphe where I could see it at the end of the alley of autumn trees. Children school satchels in their hands scuttling along with their mothers—the donkeys in a little huddle their eyes closed—napping. I used to watch Doto sleep in the same way—her eyes just closed—ready to wake if the world called. . . .

Oct 4

Today's *Figaro* explained the tents of the campers which I saw on the quai: 93 Familles de Travailleurs—Groupant 240 enfants campent sur les Berges de la Seine! So much for Mme G.'s boy scouts. C'est la nouvelle cité de l'abbé Pierre.

One worker is reported to have said that he could pay 5000 or 6000 francs a month rent—We pay Mme Gouzien 32,000.

The paper quotes the worker as saying that he would need 150,000 francs to get lodging. I wonder if the workers have to pay as we pay by the quarter or even by the half year?

The woman across the court played Bach while the old woman underneath wandered around in a grey dressing gown—a purple scarf about her waist—a cigarette

Wilfred on the ledge outside their flat.

hanging from her lips—and always the monstrous unmade bed—its strewn quilts and twisted sheets. Jean came in at dinner time and ate lots of meat from my hand.

Today I went into a galerie on the Faubourg St. Honoré—a Rouault head with a ferocious eye—a small Renoir—two nude bodies and a child's head alone—another small Renoir head—also a bowl of flowers.

The galerie was full of girls in turtle neck sweaters—their hair tinted and hanging in great horse tails down their backs. I see them often round the galleries.

The day was cold with autumn—the sky above the buildings a flat clear blue thinning into a greyed white—

This evening I spent some time studying the mysteries of French fish. In Canada we are spared most of the primitive cooking rites—the fishmonger has saved our sensibilities and our hands. When I read about beheading a fish and holding its "nuque" firmly on the table, I think of how we become insensitive to words and things. I thought too of the flounder-like figures in Klee's "Sacrifice barbare."

Today too I had to get a strap for my watch. Several people looked at it and shook their heads sadly: "C'est impossible. C'est un peu spécial—"

Finally a girl in a little bijouterie on rue Tronchet took off the old strap and put a little new lizard strap on. She was pleased with the change: "C'est chic—maintenant."

I walk around under my new haircut and now look at the strap from time to time. What curious and superficial defences the human heart builds to hide behind. Last night I had a terrible dream and woke crying. The room was full of moonlight.

Oct 6

Bought three branches of mimosa from the woman at the door of the Madeleine market. She is bundled up in a tricot now because it is cold in the streets. Her voice has a caressing cadence as if she were carrying on a conversation with the dahlias and chrysanthemums—"mes jolies fleurs—achetez mes jolies fleurs."

The mimosa has a strong stem and leaves like willow leaves only longer—the willow reflects the light. The flowers are a sulphur yellow.

The man from whom I bought the little red roses was not in the street this morning. Yesterday the man in the fish market picked up a live shrimp and held it out to me. "C'est bonne," he said, "C'est vivante." Yesterday, too, I saw a huge detachment of policemen with white belts and holsters coming off duty—or going on duty in the neighbourhood of the Louvre—two files of children with their teachers—one group small children in too large coats and bérets and tabliers.

Oct 7

Last night saw Jean-Louis Barrault's company at the Marigny in Obey's translation of the *Orestia*. It was a cold evening and we walked to the theatre through the threat of rain. Still the sky was not black—the street lights shone up through the green and terra-cotta brown of the leaves. The bit of street beside the black wall of the Palais has its inscape: on rainy days when the leaves are wet underfoot—on windy days when the leaves twist on the pavement and the sky is pigeon blue—or on still days when everything is drawn up into the arch of the black boughs.

Barrault himself is curiously fascinating. He centres in on himself. His art is the art of concentration. When he declaims the spell is broken until the gesture re-establishes his central remoteness again. He compels attention by looking at himself as a man in the street can draw attention to a cat on a fence simply by staring at it.

In the *Agamemnon*, Cassandra at first, as she stood silent in the chariot, had managed to capture the essence of his method, but when Clytemnestra went in and the Chorus persuaded Cassandra to come down from her chariot—she became, not one possessed by Apollo, not one caught in the web of Clytemnestra's hate, not the despised prophetess, or the bird wantonly destroyed, but a fake epileptic—revolting—unconvincing because she couldn't follow Barrault beyond the first silence. Electra, on the other hand, played as Barrault played.

The method, if it could be called method, seems dangerous. When it succeeds, as it did in the first scenes of the *Libation Bearers*, it defies criticism.

Today when I went to the theatre to get tickets for next Friday, I saw Electra in a black corduroy coat—a little grease paint still just below the hair line in front of her ear. She was standing at the wicket waiting to get change to make a telephone call—for when she got her change she ran off to the telephone booth.

The man at Fauchon's vegetable stand gave me a lesson this morning—not because I couldn't ask for what I wanted but because my accent was not just. I got some brown russet apples—Braque apples—called "reinettes," some spinach and some parsley. And cent vingt francs of "bifteck haché." But I had to go back to the Madeleine to get mushrooms because the great ones at F's were all 'extra'—brown and gold and swirling upward at the edges.

One still sees tourists writing letters and addressing postcards in the various cafés. They seem to haunt the reaches from the Louvre to the Étoile and from the Seine to the Faubourg S. Honoré. How do I know? I am often there myself.

It seems strange to think of Proust living on Boulevard Haussmann. It is probably more strange to think it strange.

Henri Michaux says that when a Hindoo has to explain anything which he does not understand, he begins by dividing it into 64 parts. An Englishman divides by three. I smiled thinking of Mr. Woodhouse.

Oct 8

Saturday—today Knopf sent word about the mss. So it is where it was—and no doubt will be—and one stands like a cow while the owner mutters "Pauvre bête" and signs it away. I ask myself again this morning whether such complete destruction is necessary . . .

And below in the court Mme la concierge's husband hushing the crying of la petite Claude, interrupted by her grief as he went about the careful polishing of his car while Mme la concierge cleaned the circular staircase with her "aspirateur."

She is to go to the country again—la petite Claude—so that she will grow strong—so that her cheeks will be fat and pink, her father said holding his hands at the sides of his own placid face; but she buries her own little face in her small hands so that only the little rings in her ears gleam—and gives herself up to misery. She was to have gone for a walk with Patrick's mother, but Patrick's mother has not emerged from the 6ème.

. . . .

Then Patrick's mother came down. It had all been Patrick's fault. He had cried in the hallway. He had cried in the little room up under the slanting roof. He had cried for no reason at all since his cough has gone. He had simply cried and there was no coming down with him.

One of the sheets which came with us by chance had slit so I had to go in search of others. I am impressed by the thrift of the ordinary French man or woman. The man at the linen counter spent endless time when I told him what I was looking for. The unbleached sheets he said were not "douce" enough to put on the bed right away. Then he looked at me and said in English, "'sweet,' you understand." The pillow cases are immense white pouches—big enough for the biggest of Mme Gouzien's strange assortment of pillows.

I walked down past the Marigny and along rue Gabriel to smell the leaves. In the space around the Marigny a stamp fair had been set up and the collectors were there with their glasses and their albums. There were in all dozens of little booths with stamps of all kinds. More adventurous souls no doubt were inspecting the sous-marin de poche at the Salon Nautique or the décapotables at the Salon d'Automobile or even perhaps the paintings of artists "qui ne vaudraient ou n'oseraient affrontu

Sheila looking down on rue Vignon—see entry for 18 September 1955.
PHOTO TAKEN BY WILFRED WATSON

un tribunal artistique"—at the Salon des Superintendents.

On the way home I stopped at the little button shop across the street—again thrift—"Ceci sont trop chères"—as indeed they were—then the story of a woman who had come to buy clips and spoke not a word, not a single word of French—then the fun of trying on a number of earrings quite different in their construction from anything I have ever seen—a brief moment like a bird flight—the shop empty and the woman disposed to talk—the impersonal comfort of a moment of human contact—the turning of the heart over a button into the ordinary commerce of human being with human being.

I get up again. It is two o'clock. There is a curious light as if day were breaking—or was—because it is dark again now. The rain has begun to beat on the roof. Paris rain too has its own inscape. It rains then the sky seems to clear completely. Then it rains again. The light was probably moonlight. I could see to the bottom of the court and plugged in the lamp without fumbling because I could see the white gleam of the socket. For some reason I have not learned to cat walk in these rooms but stumble into walls and errant chairs.

Every time I come up on the ascenseur . . . I am fascinated by the statement "Poids trois personnes."

Today I walked down the rue la Ville l'Évêque to the place des Saussaies. Crocodiles of children were coming out of an inner court from a school of the Sisters of St. Vincent de Paul. They were herded along by an old Sister with a heavy portfolio under her arm. Other children were being called for by their mothers. It was some time after five. I had intended to walk down Ruth's rue de Surène.

In the paper, news of the salons, of the comings and goings of Wm. Faulkner, Ingrid Bergman and Colonel Townsend make easier reading than the Morocco crisis and M. Fauré's public statements about policy.

For two days men have been repairing a clock at the Haussmann end of rue Vignon. The frame bears the sign "Aeterna." No two clocks in Paris agree. Many seem to have conspired in a private grève.

Oct 9

I come in tired out with walking after having walked to the Bastille and back—not to the Bastille to be sure though I had not thought of it being destroyed and somehow thought I would see it, a fact I record with humility. I saw then only the Colonne de Juillet—and the crowds of children riding merry-go-rounds in the space at the end of the Bd. Henri IV and the Bd. Bourdon—and crowds of people drinking beer and coffee and eating little cakes—and crowds just walking in the warm sunlight after the rain.

I had gone down the Avenue de l'Opéra to the quais where I watched the fishermen and poked about in the book stalls and went down on the banks of the Seine at the Quai des Célestins to smoke a cigarette. Here I saw a cat asleep in a box—its striped body at peace in the sun. Then up the rue Fauconnier to where the rue de l'Hôtel de Ville and rue Figuier come into it. Here is an extremely beautiful old building which is at present being reconstructed—only a few scaffoldings at present—no obvious sign of renovation. In the rue Ave Maria a man and two children were throwing a ping pong ball against the wall of one of the buildings. The man told me that the building was the Hôtel de Sèvres and was thirteenth century. I am not sure that I understood what he said. Then down the rue des Lions and by mistake across Henri IV and down the rue de Sully past some sort of military establishment—the street empty and peaceful after the crowded quais—back to the Bd. Henri IV and finally to the Colonne de Juillet—abortive search for the Bastille in the merry-making crowd—across to the rue St. Antoine and up the rue Birague to the Place des Vosges. The pink houses still too much obscured by the trees. A brief essai into the rue de Béarn where an old woman was helping an old man from his chair in the street into a house. Paris is filled with reminders of old age and poverty and of ill and sometimes witless children. A young woman wheeling a girl of four or five years in a pram which was too small for the heavy desolate body—a face empty of everything but misery—the body slack on the dirty covers.

. . . .

At various spots on the upper reaches of the rue St. Antoine venders were selling hot chestnuts—some a dark crackling brown, some burnt black.

I followed the rue St. Antoine into the rue de Rivoli. Just before the rue de Rivoli passes the Hôtel de Ville there is a park and in the park what appears to be the centre of an extremely old church. The gargoyles are worn away like the gargoyles of the Musée de Cluny. In the gardens too are the ghosts of old stone lions—brothers in stone I suspect of the Cluny lions. In the centre of the building facing out on the rue de Rivoli is a statue; I must find out what this place is.

On the wall just in front of the statue is one of the plaques which I have seen on the walls of the quais on the rue de la Cité: "Ici est tombé pour la liberation de Paris Le Cdt F. T. P. F. Marcel Faucher dit Bara le 21 Août 1944." I can only suppose that these men were shot in the street. At first I thought there had been fighting in these places. Apart from the obvious ravages at Le Havre, these quiet plaques and the barbed wire at les Invalides are the only indications of what happened in the small part of France I have seen. The city seems to belong to the Revolution and to Napoleon. Here the gargoyles and the lions and the plaque come together as the plaques on the rue de la Cité and the towers of the Conciergerie do.

Eventually I went down the rue Arbre to examine some more gargoyles, which turned out to be the gargoyles on the church of St. Germain L'Auxerrois—and down the rue des Prêtres St. Germain L'Auxerrois to the front of the church. Inside the church a priest was saying mass in a red vestment and another priest was reading the epistle from the pulpit.

I begin to think that French is the language of declamation—and explication. A sermon on the text "Be ye perfect as my Father is perfect"—I understood very little but was moved by the cadence of the priest's voice—its urgency—its persuasion and its control.

Oct 13

Today to the Church of St. Eustache—down the rue Danielle Casanova, rue des Pet.-Champs past the Banque de France, Pl. des Victoires—then along . . . to the rue du Louvre—down the crooked rue Coquillière to where St. Eustache stands, its feet strewed with the debris of the market—the street slippery underfoot. There must have been a marriage in the church because the high altar was banked with white flowers, and someone—a man in a blouse and a small boy—were rolling up a long red carpet from the central aisle.

At the door there is a plaque:

> Cy gît
> Francois de Cheveret
> Commandeur Grand Choix de l'ordre de St. Louis
> Chevalier de l'Aigle Blanc de Pologne
> Gouverneur de Givet et Charlemont Lieutenant General des
>   Armées du Roy
> Sans ayeux, sans fortune, sans appuy, orphelin des l'enfance il
>   entra au service a l'âge XI ans.
> Il s'éleva malgré l'envie à force de merite et chaque grade fut le
>   prix d'une action d'éclat.
> Le seul titre de maréchal de France a manqué non pas à sa
>   Glorie mais à l'exemple de ceux qui le prendront pour
>   modèle.
> Il était né à Verdun sur Meuse le 2 Février 1695; il mourut à
>   Paris le 24 Janvier 1769.
> Priez Dieu pour le repos de son Âme.

For some reason I thought here is what everyone hopes—here is the image sans ayeux, sans fortune, sans appuy . . . il s'éleva malgré l'envie à face de mérite. . . .

The chestnuts are falling in the parks—they are on the market stalls—they are roasted on the street—but they are used too in the shop windows—the brown nuts and the green husks.

The yellow and green of the mimosa—a green pear with the suggestion of yellow light—the branching beauty of six yellow and green chrysanthemums, the yellow of the petals darkening imperceptibly into the flame of the centre—all speak of an autumn intenser and closer to the truth than Keats's "season of mist and mellow fruitfulness." Their meaning becomes luminous in "I praise God's mankind" . . . Things don't rot away but are consumed in their own fire.

Yet I remind myself that I stepped about on the mortal remains of plants and fruits where the rue Coquillière is transformed into the rue Rambuteau.

Several days ago I saw some interesting paintings of Boussard and Humblot. Perhaps the Boussard evoked Van Gogh too persistently. Humblot's pictures are filled with a cold intense light.

On the 12th too I was given a "billet" to the opening of the exhibition L'École de Paris 1955 at Galerie Carpentier. Numbers of well turned out women—the painters or some of them there, too, distinguished by red threads in their buttonholes. I recognized Buffet from his auto portrait—there in front of his own "La Marmite rouge"—indifferent, his back to the picture. The only pictures I recognized, of course, the Picasso, the Utrillo and two pictures of Vlaminck. I am much drawn to the still lifes of Agostini and Oudot.

Crowds of people collected so that there was hardly room to breathe. I stayed for about an hour and a half, then hurried back by the Madeleine market to get two slices of cooked beef—nature morte after nature morte. It was an exciting day and dinner didn't seem to matter.

One might suspect from looking at the fish—Agostini's "les poissons bleus," the great fish in Buffet's "La Marmite rouge"—that the fish had taken on some of its old symbolic significance: the note only really sounded in Oudot's "Nature morte au poisson"; in Goerg's "La Marché aux poissons" the fish are Yeatsian.

My mind goes back to the school of dolphins cutting the waves like dull gold and ebony swords—I can close my eyes and see them rising and plunging at the side of the ship. I think, too, of the drunkard with his hacking cough, his spit and snivel sitting in the shadow of the pillar in St. Eustache's while the man and boy rolled up the wedding carpet and the young man in the black suit praying before the altar in the chapel of the Virgin.

Oct 15

. . . .

It was a warm day—only a drift of mist and the yellow of the leaves on the trees along the Seine said that the days were drawing in and that the time might come when I would be less free to wander at large. Tonight it rains.

Yesterday the fishermen were out in numbers—some sitting below the edge of the quais on round hoops which I suppose are used for tying up boats. A long barge slipped by flying a pair of man's drawers—a shirt and some towels—

Oct 16

Today the first real cold in the air—women here and there in fur coats and thick woolens. This morning—Sunday—men were out getting bread and carrying home pastries in flat boxes. The string bag simply won't do—nor the sac either. The two women at the door of the Halles had their baskets heaped with dahlias and mimosa—one, too, had a great box of white carnations. I brought back six flame-coloured dahlias. Light slips along the leaf into the dark central fire of the chrysanthemum. But the dahlia head is luminous. The fragrance of the chrysanthemum and the dahlia is really in the stem and foliage—it is by this fragrance at least that they become familiar.

On the Pont Neuf I saw a man carrying some fish in a wire basket like the basket in which Patrick's mother hangs out her lettuce or oranges across the court. The man was walking along nimbly on a curious twisted artificial leg—which was constructed as it was, I suppose, for ease in sitting.

Today the Ste. Chapelle was crowded with French tourists. By half past three most of the light gone from the windows—the gargoyles though basking impudently in the afternoon shadow—a curious glimpse of them on the side next to the Conciergerie, up between the walls.

. . . .

Oct 17

Today a bitter chill in the streets—a yellow fog in the chimney pots—the buildings along the rue de Lille grey against the yellow light. The Place Vendôme had this curious greyness—a something more than the sum total of the grey buildings.

. . . .

Oct 20

Today in the garden of the Tuileries men are raking the leaves and sweeping them into piles with their red twig brooms. A group of students in paper hats and aprons marching à gauche, à gauche, followed by a huge crowd of small children and parents. Ragged tailed sparrows tossed about by the wind—a warm liquid day after the cold of the past two days.

Last evening I went with Mme Gouzien to the parish film society organized by the curé of the Madeleine—a documentary on the subject of capital punishment. A crowd of people—some young, some old, and much heated discussion after the film. The sound track was poor so that I could not follow the dialogue easily. Some terrible scenes in which one saw the way in which the French criminal is taken to the guillotine. The very idea of the guillotine seems barbarous, but what M. le curé's parishoners would have felt about hanging I can't say.

. . . .

The fish in the market still fascinate me—the huge artificial looking eyes of the dorades—the speculative eye of the grondin—its pale brick-coloured skin—the prickly red-black oursins.

Today I saw a tray of large heavy-legged crabs which looked as if they had lived long in the sea.

Peripatetic speculators too.

Cocteau's books—some manuscripts too—displayed in the book store windows. He has created a certain sensation by refusing to wear the "col case" of the academician.

Some baby poodles—black ones and white ones—asleep in the window of the Cat and Dog Store on the rue Godot. They made me think of Doto. Jean came for some meat at dinner time and returned later to sit for a while on a chair in front of the gas heater. He loves to have his head stroked but becomes nervous and angry if he is touched anywhere else.

Oct 21

Another visit to the minister of foreign affairs on the rue de Lille—then again to the préfecture. There was a curious little man in charge of the outer office at 82. He knew what an "écrivain" was—not someone attached to a school—not someone studying under a master—but a man who lived in the city, who went here and there, peered into this corner and that—walked about looking, looking.

He was seized with the poetry of his own image—walked a step or two—himself for the moment the "écrivain" peeping into this corner and that.

In the office, too, a plump woman in a light suit—a fur knotted about her throat—a thin umbrella furled and poised like a rapier in front of her. Angry because the inner office sent out word that she had asked to stay an unreasonably long time in Strasbourg. Not an "affaire de plaisir," nothing of the sort—but "un enfant malade," the mother having written her to come—a pressing affair. No satisfaction apparently in the inner sanctum where the little man finally ushered her—out again with a twitch of the hips and a jerk of the long jointed latch of the outer door.

The trunks of the trees along the Seine black in the rain and the leaves falling gold on the pavements. The trees twisted outside the big semicircular window of the office in the préfecture of police—three harried women attending to the affairs of her Britannic Majesty's subjects—the elderly male receptionist sleeping quietly at his desk by the door between the interruptions.

A good review in the *Times Literary Supplement* of Oct 21—to take the edge off the *New Statesman's* thrust.

Tonight I packed up the mss. of "The Black Farm" to send it back to Malcolm Ross—also the mss. of the D. H. for Chatto and Windus, but when I got it ready for the post, noticed that the address is the same as that of the Hogarth Press. Again Tant pis.

I am not sorry that I did not go to the *Orestia* tonight. It has been peaceful here with the rain falling on the roof—more and more I want to be alone—freed for a moment from the burden of feeling the need to excuse myself for being what I am—indeed for existing at all.

. . . .

The wind is blowing in the court—and whistling in the flame of the gas heater.

Oct 23

The man from whom I bought the bushy yellow chrysanthemums yesterday had spikes of gladioli buds in his basket this morning. The chrysanthemums still dance like flames in the pewter jug. A dull grey day. I went out this morning to get bread, but otherwise stayed indoors. Heard a mass broadcast from Lille—a sermon on giving—without thought of the past, without thought of the future. Also the orchestra of the conservatory played Handel and Vivaldi—the flautist Rampal whom we heard with the Ensemble Baroque.

Began Golding's *The Inheritors* after finishing Duncan's *Way to the Tomb* last night.

This evening a long discussion with Mme Gouzien when I took her the papers, about anti-semitism, the Dreyfus case, old Dominici and French justice. We stood talking in the hall with the draft curling along the tiles and climbing our ankles. Mme G. was wearing the long red belted coat which her friend in America had sent her—and which, she says, is an excellent garment for warding off drafts.

Oct 26

The reflection of night thoughts which plays on the surface of eternity—or lights a small space in the darkness of unknowing—must be held like precious fire during the day—when the reason of things clamours for attention.

When Thebon says [of Simone Weil] that the contacts in time with eternity have a fearful fleetness he speaks not only of the contact of mind with mind—of person with person—in the eternal present of comprehension—but of those moments or that moment when the soul by an act of faith stands for that moment in God's eye—

Ruth [Humphrey] is quite right when she says: "We live in time not in eternity, but if we are to live in time at all we must live by eternity."

Today there was a note from Chatto and Windus. The letterhead explains the mystery of the Hogarth Press address—L[eonard] W[oolf] is one of the directors of Chatto and Windus.

My heart is filled with misgiving—with a sense of disaster—not personal—that is, not a question of the self—but of the other.

As always last night the Bach brought past and present together—adding now to the then of the days at Mrs. Clark's and the second Christmas eve in Calgary.

October 27 [1955]

This is a fat book [the new notebook she is starting with this entry]. It suggests a great stretch of life ahead—an act of hubris in its beginning.

There are two pears on the table. They remind W of breasts—and life and love and motherhood no doubt, like the breasts of Renoir's Gabrielle in the print he has asked me to look for in the shops. I remember what Simone Weil says and concentrate on the pears, which are beautiful in themselves—red and yellow and freckled and brown like the breast of a thrush. So, one comes back in another sort of circle, round the curve of the pear to the word breast. [See Appendix A—note 4]

Last night I managed to read through the poetry again by an absolute act of the will—as one wills to go underground into the Métro.

Today a final session with the préfecture of the police. Now we are "résidents temporaire" in France. I had not realized until tonight what idea W connects with residence—my residence in particular.

This afternoon I wrote to the Secretary, Association of Universities of the

British Commonwealth . . .—about application forms for the lectureship in English lit. at the University of Witwatersrand, Johannesburg. The closing date for applications is 17 Nov.

Chatto and Windus sent a receipt for *The Double Hook.*

In the bird market the age of plastic comes into its own. Solitary goldfish ready for transportation in small plastic bags of water. On the ground an enormous goose—its breast curved against the bars of the cage—preened the feathers under its wing. A red crowned rooster cried defiance at the passerby. In one of the boxes peony tubers showed pink shoots through neat wrappings of straw.

I have been thinking about Golding's *Inheritors*—sentimental pseudo-anthropology looking back into a lost paradise—the heir of Fraser and Rider Haggard—the white innocence of the monkey—the wolf people—the tree dwellers and the plainsmen—

Oct 30

Today is Sunday. I went out to the bakery to get bread. M. la Concierge's husband was polishing his car as he does every Sunday morning. Yesterday Mme was waxing the parquet while he bustled about with his feather duster. She is steel and he is soft wax. La petite must have gone off to school in the country because she has disappeared. M. the husband seemed to love her with concerned gentleness, Mme with a fierce and passionate intensity. He smiles and strokes his car as he used to soothe the child's crying.

I found a bunch of dahlias in the market place for Mme Gouzien. A man in a beret and a long blouse bent over and smelled the flowers as I carried them off—"jolies fleurs, jolies fleurs—vous avez un vrai bouquet—"

There is a sense of community in the market. It is not difficult to see what Simone Weil means by "attention."

Mme G. says that she got used to being cold during the war. She loves heat but she got used to being cold. She was in the kitchen boiling a fish when I took her the flowers—and cooking a piece of meat for Jean. She seems isolated and alone at the end of the long red-tiled corridor. The world outside was steaming with mist. The sun has broken through the haze now and the chill air becomes warmer. I like Sunday morning, when the streets are empty except for people on their occasions and the street sweepers with their red twig brooms.

October 31

A clear day after mist in the morning—.

Today I found the small Skira *Renoir*—then walked on the river banks. The Seine like a gold cloth blown in the wind—the sun angled at 45 [degrees]—shining from the left bank so that under the arches of the Pont Neuf the darkness was edged with light. Tramps asleep with their shoes off, like dogs in the strips of sunlight—a man wrapped in a heavy black cloak fishing off the point of the island. It is curious to see the huge black trunked tree there reaching out as if to support the bridge. Piles of burning leaves—and still leaves crackling underfoot. A little boy frozen in wonder before the carved heads on the bridge. . . .

After I crossed the bridge, I walked along the two Gds Augustins to the rue Gît-le-Coeur, along the rue St. André [Des]Arts to the Carrefour de Buci, down the rue Mazarine to the rue Guenegaud. Here there are small galeries and shops selling artists supplies—shops with African masks and tooth and shell necklaces. In one gallery an artist busily putting finishing touches on canvases which were about to be exhibited—like a woman arranging flowers before a party. The canvases showed the influence of Henry Moore.

At a shop on the rue Guénégaud I stopped to ask about Abelard's *Historia Calamitatis*. The bookseller specialized only in regional books. He spoke good English and asked about sending catalogues of regional books to Canada. Had we a bibliothèque nationale? I gave him . . . the address

Sketch by Sheila.

of the archives in Ottawa. Then we talked about Paris and the occupation and he told me that the plaques on the quais and elsewhere were places where members of the maquis had been shot during the days of the liberation.

I see in Hillairet that Ambroise Paré lived on the rue de l'Hirondelle—at least the part of it which was cut off by the construction of the Place Saint-Michel—and that Helvetius feasted his friends at #4 Carrefour de Buci (also, incidentally, that his *De' l'Esprit* was burned by the executioner).

When one is very much alone ghost hunting becomes a family affair.

Mme Gouzien tells me that tomorrow (Toussaint) there is to be a grand mass at ten at Notre Dame des Victoires.

Sometimes the Seine is stone green, sometimes shot crimson and gold—today gold as the stalks of wheat—not gold really but transparent yellow like the yellow of Van Gogh's "Tournesols."

Flux is not opposed to eternity. It reflects it as the Seine reflects the changing light of the sky. As W would say: "This is not a very profound thought."

Today I was happy because I found the Skira—because I talked to the girl in the art shop on the rue Gît-le-Coeur and to the man about his catalogues—and because autumn sat on my shoulders like a coat while a tug passed—and a dog retrieved leaves—and the gardeners burned leaves and painted the fence around the square at the tip of the island.

M. la Concierge's husband is M. du Cas. Mme G. says he comes from Marseilles.

Nov 1

This morning I went to the mass at Notre Dame des Victoires. At ten o'clock the food merchants were just opening their shops for Sunday hours. Le marchand de gibier was hanging up his rabbits and partridges and setting out his "gigots de cerf." Deer is not skinned but cut whole into joints, which are offered for sale. A man speeding along to Fauchon's on a motorcycle with boxes of vegetables balanced on a tray in front of him, spilled a whole box of endives into the street—pauvre homme. The folded white shoots crushed as they fell—not a matter of annoyance but of absolute loss. Exclamations of pity from both sides of the street. I followed the rue des Petits-Champs keeping Henri IV in sight. The streets—especially the Opéra—had their empty Sunday look. . . . People were gathering from all quarters to the Place des Petits Pères. The church itself was crowded, people pressed into every corner—in and around various altars. The Mozart mass indifferently executed because the voices strained in the execution. I thought of Lois Marshall singing the St. John Passion with the Mendelssohn choir in Toronto. An old priest in a black shoulder cape edged with red—an angle of blue ribbon suspending the cross on his chest—preached on the texts of the epistle and gospel. Below him faces massed—a wall of faces—a circle of faces—pyramids of faces. At the foot of the pulpit a blonde boy with a red kerchief knotted about his throat. Before the communion, altar boys carried round baskets heaped with bread, which people took—then blessed themselves and ate. In one corner two children who looked just like "les Enfants de Pulbot" tussled over a piece.

Men and women pressing through the crowded congregation to light their candles before the altar of Notre Dame des Victoires.

I have always hated white marble statues—the weight of metal crowns—fat murals—Sister Mary Zenade and her sodality of angels with their pink paper wings—the ribbons and medals of the Children of Mary—the pomp and shabby circumstance: have felt for the men who let the fires burn and hammer fall. But somehow this morning the people there, the crowded and mobile faces made the statue seem insignificant—not insignificant really, but a part, however shabby, a symbol however insignificant, of a vision—.

Nov 4

The roofs are wet with the late afternoon rain. They shine against the yellowed grey of the city sky. This afternoon I went to the Hébertot on the Bd. des Batignolles to get tickets for the Kabuki, which opens there on the 10th. This is the first time I have explored the city round the Gare St. Lazare. I asked in the station about the trains to Chartres. The "aller et retour" is 544 francs. The rue de Rome seems to be the home of music stores. There are book stores too in one of which I found Michaux's *Nouvelle de l'Étranger*. On the left side where the rue de Rome meets the Bd. Batignolles is a curious dungeon-like building called the Collège Chaptal. In a narrow passage just past the Hébertot there are a number of workshops—men working in wood—a cobbler in a shop no bigger than a cupboard—four women ironing clothes with flat irons—the wooden clack of pigeons' wings as the birds settled precariously on the narrow windowsills—the smell of sawdust—the uneven thrust of cobble stones against the soles of the feet. I sat in a café at the corner of the avenue de Villiers and the rue Levis for a while reading and drinking a cup of café noir express. At the end of the rue Lévis I bought an armful of red chrysanthemums from one of the stalls set up in the street—roses, chrysanthemums, mimosa and anemones in the barrows. Down the rue de Miromesnil to the Bd. Malesherbes—.

Today a letter from Louise [Riley] saying that Doto had had an accident, but has recovered.

A young man with a scarf about his throat and a plump elderly man in a tightly buttoned coat kissing goodbye in front of the Bureau des Postes—the right cheek, then the left. An uncommon enough occurrence to be noted. In the Marigny theatre, too, I saw two women greet one another with kisses and their husbands bow to the women and kiss their hands. One of the women was extraordinarily beautiful—her feather hat like a pink bird in the black nest of her hair.

This has nothing to do with the kissing one sees in the parks, the cafés and on the Métro. These are public kisses—the others only accidentally so—the domestic kiss without location—the ugly little man in a shabby coat consoling an ugly little woman, her face blank with misery, as one might console a child, simply holding her quietly in his arms while people passed on their concerns.

In an article in *Figaro* the following curious phrase occurs: "En contrepartie d'un renforcement des réquisitions, l'action squatter ne sera plus tolérée."

La "tactique de harcelement" de l'abbé Pierre is having its effect.

Nov 7

It is three thirty. I woke in the middle of a terrible dream crying with the tears running back into my eyes like knives. The moon is low in the sky behind the left corner of Patrick's chimney pot. Before I turned on the light I could see the moonlight lying on the floor in shattered pools as it fell through the chinks and slits of the shutters.

It rained this afternoon. I went out only long enough to post my letters and to do the shopping—then to walk down to the store behind the Madeleine where W said he saw "mandrakes." Tonight he said it was only a jest. I suppose if someone told me that there was a unicorn in the Place Vendôme I would go there to make sure.

Utrillo is dead. Tomorrow he is to lie in state at the Sacré Coeur.

November 8

I get up again because I can't sleep. The lights have just flicked out in the rue Vignon. It must be one o'clock. The sky above the inside court is blue with moonlight.

This morning it rained and at noon the rolling of thunder and flashes of lightening. Just after lunch I set out in the rain for Montmartre—up the rue La Fayette into the rue Laffitte, through the Sq. St. George and up the rue Notre-Dame de Lorette to the rue Pigalle, along the Bd. Rochechouart to the rue des Martyrs, to the rue Antoinette, across the rue [Des 3] Frères and up the rue Chappe and across the rue St. Eleuthère to the Sacré Coeur. By the time I reached Pigalle it had stopped raining. In the rue des Martyrs some workmen were repairing a building. Four or five men were working on a balcony, which seemed feebly supported by a rough scaffolding. One of the men on the ledge was lowering a pole to the single work-man in the street. It is really no wonder that there are so many construction accidents in Paris. The pole swung out into the street—swung back at the man who was trying to put it in place. Much shouting and direction from above—then argument above about the diverse directions while the pole swung and the unhappy man beneath tried to pull it into place.

The Sq. Pigalle and the upper end of the rue Pigalle is a curious place, with its nudes, its striptease, its elephants and its chimpanzees. At the moment I can't remember whether it was the elephants or the chimpanzees which belonged to someone called Smith. There seems in the matter of nudes to be a sort of *reductio ad absurdum* since the province of nudity—as someone said of the province of obscenity—is particularly limited. There are probably more mutations in Chinese boxes or jig saw puzzles. One establishment in the Place Pigalle—and it is not the Nouvelle Eve—nonetheless claims to have "les nudes le plus osées du monde."

It was like passing through vanity fair on the way to more human concerns. The steps up the hill led into Utrillo's world—and there he lay in the crypt of the Sacré Coeur—while the very old, helped sometimes by the middle aged, sprinkled the coffin with holy water, made the sign of the cross and said a prayer. Round the coffin lay official chrysanthemums, but at the head of the coffin someone had placed a small bunch of violets. A policeman came in and stood watching for a few minutes, but apart from a few women sitting at the back of the crypt, no one seemed to watch with Utrillo while his friends or "les simples curieux" called. One woman passing left a coin on the "cercueil."

I remembered seeing two oils of Utrillo in a shop not far from the church. A month ago they were hanging with other pictures for sale—not good Utrillos—the work of a man who has lost his power. Today they had small cards on the frames—"réservé."

It is the Utrillo in Boston I remember best. In many ways I remember Boston because of the Utrillos. The Utrillo print which Jean has now is the first picture I ever owned. Anne Angus gave it to me—and afterwards the Moore blue ponies.

Matisse is dead and Utrillo is dead and last month Picasso had one of his caretakers jailed for destroying his doves.

Tomorrow Utrillo is to be buried in the Cimetière St. Vincent from St. Pierre de Montmartre. W says he wants to come with me.

Today when I thought how hard it is for an artist to live at all, my heart was filled with compassion. There is always someone to kill the doves—sometimes merely a clumsy hand—sometimes, as Simone Weil points out, pain turned to destruction—or as Iago: "He has a certain beauty in his life."

November 10

Yesterday we took the Métro to the Place des Abbesses. It is a straight run on the Métro from the Madeleine. The streets were still fresh with yesterday's rain.

At half past nine the police were standing about in the Place de Torcy and in the opening of the rue Mont-Cenis. At the church itself people were busy at work hanging the black draperies over the door, hanging the "U" above the entrance—setting up the black canopied stand where M. George Petrides and M. Heuze were to deliver

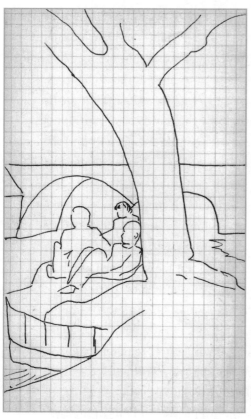

Sketch by Sheila.

their brief "allocutions" after the service. We went into the church and sat down. People began to come in. Men brought in a cross of violets and red roses and moved away candles so that they could place the cross at the foot of the bier. They came in with mammoth wreaths from the Municipal Council of Paris, chrysanthemums with great splays of fern. Officials in black suits and silver chains moved people away from the mourners' chairs. More people came. The church filled. A sense of bustle and preparation—lights turned on and off. Then someone began lighting the candles just as the bell began its seventy-two strokes. I counted the strokes to twenty then lost count watching the sacristan trying to light the candles, which didn't burn easily. A plump woman in a tweed suit and a bare-headed girl climbed over us into seats. The woman took off her scarf and gave it to the girl, who tied it about her head. The bell went on tolling and people began to move restlessly.

Photographers came in and stood on the steps of the pulpit and at the front of the church, behind the sanctuary railing. Finally, drums began to beat and the men of the "guard champêtre" of the "Commune libre" of Montmartre came in quickly with the coffin—came quickly, bent down under its weight. Then I saw Lucy Valore—a small old figure in black between M. Petrides and M. Heuze—then people crowding behind them—just a glimpse of the sans culotte caps of the P'tits Pulbots who beat the drums—then nothing until the voice of the curé de Vesinet came strangely, I expect over a loud speaker, because the pulpit was empty, the steps crowded with photographers. The violin, the voices of the choir singing I don't know what—not certainly the traditional requiem music—people turning disapprovingly towards the choir—people changing their places—people deciding to go out into the courtyard, which was already crowded.

Photographers on the fences and any ledges which would support them—an old man and woman standing at a window looking down into a courtyard—people in the windows of the buildings on the rue Mont-Cenis—the police moving people back out of the centre of the court: "Retirez s'il vous plaît"—then the persuasive "M'sieurs Mesdames." Then when the allocutions were over, people jostling out the gate—flowing out—dividing into groups—some going this way some that down to the gates of the cemetery—past the shop which sells potted plants—up through the crowded and climbing graves to drop roses or merely to look down what seemed an interminable depth—onto the pale oak coffin below—a policeman at the foot of the grave trying to keep people from crowding. It was a real funeral, not a ceremony— a "peau véritable" of a funeral—domestic and disordered. The cemetery was pink and grey with the ghosts of the Toussaint chrysanthemums. Certainly, as Mme G. said, "the cult of the dead" is still strong.

. . . .

November 12
Yesterday and the day before I watched people crowding round the windows which begin to display their Christmas goods. Windows of dolls—but first in attraction the windows of mechanical toys, meccano and construction blocks.

At the Galeries Lafayette some young men were dressing the windows for displays of electric trains. They were working with all the enthusiasm of boys—as if they had never had a chance to handle trains before. It was almost impossible to get through the crowd, who were watching them work.

Yesterday crowds had gathered in front of the windows of the department store of the Louvre. People were clinging like flies to the windows where the toys were displayed. In front of the neighbouring window of books stood an elderly man and a little girl. He was reading the titles of the books to her and suggesting the exciting stories hidden behind the covers. They seemed remote—isolated in a world of their own.

Today I had my hair cut. Etiquette requires that one shake hands with the hair dresser when he has finished the work. Everyone does. I found a book of luminous pictures (La Fontaine's *Fables*) for Mme du Cos to take to Claude when she visits her tomorrow. She has been telling me about the visit for some time now. Because of the visit Monsieur has altered his schedule. He hosed the court and polished his car this afternoon.

Nov 14

It was cold and damp this morning. It has been a grey day. I shopped late this afternoon because the stores were closed this morning. At five o'clock the sky was a swirl of pink—a damp moleskin day washed pink at sunset.

. . . .

This evening we went to see the Kabuki dancers at the Hébertot. There were a great many empty seats in the theatre. Dances like the lion dance and the spider's web didn't seem terrible or strange. They belong to the same world as the North American Indian dances which I saw at UBC—the same element too of transformation by slight of hand. There is in the Kabuki as we saw it a combination of prodigality and economy—in staging—in gesture—in facial expression.

. . . .

Nov 15

Today the mss. of the *D. H.* came back from Chatto and Windus.

. . . .

It was very cold—quite grey—the trees, black shapes against the sky, and the leaves black too, as if they had burnt out. I must look tomorrow to see if this was a trick of the afternoon light—or if frost had drained the colour from the leaves. I'm not even sure whether it could.

As I walked along the street today I kept looking at the thick soft dressing gowns made of wool from the Pyrenees—and the heavy sweaters which button to the throat—like a person without enough clothes when cold begins to set the bone.

November 18

On the 16th I went to Galignani's and came back with Wyndham Lewis's *Monstre Gai* and *Malign Fiesta* and Dorothy Sayers' translation of the *Purgatorio*. Yesterday I read the first part of the Lewis. It is the best thing I've read for some time. There is no malice, no excitement, no castigation. The Third City is built on familiar ground.

Today it was bitterly cold outside. At five-thirty a thin pale moon hung in the purple grey sky at the end of the rue Vignon. I had gone to see Oudot's exhibition at Weil's, and Humblot's at the Galerie Ramanet. There were a good many people in both galleries—some merely curious, some with the speculator's meditative mouth and arched eye brow.

I am much attracted by Humblot's use of colour—the sine qua non of the terra verde—which controls the picture. Some of the pictures were of Baux—just as I'd imagined it would be—just as it could have been for Dante. There is a certain dissipation in some of Oudot's painting. I want to see both exhibitions again—although I really have no doubt about the Baux landscapes.

When a Frenchman says "C'est incroyable" he really means what he says. We tend to do away with things in which we can't believe. Simply don't exist—so we use the French "C'est impossible." And in circumstances in which he says "C'est impossible," since we don't recognize limitations we say: "I wish I could . . . ."

On the 16th went with Mme Gouzien to the second of the Madeleine Film Society films—one of Georges Simenon's novels. I understood very little of the dialogue. After the film, a bulky man with a red face and greasy colpons of flax-coloured hair rose to his feet, carefully buttoned a light black coat he was wearing, and then hesitantly announced that the director of the film had grossly misrepresented ordinary legal procedure to secure the sympathy of the audience. He spoke, he said, as a lawyer. As far as I could make out, he maintained that the purpose of the law was to effect justice with as little scandal as possible. Followed a good deal of heated discussion about juvenile delinquency—the economic pressures which forced both parents to work—the evil influence of films etc. etc.

W begins work on Cockcrow again. . . .

Sunday Nov 20
Wyndham Lewis's satire is particularly concerned with the literature of ideas—Eliot, Charles Williams, C. S. Lewis—perhaps one should say the literature of salvation— the withdrawal of Eliot—the satanism of Williams and Lewis—the French writers like Mauriac. He has, as it were, turned the glass on these violent critics of modern science. He has, of course, done more than this. The nature of his satire is suggested by countless clues—his choice of form (the inter-planetary romance)—his choice of Pulman—the Freudian-Jungian overtones—the Dante passages in *Malign Fiesta*—

the fag . . . (the eternal running-shoe & sweatered adolescents Auden, Spender, et al.) who turns in the end to gardening.

Yesterday I noticed the woman who sells flowers at the corner of the rue Havre and Bd Haussmann. It was bitterly cold. She was wearing a pair of wool lined "pantoufles" and these were thrust into heavy wooden sabots lined with newspaper. Tonight in the vicinity of the Châtelet I saw four men sitting on the pavement in the rain having a party, with a bottle of—wine perhaps.

In the central part of the market at the Quai aux Fleurs a bird market was in full swing despite the cold and rain.

Notre Dame Cathedral was packed for the commemoration of the five centenaire of the beginning of the process of Jeanne la Pucelle's rehabilitation. The Bishop of Beauvais talked for nearly an hour—while Cardinal Feltin, the Papal Nuncio and a huge assembly of bishops and archbishops, General Weygand, and other dignitaries sat listening in state. There were many curés and nuns in the crowd.

After the benediction, I saw a bishop hastening down the central aisle of the cathedral. Near the door a number of women came up to him and kissed his ring and the lace on the edge of his sleeve. He looked aescetic, saintly, and pleased. Sometimes it is not difficult to understand violent anti-clericalism.

The ordinary man (the phrase betrays) must worship and pay reverence—to God—to Joan—to the lace-edged bishop—to the spirit of the free West (the Calgary Stampede)—the Edmonton Eskimos. There are buff-orpington displays, too, at every provincial convocation.

Nov 23

. . . .

The African marigolds which I brought back from the man who sets up his barrow at the corner of Tronchet and Castellane burn in the pewter jug. They have a wild civility. Their heads bend down from the stalk but the flame-coloured petals rayed out from the disked jade centres are lion faces. Most people have lost the fierce and humble magnificence of certain flowers and certain animals.

The trees are almost naked now and today even the banks of the Seine were almost deserted. I walked down the rue de Seine past the galleries and down to the end of rue Tournon to the gardens of the Luxembourg. At quarter to six the rue Seine was crowded with people buying vegetables and meat in the open stalls. On the rue Tournon I saw the first automatic laundry I have seen in Paris. On the streets and in and about the galleries there were numbers of young girls in tight-legged pantaloons and duffle coats—sometimes alone and sometimes with boys in duffle coats and cords.

In the Galerie de Seine an exhibition of Colombatto Rosso "Maison des Fous"—the only gallery I stopped to look at since I had set out to find a Vulgate for W. Born in Turin in 1925, Rosso has had exhibitions in Turin, Rome, Milan, Paris, New York. I suppose the impulse is a survival of a feeling of social protest which has lost its direction. The figures have no context except the age of Rossa himself. Bosch's fous are engaged in nefarious commerce or the victims of it—Breugel's dance or feast or rest.

A letter from Malcolm Ross came on Monday. He is going to publish "The Black Farm" and says he will see if Weaver will use it too. He gives me courage again.

Brought back this afternoon, too, *The Apes of God*—in format, a horrible, bulky, ugly volume. Books should never appear in such degraded dress.

On Monday night we took Mme G. to see the Kabuki. Again I sat next to a man who maintained audibly that the whole affair was grotesque. This time we had a much better opportunity to see the actors' faces.

The libraries have put all their books on Japanese art in their windows—the dealers in antiquities, all their Japanese objets d'art—the print sellers, their Japanese prints.

Today I found a lion, a mouse, and a thin-faced black poodle—red amber, grey and black.

Nov 25
It is two o'clock. It is always two o'clock.

Dec 4
Today is warm again. I went out intending to walk to the far end of la cité but got no further than the Pont Neuf. People out again in the gardens and fishing along the banks of the Seine—a man in a rowboat pulling up cages which looked like lobster pots—lovers loving and a tramp in a blanket under one of the arches. A Saint Nicholas in front of the Louvre looking like a nun in red—a thin, short figure bending forward to listen to the children as a nun bends.

I came back by the rue Pr. St. G. l'Aux to have a word with the gargoyles. It is from this side that I like to look at the church. The front is narrow shouldered and ordinary, but the back on the rue Arbre Sec and this side have more purpose, more mystery, more amplitude.

Just below the tip of the island the fire boats were gathered all together—behind them one of the low narrow cargo boats.

W says the Seine is a dull, stagnant, ugly river. He can't really have looked at it. It is not like the Fraser—it is not like the North Saskatchewan certainly, but it has its own necessity, its own inscape. Today I walked below the quais on the river banks. When a boat passed, the water was cut with blue—the greyed blue which can be seen so often roofing the Place Vendôme.

When I looked at the crowds in the streets I wondered how anyone could possibly conceive of himself in the role of "extraordinaire."

Yesterday Faber sent an envelope of reviews of *Friday's Child* from a clipping agency. We read them after dinner when Mme la Concierge brought the letter up. W was pleased—especially, he said, with the *Listener* review. He seems happy and sings a good deal about the flat. I think of the sign in St. G. l'Aux: "Quand on aime, on chante. Chantez ensemble."

Dec 6

How long? Today anguish of the bone. Nothing to record—absolutely nothing.

Dec 8

Have had a vile cold and general misery for several days. . . .

Today J. Lehmann sent back the Haemon story ["Antigone"]. It is not completely satisfactory. Perhaps he is right.

Dec 9

Took a root of parsley cut below the ground so that the green stems with their tasselled heads spring from the yellow-brown knot. Put it on the table with a tomato.

December 11

. . . .

Last night I began to write "The Landscape" again. I have finished about four pages. The writing seems slack and rhythmic. It is probably a false start. I think of UBC and the cliffs crumbling down to the beaches, the skull brow hill in the field beyond the cows and the pigpen.

It was beginning to rain when I went out to the bakery. Now the rain is falling steadily on the roof. This morning early Mme and Monsieur Du Cas went off to visit "la petite." The court yard wore its scrubbed and quiet Sunday look.

Dec 22

When I write at night I lose track of the days. It seems an eternity since three o'clock in the morning of yesterday.

. . . .

Today I went to the Louvre to see the Avignon Pietà. The Virgin (Notre Dame de Pitié) has an old and tortured face—not a face of compassion—but a face still with anguish. It is the face of St. John which is softened with compassion. The long arm of the Christ with its half-closed hand made me think of Donne.

At the far end of the gallery there are a number of Memlings—La Vierge de Jacques Floriens—a triptych, Le Martyre de St. Sebastien—the resurrection du Christ—l'ascension—portrait de femme âgée. Memling's faces are all in repose—as if he had a vision of innocence which became sober and more intense with age.

In another section of the gallery were pictures of le maître de Moulins—one of St. Marie Madeleine and a donatrice—another called "enfant en oraison." The picture of the child is exquisite in its simplicity. I would suspect that Renoir had learned something from it. Perhaps it has been reproduced, but I have never seen a reproduction.

. . . .

The streets become more and more crowded with people and automobiles. According to the paper many provincial motorists have been victims of "l'opération papillons," that is, their cars have been towed off by trucks and impounded.

. . . .

Dec 23

It is two o'clock and the rain is beating down on the roof.

See the Avignon Pietà—the blue and the red coming together behind the figure of St. John.

"En vérité, en vérité, je vous le dit: si le grain de blé jeté en terre ne meurt pas, il ne donne rien; mais s'il meurt, il donne du blé en abondance. . . ."

"Maintenant, mon être est en émoi, et que dire? Père préserve-moi de cette heure! Mais c'est pour cela que je suis arrivé à cette heure. Père glorifie-toi. Marchez tant que vous avez la lumière pour n'être pas pris par les ténèbres, car celui qui marche dans les ténèbres ne sait pas ou il va."

I have never quite understood why Dostoevsky used this passage at the beginning of *The Brothers Karamazov*.

It is always easier to understand man's weakness than his strength, his despair than his hope, his hate than his love—all the brothers except Alyosha—and Alyosha is the key to Dostoevsky. When we say, It is only human to do this or that, we usually excuse a weakness or a perversion. For this reason we attribute the strength of Christ to his Godhead, not to his manhood. This is probably what W means: If an artist walks in the shadows of men, he can achieve nothing because he has lost—or has never found—his direction.

When I saw the Pietà today, I understood that it is not the light which one fears but the terrible moment of darkness before the light comes.

The rue de Casanova and the rue des Petits Champs were crowded with people this afternoon. Just after three the butchers were beginning to open their shops. They always seem to be beginning another day. In the restaurants on the rue Coquillière men who looked like truck drivers were eating oysters. The edge of the street was piled with baskets of shell fish. The markets, of course, were closed. Here, in one of the shops was the final comment on larks—a plate of alouettes au fois gras—the whole bird on a pillow of pastry—the head and long beak delicately poised—the body garnished with a few feathers. . . . I spoke to a woman who was coming out of St. Eustache into rue des Juges. She told me that one had to have tickets for the Christmas mass. She took me round to the entrance on the rue Rambuteau where we got tickets from a woman in the church entrance. The woman who helped me said that she did not belong to the parish either, but that she wanted to go to the midnight mass there because it was the finest in Paris. She was a tall gentle-faced, middle-aged woman in a grey coat and black felt hat. Like many of the simple looking women in Paris, she was carrying a brown leather brief case. After I had left her she called me back to ask where we lived because she thought she might be able to help us reach the church tomorrow night. I imagine she thought I was a complete stranger.

Inside the church a woman was building the crèche. She had made figures out of wire netting and paper. The Virgin and St. Joseph were sitting under an arch of vegetable crates, and about them were figures dressed like the people of the market coming with baskets of flowers and bunches of leeks and vegetables as offerings.

In one door of the church a man was begging, and at the back of the church—in front of the high altar—a "clochard" slept with his bag beside him. Men were moving chairs and someone was playing the organ.

I walked the circle of the rue de Viarmes—just where this opens out on the markets, a man was lying asleep on the pavement, his head on a damp sack. The truckers moved about him without disturbing him. Just behind the Louvre an old woman stopped me. She was looking at the columns of the facade which men have been repairing for some time. "C'est un massacre," she said. "O mon beau pays." Then she called upon the government to witness what had been done. Then suddenly she said, "But perhaps you don't speak French"—and then she said that such things must happen elsewhere because the whole world was "mal équilibré." There were tears in her eyes.

Apart from the noise made by two men chipping in the entrance, the Church of St. G. de l'Aux was quiet and undisturbed. In the late afternoon the windows above the high altar burn like flames. I had no time to speak to the gargoyles.

Dec 25
Veille de Nöel and Messe de Minuit at St. Eustache.

We left the flat about 9:30. There were not a great many people in the streets. The girls on the rue Sèze were twittering like birds. It had rained in the late afternoon, but by nine the rain had stopped and the moon was out. The city was washed and grey like mother of pearl. At the end of the rue Catinat in the Place des Victoires we overtook two night watchers, one with a lantern, the other with a bunch of keys and a revolver at his hip. They were strolling deep in conversation. Behind the window of the confiserie we noticed a man, with the face of a lover, trying to make a decision between two iced logs decorated with mushrooms and flowers. By quarter to ten quite a large crowd had collected at the church. The rue Coquillière was crowded with people buying and eating oysters—baskets of oysters and baskets of empty shells.

Outside the church we stood next to two Americans—a woman in a fawn corduroy coat with a white wool scarf over her head—and a middle-aged man in a black roll brim felt. The man said he had come to St. Eustache five years ago to hear the Berlioz Requiem. The woman had spent the day at Fontainebleau. She spoke of the ferns, gold under the trees, and of the rock. While we were waiting, the patrol went by honking its misery—the gendarmes with two girls in their van. Our tickets let us into the church behind the high altar so that we did not see the mass and could hear only the shattered echo of the curé's brief "allocution." I thought of spending all eternity behind a pillar in the Renaissanced gothic heaven while St. Peter in a black overcoat with "haussement d'épaules" and "hochement de tête" admitted bearers of white tickets into the sanctuary. I thought of sitting behind a pillar while the scraping of chairs and the mutter at the barricade muffled the notes of the flute, the hautbois and the lute and only the ghost of Vittoria's "O Magnum Mysterium" whispered on the far side to the blessed before the altar.

Sketch by Sheila.

For two hours the woman who had spent the afternoon at Fontainebleau slept—her head in its white scarf flat on her husband's shoulder.

Behind us sat the woman who had helped me with the tickets on Saturday. We shook hands with her and with her son. The son was very lame—and after the communion the two crept away before the "sortie au grand orgue—the concerto posthume en ré mineur d'Handel."

As I have seen happen in French—at least Paris churches— . . . the crowd going out met the crowd coming in to the next mass. On the way back we passed two cafés where people were dancing—crossed the rue de la Paix—the avenue de l'Opéra and the Bd Madeleine through flights of roaring cars, but otherwise the streets were quiet.

. . . .

Apparently the clochards met five hundred strong under the bridge de Tournelle for their Christmas Eve party. I wish that I had been with them. It is a sad truth that the Goncourts, who saw everything, wrote nothing of any account.

Dec 27

. . . .

W gave me a scarf like a lion's mane—gold and tawny. I wonder whether or not it will make me feel like a lion—brave and royal. Still one prays to be delivered from the mouth of the lion.

Mme Gouzien told me this morning that the young butcher in the Madeleine had died over the holiday. I had noticed that he was not in the shop on Saturday. Maurice, the younger brother, waited on me. He had put on something of his brother's manner and spoke in his brother's phrase: "un petit os d'veau avec?" Today at four Maurice and a tearful girl were opening the shop. M. & Mme Dumain were not there. Maurice has the face of a harlequin.

Dec 28

This morning I read the notice of André Dumain's death posted on the door of the market. The father was cutting up meat, his face red and swollen with weeping. Maurice has inherited André's work. He moves about outside the shop—cautiously and sadly important.

. . . .

The wind was blowing and the Seine was cold gold—the sky grey, then slit with blue sunlight. Children off to the gardens with sailboats under their arms. On the way to the Pont Neuf I went down the rue Richelieu and for the first time noticed Molière with his two muses at the angle of his street and the cardinal's. On the Quai du Louvre a woman—pulled into the wind which was blowing from the Eiffel Tower by a wire-haired terrier—carefully managed a large goldfish in a plastic bag.

At the shop which sells fishing tackle (Quai de l'Horloge) I bought two double hooks ("hameçons doubles") for good luck. A black and white spaniel puppy was tied up at the back of the shop, in a dog jungle of hanging boxes. Here one could get a fish basket like the ones the men on the river bank use—wire—or the long-necked net bags hooped with willow or bamboo of some kind.

At the Hôtel Dieu a hearse was picking up a body.

. . . .

W said tonight that all people live in the imagination and that men write real poetry only when they break through the imagination into reality.

I can see what he means relative to himself—

[1956]

January 4

I like the night because it fits tight. The day is loose and ill-fitting. I like the feel of the night lying close to my skin. When one loves, the night is something else, and the day too. No word comes from South Africa. [See entry for 27 October 1995.] I begin to think of the Arctic again. Seeds and roots need winter to gather their force—light and heat contracting to the centre. Except from an abundance like that of God, one cannot give when the cup is empty or the lamp has burned its oil—one couldn't even receive because the action is reciprocal. The widow's curse and the miracle of fishes require more than human hands or nets—though the hands and nets are instrumental.

Mme Gouzien terribly upset by the elections . . . .

The papers report American, English, Italian reaction to the elections. Any Canadian reaction seems a matter of indifference—as perhaps it is.

. . . .

Helped by a friendly housewife I bought a grey turtle neck sweater—definitely "en solde"—from a tumbled mass on a trestle in front of the Maison Roberts. It actually looked and felt warmer to the hand than it does on. Coming home I met W emerging from the Post Office of the Blvd. des Capucines. We walked back as far as Fauchon's together.

January 6
Nothing except a cold wind—reports of smog in London—agreement of the Front Republican.

Since today is Epiphany I brought back a handful of African marigolds. The Italian was at the corner of the rue Castellane with a barrow of mimosa, marigolds and anemones. The mimosa and the marigolds burned like fire.

People crowded round the barrow and reached out towards the flowers.

The Italian seems to know. He comes only on the coldest and dullest days. He sells all his flowers too for the same price, so there is no decision—after the first decision is made.

January 7
Began writing the "Landscape" again—using the tentative attack of a week or so ago.

. . . The marigolds glower like rain-soaked lions.

Sunday, January 8
Listened to the Vivaldi *Seasons*—then to the Châtelet to hear l'Orchestre de l'Association des Concerts Colonne directed by Charles Munch play Haydn's *London Symphony*, Debussy's *La Mer*, and Brahms IVth.

It rained most of the afternoon. The Métro stations and the trains themselves were packed. The Métro world, like each of the streets, has its own ambience—the world of the advertiser driven underground—twenty insistent pictures of a girl drinking Koninsberg beer—a girl from the Continent Perdu—duplicated, quadruplicated—la vache sérieuse—the Metro women in their caps with the inevitable black knitted shawl round their shoulders—and their round faced signal sticks. Children in capes—a woman in a plastic raincoat standing on the scales while she adjusted her lipstick before the mirror set over the gauge—men in berets—lovers kissing and holding hands—an old man with a beard squatted in one of the tunnels while he read a newspaper.

I have never seen a conductor quite like Munch. It would have been possible to recreate the fourth symphony merely by looking at his back. He is a tall, massive man with a cap of thick silver hair. He conducted like a demon—moving quickly from movement to movement, from number to number after he had played the first movement of Honneger's Seventh Symphony. The theatre was hot and smelt as all French theatres do of feet and sweat. An old English woman sitting next to W produced a handkerchief heavily scented with eau de cologne.

Superb passages in the Honneger when single instruments carried the theme like flames out of the massed fire.

We came home through thick rain. When I went to close the shutters after supper the roof across the court was white with snow.

Every day I realize that when W called me at the beginning of May, I should have been strong enough to break the promise which he reminded me of.

> Beloved, may your sleep be sound
> That [have] found it where you fed
> What were all the world's alarms
> To mighty Paris when he found
> Sleep upon a golden bed
> That first dawn in Helen's arms[?]

Yet Yeats, too, remembers the skein that "binds ghost to ghost." The singers and writers of the ballads knew these ghosts—but they knew that they could be locked out.

Suppose one thought: We were on the Métro—at Concorde the door opened and he got off. I ran and caught up to him. At the "correspondance" we were standing together. People got off. We went to get on and I found myself alone in a group of strange people. As the door was about to close he got on. So, too, among the crowds at the theatre. Just like the last day in the station at Vancouver.

And I remember thinking that day in Vancouver. It were better to be lost. As a child knows when other children run away from him.

January 10
Sometimes I think that if I did not write I would lose track of the days. Today there were great flakes of snow and then rain.

I bought a dorade at the fish market. The man cleaned and scaled it, but when

135

I opened the package, it was staring at me out of its great round eyes.

All day today W was looking at me as the dorade did—as if my existence was some frightful crime against humanity.

. . . .

Whatever came or did not come in the post this morning has loosed W's anger against me. The climate is the climate of March 14th. There is no need for his anger. It is "gratuit." His anxiety I can understand. What should I do?

It is absolutely necessary to liquidate anger, chagrin or contempt before writing. In short, a writer must have mastered the emotions before he can use the insight which the emotion has given him. Graham Greene, for instance, is never completely master of the emotional content of his books. He writes disturbing stories, not satisfactory ones. Perhaps love is the only emotion out of which one can write without this control—since it masters and does not have to be mastered.

The word "satisfactory" is a blank. Perhaps W's image is better. He writes books which don't hatch. They are full of the heat and suspense of the brooder sheds.

. . . .

Today at lunch I thought of the laundress' remark, that it was easy enough to drive round in Paris, but very muddy and difficult in the "banlieue"—so [I,] too, thought. It is easy to think where the streets have been paved by others. It is in the suburbs, in the expanding fringes that the going is difficult.

As a corollary one might add that there is no doubt that even paved streets fall into disrepair and that lids can be knocked off manholes.

Tonight the wind is breathing like a trapped animal in the court. The clock and the beetles compete in the silence.

. . . .

January 14
Fog drifts in across the roofs.

It is not difficult to understand why Saurès wrote letters to himself. Keeping a journal is a sort of private correspondence.

When I write or read or listen to music, a chain tightens round my throat. Life and feeling are knotted together—and what I feel I must feel alone. The only safety— to let life ebb into the eyes and finger tips—to walk as many hours as the streets stretch round the corners. W takes for granted what he hopes is the truth—or tries to—for he is miserably unhappy, except in the future he plans, in the work which is his guarantee to [his young friend].

When I am too tired to go out, as I was today, the walls bend in. It is a dreadful thing to outstay one's welcome.

January 15

. . . .

Today the sun shone again. About 11:30 I went to the bakery and the market. I brought back a hyacinth—two tall spikes and a third folded in the leaves.

The Italian by the bakery had a small barrow filled with hyacinths and pots of red tulips. The hyacinths had been taken out of their pots and the plant and the soil from the pot wrapped in leaves of technical books. The hyacinth is on the table now in one of the white powdered milk tins. It is not a cut flower or a picked flower but a living thing. The colour of the flowers seems to flow from the bulb through the stalk.

One shares one's life with the flowers too—and the artichoke—terra verde burnished with purple—the smooth pointed leaves half opening—half closing into the centre.

I think of Hopkins and how well he understood the fragile and gleaming beauty of things—and their strength, too, for I carried the delicate plant back in my basket with the bread and the artichokes and the sausages—and the pink flowers glow remote and contained now in the pale fold of the leaves.

. . . .

January 18

Went to La Hune to see Michaux's graphisms. Saw Cocteau and came back with Michaux's "Misérable Miracle." . . .

La Hune was not empty. There were young men looking at books—a man and a woman inquiring about prints. Michaux's graphisms were hung in the gallery behind the main part of the shop: several delicate oils—some coloured ink sketches and the black graphisms like the illustration of the "Misérable Miracle"—and some from which the prints themselves have been made.

A girl came in and whispered something to the man who was discussing prints with the two customers. The shop had suddenly become quite quiet. Then I saw Cocteau talking to a group of boys. There was no mistaking his profile and the grey curling hair. He holds his head just as Sedgwick used to, his face turned, his chin tilted upward. Then I noticed his hands and his small feet in their soft polished black shoes. So here was the eulogist of Colette and Mistinguette, of Honneger in a steel grey coat—or rather a charcoal black—cut like a doctor's gown, with great folds over the shoulders and a sort of pleat falling from an elegant tailor's arrow in the middle of the back. With him was a tall, thick-set man dressed in an ordinary overcoat and hat. While Cocteau talked, his companion looked at Michaux's "Troubles."

First Cocteau talked to the proprietor, I suppose, who had excused himself and left the customers with their print—then to a grey-haired young middle aged woman with a Mamie Eisenhower hair cut and long pink fingernails who had been smoking a cigarette in front of one of Michaux's "Miseries." They talked about the coat, which the woman admired. Then the proprietor went for a picture of Cocteau in his academic dress. He had had the coat, he said, cut like the gown. He swirled the skirt of it about his shoulder. He put his hand in his pocket and pulled out a pencil sketch which looked as if it might have been drawn by Picasso—himself in his academic gown and hat—mostly hat in the sketch. He spoke about a picture in *Life*. He swirled his coat again; then let it drop and held out his delicate hands with the fingers extended.

Meanwhile one of the helpers had brought the master of La Hune a copy of Cocteau's collected works, but he did nothing with it, simply carried it about under his arm. Cocteau's voice was so clear and so delicately and precisely modulated that it would have been difficult not to hear what he said.

His presence filled the whole room—and he knew that it did.

When he left, people who had politely gone about their business while he was there, twittered to one another and turned to watch him go—lifting his hands and shaking the folds of his new coat and stepping delicately over puddles because it had begun to rain.

When the chauffeur closed the door of the black car, which had been waiting in the side street, everyone began to talk. There was great excitement, too, among a crowd of girls who were being brought by an elderly woman to see the "Troubles," for it was among them that Cocteau had to make his way to reach his car.

I don't know why but I thought of Mrs. Dalloway.

Then I drank coffee and came back laughing on the Métro because I had been staring at Cocteau and listening as shamelessly as Boswell, while a poet [who] was writing a satirical novel which might portray Cocteau was waiting at 28 rue Vignon for his dinner.

. . . .

Tonight on the National we heard Milstein play the Sonata #1 in F minor and the chaconne of the Partita #11 in D minor of Bach. W lit the candles and turned out the light. In the candle light the hyacinth became a witch-like translucent gleam. The blooms at the tip of the flower open and the leaves fold more tightly against the spikes. The sonata had none of the fierce nobility which Szegetti gives it—and the chaconne, none of the sweeping grandeur of our Menuhin.

A good deal of my life is laced together with this music. The sonata is like a central knot. I heard it accidentally in Calgary on the Christmas Eve of the year we lived in Rae Chittick's flat. That day the music was like a noose. Tonight is this side of abnegation.

. . . .

Jan 25
Il faut avoir eu par la joie [la] révélation de la réalité pour trouver la réalité dans la souffrance.

It is not humanly possible to live in the present for great stretches of time unless there is some one strand which persists, some sense of continuity and direction. The clochard, for instance, may not know under what arch of the bridge he will sleep, or where he will get his next meal—but, for better or for worse, he is a clochard. He might, of course, be a clochard by accident. He might, however, be rooted in his state. He might move only in a small circle under the bridges and beside the river.

This is probably a bad illustration—but it has an element of truth. I thought of the tramp because he seems the most rootless of men—yet in a sense he is rooted in place and in a way of life.

The fault of the analogy is in thinking of the clochard's life as a vocation. He probably makes it bearable by an active choice of his arch, his river, his particular jungle.

S[imone] W[eil] is quite right when she says that it is the cutting up of life, the "morcellement," that makes life an intolerable misery.

People can't start life again. She is right when she says that "l'acte de jeter le clef," "l'acte où la faculté de mettre à part" is the most destructive of actions—the beginning of unhappiness and evil.

The "faculté de mettre à part" is the disease of the age—clear everything out, begin over.

The mind wanders among fragments of thoughts. I think of life as a piece of metal which must be shaped, not thrown away—of work even as something which must be shaped not thrown away—the something to write once given or elected, turned until it has form—until it lives. One simply can't drop it and look for something else. This way man wears his life or his work like ready-made clothes. He shops around until he finds something that fits—that will do with a little adjustment here or there. It is life off the rack—work off the rack—not living or creating.

I went to the Champs Élysée to get tickets for *Ornifle*.

January 26

I have a great fear that, like the adolescent, I am not quite in control of the ship. If the hands of the two navigators are unsteady, then the chances of collision assume the character of a nightmare. One can't and shouldn't control another's ship, but [one's] own hand must be steady enough to prevent collision.

Tonight we went to *Ornifle* only to find that the seats were mere flaps against a back wall at the corner. W came back, but I stayed, then came back through the rain by Métro.

Fear panics. I think the door will not open when I press the outside button—or the key, which is uncertain, will fail in the lock—that 28 rue Vignon will have disappeared.

It is three-thirty and the rain still beats down in the court.

Jan 27 (Vendredi)

. . . .

S[imone] W[eil] knows the dangers which destroy the heart—

Read Cocteau this evening after a day when the flat was too small for the number of presences in it.

I thought of crossing the Fraser river when every crack and knot hole in the bridge opened on terror.

W came back with a duffle coat from the C. C. C. He looks as young in it as he is at heart.

Jan 30

. . . .

I record that I still can't stand the shock of physical evidence which thrusts itself into my consciousness from time to time—as today. Evidence is the wrong word since the meaning has been circumscribed—physical witness. I recall S[imone] W[eil]'s words: "Quand on a péché par injustice il faut souffrir l'injustice." Intellectually I know, as a person I understand, but my heart shies as a horse shies when it sees a paper or small animal on the path.

I watch the transformation—what does it mean? The curly 'W' has now become the 'W.' These are the things—light as a mosquito's breath. Perhaps it came to me from W in the first place—besides, it is the commonest W in the world. . . .

Brought back two bunches of anemones from the man with the barrow—à prochain. His barrow was loaded with tulips—bulbs and all.

. . . .

The anemones open—wind flowers—strange precious fragile things. Beyond all flowers they seem to have an aptitude for living.

Feb 5

. . . .

Our life, S[imone] W[eil] says, is an impossibility and absurdity. Everything that we want is contradicted by the conditions or consequences that are attached to it. It is because we ourselves are contradictions, being creatures being God and infinitely different from God.

Thebon says: Improve the material condition of a people and you run the risk of changing its soul—devote yourself entirely to someone and you cease to exist for him. Only imaginary good is without contradiction: the young girl who desires many children ("nombreuse postérité"), the social reformer who dreams of the happiness of the race—encounter no obstacle until they begin to act—they fly wide-winged in a pure but fictitious good.

It is across the absurdity of the world, conceived of and suffered as an absurdity, not only that man finds "the Kingdom which is not of this world" but also that the artist finds his world of discourse.

The circus becomes the symbol of life for the writer—for me at least. There is no message—there is the impossible—and men lifting it like a weight or jumping through it like a hoop—or trying to tame it: torn faces, falls from the tight rope—spectacular manipulations—tigers bowing humbly before men—clowns drooling.

That is what Mr. Salter didn't understand about *The Double Hook*. He thought that my people were stripped of society—conceived of as progressive. I meant that they were stripped of their bridges or centre, roots, traditions, which Thebon describes as bridges, S[imone] W[eil] as "des métaux" between earth & sky—and between one another even.

As S. W. says so often: "C'est autre chose." Hence the argument about the end of the book—and, I suppose, why Day Lewis [who responded on behalf of Chatto

& Windus] found it difficult to understand the relationships between the various characters.

Today we went with Mme Gouzien to La Bruyère to see Susanne Flon in Audibuti's *La Mal Court* .

It has rained gently all day. Now at two-fifteen the rain pours into the court. I bought a bunch of tulips from the man with the barrow—some with the bulbs attached. The flowers were in bud and just begin to open. They are a mat and richly delicate pink—the pink which suggests blue.

. . . .

A writer cannot will a work, he must wait for it—not as a man who sleeps and distracts himself—but as one waits for a person one loves. The writer must watch and wait. Then he must attend. He must, if he attends, believe in the existence of his characters—and respect them.

For this reason he can't manipulate character—or plot, which is the action or living of his characters in time. He can't compel his characters to carry briefcases full of tracts—or to give radio talks on religion or politics or science or the way to get on with the neighbours. The moment he does, his characters lose their identity—as they do, too, when he pities or despises or exalts them.

If there is any miracle—it is the recognition of existence—not the shaping of it to one's will.

This is my answer to Kilgenius Dobbs. [Her reference is to Kildare Dobbs, who, as editor or Macmillan's Canada, had rejected *The Double Hook*.] This is my answer to any one who asks.

It is possible to withdraw, or rather to suspend the material operation of love which compels attention—or seems to compel it.

Again the absurdity—only to be born at the human level of mutual comprehension.

I remember walking with Doto through the mud to the river and trying to explain to her what Eliot meant when he said: "Say to your heart be still."

If she were here she would come stumbling from her box to see if all were well. She came and stood at the living room door for a few minutes and then went back to her rugs. We assured one another without the slightest gesture—not a word—only the silence of complete comprehension. Despite Eliot, too, we used to sit on the horses' brown hill and look out across the river into the distance.

. . . .

Feb 6 (Monday)

Chamber music at the Musée des Arts Décoratifs: the Pasquier Trio—Purcell—two Fantasies; Brival, about whom I know nothing, three "trios concertants"; a Boccherini trio (op. 14); and then after a stroll through the cabinet makers' clutter, the Mozart Divertimento (K 563).

The Pasquiers remind me of the Indian dancers I saw in Vancouver. They have tension without strain. Like the dancers, they made signs to one another with quick movements of their heads and bows. The second of the Purcell fantasies was extraordinarily beautiful, but it is in the Divertimento that the Pasquiers and the music meet. Here is passion like a bird held in the hand. Today—tonight just before we went out—I missed my green note book. I wanted to slip it into my pocket so that I could sketch a little before the concert began—faces all about, angled and turned and superimposed on one another. The book with the Tuileries sketches, the lovers, the woman with the poodle, the children, the students in the cafés on the Bd. St. Germain has completely vanished.

Feb 9

. . . .

La Peste—tremendously moving. I think of sitting in the flat at Mission reading Defoe's *Journal of the Plague Year* and hearing Churchill speak, and thinking at the time when W and I would be together as we never had been—then the long spring and the troubled summer and the long wait between September and Christmas.

Today it was bitterly cold—the wind rioting through the streets. I went to get tickets for the Petit Marigny.

Outside the Salle Gaveau I saw a curious looking young man in a black plush hat and what appeared to be a pair of black jodhpur pants. In one hand he carried an umbrella, in the other a brief case. He and the girl with him were talking in English:

> "He seemed a pleasant man."
> "Yes. I made everything quite clear. Nothing left unsaid."
> "Nothing."

Everywhere strange people moving in the intensity of their own lives. People in pairs reassuring one another.

[February] 17

Walked along the banks of the Seine. The sky a fragile blue above the snow—men were dropping long lines into the river from the quais above. One man, as I passed, drew a minnow from between the floating mats of ice. Only a few dark figures prowled by the water. The man with the three donkeys waited about in the Gardens of the Tuileries but there were no more than a dozen people in the gardens. The snow was netted with the marks of birds' feet. The fountain at the Concorde end of the gardens was sending up a great jet of water. Winter fountains are prodigal and unexpected. I passed two men engaged in animated conversation but caught nothing except the inevitable "Moi j'ai des—."

Mme Gouzien told me that W had given notice for May 14. He has said nothing.

. . . .

Feb 21

Went to see Buffet's "Cirque" at the Galerie Durand-David in the Faubourg St. Honoré. The gallery is not big but it is spacious and well-lighted. The pictures were well hung—twenty-six of them, all dated 1955. More than twenty of them have been sold. I note this as a fact because the pictures in general would be adapted only to large wall spaces. They would, in any but the largest room, assume the proportion of a mural. In the exposition the pictures form a unity. Each painting draws strength from the others. At the far end of the gallery, a clown with a trumpet attracts the attention of the crowd. Some are already seated—three or four men and a girl—a woman and a child. On the step below the clown a monkey sits playing by himself. The clown is flanked by the attractions which the circus offers—a man in gym strip, two long-faced women in skimpy underslips—and in the centre, two acrobats, one balancing the other like a seal on his upraised hands. A sign announces "Cirque—100f." Down either side of the gallery the circus unrolls itself—the clowns, the equestrian lady, her foot held by the hand of a kneeling dwarf, the dwarfs, the conjurer with his baguette and hat, the trick cycle rider with tea cups balanced on his chin, the elephants, the rhinoceros in his cage, the clowns with their fiddles, their saxophone and their guitar, the men on trapezes, a woman hanging by her teeth from a rope.

The picture I liked best, I think, was that of a clown seated before a music stand and playing a saxophone to another clown in an orange tunic.

Behind the clown in the tunic there is a yellow-green screen, and under the

144

clown with the saxophone, a square blue mat. The figure in the sleeveless tunic—his long bare arms and false cuffs—is charged with pathos.

The thin arm and the great curved flat hand seem to be the central symbol in most of the pictures. Buffet's pictures are in some ways the *reductio ad absurdum* of the flat surface. His vision is that of a world rolled flat—not accepted as flat as one accepts the length and compression of the jackfish. In front of one of the most mournful heads, a small girl in a black teddy bear coat with a capuchon was busy making a copy in a minute notebook. [See Appendix A—note 5]

Today the cold has increased. There were no vegetables in the stores, only a few bags of onions and some potatoes. Red bags of five or six large oranges at 215 francs—some withered apples and green, sad looking bananas. I did not go to the market.

. . . .

Feb 25

. . . .

The cold continues. Reports come of the world one does not see in Paris—rabbits, pheasants, partridge so weak after three weeks of starvation that in many places they can be trapped by hand. The seagulls desert the banks of the Garonne and fish for carp and red fish in the ponds of the gardens of Bordeaux. . . .

In Italy wolves attack the farms at the base of Etna, and at Vasto 150 houses are menaced by a huge mass of earth and snow. . . .

Today a letter from Mr. Salter. He said he had spoken to Jack McClelland in the summer about *The Double Hook*—but had obviously not been able to follow up the affair. He sounded tense and remote. . . .

In the late mail W had a letter from Mr. Monteith [of Faber & Faber] congratulating him on the Governor-General's Award—sending Mr. Eliot's good wishes and asking with concern about work in progress. . . .

Feb 27

On Sunday we went to the Passion Play at the gars[?] de Mélimontant. The hall was filled with children, nuns, and priests.

The Christ reminded me of Roy Daniells—troubled, perplexed—a Roy in a situation where he could see no way out and had to drink the cup to the dregs. Pilate was the typical French official—much shrugging of shoulders—"soyez raisonable, I can't stop you. Go ahead, I wash my hands of the affair." Judas was a small plump man in blue and brown—with the chestnut hair and startled face of a girl suffering from hurt pride—wanting too to make something of himself in the world. The play lived in spite of the heavy weight of some pious curé's text and the fleshy images of an inadequate iconography. The Christ did not sound the "populus meus" note, but felt only the conflict of Christ's manhood with God's power—or with the design of God, which was not clear to him. Within the world of the play, the betrayal was fictitious. There was no real tension between Christ and the Jews—the Roman soldiers played with the Christ figure, they did not strike him.

W thought that the play was the negation of Christianity. The feeling was in its very essence the symbol of the complete triumph of Christian love.

The "populus meus" is the cry of an outraged David—the God-king.

The Christ of Gethsemane is the God-man.

On the way to Gambetta we travelled in a Métro car filled with cubs. The French school boy cape gives way slowly to the duffle coat. The boys shoved and pushed and chattered like birds.

The papers have new accounts of the cold in Geneva. Gulls trapped in the ice were attacked by crows. The police killed the crows. Then they had to kill the gulls since, caught by their feet in the ice and mutilated by the bills of crows, they were dying of frost and hunger. The swans fared better. They were taken by taxi to the Grand Théâtre where they were warmed and fed and bedded down.

For myself I write: Le froid, toujours le froid. Bad begins and worse remains behind.

March 1

The great cold seems to have gone as quickly as it came. Today the world opened its window into the court. Patrick's mother hung out his woolens on her short line. People abandoned their scarves and unbuttoned their coats and drifted into the streets, their faces to the sun. I did not shop until the afternoon. The bakery door was open and the tall dark girl had taken off her shawl.

W brought home four Vivaldi Concertos. He played them for me while dinner cooked. This morning he woke me up to read the beginning of his poem about the birds—the city of owls, the cathedral like a goose—the fields of canaries—the crossing from the field to the city of owls on a kingfisher's feather—the heron. . . .

March 6

Yesterday afternoon I went to the Musée de Cluny. . . . Another soft day—a swimming day of pure gold. Despite the soldiers with their vociferous guides and the groups of school children with their mistresses, the Museum was bathed in peace.

There is something essentially right about it. Going into the Museum is like going into a spacious and carefully appointed house. It seems to have the unity of a single personality. The tapestries are extraordinarily beautiful, and the windows, especially on the second floor. For a few minutes I felt almost in a state of beatitude. In the evening we went to l'Oeuvre to see the *Bas Fonds*. What we saw of the play was extremely moving—light flashed into the depths of man's potential despair—paradoxical despair since flame burns suddenly in the sodden wood. . . .

The people of the *D. H.*, like the bas-fonds, are below the margin of grace. There is no question of social rehabilitation, although there may be an imperative demand to feed the hungry.

The problem is insoluble in human terms.

March 26
Worked on *The Double Hook*.

K[en] Macl[ean] wrote on March 17: "one wants to be very chary in surrendering one's own forms of sorrow." I wish I knew what he meant. As I think I understand it, I would agree with him completely.

W read the revision of the first fifty pages of *The Double Hook*. He says there is good material, but a dreadful and unnecessary incompetence. Since he doesn't like the flight passage, there is not much left if one calculates in pages. . . .

March 27
Went to the Bibliothèque Nationale to see the illuminated manuscripts—a string of people waiting in line to get into the Reading Room.

The exhibition of manuscripts is indescribable—two great rooms filled with cases—image after image—detail after detail—souls breaking through the blue ice crust of a sky at the feet of God the Father, who sits in the circle of a rainbow—Andromeda and the sea beast—the Trojans—rabbits and owls and dolphins in margins—horses and horses and horses—souls being weighed in the balance—

March 28

. . . .

The images from the Books of Hours, the Bibles, the Ovids Moralized, the histories of Troy, the Froissart keep crowding before my eyes—the golds, the reds, the blues—the beasts climbing up and down the margins.

This evening again I worked on *The Double Hook*.

March 31

Fewer people in the markets and on the streets since the great flight for the Vacances de Pâques.

Today it was colder—a fine mist in the late afternoon when I went down to the Madeleine to get the English papers from the little woman at the kiosk. Stopped on the way back at Tanrade's to look for a "lapin" but settled for some small "oeufs pâté d'amande." There was a great deal of laughter at Fauchon's when I asked for "un lapin." I keep wanting to do the traditional family things—I remember buying egg dyes when we were in the Camp at UBC—then putting them away.

The French have no respect for birds—perhaps they wear too many feather hats. I saw a dead lark lying on a nest of artificial eggs in one of the confiseur's windows.

Work on the *D. H.* goes slowly. W has spoken of format, but the impulse to go back to something like the original form of the mss. came from the mss. at the Bibliothèque Nationale. This time the mss. will have to stand.

Malcolm Ross wrote today to say that he is publishing "The Black Farm" in the summer issue of Q[ueens] Q[uarterly]. The CBC thought it too difficult to be useful broadcast material.

W swings from depression to exultation. Suddenly tonight I felt terribly tired—an overwhelming desire simply to lie down like a horse, where I stood.

Tonight in the paper there was a picture of a pointer setting out with its family for the Easter holidays. It reminded me of Doto.

I try to think what I believe:

> I believe in human dignity
> I believe in human intelligence
> I believe in trust and fidelity (Maclean's Burke was the sort of man
> who walked behind his friends' bodies to the grave)

I know:

> human weakness
> the limitation of human intelligence
> the need to walk as if one walked in the presence of God—that is,
> without evasion or deception.

I do not believe in destruction, in evasion, in discontinuity. . . .

I have a terrible fear of falling into the casuistry of self-justification—or conversely, of destroying post hoc something which grew in human love and understanding.

Except under particular circumstances one does not begin with God—one ends with God.

I take it now as an axiom that one should never enter into a relationship or perform an act which needs justification—I mean justification against a conviction, justification argumentative.

April 7

A warm day—English people and German tourists everywhere. When I went into the Kodak shop in rue Vignon to pick up my film, the woman whom I know because of passport photographs hailed me with relief. An American woman with rolls of film which she had taken or exposed or confused—in Ireland—wanted the photographer to see which of the films had been damaged. After she went, leaving an address at Bar le Duc, we talked for a while. A Frenchman came in for some pictures—"intimate" the man said after the Frenchman went off with them, "but the most exquisite lighting." He said that the French Canadians who came into the shop spoke like his grandparents in the country. He said that I didn't look like an American or an English person and that, until I spoke, would be taken for a native. I suppose I should be pleased. Certainly people speak to me and ask directions too as if I belonged. He said, too, that the German tourists don't like to speak German and speak English instead if they can.

W said that poetry was a sort of potlaching—that is why he liked Dylan Thomas. D. T. was someone for him to potlach with.

The real potlach involves destruction—a great burning of blankets on all sides.

One could, I suppose, see it as offering poem for poem.

A black maria is called "le panier à salade."

April 12

Conversation about May 13. I am quite sure that only unhappiness will be the outcome. I remember thinking on the steps of the Courthouse in Vancouver, without more than natural grace, this is for always—whatever I have thought since, this thought has never been in question. There is no comparison with other contracts, which are in their nature material and temporal. What I think about contracts, terms of tenure, wages, has no relevance.

There is marriage and there is a marriage contract—the contract is material and temporal. Marriage itself is an act of faith and consequently an act of perfect love—or inversely and perhaps more truly, an act of perfect love consequently an act of faith. Only a belief such as this would have made and did make the first years of our marriage possible.

When a parent has a child, he knows that at a certain age the child should leave him, except under unusual circumstances. Even these circumstances are a violation in a sense—as the parent realizes, as mother for instance realized. . . .

There is no analogy between the relationship of child and parent and the relationship of husband and wife.

[Wilfred's young friend's] heart speaks to her now. This she will know whether she marries W or not. . . .

The law does not make marriage. It protects or rather tries to protect, often bunglingly and inadequately in a temporal world, something which is not temporal, although rooted in beginning as human life—and, I suppose, even the soul is—though one does not think of soul as temporal. Whatever suffering three acceptances would imply or entail now—my acceptance of W's state of heart and mind, [his young friend's] of W's and mine, and W's of [his young friend's acceptance] and mine, there would I think be less suffering in the end—and less negation.

All human social wisdom to the contrary—

[See Appendix A—note 6]

April 15

More work on the *D. Hook*. The first section is almost finished.

W finished the first draft of the rabbits.

This morning Père Doumain was showing the two little boys how to separate the hind quarters of a beef. Maurice was waiting on the customers—his harlequin face gentle and kind. Maurice always decides in favour of the customer—trims, weighs under rather than over—without paper rather than with. He had just finished trimming the rumpteck—Père descended.

"Alors mon petit Maurice!"

He picked up the trimmed edges and threw them on the scales. "Alors!"

Maurice bit his lips and wrinkled his eyes but said nothing at all. The boys' aprons like Roman togas. . . .

April 17

Worked on the *D. H.* most of the day while W put the first two chapters of the rabbits into shape.

The new *D. H.* manuscript is cleaner, but even the slightest alteration entails countless others. W as always works like a fiend. . . .

April 21

Yesterday I spent the afternoon at the Bibliothèque Nationale looking at the manuscript books—two magnificent crucifixions, the dark blue skies filled with the insubstantial shapes of angels. It is not difficult to see why people became medievalists. The books belonging to St. Louis are of extraordinary beauty. The Trojans had been turned over—an alabaster statue of a monk, his face shrouded by his hood: I noticed the hands particularly—the delicate almost imperceptible lines and the mark of the finger nails.

Today through the Tuileries and along the banks of the Seine in sunlight. The river is full and swift. The trees in leaf. An old woman asleep on a bench under a tattered fur coat, her belongings in great paper parcels beside her—a man in rags with his shoes off asleep under the ivy-covered wall—people walking their dogs—or reading—or making love—the chalands going up and down. For the first time I noticed the monument to Rousseau in the gardens—the inscription wearing away:

Nous avons choisi la liberté faisons lui confiance devant de devenir—

What followed I couldn't read.

Beyond Augustus and Cincinnatus, Agamemnon bearing off Anchises, a satyr decamping with a struggling maiden—

The pigeons being fed not by tourists but by a plump French woman—a solitary pigeon watching the play of water in the first fountain—children sailing their boats in the second.

A fresh cold wind—a day like a day on the coast.

I am working on the fourth part of the *Double Hook*. I wonder now how I let it stand. Now I ask myself if I have the power to make it come whole—to fuse completely character, event, setting. I couldn't help thinking that if inscriptions such as "Nous avons choisi la liberté faisons lui confiance" become part of a person's iconography so to speak—that existentialism is an obvious step.

I thought of the phrase iterated and reiterated in Bede—"Servant of the servants of God."

It seems to me that in some way the two concepts have to be welded into a single whole.

Vivaldi's "La Stravaganze"—the Sainte-Chapelle and the illuminated manuscripts—the tattered old woman asleep on her bench—. . . .

[Between April 21 and 28]

Today I decided to go back to the Place des Vosges before the leaves had come into full leaf. A cool day but sunny—not as many people abroad as there usually are on Sunday, although beyond the Hôtel de Ville queues of people waited outside theatres and, comme d'habitude, filled the pavement and disputed their respective rights.

The Place de la Hôtel de Ville was crowded with children and people and pigeons. It is ridiculous to say that the pigeons are a tourist attraction. They are the familiar spirits, the gentle clowns—even the intangible beloveds of the poor and not so rich. One old man had coaxed a pigeon onto his finger. They went off together kissing and rubbing cheeks, until some casual intruder frightened the bird. The old man was very angry. He came back to the square and tried to coax another pigeon to go with him—but a small girl in a yellow coat was running about among them distracting their attention.

At the corner of the rue de Rivoli and the rue St. Denis a man was lying crouched on the pavement against the wall. Everyone who passed looked at him. He did not seem to be sleeping although he did not move. I saw two priests come up to him, and thought they at least will stop, but they passed him without looking—their soutanes blowing about them in the wind.

On the traffic island—just where the rue de Rivoli runs into the rue Antoine— three tramps were having a meal of bread and wine. They had two bottles of wine and a great round loaf set out on a newspaper.

In l'Église St. Paul-St. Louis a pigeon was wandering slowly down the central aisle.

At the side of the church I noticed the entrance into lycée Charlemagne.

Found a curious little street with steps, an iron railing and a view into what must have been the remains of some extremely old buildings—one with a small barred window like a dungeon window. It is called rue Cloche-Percé.

The Place Baudoyer was completely empty except for the incredibly small figure of an old Sister of St. Vincent de Paul in her great white head-dress and prim black knitted shawl.

On the rue Birague I noticed for the first time the horse butcher's shop with the three horse heads looking down into the street.

The Place des Vosges was filled with people knitting, watching children who have brought out their wooden hoops again. I sat for a little while under the tree near one of the fountains, and watched the people and the walls on the pink buildings.

When I came back from the market this morning, M. & Mme la Concierge were looking at a paper in front of the elevator. Mme showed it to me with great excitement—a picture of a man who lives above us delivering a dress to Grace Kelly. M. described him. Surely I had seen him, but "No" Mme said, "he goes out very early and comes in very late."

M. la Concierge had a gentle fancy. He begged me not to go away without seeing the fields of tulips in the Bois de Boulogne. He described them as if he saw them before him. . . .

Last evening went with Mme Gouzien to the théâtre en rond to see Sartre's *Huis Clos*—a good performance on the whole—a small theatre, five rows of seats.

On the way to the theatre we looked through the doors of the rue Pigalle into the gardens.

Curious because the whole district seems to be without charm except for the gentle rise of the hill towards the Butte.

April 28
For two nights before yesterday I dreamed my dreams—the ones I have not written down. This after two weeks of relative peace while we both worked on mss. Yesterday I decided to go to England. When I told W, he said it was just what he expected. . . .

May 5
Today I got a ticket for London. It is three o'clock now and I leave in a few hours— 6:40 at the Invalides. Now I ask myself why I am going since I say I will come back and go back to Canada on the 15th of May so that W can be sure of the divorce. I feel terribly lost—more troubled than I care to think.

On the first of May everyone bought sprigs of lily-of-the-valley for happiness—this year a thin green forced happiness if the flowers are its symbol.

A wire to W last night—his birthday. [Wilfred's birthday was May 1st.] The man rang while we still sat over dinner—and now going for a week. I feel as if somehow I were abandoning him—as I must.

[See Appendix A—note 7]

Thursday May 8
Yesterday afternoon went to see the Spanish paintings at the Arts Council Gallery (4 St. James Sq. SW 1)—a heteroclite mixed-bag. . . . The traditionalists triumph when the experimentalists fail to impose—or to exact their vision—neither word is right—

Walked by the pond in St. James' Park and conversed with the ducks—one great yellow fellow with green tipped wings and a voice like an oboe—.

The pigeons were making love growling and swaying and puffing their rainbow necks—a black, pink-faced bird with grey frog feet followed by a handful of birdlings—a white goose with the face of a Mona Lisa.

Then on to Westminster Abbey and the sudden surprise of Wordsworth's marble presence—Spenser comes off best and Chaucer with his canopy and Purbeck marble altar.

At eight Lucienne Hill's translation of Anouilh's *Dance of the Toreadors*—at the Criterion—an interesting set designed by Paul Mayo—the play except for Beatrix Lehmann's possession scene not convincing—

A run for the train—a subway car which pounded on to the Elephant and Castle without stopping at Waterloo—a swoop back on the almost-last train because it was nearly eleven.

Vision of life in a black bowler hat with the escape clause furled in a black umbrella.

Meditation on escalators—especially the long ones in the Picadilly Circus station.

. . . .

Leith Hill and a carpet of bluebells under the trees—the curled fists of bracken and other fern in young leaf—a cuckoo's voice somewhere in the thicket—a surge and fall of blue and green as far as the eye could see—blue and green and terra cotta of last year's ferns.

We walked looking for the rhododendrons—saw a man his wife and a child eating lunch beside a motor cycle—flat on the bluebells under a tree—and on the way back the man and the child hunting for white bluebells in the sea of blue—the child clutching the three white bluebells we had noticed by the path and the only flower of ragged robin—

We ate our lunch in an Emily Carr thicket at the top of one of the hills—then climbed about over the moss under the oaks.

I remember the swan in the gardens of Hampton Court which came to have its head stroked—then swam about—kicking its black legs and twisting its neck simply because someone was watching it—the sweep of country from the top of Ditchling Beacon—Meredith's house and summer house at Box Hill—Abinger the Georgian houses and the view of the river from the top of Richmond Hill—dinner with Mrs. Lawrence in the Inn at Bray—Chablis and duck and conversation—

Not until I wrote this down did I think of "roast duck" in the same way I thought of French larks. It seemed strange to see Strawberry hill—now a Catholic boys' school—and Pope's gardens.

May 9/56
Hillcroft College, Surbitan, Surrey
It is raining. On the lawn the yellow-nosed blackbirds are looking for worms. Beyond the copper beech a cherry is in bloom and a lilac just misted with flowers still in bud. In the bed at the corner of the great sweep of lawn wallflower and tulips and bluebells and forget-me-nots and primroses riot together. It is last year's spring across an ocean of distance—the rain loud with bird cries and heavy with the scent of flowers.

This afternoon we walked across Epsom Downs against a level wind—past a great sweep of brown hill lit by a solitary green bush—fields and flat topped black pines and long distances—a road as red as a flowerpot.

This morning I took the *D. H.* in to Mr. Monteith [of Faber's]. The wind was blowing even then through Russell Square in great draughts which caught at the throat and set the leaves in the square into a desperate whipping frenzy. Mr. M. told me about the arrival of the ms. of *Friday's Child*—how "Tom" had read steadily for two hours and came in wonder at the discovery—the first real Canadian poetry—that is the first real poetry written in Canada. He took me into T. S. E.'s office—the one next to his— a little room piled round with books—and hung with portraits—the easy chair gone to the cleaners because T. S. E. is in the States. We talked for a few minutes—He seemed to understand that I had come alone on my own concerns—to grasp what I wanted to do—. If the MS. goes under this time I think I will know the last desolation of failure.
     . . . .
I had gone to Russell Sq. in the morning to make an appointment with Mr. Monteith—had lunch with Aunt Agatha [Myatt] at the Wellbeck and then gone with her to Paddington to see her off on the 4:10 train for Birmingham. . . .

May 11
Came back by plane to Paris. Constance and Peter [her son] drove me to the London Airport. . . .

C and P so good to me I could have cried.

Le Bourget—then the Paris streets at 1:15—a crowd of men coming out of a picture show—"Au delà de Missouri"—people still sitting "en plein air" outside the bars and café tabacs. The streets seemed less narrow, less dark, less unexpected than

155

they did in August. I could have climbed off the bus at the corner of rue Tronchet but my bag was with the luggage.

May 18

. . . .

When I came in a letter to say that Faber would not publish the *D. H.*

I went to bed and slept and dreamed that I was going up and down the Dunbar hill in a bus. The bus finally went in through the University gates and along the road, through the farm into an area of factories, which seemed to have sprung up near the skullbrow hill.

W says that when I read certain books, they bring out the worst side of my nature—Lawrence at Goetts' and now Simone de Beauvoir.

May 19

Explored the region round St. Eustache again—the great flower market with its array of wicker crates. The rest of the market was closed. The flower sellers seemed to be setting up their stalls. Each seller had his place marked out in chalk on the pavement—peonies in tight-fisted buds, lily-of-the-valley in huge round bunches—roses—calla lilies—carnations—yellow and white daisies. In one spot only a small basket of wallflower—branches of leaves tied up in canvases—much pleasantry and back chat.

Walked down the rue Balard, through the Halles and along the rue St. Honoré past the central Tripierie and a wholesale meat market to the Place de la Croix-du-Trahoir[?] (le carrefour des rues Saint-Honoré et de l'Arbre- Sec.)

In St. Eustache people were gathering for confession. I sat down to copy the Litany of St. Louis, and a wizened little verger told me that I was in the wrong place for confession. In front of a news stand on the rue St. Honoré, two men and a woman were laughing and talking. "La jalousie le rouge" the woman kept saying. Then she would slap her thighs and roll with laughter.

[June 20]

I sit listening to the broadcast of the Mozart C minor piano concerto and looking out onto the roofs across rue Vignon. The Strasbourgians cry out and stamp their feet calling Casadesus back again and again. The roofs are wine grey—behind and over them a dusty yellow sky. W lies on the bed, his hands under his head.

Les hommes ne sont pas mes semblables, ils sont ceux qui regardent et me jugent; mes semblables, ce sont ceux qui m'aiment et ne me regardent pas, qui m'aiment contre tout qui m'aiment contre la déchéance contre la bassesse, contre la trahison, moi et non ce que j'ai ou ferai.

The enormity of the sky weighs down the city—the city as one sees it from the high windows.

June 26

. . . .

A note from J. T. Jones enclosed in a letter to W—asking me to take the night class next winter in Edmonton. I meditated on the irony.

July 11

. . . .

Gallimard had finally delivered the Ionesco *Théâtre* to the man at 3 rue Marivaux. Stood about for a while thumbing books. The little man is rather morose. He put a cover on the book and gave me a paper knife. The French always seem to understand that a customer might want to read on the way home.

The clochard has taken possession of Beckett—the infinite misery of unaccommodated man. . . . Today I saw the blind man with his dog at the corner of the rue Roche. The dog sits alert and elegant—vigilant and self-possessed. After the spring clipping, her coat grows into soft black curl. Her winter coat was dull and thick-matted as a bear's. Now I go particularly to see them; they are part of my life—though we do not speak.

A letter from Jack [Shadbolt]. He and Doris think they will go to the Maritime Alps after a short time in Paris. . . .

July 15

Last night I thought more than ever how to draw to conclusions—a curious voluntary death, which one can only hope has its resurrection.

The Republican Guard in plumed helmets—I think, though the men are indistinct. What I remember is the movement of the horses—the chestnut bodies flowing together, rising and sweeping forward like a brown wave.

The woman at the kiosk while I was picking up the English papers when the Guard passed: "we need them too. In a big city not everyone is reasonable, malheureusement."

Walked back through the flower market to pick some African marigolds. "Les rouges" the man called the orange ones to distinguish them from the yellow.

At 9:30 we walked down through the Gardens of the Tuileries and across the Pont des Arts to watch the fireworks—the "flèches, gerbes, bouquets de feu." People were beginning to take up their stand on the bridges and along the quais. The police had blocked off the river banks. The crowd as usual consisted of those who found and resolutely maintained a place of vantage and those who swirled in a restless current along the streets. In the Place de l'Institute children were staging their own feu d'artifice while they waited for the big show to begin.

Only when the rockets burst into successive fires did the crowd become really excited. Then the children began to chant "un, deux, trois, quatre" as they do when they run up and down the steps in the gardens. There was no real sense of a fête. The war in Algeria is too much a fact.

In the morning Mme & M. Ducros came up as usual on Saturday, armed with vacuum and feather duster. They allowed themselves—in the slackness of the holiday—to chat across the court with Patrick's mother, who announced to all who could hear that she had a "poulet" for the celebration. . . .

Today I brought back a crab from the market—dark brownish red—the shell pinched around like the edge of a pie—two large blue-black eyes under the shadow of its shell.

July 17

. . . .

In the evening the street is filled with the chirping of the sparrows who hustle in and out of their nests in the ventilators. From the bottom of the pit between the two rows of walls comes the noise of cars—the sound of feet on the pavement. The light slides yellow between the chimneys and spills down the dove grey roofs. Sometimes the black and white cat sits smelling the potted geraniums outside his window—or stretches out over the gutter to look down into the street below. . . .

July 18

It rained all day. I finished tidying the mss. of *The Double Hook*. Rewrote the final passage.

. . . .

July 20

Went to the Comédie Française to get tickets for the Sunday matinee (*Le*

Misanthrope). It seemed a pity not to see one Molière this year.

Then on to the Louvre to visit the Egyptians, who continue to fascinate.

Between Henry Moore and the Egyptians there is only a difference in time. The disposition of feet and hands—the attitude of gentle yet remote attention is in Moore's seated King and Queen and in the Functionary of Memphis and his wife—in the statuette of the Functionary named Piai. A French father with a child in front of the seated scribe:

> Look well, look at the eyes; look at the hands and the way the feet
> are folded—look well at the face. I want you to remember that you
> have seen the 'scribe accroupi'—that you have seen the best of
> Egyptian art.

July 22

At four o'clock this morning I was wakened by the incessant ringing of the telephone. Then Mme Gouzien knocked on the door to say the Mlle [Wilfred's young friend] was calling W "du Canada."

Light had just begun to creep through the shutters. I smoked a couple of cigarettes, then turned off the light and lay watching the light through the slits.

W's objections to the privileges of "the rich" with respect to books, music and university education applies equally to an "intersubjectivity" which is preserved in special delivery, telegraph and transAtlantic telephone.

It is a dull day—misty and threatening rain.

Figaro outraged by the statements of Tito, Nasser, and Nehru. . . .

Tonight I feel like a person who has walked too far to the final judgement—or simply walked too far.

July 26

Yesterday I went to Versailles by train from the Gare St. Lazare. It was a hot day and the 11:30 train was crowded enough.

A tiresome old man in a suede vest and tweed jacket and his middle-aged daughter, or wife perhaps—for she wore a wedding ring jammed down on her finger by a heavy square gold signet ring—sat opposite. The woman was reading a paper. All the way to Versailles the old man grumbled about the universe. Every few minutes he would catch the woman by the sleeve to compel her attention. She smiled politely and pretended to listen. I thought of them together day in and day out—the woman's frozen smile and the old man tugging at her sleeve.

At Versailles, the apartments of the King and Queen. Louis' face on the door knobs—on the carpets—Louis as Jupiter—as Neptune—the glass gallery—the chapel with a sparrow flying through the sunlight about the altar. . . .

Then I went down the staircase and through the gardens, where children played and women knitted, to the little Trianon and then to the big Trianon—not directly but by the side garden where gardeners were sweeping the paths—and out to the terraces bordered with geraniums on the right of the palace. This part of the garden was quite empty. I sat for a long time in the broken sunlight under the trees to watch the geraniums flickering and flaming along the edges of the grass. The long alley down to the pink marble fountain, too, was deserted. Here on both sides of the alley a trellis fence weathered blue as if it belonged to the place—in front of the pink marble palace, beds of verbena and heliotrope.

. . . .

Today to the Louvre again because of pictures I wanted to see—perhaps for the last time. . . .

Outside the Ministry of Finance, a harried starling was feeding an enormous still grey nestling. For the first time I spotted the birds' nests, tucked usually between the rumps and shoulders of the various statues perched along the facade.

July 27

. . . .

"L'amour qui adhére au desir d'autrui, c'est compassion" (S[imone] W[eil], *Cahiers d'Amérique*).

If one writes at all, it is only to make the passionate suffering of men intelligible. Some poets, and W I suspect is one, can make clear the vision beyond the suffering—to wit *The Canticle of Darkness*—Je me demande—.

I note S. W.'s comment on compassion because it is of compassion that W always speaks when he speaks of literature or art:

"Renoir has compassion."

"A writer must have compassion."

He finished the correction of U[nder] the R[abbit's] P[aw] yesterday. Today news of the British Arts Council Award. The telegram came while we discussed eschatology between visits of Mme Gouzien about the installation of a not-new bathtub. . . .

July 28

Went to bed late last night—the moon filling the court and spilling through the cracks of the shutters. Read *L'Innommable* until the alarm upstairs went off—and then to sleep. At five-thirty was awakened again by the telephone. It was daylight and the birds were talking in the court. W answered the telephone. I heard Mme G. get up and go to the bathroom, and then W clicking the receiver too. At breakfast time a man came with a wire.

Tonight it is raining.

Aug 9

It is four o'clock in the afternoon. We dock tomorrow at seven. The boat is in a fury of excitement—the bath steward argues with the cabin steward in the hall—people wander about with bits of clothing in their hands. W is in the cabin doing his packing. Yesterday's indigo sea is blue under the sun. For the moment I have the sense of going nowhere—while the world packs its bags and people stand scenting their purpose.

The decks are salty and clean after the storm. From the front deck one can peer down through the anchor holes, across the clumsy anchor chains into the water below—a blue sea—a sand-coloured deck—the yellow arms of the booms—the black and white mushroom ventilators.

Aug 26

Nothing written since the day before we got off the boat in New York. Nothing much in my mind except the memory of sitting most of the afternoon on someone else's trunk in #14 Luggage Shed—sitting and waiting for the trunks to come up from the dock so that they could be sorted out—. W's for Edmonton, mine for Toronto. It was hot and, except for the agent who quibbled about my ticket, everyone seemed particularly kind. In the middle of the afternoon I felt the horror of stamping out the last of a life under the blowzy ceiling of the Grand Central [Station].

Now I'm sitting in Ruth [Humphrey's] room [in Vancouver] again looking out into the trees where the robins nested last May—not last May, though the birds may have come back as they do—but the May of 1955. I sit thinking of the grain ripening to gold across the prairies and the folded rise of the foothills, and W getting off the train at Calgary bird-dog eager—as I remember him years ago on the station platform at Jasper.

~ X ~

WILFRED'S BIRD-DOG EAGERNESS WAS SHORT-LIVED. WITHIN DAYS of Sheila's reflections upon it, he telegraphed her to Vancouver from Edmonton: "Want you to return to me Stop All else is madness." Over the next two weeks, in letters as well as in telegrams, he pleaded with her not to carry out her plans to go to Toronto. Sheila had settled on these plans during her trip to England in May. She had gone to consult with her aunt, her father's sister Agatha Myatt, fully intending to take up residence in England after their time in Paris had ended. She would look for employment in a bookstore or with a publisher or as a teacher. Her aunt discouraged her from considering such possibilities, and insisted that, in view of Wilfred's conduct, she must prepare herself to fend for herself. Accordingly, she advised Sheila to complete her doctorate—not in England but in Canada, where she was known.

Wise as Dr. Myatt's advice was, it resulted in Sheila remaining for a time in the line of Wilfred's increasingly erratic fire. "Yesterday a wire from W," she noted in her journal on September first. "He lives in images which will not bear the strain of use." The images in which Wilfred was living and with which he attempted to persuade Sheila to return were often only pale shadows of images of her making. "I think at this moment in an image," he wrote to her in early September, "the French flowers, les jolies fleurs, the African marigolds and the wind flowers." This same letter included a gesture towards capitulation which fell wide of the block: "[I]f you wanted it," he wrote, "I'd become a R. Cath. and marry you again. . . . I think of the marigold flowers and then of all the furnitures we hold in common, and thus of all the bonds there are between us, still unbroken and not to be broken." And then there was the appeal to Doto. "I'm calling you," he wrote on 13 September, "as we used to call Doto. I did buy Doto for you. You can't think of Doto without thinking of me." An attempt to elaborate whimsically upon a domestic detail must have confirmed Sheila in her sense of the meanness of his image-hoard. "I couldn't possibly leave you until the socks you knitted me were worn out and finished—so if you knitted me some more from time to time I wd always be yours." Penelope weaving and re-weaving a shroud for her father-in-law in order to keep her suitors at bay, and Sheila endlessly knitting socks—woman's work.

Wilfred had soon found himself in what he perceived to be an untenable position. He wrote to Sheila, "From the moment I left you on the train [at Calgary, while she went on to Vancouver], I felt like Macbeth, destroying when I knew I was destroying peace, honour, everything." In light of this perception, he claimed that he and his young friend had agreed to part, "for good." What he did not admit was that she and not he wished to end the relationship; absence had apparently not left her heart fonder. As he admitted years later to a friend, and with some embarrassment, she was disturbed by the fact that he had let his hair grow while abroad—a sign for her perhaps of his incipient unconventionality. Wilfred foundered, like a character in a Chaucerian fabliau. "I lead an incongruous existence among bachelors," he wrote to Sheila from Edmonton on 8 September. "I see the attractions of the bachelor's life. But it isn't for me—give me any sort of folie a deux, even a la *les Chaises*."

Sheila's responses were more to the point and less allusive than Wilfred's overtures. "Perhaps neither of us is or has been strong enough to face spiritual truth in its physical body," she wrote on 10 September; "For this reason I think I should go this time as I said I would."

⌒

In this late summer of 1956, they had been married for almost fifteen years, and Wilfred was enjoying a type of recognition which Sheila was never to receive. He had won the Governor General's Award for poetry in English and a British Arts Council Award, his work was being reviewed extensively in England and in the United States as well as in Canada, and Faber and T. S. Eliot were considering his next work. Sheila had completed revisions to *The Double Hook* in Paris, but she had not yet found a publisher for it. She had published a poem and a short story in the thirties, and "Brother Oedipus" in 1954, and now she looked forward to the publication of "The Black Farm."

The revisions to *The Double Hook* that Sheila had completed in Paris, and Wilfred's response to her second novel formed a part of the gnarled texture of their relationship during this time. Her Paris journals provide evidence of her sense of his reservations about her work and of assumptions that he believed lay behind it. What the journals do not reveal is the extent to which, even before it had reached its final state, and certainly before its publication, this novel had lodged in Wilfred's imagination like a canker. The draft of a poem in seven stanzas entitled "The double hook" survives among his papers at the University of Alberta. It is not dated, but presumably it was written during their time in Paris. Its banality provides a commentary—even a judgement—upon the central conceit of his wife's novel and upon their relationship. These are the last two stanzas:

The yellow sun looks on the sliding Seine
The sliding Seine looks on the yellow sun
The ragged poster[ed] walls by a return
Smile up at skies which smile politely down;
The poverty of this city seems urbane
Although it is a poverty most evil
Under a heaven which [is] doubly civil.

But in this city I learn a sort of madness
Which suits me well, resigned past common sense;
Singing a little, as if we once knew gladness;
Weeping, because we did, and not from sadness;
But nothing long the same, having an intense
Impatience with everything, that endures,
Catching a[t] flies, shadows, bits of string, and doors.

More puzzling evidence of his uneasiness about aspects of their relationship, and possible refractions of these in *The Double Hook*, is to be found in the work with which Wilfred occupied himself—while Sheila wandered the streets and markets and quais, the galleries and gardens and churches of Paris—the work that occasioned these wanderings. He was well into the writing of it before they went abroad: "past the hundred pp. today," he observed in a letter dated 16 May 1955. Sheila refers to it as "the rabbits" or "URP" in her journals, and while she mentions Wilfred discussing it with her and reading to her from it, she never comments on the work. Its full title is: *Under the Rabbit's Paw: Parapsychotransmitted from the Canamerican of Everett Howard by Wilfred Watson.* It is a lengthy and not always clearly focused satire, indebted to Swift, especially to the fourth book of *Gulliver's Travels.* Rational horses give way now to giant rabbits—twelve to fifteen feet in height—and Swift's Yahoos, to a selectively puritanical equivalent called Gottas, who are described in an editor's note (a role Wilfred assumes, as well as that of transmitter of Howard's narrative) as thinking of their offspring "as punishment to the mother for her sexual appetite." The narrator, Everett Howard, a disturbing blend of Lemuel Gulliver and Wilfred himself, has been living, like the Gottas and the rest of human kind in Canamerica, "under the shadow of the rabbit's paw . . . under the shadow of a great curse."

The curse, as one might expect of rabbits, is fecundity: "the ever-increasing rabbit hordes," Howard tells us, "[have] swallowed up the whole of the North

Canamerican continent, from the Isthmus of Panama to the arctic circle in Canada."
More serious than numbers, however, is the fact that this change has also seen the
decay of "the great mechanical age," and its replacement by what the narrator calls
"Huck-Finn-ism," a kind of bastardized romanticism—as distinct from the true
romanticism of Bacon and Descartes and Boyle, in short, of the philosopher-
mechanics.

Wilfred appears to have written his novel—like his protagonist—"under the
shadow of a great curse," and Sheila seems to have formed a part of that shadow.
Near the end of his novel, Everett Howard extols the advantages of life among the
Gottas in terms that must have seemed as pointed to her then as they appear trite
now. "It gave one companionship—not intellectual companionship but a better
sort, the sort which doesn't wear itself out in squabbles and arguments. The sort of
companionship shared by Brigita and Sallyjohn and Annajohn and me, as we sat
over tin mugs of beer."

Under the Rabbit's Paw—"under coyote's eye": It is odd but inescapable, the possibility of the subversion of a novel which had not yet been published, which was still
in process of being revised. Years later, after her novel's place in Canadian letters had
been established, Sheila remained uneasy—even apologetic—about the attention it
had received when the one she considered the real writer in the household continued
to labour—now relatively unnoticed. What some of her friends took to be jealousy on
Wilfred's part was rooted in a response to *The Double Hook* which predated its publication—and even its completion—and which reached back to what Sheila remembered as "the cold horror" of their time in Calgary and Wilfred's "sudden wild furies"
there. It is not jealousy that underlies much in Wilfred's novel—but anger, and, as
Sheila wrote in Paris in January 1956, "It is absolutely necessary to liquidate anger,
chagrin, or contempt before writing. In short, a writer must have mastered the emotions before he can use the insight which the emotion has given him."

Wilfred's anger—like so much in his nature—was more erratic than it was
persistent, and his evaluation of Sheila's novel followed a similarly irregular course.
His responses provide a register of his intentions, of his emotional state, of his relationship to Sheila. In the spring before they went to Paris, when he was attempting
to persuade her to return from Vancouver to Edmonton, he wrote: "I thought today
how marvellously and in how unequalled a way *D. H.* fuses together the earth and
land and its people. Does any book do this so well? Thoreau's *Walden* has the
land—but where are the people?" At the time of its publication in 1959, when they
had effectively been separated for three years, he described for her his excitement at

165

reading it again. "I and Wyndham Lewis and a third critic (E[zra].P[ound].?) approve of this book," he concluded in a letter to her.

Meanwhile, more pointed than either his novel or his seven-stanza poem is "a dramatization of *The Double Hook*, for 2 narrators, two choruses and rock band" entitled *The Rock Hook*, which also exists in draft versions in Wilfred's archives in Edmonton. Its title-page reads, "authorized by Sheila Watson," although it is not clear when it was written. There are thirteen pages of a libretto, and it is difficult to determine whether Wilfred was being more contemptuous of Sheila's novel or of the genre he himself was playing with. What there is of the story (and there is very little) is told alternately by Kip and Coyote, and the central presence is Lenchen, who sings the big number:

> The double hook, the double hook,
> What does it mean, what does it say?
> The double hook, the double hook
> means something like this, it yells out—etc., etc., etc.

The "show" ends with this choral rendering:

> If you double hook the moon
> if you double hook the moon
> you'll double hook a stone
> you'll double hook a stone—etc., etc., etc.

Even if this was a later attempt to bring Sheila's novel into the Age of Aquarius— and there is unquestionably a populist strain here as in his playing off *Harvey*, a popular play about an imaginary giant rabbit, in *Under the Rabbit's Paw*—Wilfred's rock opera must be judged a feeble attempt. It is, however, typical of his restless experimenting with forms of drama, and of his uneasiness with *The Double Hook*.

In the same archival folder that contains drafts of Lenchen's song—a folder whose contents are described as "Poems from the fifties and early sixties"—there is a "verse-letter to s w p," Wilfred's nickname for Sheila, and a shortened form for Shuswap. It is a poem which James Potter might have written, had he the skill to express his anger in words rather than in whippings, blinding and murder. It is in fifteen stanzas, and ends,

> All he wants now is to escape. A shot
> rings out, and carelessly finds its slot,
> and she becomes a bloody myth,

which I recall, but not the truth,

as truth. I place my anger against hers.
The facts are otherwise, New Westminster's,
twisted and wrong. They always are.
You tell them better, if you dare.

⌒

We have read in her journals Sheila's own accounts of her activities and of her thoughts during the Paris year, including her reconsiderings and reworkings of *The Double Hook*. What began in the isolation and loneliness of Dog Creek, and developed in response to her dissatisfaction with her earliest attempts to give voice to that experience; what grew out of voices heard on a street in Toronto, and the pain and loneliness of two years in Calgary—reached its final form in the revisions that Sheila undertook in Paris. These were provoked by, but they were certainly not limited to, suggestions Salter had made to her. In her journal entry for 5 February 1956, she had played her own sense of her art's affinity with the daring and the playful contrivances of a circus off against his invoking of Shakespeare, and more specifically, of *King Lear* as her source, or at least as her model. She was unhappy with what she believed to be Salter's assumption that disaccommodation represented a "progressive" rather than an alienated condition. A sense of her novel's affinities with drama had, however, influenced her revisions as it had informed his praise. What is more, the text of the novel that he had commented on was luxurious in its detail by comparison with its final state.

Much of what she did not withhold in earlier drafts Sheila now withdrew: the name of a cow, a type of chair in Ara and William's parlour, the pieces Felix played on his fiddle, scraps of personal and family history, and details of national and racial origins. Gone too are possibilities: the doctor who might have been called by William to certify his mother's death, and the law that Kip might have brought on James if he had known "how to go about it." Two versions of a scene involving the Widow Wagner and her son, Heinrich, illustrate something of the differing natures of draft and final text. In this scene (Part 3, Section 6) the Widow tells her son to find his sister, Lenchen, who has gone in search of her lover, James Potter, and to bring her home: "Then together we will think what to do," she says. In the draft, the scene is remembered by Heinrich; and the memory—framed by the Widow's final cry ("Come back. Come back whatever you find.") and the repetition of this cry in the sound of his horse's hoofs—is of a confession which his mother had made to him.

Heinrich, she said, flesh calls for flesh, but we don't always choose. In my country, she said, custom held one so and gave one so. Once in the summer when my father was out on the river with his nets—but when Wagner knew as he must he closed his mouth and shut his eyes and we came leaving the shame behind. The child died, she said. Of such things Wagner would not let me speak. Of such things I thought no longer. Why should I speak so to you? I have done wrong. I have seen the wrong. You do not judge. It is God who judges, she said, and covered her eyes with her hand. I have cried against God, she said. I have set wrong on wrong. Heinrich, she said, I have seen the judgement. Eyes looking from the creek bottom. God's eyes looking out from the body of an old woman. The knowledge. The silence. The shame.

In its revised form, the framework of memory and the Widow's confession both disappear as the scene is compressed and internalized:

Flesh calls for flesh, she thought. She had paid enough. Had come with Wagner. Her lips closed. Her eyes shut. Had come into the wilderness. She had done wrong. She had seen the wrong. It was God who would judge.

She covered her eyes with her hand.

She had cried out against God. She had set wrong on wrong. She had been judged. Eyes looking from the creek bottom. From the body of another old woman. Knowledge. Silence. Shame.

The nature and circumstances of a past sin have become less important than its consequences. The Widow's experience of guilt issues now in urgent compassion for her pregnant daughter: "Heinrich, she said, Go. Go."

The Widow's new urgency, like the novel's new vividness and economy, follows from the disappearance of the prospects that every condition must have a cause and that the past will always make room for regret even when the present has room only for fear. In her final, extensive revisions, Sheila moved away from the prospects provided by possibility, causality, and memory in order to express more vividly the spareness and immediacy that come to characters when they have no alternative but to be in their time and place, when they have no history apart from the experience of their readers. It is the spareness of Beckett—whom she was reading and seeing performed at the same time in Paris that she was doing this final work on her novel—rather than the deceptive spareness of Lear's heath that is a quality of *The Double Hook*.

In his last publication before a devastating stroke in 1979, Marshall McLuhan proposed that, as T. S. Eliot revised *The Waste Land* under the influence of Ezra Pound, he discovered "the public outside the poem" as the poem's "real ground." His perception recalls comments of Stephen Dedalus in Joyce's *Portrait of the Artist* on "the dramatic form," wherein "the artist presents his image," not "in immediate relation to himself" as the lyric poet does, and as Sheila believed she had done in her first novel, but "in immediate relation to others." Eliot's revisions to his poem and Sheila's to her second novel moved their works closer to such an "immediate" relationship to their audiences, closer, then, to drama.

Joyce, incidentally, was a fairly obvious presence in Sheila's unrevised text. But cadences and turns of phrase that recall *Ulysses* in particular disappeared. Angel no longer "dropped her children to the tune of Over the Waves," and a homage to Joyce's taste for heraldry—"Terrier rampant in the field azure of Prosper's glance"—vanished. "Sainted in the no-struggle of it" became "Simply redeemed." Even her use of a strategy familiar to readers of *Dubliners* and *Ulysses*—as well as of Faulkner's Yoknapatawa county fictions—the strategy of recalling characters from an earlier in a later work, also disappeared. In the draft, "a man called Farish" figured in one of William Potter's anecdotes, presumably a reference to Nicholas Farish, a character in *Deep Hollow Creek*. He vanished in the Paris revisions to *The Double Hook*.

⌒

Sheila also attempted to rework her own Paris experience in the midst of that experience. In a notebook with the date "Mardi 30 août 1955" in her hand on its cover, only days into their occupancy of the flat on rue Vignon, she wrote of a couple, Paul and Susan—they have no surname—who like themselves were newly arrived in Paris, and of their landlady, Madame Maillot. The fragment is ten pages, and much of it by now is as familiar—and seemingly untransformed—as the materials of *Deep Hollow Creek* would seem to Sheila's friend, the model for that novel's Miriam. Susan, the wife, speaks in this fragment as if she too had lived in Toronto, on Admiral Road in the forties:

> Do you remember how you blocked off the corner of the house in
> Toronto to keep the pigeons from cooing under the roof in the
> morning[?]

He had said then as he always said: It was your idea. You couldn't stand the way they messed up the wall with their droppings. You never see anything but the dirt things make by simply living. I remember how I wired up the corner, he said[,] and Venus has punished me for my pains.

The fragment has a young friend of Paul (who remains nameless) more present to his wife, to the reader, and to Paul himself than her counterpart is in Sheila's journals. The young woman has imagined herself in Paris. Paul reads a letter from her at the beginning of the fragment: "She wrote, I am in Paris before you. I will be standing at the door and my slippers will be under the bed. Can you see me?" "His heart," the narrator observes, "was filled with tenderness as his eyes followed the round unformed script." But it is his wife's consciousness—her memory and her imagination—that drives the narrative. Susan is obsessed by the young woman:

> She saw the face everywhere. . . . The face appeared at street corners—at counters—in the queues waiting to be served at the market stalls. It was the face of a squirrel, the face of an owl, the face of a half open flower. . . . It came saying I am Helen and Heloise. I am the eyes of Beatrice and ear of Stella. It said I am tower and the stairs—the lamb and the light of the first day. . . .
>
> With all the passion of jealousy she imagined a perfect love. She had no defence. When she saw with Paul's eyes she saw what he saw or what, at least, she thought he saw: Heloise among her nuns, the child, the pupil, the lover.

We have heard Paul's rebuke before in Wilfred's "Your tragedy is the tragedy of Othello": "You destroy yourself like Othello."

There is nothing petty or vindictive in Susan's imaginings, only authenticity consistent with her own love for her husband. The author of this fragment knew that to trivialize the object of Paul's infatuation would necessarily diminish Paul—as well as his wife's judgement and her love for him.

⤸

When they returned from Paris, Wilfred had gone first to Alberta—to Calgary to be reunited with his friend, and then to Edmonton—while Sheila had gone on to Vancouver to see family and friends. Wilfred then went on to the coast to visit his family, and to retrieve his car, which he had left in the care of friends who lived up the Fraser Valley from Vancouver. Despite his epistolary pleas, he seems to have made no attempt to see or contact Sheila during this time. Shortly before she proceeded to Toronto, she spent a few days with these same friends, just days after Wilfred had visited them. He and his host, she was told, had "talked for eight hours like Milton's devils about time and eternity." Journal entries dated the first and second of September 1956 suggest that she had spent her time otherwise:

> We ate our supper on the bank by the Ruskin Dam—an old spaniel with a half paralyzed face came wagging his tail and giving tongue to all the misery of the ages. Behind us the rounded humps of the hills and across the river in the distance the Hope mountains snow topped above a low blanket of mist.
>
> This morning Elena dug iris roots—the air thin with the first autumn cold. I tagged the roots as she dug—some were small and compact, others large and ridged in the hand. Now I sit on the lawn out of the wind behind a hedge. The hills are shadowed with clouds. Everywhere now patches and slashes and reaches of colour—a field of dahlias in full bloom, the ageing copper peony shrubs—the fragile Byzantine cups of autumn crocus.

And the next day, it is as if the streets and flower markets of Paris had given way to a more familiar landscape:

> This morning the contracted warmth of summer—slim elegant branches of Japanese anemone—a robin opening the hedge with its wings and disappearing with a cry—the striped cat ravening a mole in the shade of the pergola—out over the valley the grey shadow of a heron dropping to the lake edge.

‿

Sheila travelled by train to Toronto from the coast, stopping in Calgary to have a final visit with Doto, and to make over her registration papers to Louise Riley, uneasy that a single signature might not satisfy where joint ownership had existed. Her first journal entry written after her arrival in Toronto includes impressions of her journey, and is dated 30 September. It deserves to be quoted in its entirety by way of prologue to this chapter of her life. She starts by quoting George Barker:

I sent a letter to my love
In an envelope of stone
And in between the letters ran
A crying torrent that began
To grow till it was bigger than
Nyanza or the heart of man
I sent a letter to my love
In an envelope of stone

Great summer sun. . . .

My one, my one, my only love,
Hide, hide your face in a leaf
And let the hot tears falling burn
The stupid heart that will not learn
The every where of grief.

Left Calgary on the night of the 26—that is at 3:30 in the morning.
The train had been held up six hours by a mud slide somewhere out
of Vancouver. On Wednesday afternoon Agnes brought Doto in and
left her with me at Louise's flat while she went to a meeting. It was
as I had thought. After a little D. licked me all over, lay on her back
so that I could rub her armpits, then went to sleep pillowed against
my foot. She sat beside me at tea and when L. began to make a salad
for dinner she asked for celery as she used to do. Made over the registration papers—Perhaps the c[anadian] k[ennel] c[lubs] will not
accept a single signature.

For the time being all is a state of paralysis—Geo. Barker speaks
my heart—have been reading Blackmur with a great deal of difficulty—His criteria are remorselessly exigent.

Here in Toronto the Travellers Aid woman sent me to a Mrs.
McGill 143 Spadina Road—just below Bernard. Today a wild
windy day—alternate sunshine and rain. Toronto is still a shriek of
irresponsible breaks—a roar of jets since early this morning. Mrs.
McGill's boys are remarkably quiet. I have heard nothing except a
bath running and the tap of the Swiss boy's typewriter in the next
room.

For the time being all is a state of paralysis—Geo. Barker speaks
my heart—have been reading Blackmur with a great deal of difficulty—His criteria are remorselessly exigent.

A man on the Dupont streetcar tonight:

He walked around the world throwing his weight about; now he's pushing

up daisies.

A man on the CPR: (looking at the white edged waves and torn trees on the shore of Lk. Superior):

It looks wild out there
His wife:

Well, it's beginning to come in dusk.

Near Terrace Bay I saw two moose up to their shoulders in a black lake. Red rock, red sumac under the yellow birch and poplar.

A man speaking of war:

It doesn't really matter. You only die once.
A woman beside him:

But nobody wants to die. It's not natural.
A pause and an amendment:

It's not natural to die of unnatural causes.

The hills glowed like the windows of Ste. Chapelle—flamed like the windows of Chartres.

I can't persuade myself that being here is right—Only the will born of last year's experience brought me across the prairies.

Teach us to care and not to care
Teach us to sit still.

September 28/56. Lake Superior.

Leaves fire the bush
And heron heavy wings
lift from the ground
Leaves burn down rock
where shouting waters rise

spilling their fear.

Cry paraclete
Cry wings caught crying
in the waves of air
while body stands
moose shouldered in a sponge of moss
Chafing the rooted year.

~ XI ~

SHEILA LIVED IN TORONTO, SEPARATED FROM WILFRED except for Christmas and summer visits, from September 1956 to August 1961. It was not nostalgia which brought her back to this city. Shortly after her arrival, she wrote to Wilfred recalling and confirming his feelings about this place: "The existence under concrete here is almost too much as you found." But, as she admitted, such entombment was not entirely undesirable: "It has the advantage though of making books speak as people do. In a city like this, one moves from seminar to seminar in silence. . . ." She found in Toronto little of the garrulousness of Paris, and even less of its vivacity: "It is not a speaking city like Paris," she wrote to Wilfred, "only a noisy groaning silence—except for the squirrels and the white winged pigeons—."

Sheila had maintained contact with Norman and Betty Endicott during the seven years since she and Wilfred had left Toronto. Her interest in Wyndham Lewis, which had recently been confirmed in Paris when she read the two newly published parts of *The Human Age* trilogy, led her to assume that she might do work on him under Norman's supervision. Endicott was a reader and a collector of Lewis, and it is not entirely clear what influence this had had on Sheila when she had studied with him in the forties. What is clear is that she returned to Toronto in 1956, intending to do her doctoral thesis on Lewis under her old friend's supervision.

The Endicotts had booked a room for her at the Ford Hotel, across from the bus station on Bay Street. It was a more colourful place than they might have realized. Female and male guests were assigned to different floors, in a public show of decorum, and an omnipresent manager commanded the cavernous lobby with a parrot perched on his shoulder. Almost immediately, Sheila found a room with a Mrs. McGill and the group of male students she referred to as her "boys." Here she spent the first year of her second sojourn in Toronto.

Norman Endicott was a member of a distinguished left-wing family. His brother was at this time head of the Communist Party of Canada, and both he and Norman had been born in China of Canadian missionary parents. In the fifties, his brother's political affiliation and the fact of Chinese birth made Norman seem a more exotic—and in certain quarters, a more threatening—bird than was borne out by his absent-mindedness, his gentle, although at times intense, irascibility, and his passion for the works of Sir Thomas Browne. He was the sort of person who remained oblivious to the lore he generated, a "character" in spite of himself. And he was a passionate reader of literature.

When Sheila spoke with him about working on Lewis, Endicott insisted that Marshall McLuhan's friendship with Lewis and work he had done—including a 1953 essay, "Wyndham Lewis: His Theory of Art and Communication"—qualified him, alone among members of the English Department, to supervise her work. It was advice justly and dispassionately given. Endicott was for temperamental and other reasons no admirer of McLuhan.

At this time, the Faculty of Arts of the University of Toronto was divided among four colleges. Three of these had strong denominational ties: Trinity College, with the Church of England; Victoria College, with the United Church of Canada; and St. Michael's College, with the Roman Catholic Church. The fourth, University College, was precisely that, the University's non-denominational college. This collegiate system recalled certain British universities at the same time it reflected characteristics of the federal structure of Canada itself. The colleges had clearly defined responsibilities and powers, while remaining answerable to the University's Faculty of Arts. They enrolled undergraduate students—and all Arts students had to be registered in a college—and taught only courses in what were defined as "college subjects": Classics, English, French, German, Religious Knowledge, and Philosophy. Students had necessarily to go outside their colleges to take courses in so-called University subjects. The colleges had the right and responsibility to hire their own faculty, but curriculum and examinations were common to the college departments of each discipline. Graduate students were not affiliated with colleges, except as dons in college residences and as tutors.

Their affiliations, their traditions, and their staff gave to each of the colleges its own colouring. The system led to remarkable variety among the staff appointed by the colleges, and among the so-called Combined or Joint Departments that administered the curriculum and examinations for English and the other college subjects. The system led to remarkable discord among members of this federation. For Norman Endicott of University College to send Sheila to study with Marshall McLuhan at St. Michael's College was then a more significant gesture than it might seem now. Endicott's chairman at University College, A. S. P. Woodhouse, who was also head of the graduate program in English, commenting on McLuhan's appointment by St. Michael's in 1945, had said that he was "not the sort of person we want at the University of Toronto."

↬

"Everything more or less settled with M. McLuhan," Sheila wrote in her journal on the 5 October. "He had gone to the library so I waited for him in the 'parlour'—varnished and hung about with lithographs & crucifix. . . ." The parlour she refers to was in the oldest building on the University campus, Cloverhill at St. Michael's, which then housed parish facilities as well as academic offices, seminar rooms, and student residences. McLuhan's office was crammed with books. Perched above them was an oar holding two crates apart, a memento of his Cambridge rowing days, and there was a chaise on which he would recline, all but enveloped in cigar smoke and words.

He agreed to supervise her work and, in return, Sheila thought it only reasonable to enrol in his graduate course, that he might have the chance to see her at work, and she might acquaint herself with his methods and expectations. This was to be an extra course, as the work she had done in the forties left her with only two courses to take in the doctoral program, one outside the English Department, and one in the area of Old and Middle English literature. Accordingly, she enrolled to study Chaucer with Harold Wilson at University College, and Flaubert and Zola with William Kennett at Trinity College. McLuhan's course, entitled "Modern Poetry," was to deal with Joyce and Pound. Joyce, however, became its sole concern. In the second term, at the urging of Professor Woodhouse, with whom she had studied in the forties, she added a course on Swift being offered by a visiting scholar who had once taught at the University of Toronto, Herbert Davis of Oxford, the editor of Swift's works. Sheila participated as fully in these "extra" courses as in the courses she was required to take.

〜

Sheila was forty-seven when she returned to Toronto. After the year in Paris, the city seemed provincial, ill-at-ease, and ungainly in its still developing skin. "The traffic rips and grinds along the streets," she wrote in October. "At the corners the halt and feeble wave ineffectual pandybats while the children scramble across the streets. Restaurants are staffed by the oppressed, the subnormal, and the disinherited." This Toronto sounds more like a suburb of hell—populated by the damned—than like the next best place to heaven it was in time to become for her. But even then the city had means of relieving her loneliness and rare bouts of bitterness. In this same journal entry, she sees from her room on Spadina Road "a ragged and bundled nest. A blue jay and some sparrows peck about the eavestrough—the blue jay metallic and mottled, svelte and imperious. Thank God for the companionship of birds." Human actions, including her own, seemed more ambiguous, and human presences more uncertain before the constancy and unselfconsciousness of animals. At the end of her first month she wrote:

> October is finished.
>
> How can a month be finished? October has finished me. I have written nothing. The girl with the helmet of auburn hair who made love in the dip near Philosopher's Walk has gone off—the squirrels turn leaves with nervous haste—They sit up; life flows along their tiny muscles to their fingertips—they look—they fold their hands into the apex of their bellies—The air is filled with smoke—leaves break under the foot or lie drowned in the gutters.

These Toronto years were to be as full as any in Sheila's life. A chronicle of the events of this time can give little sense of their colour, their shape, their density. A list of her activities and responsibilities is meaningless unless it communicates some sense of people and books and places weaving in and out of her consciousness and her life, of newly discovered and familiar authors providing words and images for what now passed before her eyes or through her mind, of old ties and old friendships being modified by new relationships, of the changing appearance of a bird's wing in a changing light, and—as we shall see later—of a blade of grass recalling Yeats, anticipating McLuhan and her still unpublished second novel. Patterns and preoccupations recur, sometimes obsessively and sometimes merely predictably.

Sheila lived in three different places during these five years. She lived with Mrs. McGill and her "boys" during the academic year 1956–57. From 1957 to 1959 she shared with two young Dutch women the ground floor of a house on Willcocks Street, where New College now stands. From 1959 to 1961 she lived alone in a flat in an apartment building at the corner of Sussex Avenue and Huron Street. These places had in common their proximity to the University, whose location in the centre of the city left her within easy walking distance of what was most familiar and important to her.

During these years, Sheila spent a summer with Wilfred near Victoria, and shorter intervals with him in Edmonton and in the mountains, and he spent parts of two summers with her in Toronto. And when they were apart they corresponded. Sometimes as many as two or three letters a day passed between them. "Your letters come in threes," he observed. "A day without a letter," she wrote to him, "doesn't seem to be a day somehow . . ." Letters made possible a kind of communication which, as her Paris journals show, proximity seemed inevitably to threaten. In Toronto, except during the first summer he spent with her there, in 1959, Sheila was relatively free of reminders of his other attachment, which had not ended. There were none of the long-distance telephone calls that had left her sleepless in Paris, or of the envelopes addressed in a recognizable hand. But nor was there the casual, random, unselfconscious pleasure of what she termed a "usual affinity of observation" which she believed they shared, and which flourished in presence, when the observer might be observed.

With few exceptions, their letters followed a pattern which was common to both of them. Only in the most formal or most tense of circumstances would they refer to one another by name. Normally Wilfred addressed Sheila as "Swp"—the shortened form of Shuswap (which sometimes he used) entwined with her initials—and she inevitably addressed him as "leopard." After familiar salutations, they tended to focus on intellectual or aesthetic issues, the argument of a book, or Sheila's response to a poem or a story written by Wilfred. There was occasional news of friends or family, but the telephone was the more likely medium for such matters. Sometimes there were drawings and often a playful sign-off by Wilfred and drawings and a description of a bird or a leaf or a shaft of light from Sheila. Because they wrote so often, and because readers are inclined to read such letters as if they formed a single document, their epistolary conversations might seem now more repetitive and protracted than they must have seemed to them then.

Letters made possible the continuation of what in their relationship survived separation, their intense intellectual compatibility. Each became so immersed in the interests of the other that it is sometimes difficult to determine where an interest which has become associated with one or the other had its origins. Wilfred was the first to meet and very likely the first to read McLuhan, and his interest in Lewis raises the possibility—as he himself did—that it was he who introduced Lewis into their world. Sheila's copy of *Tristram Shandy*, which is so much more extensively annotated than Wilfred's, gives some sense of her commitment to his interests when he had worked on his thesis in the late forties and early fifties. Even when relations between them were most strained, they did not lose interest in each other's interests. This was the stuff of their letters during these years, the glue that sealed them.

Sheila's journals provide an important adjunct to their correspondence. In the first months of her time in Toronto, these journals read less like exercises in keeping back the darkness—as she had described them in Paris—than as accounts of her defeat by it. On New Year's Eve of 1956 she writes: "The mail has come this morning and no letter from Wilfred—These two weeks have been a torment—time stretched like a thin rope over a pit—feet on sliding shale—darkness behind and darkness still ahead—the fear the knowledge perhaps that the flaw is in myself—." She seldom indulged these feelings, or others like them. Inevitably she would attempt to focus her mind on something outside herself, on a book, or on some phenomenon in nature which had caught her eye. The next sentence after the passage just quoted reads: "The horror of a vision like that in Germanie Lacerteux—the prayer for an insight that can root out such images." Earlier in this same month, December 1956, she admitted to "a terrible loneliness," and then immediately noted: "Read *A Tale of a Tub*. I can't believe that the narrative passages and the digressions are not closely connected." She ended this entry: "Satire, Swift says, is a sort of glass, wherein beholders do generally discover everybody's face but their own. . . ." The ellipsis is interesting, as are the thoughts that supplanted her darker feelings.

Scott Fitzgerald's claim that in the dark night of the soul, it is always three o'clock in the morning was as true of Sheila as of his revelers and of himself. She seldom reveled, but she as seldom slept a night through. Sometimes there were compensations for this sleeplessness, as when she recorded: "It is four o'clock. Because I can't sleep I work on Swift—and because I can't sleep I hear the private talk of birds." A few years later, when she was living on Sussex Avenue, she set down childhood memories of her first home and her first school that had supplanted sleep:

> For some reason I couldn't sleep—perhaps the sound of a voice I don't know—My mind went back as it is supposed to do when one is dying—the blue flowers—periwinkle I think in the circular flower bed they made when the hitching post was taken down—the giant shasta daisies running in rows and throwing themselves down the mountainside of the terrace—Lawn House Miss Filmore and Flip Toppy and Smith—Jack and Trini—the airing-courts and the swing doors—father in his uniform saying I can't wear it but I'll put it in my pocket book—the tiles of the dispensary and the black smell of the nuns—Sister Mary Zenade and every one in white dresses—and a girl at the piano thumping out a grand entry for old [Bishop] Casey—

Often a dream, or more frequently a nightmare, wakened her. "Last night I woke about three-thirty filled with terror," she wrote in December 1956. "I dreamed that a cat had jumped on my back. Its hind feet were hooked in the small of my back—

its head over my head like a cap." "It was a physical dream—an involvement not a detachment," she added. She also had recurring dreams. "Dreamed the old destruction dream," she wrote at one point, and referred at another time to "crying dreams" that inevitably wakened her. After one of these, she mused: "Calamities of the heart are like fires in a house. They send consciousness groping against the walls." An "old destruction dream" left her feeling as if she had "set up housekeeping while the walls tumbled and [Wilfred's young friend] in the hall in Calgary staring and staring."

Her Toronto journals helped Sheila to achieve something of the formal feeling that comes after great pain, a feeling which expressed itself through generalization or image in an attempt to free itself from its own weight. "There are moments of desolation," she wrote in the spring of 1959, "as when the sea has flown from the clam flats—when even the light is shallow and the depth of grief the depth of a grain of sand." And then, "To live in an abstraction of suffering—the life of a cameo or an engraving on copper." She had commented in her journal, "The emotion from which W's poetry springs is always stronger than the 'objective correlative' he finds for it." In her own case, the "objective correlative" inevitably evoked a wider range of emotional and sensory response than the emotion that occasioned it. She commented to a friend, Pat Brückmann, one day, when a white pigeon settled on the porch of her Sussex Avenue apartment, that the bird reminded her of Wilfred's friend. Later, in the summer of 1959, when Wilfred was with Sheila in Toronto, in a flat they had sublet from friends, Sheila observed: "A white pigeon—a stranger to these roofs—like a flying tulip comes in its cinnamon streaked and spotted whiteness as someone else's observed ghost." Within weeks, more material evidence of the ghost appeared: "Came a letter on the 27 from Calgary dated Aug. 24—Only the shock of seeing the handwriting made me look at the date and postmark." The next January, of 1960, she reflected back on the recent Christmas break she had spent in Edmonton as "the days of the white pigeon." "When I opened the cupboard door and saw the picture [of Wilfred's young friend] there the lines of Pope's 'Rape [of the Lock]' sang in my head 'On her white breast etc.'—and I thought how always my thoughts were a kind of blasphemy—Sometime during the two wks. [that Sheila was in Edmonton] the picture was taken down." Image and allusion were means by which she attempted to make bearable a situation which otherwise might have maddened her.

⌐

Wilfred and their painful past were not the only concerns of the journals she kept during these Toronto years. More immediate persons and places recur like threads, contributing to an almost palpable sense of a time and a community. Philosopher's Walk, that links the campus to Bloor Street along a buried creek, running beside Trinity College and the Faculty of Music and behind the Royal Ontario Museum— a green and wooded place in summer, a short-cut in winter—this was such a place. Only days after her arrival in Toronto in the fall of 1956 she met an old friend there: "The leaves burn along Philosopher's Walk. I saw Ken MacLean. We talked—about Wordsworth—about poetry and sacrifice—He knew instinctively why I was work- ing on Lewis." MacLean, Wilfred's one time thesis supervisor, had remained Sheila's friend since the forties, a friend at a distance although not a distant friend. "This afternoon I went to hear John Sutherland lecture on [eighteenth-century] prose," she wrote early that same December; "I sat with [Ken MacLean] who rubbed his hands softly and muttered 'What prose' when Sutherland read a passage from Hobbes." And then one May day in 1958: "A day of bright sunshine—Walking behind the museum I saw every leaf on every tree—." And in the same month: "Sunlight and a cold breeze—behind the Museum on Philosopher's Walk a woman carrying two bags—singing in Yiddish—in German—a hard wailing chant—the surge of a contralto art-voice—laughter—the cold quick tempo of the music hall— 'Ach Herr Docktor.'" And then she adds, "[Marshall McLuhan] said, 'If this was in a play one would stop and listen to it, but one is ashamed to listen so to another human being singing so.'"

Sheila did listen, though, and she observed and recorded. "The problem is to produce the effect of drawing," she wrote, glossing the following passage in da Vinci: "And you who wish to represent by words the form of man and all the aspects of his membrification, relinquish that idea. For the more minutely you describe the more you will confine the mind of the reader, and the more you will keep him from the knowledge of the thing described. And so it is necessary to draw and to describe."

Her aim—in her journals as in her fiction—was what she called "writing spa- tially." "Characters out of space," she wrote, "become mere abstractions—an accu- mulation of detail—." "Figures in a ground" is a phrase we have met with already. During these years, Toronto was her ground, and Sheila's eyes and ears received the details that she translated into images and vignettes, the stuff of her journals.

One wet April day in 1961:

> Two, four, six, eight—twenty two, four, six, eight—thirty two, four,
> six, eight—forty

Children skipping outside on the asphalt-court of the store across the street—the tree trunks black in the rain, the brick absorbing the light until it burns with a deep red concentration.

In the autumn of 1959:

> The inarticulately malignant chatter of public machinery—the road outside mending—one fat character in a peaked cap bellowing through the road sign which is hollow and shaped like a megaphone: "Ladies & etc. come and see the elephant which hasn't made water for fifteen years." Another character dances up to him with a bucket and a tar brush. Sob, sob through the megaphone—.

In an undated note: "men in overcoats huddling a coffin (grey composition) into a hearse in the rush of the traffic—furtively the hearse pulled into the gutter." In a short space of time she sees two women on the street: the first, "a small dump of a woman in a gnawed fur coat feeding a ginger, a grey, and a white cat from a tin of cat food which she was carrying in a battered but elegant hand-bag. She had piled the food in little heaps on the pavement—and stood guard while the cats crouched down to it." And then: "Another woman—this time pudgy and blonde—a tooth or two gone—standing drunk against the lamp post at the corner of Harbord and St. George. She wore a stylish hat, lace mittens, and had some sort of fur about her throat. She was mumbling to herself—and calling imprecations down an empty street—." "I hope I don't see a third," she added.

She recorded names that caught her eye: The Venus Grill, Trinity Poultry, Litera Printing Co.; and phrases and scraps of dialogue that revealed the texture of the place and time: "We like to assure ourselves that we believe in—" and "franchised body dealer" and "the great broad fact stands out." The place where she often ate supper yielded glimpses and snatches of campus life: for example, phrases from a conversation between "two BBC voiced girls":

> "I may be a purist—but"
> "so extremely serious and ruthless . . . so learned and erudite"
> "human kindness must be the vortex—Shaw does show pity . . ."
> "Mr. P. said etc. etc."

She noted beauty in surprising places: "A drift of white broom on the high bank where the train comes out of the Bloor Street subway station—suddenly falling on the eye in all its whiteness." She noted the rhythm of the seasons and the impatience of planters:

"The forsythia falls over the fence—spray of light—the bushes leaf and the peony in the back garden shoves through the winter-baked earth—everywhere things grow, but the daffodils about the fountain on University Avenue cheat the season—They've been set out—seem gathered together like wedding guests in a rented hall."

Sheila's life during these years focused on the University, and it fed her eyes and her ears as well as her mind and imagination. Her Toronto journals, like those she kept in Paris, are filled with vivid verbal sketches. The Rare Book Room of the University's main library was then presided over by a Miss Brown, whose criteria for rare books prevailed even as they puzzled. She refused to accept into her collection a first edition of Alexander Pope's *An Essay on Man* because it was too recent to be considered rare. She was interested only in incunabula: printed books really did not interest her. "Miss Brown of the Rare Book Room said that she thinks all books now being printed will be self-liquidating," Sheila recorded, adding, "she spoke with a dull sweet relish." She talked with the Chancellor of Victoria College at the installation of Northrop Frye as its Principal: "He spoke of the anecdote of Swift—the tree going at the top—'I begin to go,' he said, 'more ignominiously in my left hip.'" She described the laugh of the man with whom she studied Chaucer: "Mr. Wilson's laugh—thin silence, then ou-ha, ha, ha, ha, ou ha ha ha ha—long drawn like a loon's cry. Almost frightening in its persistence—again and again and again." After a recital by the renowned harpsichordist Greta Kraus, in early February 1957 in the Great Hall at Hart House: "I met G. K. and her gentle faced Austrian husband—she a thin blue match tipped with flame. Her husband said: 'The program was too much—Couperin, Bach, Scarlatti.' I noticed her hands—wide and long fingered yet thin to the bone." At another concert, in January 1958 at Victoria College, "In the row behind sat Jay Macpherson—her hair coiled, a look of Byzantine sorrow on her face, a Sitwell medallion on her breast." In May 1960: "Met Margaret Avison in the street looking deathly pale—she was she said trying to find a room—She had just finished ghosting a book and didn't know what she could find to do. She has a terrible solemnity—as if poetry was a sort of anguish and her principles a heavy Cross." "Met Barker Fairley twice today," she wrote in March 1958. "He says this is not economical—We listened to the song of a cardinal which he says lives on Willcocks Street with us—I've not seen it, but then only the pigeons would venture into the cul de sac beyond my window—I might, however, have met it in the trees when I was interrogating the branches."

I met Sheila for the first time in the fall of 1956, in Marshall McLuhan's graduate seminar. I had come from Vancouver to begin graduate work, and a cousin who taught in the University's History Department and who was Secretary of the Pontifical Institute of Mediaeval Studies recommended two professors with whom I should study—McLuhan and Norman Endicott. I knew nothing of Endicott except that he was offering a graduate course on John Donne and Sir Thomas Browne and that he played tennis with my cousin, but I had heard Marshall on the radio. It was in Vancouver, on CBC, a program called *Critically Speaking*, I believe, and he spoke of the generation gap (this would have been in 1955 or early 1956) in terms of a generation now attending university being the first in their families' histories to do so. I remember listening to it with my father, who already dreaded the prospect of my going East to study. McLuhan made more painful sense to him at that time than to me, but he did make sense to me. And so I registered in his seminar, and nothing since has been as once it was.

Sheila was the oldest member of the seminar, older even than McLuhan. There were about twelve or fifteen of us in all, including a young Jesuit scholastic, a fellow graduate from UBC, and a young woman from Saskatchewan who later became an Anglican nun, and who was also in Endicott's seminar with me. The young men were from Windsor and Fort William and Rochester, New York, and they were intense. One of them rather self-consciously carried about a copy of Pound's *Cantos*, which eventually I bought from him.

I remember Sheila's size, first of all; her smallness that must have seemed the more so because of McLuhan's lankiness. I remember her small hands with intensely nicotined fingers, her small, rather fat feet in sandals, and legs that seemed stocky in comparison with her smallness. I remember the mop of closely cropped hair and, in winter, the raccoon coat that buried her so that she seemed less a person clothed than one only partially metamorphosed. Not everyone resisted the temptation to pat this coat. I remember her eyes, squinting behind the smoke that inevitably veiled them, eyes that were direct and remote, that, as I soon discovered, had read so much and had seen so much of my world. She was a strange presence in the seminar, the one person who moved easily in the current of Marshall's thought. She seemed to have read all that he had read and, in some areas, books that he had not read. Work she was doing on Flaubert with William Kennett fed him as it fed her. I recall her seminar presentations—they were inevitably taken up with Flaubert's influence on, or his presence in, Joyce. They seemed to me then to be rather scattered, perhaps because I knew so little about what interested her.

Sheila provided two glimpses of Marshall's seminar in letters written to Wilfred in the fall of 1956. The first involved the Jesuit scholastic:

> Mr. Johnson . . . had announced at the end of the period that he had this summer finally come to an understanding of the bull in Picasso's Guernica sketches:
>
> Yes, said M. McL.
>
> The threat to a man's woman, said Mr. Father Johnson.
>
> Eh? said McL. What do you mean? A man's woman?
>
> The anima, said Father Johnson.

Such an exchange (or non-exchange) was not unusual as students or occasional visitors to the seminar tended to overlook or misunderstand Marshall's literalness, assuming that he was "far out" when he was invariably very close-at-hand. I remember a young woman appearing one day with a carved pumpkin, seating herself at the opposite end of the table from Marshall, and announcing that this was the last vestige of the mask in our culture. Marshall looked more uncomfortable than interested.

Sheila's second glimpse is more revealing of McLuhan's method of teaching. "The method here seems divided," she wrote to Wilfred: "Mr. Wilson and Mr. Kennett use the seminar. Frye [whose graduate course she was also auditing] and Mr. McLuhan both lecture—at least Frye lectures with blackboard et al. and Mr. McLuhan gives a running explicatio of text—meander of text and a meadow of *explicatio*." It was a just description. But, while there might have been much by way of meandering, there was little aimlessness. More by example than by exhortation, Marshall encouraged us to move freely in a text, to recognize and savour patterns, to see the text in its larger, cultural contexts. Because it was Joyce we were reading, the contexts were varied indeed. Because it was Joyce and Marshall and St. Michael's College, and a seminar room with a crucifix on a wall (as a graduate of UBC, this was the first such I had encountered in a university classroom), what we read and discussed seemed imbued with that same odour of sanctity (roughly speaking, a mixture of black serge and waxed floors and incense) that had permeated much of Sheila's—and indeed of my—earliest schooling. Marshall's sense of the necessity, the integrity, the power of the individual reader, his sense of the transformative power of reading, of Henry James become a Canadian in a Canadian's reading of him (a favourite example of his), began my liberation from those vestiges of colonialism that had continued to colour my own relationship to literature. I found myself now at ease in my own skin, easier even with my own inadequacies. I recall talking with Marshall during this time—about what I don't recall. He mentioned Shakespeare's *The Winter's Tale*, and when I confessed that I had not yet read it, he said simply, "I envy you."

⌒

Sheila soon became a part of the McLuhan family. I don't know if an evening the members of the graduate seminar spent at their house on Wells Hill Avenue, drinking white wine and eating figs, was her first visit there. Her first reference to a visit comes in a journal entry, dated February 1957:

> To dinner with the McLuhans—When I went up the path Mike and the little girl with braids [Stephanie] were looking out of the window—Eric was going off to his judo—Mary, Theresa, Libby—Mrs. McLuhan in a red dress with the children all about her. We drank rye in the kitchen, had dinner and sat about the fire—anecdotes of Wyndham Lewis [who was to die in the next month] coming to dinner—Mrs. L[ewis] walking breathlessly behind abandoned in fury—I like C[orinne]. She spoke of spring in Texas [where she had been born and had grown up]—the nigger-toes and the indian blankets—the long death of a Toronto winter.

Corinne McLuhan embodied much that Sheila admired in a woman—beauty and style, a sense of the details of life, a capacity for friendship, ease in her own being. They were in many respects a study in contrasts—in their physical appearances, certainly, in their domestic responsibilities, in what was uppermost in their minds. But despite these differences, they shared a capacity for fierce and protective loyalty to their husbands. Sheila had from her own experience an appreciation of the tact that Corinne exercised in dealing with Marshall, while Corinne in time became indignant as Sheila would not allow herself to, about the extent to which Sheila had been betrayed by Wilfred. They confided in one another, like sisters who were determined to protect a towering and demanding brother. There could be no jealousy between them. Marshall respected and felt affection for Sheila, and he remained protective of her, as a tall man often instinctively does of a small woman.

Sheila liked to tell the story of his later attempts to prepare her to find her way in the academic marketplace. He was concerned that her age would tell against her, and so he encouraged her to dye her hair blonde. She relished the absurdity of the idea, and asked him if he had ever made such a suggestion to Corinne. "But Corinne is a naturally beautiful woman," was Marshall's incredulous reply.

Perhaps in the wake of this exchange—or in anticipation of it, for I have no date for it—during the summer of 1958, when she house-sat Wells Hill Avenue while the family was with Marshall, who was lecturing in Santa Barbara, Sheila wrote in her journal:

> 29 Wells Hill is a temporary ark—Marshall laughed at the feminin-
> ity of V[irginia] W[oolf]'s "My back is against the wall"—I would
> not write as a woman and yet this is a fact—more fundamental say
> than the fact of a one legged man—or a blind pianist—or a two-
> headed calf—

Deeper than disability or aberration was the inescapability of gender—and this after her attempt in her second novel to dispose of her own personality, a presence which she believed had marred *Deep Hollow Creek*. And she had appeared in Toronto in a sexless guise—with her hair cut short, baggy sweaters and overly long skirts, and the raccoon coat that almost submerged her gender as well as her nature. Years later, in response to a question about feminism, she appeared to downplay the significance of gender—for hers or for anyone's consciousness:

> I've never thought of myself specifically as a woman. There's not
> much difference between being a man or a woman. I mean you live
> and you breathe and you have to cope. . . . The things in people that
> are similar are more important than things that are dissimilar.

At about the same time as McLuhan's well-meaning although tactless attempt to prepare Sheila to enter the academic world, another member of the English Department spoke with her of the difficulties she must expect in making her way in what was very much a man's world. A. S. P. Woodhouse called her to his office to discuss her future. Like Marshall's, it was a well-intentioned, avuncular gesture. Woodhouse advised her—and Sheila relished mimicking the long withdrawing roar of his speech: "Mrs. Waaatson, in the aaacademic worrrld a wooman must beee as gooood as tennn mennn." "What men?" she asked.

Photographs of Sheila taken in the thirties show a very different image than she presented when she came to Toronto in the mid-fifties. Photographs taken at Dog Creek, some of which Michael Ondaatje reprinted in *Brick* to honour the publication of *Deep Hollow Creek*, show her at ease in the company of dogs and of horses and of men. A photograph taken at a later time, although still in the thirties and likely at Murrayville, shows her balancing cheekily—like a circus performer—on the back of a horse, Fiddle perhaps, wearing a two-piece bathing suit. On the first of April 1959, she wrote in her journal: "I remember the slippery trail and Fiddle falling and of the way he kept his weight off my left leg and rose so slowly that I came up on his back— It seems curious to record that I have been defended and consoled by a horse and three dogs—I have besides loved and been loved—this as comment."

A man's disloyalty can make a nun of his wife. There was a time when "rejected" women might enter a convent, or a beguinage, in order to recover some sense of themselves in the company of women. This was never an option for Sheila, but she knew enough of nuns to know that they were no less women for making themselves untouchable. Marshall was fond of telling the story of the Irishman who came upon a nun who had slipped and fallen on a sidewalk. He fetched a shovel so that he could lift her without touching her, because she was "a holy thing." There was nothing of what she remembered as "the black smell of the nuns" about Sheila, and certainly nothing of the sense of being "a holy thing," but there was the quality of a habit about the way she dressed that betrayed a determination not to be approached in a sexual way. "Pat my raccoon coat, if you must," she might have said, "but *noli me tangere*."

⌇

Religion was to play a very important part in Sheila's relationship with Marshall: he, the fervent convert to Catholicism, and she, the "lapsed" Catholic whose memory and imagination and intellect were imbued with the images, the odors and gestures and questions whose sources were in the practices and beliefs of Roman Catholicism. Joyce was a kind of facilitator in this relationship, the subject of the graduate course in which Sheila first worked with Marshall, but also someone who had been shaped much as she had been, who intrigued Marshall despite, or perhaps because of, his own strict observance of the conditions of Catholicism. Time and space collapsed when she recalled a time and place in her own past. Twice in her journals she went back to this same time and place. Once in response to something she had read in Maud Bodkin she wrote:

> M. Bodkin observes:
> "The power to observe accurately may be in part a product of train-
> ing in introspection under ordinary conditions."

The phrase amuses me quite irrelevantly—the memory of early morning meditation in the physics laboratory—with its high sinks and glass cases of instruments—examination of conscience—directed—then a half hour of cold meditation—with Mother Seymour pressing her plump figure against the prie dieu at our backs.

At another time she expanded upon this in the context of the difference between introspection and meditation:

In the physics lab at 6:30 in the morning we were supposed to meditate—Mother S. formulated the object of meditation. She forced us . . . into an examination of conscience in her hectoring way too—

the mysteries of the rosary
the stations of the cross
Wm James shutting himself
in a dark cupboard or
concentrating on a door jamb
How often, my child? Alone or
with another? Say three Our
Fathers and three Hail Marys
and say them slowly.
Ignatius Loyola.

The distance between Clongowes College and the Convent of the Sacred Heart, between Dublin and Vancouver disappears. The distance between Joyce and Sheila narrows. Eliot termed it simultaneity, and so did Marshall.

At the beginning of the journal entry that contained this last passage, dated 14 February 1958, Sheila wrote as a motto a variation on Tertullian's "*Credo quia impossibile est.*" It read, "*Credo quia absurdum.*" By the mid-1950s, of course, the term absurdity had, after Camus and others, come to be applied to the actions of characters performed in the teeth of impossibility: the persistence of Sisyphus, the happiness of Beckett's Winnie, the patience of those who wait for Godot. Impossibility became, in Sheila's terms, the ground, and absurdity, the nature of the responses of those figures who inhabited that ground. On 22 March of this same year, she began a journal entry: "Yesterday M[arshall] said that it is impossible to ask for faith on any terms—all one can do is to pray—the universe is not a fallen universe but one which has been redeemed." She continued: "I try to understand him but my mind does not move as quickly—or in the same light—or in light at all." Her hesitation had less to do with the "absurdity" of Marshall praying than with his certainty about the ground they occupied—that it had been redeemed and was no longer fallen.

Marshall's Catholicism was not simple, but his sense of literalness made it seem so. It was a quality of Sheila's religion as well—as it is of Roman Catholicism. Remember her account of the midnight mass she and Wilfred attended in Paris in 1955, when the church was so crowded they found themselves behind the altar, out of sight although still within earshot of the ceremony. This led her to speculate about the nature and extent of the influence of the Real Presence. How far could one be from the altar, even from the church, and still be said to have attended mass? Such a sense of literalness may strike some as risible, as the stuff of angels on the head of a pin, but neither Sheila nor Marshall was a fool. Both would have understood Flannery O'Connor's comment about the eucharist: "If it's a symbol, to hell with it."

"There is a natural literalism as there is a verbal literalism," she wrote to me later, in the fall of 1959, in the wake of my first reading of *The Double Hook.* "It is St. Bonaventure I think who makes a comment about the phrase '*Verbum Dei*'—word *of* God, word *about* God." She continued: "In some ways the D. H. is a comment on this type of literalism as I am convinced Swift's *Tale of a Tub* is—only between now and Swift's time the pseudo scientific reading of the vestigia has been romanticized and diabolized."

If Sheila hesitated before Marshall's confidence in the universe redeemed, like Hopkins's her discerning of that universe's beauty and coherence, of the rhyming of human sensitivity with the gentleness of the wind blowing back leaves, of the companionship of birds, of what she called "the seal of the 'incarnate' God" on every human being, testified to her belief in the continuousness of incarnation in nature as well as in sacrament. "This I hadn't known before," she commented in November 1958, "thinking only of God the Father at work with his compasses." It is a strange admission, almost as if she had undergone a kind of conversion, not returning to the religion of her youth exactly, but finding traces everywhere of what that religion insisted upon and, at its best, celebrated. Years later, in 1975, at the time of her retirement from the University of Alberta, in an interview with the *Western Catholic Reporter* of Edmonton, Sheila spoke of being raised a Catholic in a predominantly Protestant society. "My religious beginnings were not, you might say, extra-institutional," she observed; "My life in the convent, it was just there." The presence of religion in her life, like her speculations about the influence of the Real Presence, must be acknowledged even if it can never be adequately measured.

⤺

Sheila had been preceded to Toronto by her brother Bill, whose life in New Westminster had come to an end because his marriage had. There was about Bill, according to his sister Norah, something of what the Irish called "the spoiled priest." He had apparently failed to become what he was meant to be: he had missed his vocation and had seemingly dissipated his considerable gifts. The consequences are familiar: broken relationships, professional aimlessness, the demon in the bottle.

He and Sheila saw little of one another over the years, and her renewed relations with him in Toronto were not easy. During her first months in Toronto, however, she was, as she wrote Anne Angus, encouraged "to see him looking so well—better than he has for a number of years now." When he returned to Toronto from a short stint working on a newspaper in Sudbury, he had changed. Sheila was determined that he should not return to Vancouver, believing that he would become too difficult a responsibility for their mother. At the same time such demands as he made on her in Toronto were painful and distracting. She had inherited a full-blown situation. She could have no effect on him or on his affairs, other than to listen to him, and occasionally feed him. It was Marshall who put the most charitable and perhaps the most accurate construction on her brother's predicament when he suggested to Sheila that "a search for total relevance creates the condition of paranoia."

In the early winter months of 1957, in her first year back in Toronto, she found herself writing about the place where she and Bill had been born, and at the same time having it recalled for her by the circumstances of his present life. On 3 February, she visited him in his room in an as yet ungentrified Yorkville area. "He was in bed, two bottles of brandy empty beside him—in bed with his Plato and Thoreau around him. He was almost in tears—spoke of the horror of having to go to court about the divorce—yet he is the one who is insisting on it. I took him out to breakfast. We talked about other things. I came back and worked on my Antigone again to set a wall against the thought."

Later that month, she was told by his landlady that he was in hospital. "I called the hospital," she wrote in her journal, "and someone said he had been transferred to the hospital on Queen Street. I am to call tomorrow. This is a nightmare. . . ." "[M]y Antigone" had proved to be less a wall than a premonition. 999 Queen Street

West was the Toronto equivalent to the hospital in which she and Bill had grown up, and about which she was then writing her most famous short story.

Bill's condition was the more puzzling to Sheila because he had recently begun a relationship with a woman who cared for him deeply and whom Sheila liked and respected. With his doctor, she found it difficult to reconcile his new-found contentment with his present state. But it was not in Sheila's nature to intervene in the affairs of any person. She would listen, perhaps even attempt to distract, but seldom would she presume to advise. In time, Bill did return to Vancouver, where he died in 1974.

Meanwhile, Ween and Norah and her family continued to live in Vancouver. By 1957, Norah and her husband had five children, three daughters and two sons. Sheila and Wilfred spent the summer of that year in and near Victoria, their first time together since parting the previous summer. The last part of their stay was in Victoria, house-sitting for friends. They invited Norah's eldest child, Barbara, then eight years old, to spend some time with them. This visit was the occasion of an episode which became part of their lore.

Concerned that Wilfred not be disturbed, Sheila had told her niece that, being a poet, he required quiet in order to concentrate. Barbara knew what a poet was, and she knew what poetry was, and she now had a sense of the privileges that accompanied both. One morning at breakfast, she announced, "I am a poet." Her aunt and uncle waited. "Oh, yes," she continued. "At night I sit on my bed, and I look out the window, and I say, 'O Moon!'"

Barbara was never to be free of her poem. Sheila and Wilfred referred to her ever after, upon occasion as, "O Moon!"—a name which recalled the episode and a summer of particular happiness, and their "adoption" of the child they had never had, which was in Norah's eyes what "O Moon!" had become.

⌒

With her coursework completed by the winter of 1958, her second year in Toronto, Sheila was able to turn in earnest to the matter of her thesis. She had found in Wyndham Lewis, among many other qualities and characteristics, a valuing of literalness similar to her own. She observed him working, "as he said, like the mason-bee or the woodpecker, from a fundamental need." She found him "at his best when he talks of lions and tigers and bees—and the warm parts of pigeons' wings." According to Sturge Moore, as she notes in her journal, "Lewis thought that God has a composite back as a fly has a composite eye, so that he can be back to back with every soul and that he, God, is not pleased with those who try to see him over their shoulders but prefers those who merely lean against him and take no notice of him giving all their attention to the world in front of them." It is a vivid little parable, as applicable to Sheila herself as to Lewis. With God as her back-rest, her eyes could be absorbed by a sparrow, a pigeon, a moth, an owl. In a journal entry dated 8 May 1959, she surrendered briefly to a somber thought: "Every act carries its hell in its own hands." And then she pulled herself up short: "but this is to see darkly." The phrase evoked a "spot of time" whose vividness redeemed the time. "Yet I remember walking into the hollows at night fall, thinking of the phrase and watching the darkness creep up the blades of grass, for one's feet are in darkness while the eye is still tangled by the quick brightness of a bird's wing."

◡

A taste for literalness was only one of the bonds Sheila felt with Lewis. Where or when or with whom she first encountered his work remains unclear. What was clear, however, was her desire as a writer to learn from the man who in his lifetime had been judged by Eliot and I. A. Richards the greatest living master of imaginative prose in English. As she worked on her doctoral thesis, she referred to it as "The Passionate Image." Its title when it was submitted, however, was a more prosaic "Wyndham Lewis and Expressionism."

As her working title implies, Sheila was interested in Lewis as a painter, and in his fiction as an iconographer. She was fascinated by "the passionate concentration of attention" that brought to his remarkably varied interests and achievements what Eliot had termed "unity of underlying pattern." She admired his clear-eyed engagement with a world "being transformed by technological magic." She admired, too, his protean boldness, even though she found him upon occasion more elusive than Proteus. But she also found his contentiousness at times exhausting. "I groan under the weight of the material where every detail is an issue," she wrote to Wilfred; "Wyndham Lewis immerses me in a confusion worse than my own." She found herself, as many thesis writers have, locked in a love-hate relationship with her subject.

The ground for Sheila's work on Lewis included the novel she had begun working on before returning to Toronto. What she said of it and what survives of "Landscape of the Moon" suggest her interest in a type of isolated society unlike the isolated societies of her other novels—one which is not removed from the world of the city. A university functions here as Bloomsbury does in Lewis's *The Apes of God*.

Sheila considered Lewis's *Apes* "as great a satire as any in English literature," matched only by *Gulliver's Travels* and *Tristram Shandy*. She was at pains in her thesis to challenge those readings of Lewis's novel that assumed it was little more than "a spiteful roman à clef," as if she were anticipating responses to her own satire of the academy.

What years later Sheila described as a concern which informed *The Double Hook* and her method in writing it recalls both her concerns and method in writing her thesis. She had spoken of Lewis's work as an organic structure, developing "in a specific matrix and . . . responsive to the conditions of its existence." In 1973, she described the characters in her own novel with, for us now, the more familiar phrase "figures in a ground, from which they could not be separated." By "ground," she was careful to note, she did not mean only landscape, but "the things about them, the other things which exist." Her study of Lewis was very much of a figure in a ground "from which [he] could not be separated." His was not the driven helplessness of James Potter, with "no art . . . no tradition . . . no ritual," but Lewis's ground did share with Sheila's figures at least one characteristic. In the final section of her thesis, she observed that it "was not until he had explored the implications of Expressionist theory . . . that Lewis realized fully the extent to which men by a process of abstraction create outside themselves a reality which dominates them like a fate." Coyote and old Mrs. Potter, it seems, had cohorts prowling and angling in London's Strand.

The ground that Sheila occupied while she wrote her thesis, for a time at least, also included Lewis's drawing of a bull's head, loaned to her by Norman Endicott, and a table painted by Lewis, loaned to her by Marshall. It also included an ironing board. She wrote on that ironing board while she lived in the apartment on Sussex Avenue. Friends savoured the epiphanic absurdity of her dampening and pressing and folding Lewis, so to speak; still, they admired her ingenuity and practicality in adapting so commonplace an object to her needs. At the time, in the late fifties, an ironing board brought to mind the mean midland digs of Jimmy Porter, and more particularly his wife, Alison, ironing her way through the first act of John Osborne's *Look Back in Anger*. It was typical of Sheila that she had turned to her own purposes—and had made the stuff of myth—so ordinary an object.

⤶

Sheila had not returned to Toronto in 1956 as the author of *The Double Hook*— although she was that already—nor had she come primarily to see it published. She came to prepare herself to support herself. Still her confidence in the novel had survived what she believed would be "the last desolation of failure" when it was rejected by Faber & Faber, that bastion of modernism and—at her instigation—publisher of Wilfred's poetry. For she did not try to bury her second novel as she had her first when it had been rejected.

She could not have been surprised that an English publisher was not interested in her novel. In the previous year, 1955, she had sent the manuscript to C. Day Lewis at Chatto and Windus, and his reply was a harbinger of other responses from the English trade. "I myself admired some of the writing and the intuition behind it," he wrote to her, "but I found it difficult to get clear in my mind the characters and their responses to one another and to their situation. Commercially, I am afraid, the book would stand no chance in the British market." In the summer of 1954, she had already sent the manuscript to Rupert Hart-Davis, and his judgement, as we have seen—"all insufficiently explored, too much motion and dust"—was hardly encouraging.

Salter had attempted to interest American publishers, but again, as we have seen, with no more success. Almost fifty years after its publication, it still had not appeared either in England or in the United States. This does not mean that there have not been British and American admirers of the novel. Shortly after its publication, in the spring of 1959, Sheila's friend Toronto scholar and painter, Barker Fairley, sent a copy to an English acquaintance, a fellow student of German literature and distinguished critic Michael Hamburger. His response was everything an author might hope for, and it was strikingly unlike the bemused response of Day Lewis and the dismissive response of Hart-Davis. "This is a book which couldn't have been written by an English writer," Hamburger wrote,

> and it is a pioneering work in more than one way. It has a savage economy; I think that is the best thing about it. And it is at once poetic and realistic, the nearest thing to an epic poem which it is possible to write at present. . . .
>
> It certainly ought to be available.

Despite his admiration for Sheila's novel, Hamburger's attempts to find an English publisher even after its publication in Canada were unsuccessful. England was not a place for her novel any more that it had been in her aunt's eyes a place for Sheila.

In a letter dated 8 August 1958, Jack McClelland wrote to Sheila to inform her McClelland & Stewart had decided to publish *The Double Hook*. It had been sent to them by Kay Mathers, a friend from Vancouver who was acting as Sheila's agent. At the time, Sheila was in Banff visiting Wilfred, who was teaching there for the summer at the School of Fine Arts. She had gone after house-sitting for the McLuhans. McClelland's was a bold step, in the teeth of what he described as "a general consensus of opinion that it is not a sound commercial publishing risk." "Before we published it," he wrote in 1960,

> we submitted the book to Knopf, Harcourt, Atlantic-Little Brown Doubleday, New Directions and Grove. . . . In each case it was rejected. We finally decided that this was all nonsense and published it here anyway.

In order to minimize their risk, he and his advisers proposed to publish the novel in the New Canadian Library, a series which had begun publishing in January 1958 under the editorship of Malcolm Ross. These were to be inexpensive paper-back reprints of Canadian "classics," but McClelland hoped to open the series to "new or contemporary writing" as well. In this way he felt the novel would receive distribution at a price which would put it, in his words, "within the reach of the undergraduate market who are likely to be most interested. . . ."

The format in which *The Double Hook* was published was not as McClelland had proposed. It appeared in May 1959 in both hard-cover and paper-cover editions, the latter costing $1.75, instead of the $1.00 he had proposed had it appeared in the New Canadian Library format. Before its publication, however, Sheila was involved in decisions about the book's format and design. McClelland had indicated in his first letter to her that he and his advisers were uncertain if they would include as a preface Salter's appreciation of the novel, written when he was attempting to assist Sheila to find a publisher, and before the novel had been finally revised. Although this was decided against, Sheila's desire to acknowledge Salter's support was echoed in "A Note from the Publisher" that prefaced the novel's first edition, in which McClelland spoke of the novelty—at least in English-language publishing—of a novel appearing for the first time in a paper-covered edition. He spoke of it as an innovation which suited the innovative nature of the work. He then quoted from Salter's essay, thus acknowledging him as *The Double Hook's* earliest admirer and commentator.

Unlike the publisher's note, the novel's epigraph has remained in all its reprintings and editions. Sheila was quick to insist that the choice of Kip's words (from Part Two, section 10) was not hers. She was somewhat uneasy about their seeming patness when separated from their context: "He doesn't know you can't catch the glory on a hook and hold on to it. That when you fish for the glory you catch the darkness too. That if you hook twice the glory you hook twice the fear." Behind her uneasiness lay the fact that she had proposed another, more arcane, epigraph when she had submitted the novel for publication. It was from the seventeenth-century German mystic philosopher Jakob Boehme's "Preface" to his *The High and Deep Searching of the Threefold Life of Man*, in an eighteenth-century translation:

> If we consider the great and wonderful Structure of the Heaven, and of the Earth, and observe their Motions, and contemplate the Manifold Operations of their Powers and Properties, and the great Variety of the Bodies of Creatures how they are hard and soft, gross and subtil, obscure and glistering, thick and clear, heavy and light, we then find the Twofold Origin of the manifestation of God, the Darkness and the Light, which out of all their Powers and Wonders have breathed forth and made themselves visible with the Firmament, Stars and Elements, and all the palpable creatures, wherein all Things, Life, and Death, Good and Evil, are together. This is the third Life (besides the two that are hid), and is called Time in the strife of vanity.

In a journal entry in November 1958, Sheila referred to a conversation with her editor. Conway Turton earned her respect in the fifties as Sybil Hutchinson had in the forties when Sheila had sent the manuscripts of *Deep Hollow Creek* and "the excerpt of the new novel" to McClelland & Stewart, and as Ellen Seligman would again in the nineties, when McClelland & Stewart finally published her first-written novel. "Conway called tonight," she wrote; "She agrees that the epigraph should not stand—Kip wrings from the Cariboo what Boehme found by staring into his pewter plate." (The 9th edition of the *Encyclopedia Britannica* describes how Boehme's fascination with "the luminous sheen, reflected from a common pewter dish . . . first . . . gave an intuitive turn to [his] meditations.") It is not clear with whom Ms. Turton agreed, whether with Sheila or with someone at McClelland & Stewart. Nor is it clear who first proposed Kip's words as an alternative to Boehme's. What is clear is that Sheila was consulted about the change, and at the time accepted it seemingly without reservation.

The book was designed by Frank Newfeld, and Sheila was unstinting in her praise of his achievement. In 1973, when she gave her first public reading from *The Double Hook*, she made a point of acknowledging publicly her admiration for the cover he had designed for its first edition. According to her account, Jack McClelland had wanted a photograph of her on the book's cover, and she had balked at this when Newfeld told her of the plan: "Here I had spent many years creating an artifact separate from me, something that is a world of its own and he wanted to put me on the cover." She gave him instead one of the two double hooks she had bought in Paris, and, in her words, "[h]e photographed the hook, enlarged it, and as he enlarged it, all the imperfections—the beautiful imperfections of hand work began to show." The photograph, or rather, photographs, for there are two double hooks in the design—one black and the other a rather lurid orange-red—are set against a background which suggests a space at once aquatic and skeletal. Newfeld had, according to Sheila, photographed the cross-section of a tibia bone ("Frank's tibia," as she liked to refer to it), and in a softer focus than was used for the harsh blow-ups of the hook. There is something of Eliot's "Down among the dead men" in the very striking image. "It gave me enormous pleasure when I saw the book in this cover," Sheila commented in 1973, "because it seemed like a co-creation. It was the first thing that happened after the writing of the book, that is, it had caused someone else to make something else which I thought was in itself very lovely."

"Lovely" seems an odd word to describe Newfeld's design, and it is not one she used at the time she first saw it. What struck her then was the jagged cruelty of the magnified hook, not its "beautiful imperfections." It was as if the designer had revealed a quality of the hook—and of her novel—which she had not recognized, or at least which she had not acknowledged. She had been told something about her book by its cover, and she came to respect, even to revere, Newfeld's co-creative comment. "My first real pleasure," she commented years later, "was that out of the book something else had been created." Subsequent covers for the novel never satisfied her, for they represented in her eyes tamperings with the text.

‽

The Double Hook was published on 16 May 1959, and the most notable first response to it appeared in that morning's *Globe and Mail.* Under the headline "Left Hook, Right Hook, KO!" the reviewer dismissed the novel as "obscure," "eccentric," and "difficult," illustrating her judgements with evidence of the difficulties she had had in reading it. She found "confusion" in the circumstances of old Mrs. Potter's death, and she assumed that Greta was James's wife not his sister. "Certainly, it cannot be described as entertainment in any sense of the word," she concluded. The feeble wit of the headline, the careless reading, and the rush to judgement have earned this review a place in our literary history, but this reviewer was not alone in being puzzled by the novel's terse and sometimes cryptic style. Its opening page, and in particular the account of James Potter murdering his mother, continue to elude readers who do not expect an action whose likelier place is the third or fifth act of a tragedy to occur on the first page of a Canadian novel. Another early reviewer, Philip Child, shrewdly recognized that the author in no sense miscalculated in opening her novel as she had. "In the third line of the narrative," he wrote, "James begins to murder his mother, and the act is completed in the fifth line. But the crude reality and the horror of that deed is veiled, as if to say that no act of violence is quite real until its consequences are seized by the mind and the spirit." The deed, in other words, is veiled by its obviousness.

Child's review, which appeared in the *Dalhousie Review*, was one of a number of responses from the academy. Himself a novelist as well as an academic (he was teaching in the English Department at UBC during Sheila's first year there as an undergraduate, and taught at the University of Toronto during her times there), Child was less concerned with sources and analogues than with the novel's shapeliness and with Sheila's handling of symbols. With an eerie rightness, he ended his review with the whisper of a reference to Jakob Boehme. Among early reviews, William Faulkner and his *As I Lay Dying* were frequently cited counterparts to Sheila and her work. Sheila was never entirely comfortable with this linkage, and she appreciated all the more D. F. Theall's judgement that *The Double Hook* "achieves the kind of universality that is characteristic of Joyce's *Ulysses* . . . rather than the regionalism of Faulkner."

Not the entire academy, however, was so enthusiastic. Earle Birney, who had read the manuscript for McClelland & Stewart, and who earlier had very likely been responsible for the publication of "Rough Answer," judged it, by Sheila's account, "clever but phony"—"a stylistic tour de force," he had written in his reader's report, "monotonous, self-conscious, artificial, and lacking in real fictional interest. . . . No I would not publish this novel." And a panel consisting of Robertson Davies, Northrop Frye, and Douglas Le Pan recommended that the 1959 Governor General's Award for fiction in English be given to Hugh MacLennan's *The Watch That Ends The Night*, not to *The Double Hook*.

A voice other than these would have the final word in this matter of the early reception of Sheila's first-published novel. In the Autumn 1959 issue of *Canadian Literature*, in an essay entitled "A Cat among the Falcons," Ethel Wilson wrote:

There is a moment, I think, within a novelist of any originality, whatever his country or his scope, when some sort of synthesis takes place over which he has only partial control. There is an incandescence, and from it meaning emerges, words appear, they take shape in their order, a fusion occurs. . . . I am sure that the very best writing in our country will result from such an incandescence which takes place in a prepared mind where forces meet. . . . We do not look to an earnest mediocrity amongst us but to this personal incandescence in a lighted mind in whatever manner it shows itself. I think it has shown here, lately, by Sheila Watson in the small book *The Double Hook*. Such work as that is individual, an emergence from within, not to be copied. We can recognize this phenomenon, great or in miniature, wherever we see it.

~ XII ~

1959 WAS SOMETHING OF AN ANNUS MIRABILIS FOR CANADIAN literature. It saw also the publication of Marie-Claire Blais's first novel, *La Belle Bête* (in English, *Mad Shadows*), and of Irving Layton's *Red Carpet for the Sun*, winner of that year's Governor General's Award for poetry in English. And it saw, as well as her novel, the publication of Sheila's "Antigone," the most fully realized of her own fictions in her view.

The story appeared in *The Tamarack Review* in the spring of 1959. That January she had noted in her journal: "Bob Weaver [one of its editors] called about the 'Antigone' which he says he will send back for a final inspection. It is a long time since I've read it. I hope I don't want to tear it to pieces." We know that she was revising the story during the winter of 1957, when her brother Bill's circumstances were preoccupying her, but an earlier version, entitled "Haemon's Story," was completed in Paris. In a journal entry from that time, she commented on a day of particular tension, when the flat on the rue Vignon seemed "too small for the number of presences in it," by evoking the memory of an equivalent sensation at a much earlier time: "I thought of crossing the Fraser river when every crack and knot hole in the bridge opened on terror." The narrator of "Antigone" speaks of the same river and the same bridge: "The old bridge still spans the river, but the cat-walk with its cracks and knot-holes, with its gap between planking and hand-rail has been torn down." Still its terrors remained. In this earlier version, and in an even earlier draft entitled "On the right bank of the river," about Antigone's question "How often can we cross the same river by a different bridge?" The narrator muses: "I want to tell her to look at a map of Paris."

As we know, Sheila had written the first version of this story in Calgary in November 1953, and with the title "The Funeral" she had sent it to Anne Angus. During the same period, and in the same places that she wrote and revised the novel—in which she claimed to have drawn upon her actual experience only to the extent of a beer-drinking parrot—during those times and in those places, she wrote and revised a story whose essence lies in the place of her own beginnings; "The accidents of one's place of birth or upbringing one simply has to include—since exclusion makes one a cut not a picked flower." Haemon, son of Creon and nephew of Oedipus, and hence cousin to Antigone and Ismene, is the story's narrator:

The habitable world, as I've said, is on the right bank of the river.

Here is the market with its market stalls—the coops of hens, the long-tongued geese, the haltered calf, the bearded goat, the shoving pigs, and the empty bodies of cows and sheep and rabbits hanging on iron hooks. My father's kingdom provides asylum in the suburbs. Near it are the convent, the churches, and the penitentiary. Above these on the hill the cemetery looks down on the people and on the river itself.

It is a world spread flat, tipped up into the sky so that men and women bend forward, walking as men walk when they board a ship at high tide. This is the world I feel with my feet. It is the world I see with my eyes.

In an age dominated by *Ulysses*, a story named "Antigone" could come as no surprise. But works whose titles announce their sources do not necessarily proceed according to the same, or even similar, methods. Joyce's Dublin may contain characters, places, and situations for which there are equivalents in Homer's epic; parallels, as Eliot called them. But Sheila's method was not to play the chaos of the contemporary world off against an assumed greater coherence of an antique mythical world, as Eliot said Joyce had done. Her Haemon, Creon, Ismene, and Antigone have become naturalized: they live in New Westminster. They are not visitors—or shades or echoes or possibilities—but only what they claim to be. Sheila's method here, as in the two "Theban" stories she had already published, "Brother Oedipus" and "The Black Farm," owes more to Chaucer than to Joyce. Her Oedipus is our contemporary as Chaucer's audience was encouraged to think of his Troilus as their contemporary.

During the academic year 1957–58, Etienne Gilson, who had established an Institute of Mediaeval Studies at St. Michael's College in the thirties, gave a series of lectures on mediaeval and renaissance attitudes to the classical world. He argued that mediaeval art and thought reflected a sense of continuity with the classical past, reflected in Thomas Aquinas's synthesis of Aristotelean philosophy with Christian doctrine, as well as in painters' and sculptors' and poets' tastes for mediaevalizing classical subjects. These latter, he maintained, had been for too long viewed as naively anachronistic, when in fact they signaled the continuing vitality of classical matter. The commonly held view that the renaissance saw the rebirth of the classics mistook discontinuity for authenticity. Gilson argued that attempts to see the classical past as it had been—togas and columns and all—represented its burial—in robes of purple, admittedly—rather than its rebirth. Listening to Gilson, I felt as if I were being led by Poe's Monsieur Dupin to the revelation that things are not always what they seem—or what they have been seen to be. "I do not believe in destruction, in evasion, in discontinuity," Sheila had written in Paris. Somewhat later she quoted—without comment—from a letter of Juan Gris: "One's resemblance to one's parents is always strong enough without putting on their clothes."

~

Gilson's lectures that year, which were public and attended by a few hundred each week, formed a graduate course in philosophy in which I was enrolled. I remember sharing with Sheila—or "Mrs. Watson" as she was to me then and for at least another year—my excitement at what I was hearing and seeing (Gilson made brilliant and extensive use of slides). This would have been over grilled cheese sandwiches and coffee and many cigarettes in the Honey Dew Restaurant, on the north side of Bloor Street, across from where Philosopher's Walk leads out of the campus. This became a Saturday ritual—the same lunch at the same Honey Dew. Here she spoke of her youth, of her convent days, of her days at UBC, of Dog Creek—secure in the knowledge that I was familiar with, or at least had some sense of these places. I, too, had been taught by the Madames of the Sacred Heart, in the parochial school that adjoined the convent where she had been a student, and I had been trained to serve, first benediction and then mass, by the nun who had once played at dolls or at skipping with the Little Flower. I had been taught to perform the sailor's hornpipe by Sheila's dancing teacher of St. Ann's days, Grace Goddard, and how to read Milton by her friend and former chairman Roy Daniells, and how-not-to-read Chaucer by Earle Birney. I was even familiar with the story of the abduction of Emma Keary by George Ward de Beck. It was part of my own family's history: a cousin of my mother had married into the family of the abductor. I knew of the priest who had baptized Sheila, of the shame attached to his unsanctioned marriage. He lived across the street from a school friend of mine, and we would spy him and his "wife" occasionally—very occasionally—emerging from behind the high fence that surrounded their house and garden. I had even been taken as a child by my parents to visit a neighbour who was a patient at Essondale. I knew nothing of Charlie Doherty then, of course, or of his achievements. I remember only the verandahs (or "airing porches," as Sheila referred to them), and people calling down from them, and sheets draped on trees.

Each of us knew a great deal of the other's ground, although I had known nothing of Sheila until we met in Toronto. Our friendship was rooted in what was familiar to us both. I can remember when we realized we both knew the opening lines of a particular hymn to St. Joseph, and carolled together—"Dear guardian of Mary, dear nurse of her child / Life's ways are full weary, the desert is wild; / Bleak sands are all round us, etc., etc."—then Sheila turning to me with, "That was my first experience of the waste land." She provided me with a sense of continuity between what I took to be provincial and parochial in my own background and a world which now included Gilson and McLuhan, and many others besides, not least among them Sheila herself. It was a world summed up for me then by the phrase "total relevance," which I came upon at that time thumbing through a book on Joyce in Britnell's Bookstore. It was exhilarating—and taxing, too—this discovery that nothing was unimportant, nothing was trivial—that "trivia" itself, as Jay Macpherson was later to point out to me, contained the junction of the three roads where Oedipus unwittingly met and slew his father.

By the time Sheila left Toronto, in the summer of 1961, I had begun to teach full time. I remember her advice when I was preparing for the first time a survey of literary criticism from "Plato to the present"—"Start with what you know and with what is most familiar to the students"—start, in short, with Eliot, not with the Greeks. I remember her on Chaucer's *Troilus and Criseyde,* which I was also teaching; her sense of this tragedy was of lovers who longed to find in their relationship, and in one another, an impossible permanency, a degree of stability which no human being could ever provide. I saw through her eyes—and beyond Criseyde extolling Troilus as her shield and wall—to the ruins of Troy. I learned from Sheila that while the search for total relevance, as Marshall had observed, can create the condition of paranoia, confronted by its possibility there can be no alternative but to be totally unflinching.

She spoke to me also of Wilfred, obliquely of their trials, and at great length of his gifts and his accomplishments. And she spoke to me of her own writing.

⌐

While her focus during these Toronto years was academic, in particular her work on Wyndham Lewis, and the publication of *The Double Hook* was unquestionably the most important event of this period, Sheila's journals and letters to Wilfred reveal the eagerness with which she planned to return to unfinished projects. "I want to get at my Orpheus and the Landscape," she wrote in the spring of 1961. Earlier there were asides in her journals: "For the Landscape" in the fall of 1958, and then a phrase, "The mentally unemployed;" "—a strand in the Landscape from Wednesday's conversation," she wrote in the spring of that year; and a year earlier, "I've been seeing how to expand the articulated crab image in the Landscape." It is not surprising that the university world of Toronto would provide her with materials for her academic satire. Still, distractions and her own slow meticulousness in writing allowed events to catch up with her anticipation of them, dooming foresight to appear like hindsight, and satire to seem documentary; in short, dooming her novel as she had envisioned it.

References to a reworking of the Orpheus and Eurydice story are tantalizing because she intended to relate Orpheus to the figure of Oedipus as he had appeared in "Brother Oedipus" and "The Black Farm." A journal entry in the spring of 1958 provides a glimpse of the way she hoped to associate these figures. She begins by quoting a phrase from Charles Lamb concerning Cervantes' Sancho Panza: "the contagion caught from a stronger mind infected—the madness at second-hand." She then reflected on associations that underlay what she hoped to write: "Some of this same relationship between Oedipus and Orpheus—the problem in the story that Eurydice comes alive too—. As Daedalus was infected by Oedipus so too Orpheus— Eurydice the ground in which the ideas take root to destruction." Her reference to the infection of Daedalus by Oedipus is to "The Black Farm," which was published in 1956. This passage is complicated, however, by the chronically unreliable nature of Sheila's spelling: Does Eurydice come alive "too" or "to"? A phrase from nowhere begins a journal entry a few months later: "an imagination which riots in an over-seeded garden." This is followed by, "So thinking of the Orpheus story which still waits." Later, in November 1959, she quotes a passage from Eliot's "Prufrock": "Though I have seen my head [grown slightly bald] / brought in upon a platter." "The John the Baptist image stays in my mind—. It can't be done until after the white horror of the Orpheus."

Whatever she hoped to achieve in linking Oedipus and Orpheus must remain a matter for speculation, as must the phrase "the white horror." And so must her fascination with Eliot's John the Baptist image, as well as a story she wanted to write about "old" Mr. Laing, the founder of the Laing Gallery in Toronto from whom she bought a drawing by Henry Moore of a seated woman, and about whom she observed, "His public has been educated for him—and has educated him. . . ." Again and again in later years, Sheila was to insist that she was not a writer, that she had simply written a novel. She proposed Wilfred as the writer, someone who wrote every day; someone who had answered to his calling as she had answered to no calling. While he was both disciplined and adventuresome, her sense of her own imagination rioting "in an over-seeded garden" inhibited her. Another image that recurs in her journals during this time—as it does at other times and in other contexts—testifies to her belief in the need for struggle and in its sometimes paradoxical outcome.

> It is as difficult to work as it is to hold a hot horse in the middle of the road. The stronger the bit and bridle, the stronger the hands, the more apt the horse is to fling about, to rear and paw since it has lit-tle hope of bolting. When the feeling imagination gets its head down and the bit between its teeth the game's up.

The uninhibited artist, as she observed, "rolls his eyes—pleads total ignorance—and proceeds to dogmatize on the quaint paradigm of his own fancy." On the other hand, she believed herself to be like one of those desert plants that have "built-in inhibitors" but no rain to trigger them. For she knew that drought could be generated by the will—or its absence—as well as by weather. "There is no conceit greater than the con-ceit of decorous and intelligent restraint—the snobbery of caution" was her gloss on the image of herself as an over-prepared desert plant.

⮌

As I look back on those years, my own memory—unlike Sheila's looking back on her convent-school days—only occasionally yields "a picture in the cubist style":

The harsh, livid yellow of French's mustard that inevitably sat like a jaundiced eye ball on any serving of the ham steak Sheila ordered at the restaurant-cum-con-venience store, now the lawn on the south side of University's Robarts Library, where she most frequently ate. And she inevitably ordered ham steak, but could never work her way around the offensive stain, nor could she ignore it. It had always to be removed by an always puzzled waitress.

Otherwise:

Her first reference to Ween Doherty, her mother, as "the sort of person who expects daffodils in January," and then that she was a reader of Robertson Davies's novels, and a reader, too, of Marshall, with whom in time she would correspond.

Sheila saying that Norah, her sister, did not know their father, and noting: "That is what separates us."

"I am your Turk"—a student whom she had not recognized, identifying him-self to Sheila.

"She is not one of us"—Sheila of a graduate student presuming to be one of a group whose existence I had not sensed until that moment.

Sheila at ease with Pat and John Brückmann, relishing John's bearish presence, his mediaeval learning and the warmth of his wisdom. "A symbol is not a fetish," he had insisted when Pat was not to be consoled about his misplacing (briefly) his wedding ring, and Sheila wove that truth into her memory.

Standing with friends under her porch on Sussex Avenue late one night, chanting "Rapunzel, Rapunzel, let down your golden hair," to draw her away from Lewis and her ironing—and Sheila's stern "You're all drunk. Come in."

An October dusk on lower Bay Street, after a matinee performance of Robertson Davies's *Love and Libel* at the Royal Alex, sitting on a curb with Sheila, smoking and waiting for the starlings gathered on wires and window ledges to erupt into their migratory flight.

I remember Sheila's friend Ruth Cohen and her House of Prints, down in the old village, on Gerrard Street near the General Hospital, and the Inuit prints and the engravings of the Mexican Guillermo Silva Santamaria, whose bird girls and flower sellers and mediaeval jousts seemed to embody so much of that time.

And I remember, too, standing with Sheila outside the small Russian Orthodox church on the street behind her Sussex Avenue apartment building, where the faithful had come for the funeral of the Grand Duchess Olga, the last of the Romanovs.

In March 1961, she wrote to Anne Angus: "I will miss Toronto. It is the only place really where I have felt completely at home."

⌒

During her last year in Toronto before returning to Edmonton in the fall of 1961, Sheila made two trips, occasioned by her work on Lewis. The first was to Ottawa to see a painting by Lewis in the collection of the National Gallery. The second trip, in the summer of 1961, was to England, to meet with Lewis's widow.

Early in December 1960, she went to Ottawa, in her words, "to check, if possible, any recorded detail about Lewis's part in the Canadian War Memorials scheme which had been inaugurated in 1917 by Lord Beaverbrook," and to see the large oil (10 x 11 feet), "A Canadian Gun Pit," that Lewis had painted in 1918, during his brief stint as a member of the Canadian War Records unit of the Canadian Corps in France. She met with the curator of the National War Museum, who told her that Lewis's painting, along with other pictures in the Beaverbrook collection, was stored in a warehouse in

Hull, across the river from the capital. In preparation for her brief trip, Sheila had contacted a friend from convent and university days in Vancouver, Bunny Pound, who now lived in Ottawa and who had for some time encouraged her to visit.

Ezra Pound's cousin, Bunny Pound, was also private secretary to the then-Prime Minister, John Diefenbaker. About a year earlier, Sheila had written to Wilfred that she had heard from her old friend for the first time "since she wrote for quotations for the PM." Pound had written this time in response to the publication of *The Double Hook*. Sheila's visit to Ottawa, as it happened, coincided with a political crisis, which required all-night sittings of the Commons and Pound's all but constant attendance upon a demanding boss. Sheila saw little of her friend, but thanks to the curator of the National War Museum she did manage to see the Lewis, and she wrote to Wilfred her first impressions: "It was like uncovering a Uccello battle piece—the colour is superb—I imagine it is the greatest of all the war pictures." In a journal entry dated 4 December 1960, she wrote at greater length:

> . . . the Lewis mural striking in its colour, and composition, but it was the colour which startled me so—the pink of the negro's shirt ranging into the lemon yellow of the hill behind the men—but under the net—the blue-bottle blue of the officer's shoes—the metallic blue of the man's face—the green box—. Can one speak of lines of colour as one does of lines of force—dynamic colour—in the sense that the force of the colour is contained in the canvas—the colour is used as a line is used not to astound the eye but to move it—.

Sheila and Bunny Pound together visited the National Gallery when her friend had a brief respite from her responsibilities. She saw again Paul Nash's *Solstice of the Sunflower*—"for purposes of my landscape," as she wrote to Wilfred—and she bought a print of it for him—"as a symbol," she said. They met a long-time political adversary of the Prime Minister outside the Gallery, and he joined them for coffee at a nearby Murrays Restaurant. Pound introduced Sheila to Paul Martin, a senior member of the then-official opposition, and, more relevant to Sheila's interests, a one-time acquaintance of Wyndham Lewis. Martin's constituency was located in Windsor, Ontario, where Lewis had lived for a time in the early forties. Then Martin had practiced law and had done some legal work for him. According to Martin, Lewis wanted to paint a portrait of Mrs. Martin, and they agreed on a price of six hundred dollars, "a quid pro quo for the legal services," as Sheila described it in her journal account of the meeting. Martin told her that his wife did not like Lewis, "man or ideas," and he felt that her dislike showed in the portrait. However, she had given him some money, over and above what had been agreed upon by her husband. Martin was concerned that Lewis had refused to sign the painting, and he wanted its authenticity established "for his children's sake." When Sheila offered to be of what assistance she could in this matter, Martin offered in return to write to Lord Beaverbrook on her behalf to learn more about his dealings with Lewis and the provenance of a Lewis painting, *The Mud Clinic*, in the collection of the Beaverbrook Gallery in Fredericton. Martin also offered to send Sheila a photograph of Lewis's portrait of his wife.

She acknowledged in print the authenticity of the Martin portrait in an essay published in *Canadian Literature* in 1968. Long before this, however, she had written to Mrs. Lewis asking her to verify that Lewis had painted the picture. In October 1961, Martin wrote to tell Sheila that Mrs. Lewis had indeed "sent, in legal form, corroboration of the fact that her distinguished husband had done a portrait of my wife." "I am sure we have you to thank," he accurately and graciously observed. By way of thanks, he again proposed writing to Beaverbrook, this time in the hope that his patronage might be extended to a biography of Lewis which Sheila was planning. In response to Martin's earlier inquiry about his relations with Lewis, Lord Beaverbrook had said that he had no dealings with him at all but knew that "his eccentricities interested very many." There is no evidence that he was interested in becoming a patron to a Lewis biographer—or that Sheila was interested in being patronized.

Wyndham Lewis, incidentally, was only one of a group of "British" painters (although he was born in Canada and continued to carry a Canadian passport) who had been transferred to the Canadian War Records unit in World War I, a situation managed by Beaverbrook, which resulted in the Canadian government's entitlement to works by Augustus John, David Bomberg, and Edward Wadsworth (whose *Dazzle-Ships in Drydock at Liverpool* Sheila also saw in the warehouse in Hull) among others, as well as to Lewis's *Gun Pit*. Lewis mused wryly—and rather condescendingly—about this situation in a passage in his autobiographical *Blasting and Bombardiering*, which Sheila quotes at the beginning of an essay on Lewis in Canada: "England's artists were being 'saved' by Canada of all countries, and by Lord Beaverbrook of all people. I mean of course that we do not associate the land of the 'Mounties' and Montcalm with the fine arts, and Lord Beaverbrook I imagined fully occupied making and unmaking Governments and Cabinets." What Lewis does not mention, although Sheila does, is that he had himself requested to be seconded from the Royal Garrison Artillery to the Canadian unit.

While she was in Ottawa, Sheila also spoke with the director of the National Gallery, the painter Charles Comfort, who had known Lewis during the time he and his wife had lived in Toronto. He told her that Lewis had rented a studio from Lawren Harris; otherwise he spoke guardedly of him: "a difficult man—however, an honour to know him—to have been associated with him." It was Sheila's lot to have been attracted to difficult men—and to have been willing to see them and their work shrewdly and sympathetically, free of many of the prejudices that blinded or at least impeded the judgements of others.

⌇

Sheila liked to remind me of a responsibility she had laid on me—in the mid-sixties I think it was—to set down the details of the time we spent in London in June 1961. She kept no journals while she was there, although she did write from London to Wilfred, and to Anne Angus from Toronto of her experiences there. Years later, she wrote an account of Lewis contacts she had made on this and on her earlier trip to Ottawa, an account which has not been published.

It was a short trip—only three weeks—but for Sheila it came at a crucial time, both the time she spent in London and the time in which that time occurred. The Toronto years, or, rather, her second Toronto sojourn, which had begun in the fall of 1956, were about to end. She was to return to Edmonton with Wilfred when she returned from England.

Marshall McLuhan had proposed this trip and the project—a biography of Wyndham Lewis—that occasioned it. Sheila had been working with Marshall on her doctoral thesis, and by the spring of 1961 she hoped that the thesis was near completion. McLuhan had remained close to Lewis's widow (Lewis himself had died early in 1957), and she intended Marshall to be her literary executor. His suggestion to her that Sheila undertake this project was partly in response to Mrs. Lewis's distress with Geoffrey Wagner's 1957 biography, *Wyndham Lewis, a Portrait of the Artist as The Enemy*. ("There is definite malice in his book," she had written to Sheila.) Walter Allen had considered a similar proposal of Mrs. Lewis, but after two years he had set it aside because of other commitments.

The prospect of Sheila returning to Edmonton lent a certain urgency to Marshall's plans—that and Mrs. Lewis's poor health. She had eagerly encouraged this plan and Sheila's part in it, offering every assistance, even proposing to meet her in Montreal in order to "settle all details and cut things as short as possible," as she wrote to her: "I could not come to Toronto. It would be too painful," she added, remembering the two and a half years—the *Self-Condemned* years—that she and Lewis had spent there in the forties.

Marshall's persistence and Mrs. Lewis's eagerness combined to create a kind of pressure which Sheila admitted to Wilfred left her feeling out of control: "The whole thing has snowballed with untoward speed." She was having to set aside work on her thesis and on what beyond the thesis beckoned her. It was in this context that she wrote to Wilfred, "I want to get at my Orpheus and the Landscape."

A thesis still in process, fictions long mulled over and worked on, and a biography as a looming responsibility—these were what Sheila was juggling in June 1961. When she set off for London, she intended to take the manuscript of "Landscape" to work on, but she could not find it; not that London would have provided her with any more time to work on her novel than it did for journal writing. But she did take with her a typescript of Wilfred's first full-length play, *Cockcrow and the Gulls*, hoping to find a theatrical producer in London interested in staging it.

Sheila's flight on 3 June was cancelled because of fog. She re-booked on the flight I was taking, returning to London for a second summer of work on my own thesis. It was a night flight, one that very soon saw day break. I remember we were having a gin and tonic when the first sign of morning unexpectedly appeared. Sheila pointed in surprise to the light, and in so doing she managed to tip her glass into her handbag, which was at her feet. There ensued much drying of its contents, and so the episode ended, until we arrived at Immigration at Heathrow. When she reached for her passport she produced instead the wedge of lemon from the upturned drink. It was a small bit of comedy but it was a prologue of sorts—that and our noticing on the bus ride into London Hogarth's house close by the Cherry Blossom Shoe Polish factory.

Norman Endicott had recommended to Sheila a small hotel near Russell Square where he and Betty had stayed: the Coram House Hotel. My own plans to return to my digs of the previous summer depended upon my making contact with a peripatetic and rather half-hearted landlord. Meanwhile, I had made plans to take a week's holiday in Ireland. But first I wanted to see Sheila settled. And so we went round to the Coram House Hotel.

The hotel was a converted Georgian row-house which stood on the southwest corner of Coram and Marchmont streets. The bell was answered by an ingratiating gentleman from Bolivia, who turned out to be the hotel's manager. His name was Raoul Calvamontes, and, as we were to discover, he held a doctorate in mediaeval philosophy from a Spanish university, and he had been for a time Foreign Minister of Bolivia.

Any friends of the Endicotts were friends of Coram House. Yes, they could accommodate Mrs. Watson. But what about the young gentleman? I assured him that I was going on that evening's boat train to Dublin for a week. And when you return? I confessed that my plans were as uncertain as last year's landlord. You must come here and we will take care of you.

When I did return and was unsuccessful in rousing my sometime landlord, I went back to Coram Street, where Raoul greeted me, again most cordially. There were no rooms available in the hotel but the owner had a flat a half block away on Marchmont Street where "overflow" was housed. Mrs. Watson had already been moved there and a room awaited me.

The Coram House Hotel was owned by Stephen Heathcote, a Londoner of great grace and charm: a would-be painter, a rather haphazard businessman, a person with a quiet though fierce sense of fairness and justice. Raoul was only the most distinguished emigré in his employ. Stephen was well connected: he appeared to have access always to tickets for Royal Garden Parties or performances at Glyndebourne or Stratford, and he had a nephew in the Guards. Stephen was one of those Englishmen who sits comfortably at the centre of his nation's being—easily parodied, even more easily admired.

His flat was at the top of four flights of stairs. Its east windows looked out across chimney pots to the figure of Justice atop Old Bailey and the dome of St. Paul's. Its west side hung over the business of Marchmont Street. The flat was not especially spacious but it had many rooms. There was a lounge and there were four bedrooms as well as a kitchen and bathroom. These all led off a hallway which ran in a north-south direction. Both Stephen and Raoul occupied the flat, along with any "overflow" from the hotel: Sheila and I at first, and, after Sheila's departure, a young Spanish professor and his very pregnant wife.

The Berlin Wall had gone up in 1961, and Yuri Gagarin had been the first man to travel in space, followed only recently by the American Alan Shepard. Gagarin visited London that June, the star and centrepiece of a Russian trade exhibition being held at the Earlscourt Olympia. I can remember one evening in the lounge at Marchmont Street there was talk of the need to send a poet and a painter into space in order to give us words and images worthy of the experience. I remember the uneasiness of two friends of Stephen and Raoul, second secretaries at the United States Embassy in its then-new quarters in Grosvenor Square, who were not entirely happy about London's infatuation with Russian achievements. Like Stephen, these women embodied what was most guileless and what was most endearing in their national character. One of them, who later married Stephen and became us Consul on Malta, had an elegant Russian wolfhound she had named Edith Sitwell. We learned from them the dimensions of the sculpted eagle that perched over the entrance to the new American Embassy. Sheila was fascinated by them, as they were, I think, puzzled by her. It was a study in contrasts: the prosperous, comely, and very innocent American career women; and the small, quiet, intense Canadian who knew that birth had done away with her innocence.

Sheila had been in telephone contact with Mrs. Lewis while I was in Ireland. She asked me to go with her to her Lancaster Gate flat. Anne Lewis, or "Froanna" as she was commonly referred to, was cordial, if somewhat distracted. She was like someone who carries on energetic conversations with herself, and when others appear continues in much the same vein. Her obsession with Lewis's legacy and his reputation was like some awful inheritance. She spoke of him as "Lewis," as if he were a proper noun rather than a person. She spoke of those many who continued to malign him, but also of kindnesses—of T. S. Eliot at the end of an evening visit, tapping her on the arm and saying of *The Human Age*, "It's a great book, a great book," and of his coming when Lewis died, resting his hand on hers and assuring her that he would take care of her. She spoke of her own attempts to buy as many of Lewis's pictures as she could, but her means were very limited and, as she had written to Sheila, "my husband's work is rising considerably over here."

Froanna's commitment to Lewis's memory and the very complicated nature of the relations among his survivors made Sheila uneasy about undertaking a biography commissioned by any of the parties involved. Lewis remained as controversial and thorny in death as he had been in life. A son and daughter, children of Iris Barry (whose portrait by Lewis was hanging in Froanna's bedroom), made claims upon their father's estate, questioning whether he and Froanna had ever actually been married. Sheila tested the waters by asking her when and where their marriage had taken place. In a move which left both of us feeling uneasy, we went to Somerset House, then the repository of records of births, deaths, and marriages in Great Britain, to check her memory, her word. We found no record of the marriage she had described taking place in Britain on or near the time she had indicated. Sheila felt it impossible to move independent of Mrs. Lewis given that Marshall had introduced her as sympathetic to her interests. Somerset House was the place where, if not in fact then at least in spirit, Sheila abandoned plans to write a biography of Wyndham Lewis.

Her relations with Froanna remained cordial, however. Mrs. Lewis's suggestions about people and places to be sought out and consulted proved helpful to Sheila, especially given her interest in Lewis's paintings and drawings. We saw the Lewis holdings at the Victoria and Albert, and at the Marlborough, Brook Street, and Zwemmer Galleries. At the Leicester Galleries, Sheila bought three of his drawings—*Study of a Girl, Nude Study,* and *A Darts Player*—and a fourth, *Woman seated on a couch,* elsewhere. As well, Mrs. Lewis entrusted to her two portraits of friends of the McLuhans that Lewis had in error taken back to England from Canada. Sheila undertook to deliver these. Froanna, in turn, undertook to authenticate Lewis's unsigned portrait of Paul Martin's wife.

Shortly after her return to Toronto from London, Sheila wrote to Anne Angus:

> I had an interesting three weeks—and crowded ones in London arranging with Mrs. Lewis about the biography—hunting out Lewis pictures in the public and private galleries—talking to people who had known Lewis or had business dealings with him. The most interesting person of all was Anton Zwemmer who spent a great deal of time simply talking—although he found catalogues of Lewis exhibitions for me and was otherwise very helpful. I saw Sir John Rothenstein at the Tate, Charles Handley-Reid who made a collection of Lewis pictures for Faber, Father Martin Darcy, Mr. Bridson of the BBC and Mr. White of Methuens.
>
> Somehow, too, I managed to see *The Blacks* at the Royal Court, Sartre's *Altona* and the *Andersonville Trial* at the Mermaid—to go to a party at John Wain's at Blackheath where I met V.S. Pritchett who gossiped about Lewis—And to spend a day with my friend Connie Dyson at a C17 cottage she's just bought at Hazelmere.

Among those whom Sheila was unable to see on this trip were T. S. Eliot, who was out of London, and Ezra Pound. She had cabled Pound to Rapallo, prepared to go there if he would see her. His wife, Dorothy, replied by cable that he was not to be seen.

During much of this time I was about my own business, in Ireland or in the Reading Room at the British Museum. I did attend the plays with Sheila and accompanied her to galleries and to her meeting with Sir John Rothenstein. Otherwise, on evenings at Marchmont Street I heard of her comings and goings. I remember her speaking of the Jesuit Father Darcy gesturing floatingly, as if the souls in his care were fragile and thrilling, to be released as butterflies on the Day of Judgement. I remember her accounts of Pritchett on Lewis's son, who said of his father, "I never knew the man," and of Sheila's being driven back as far as Chelsea from Blackheath and John Wain's party in a sporty little convertible with its top down by a very self-assured Muriel Spark, who boasted of having just been "paper-backed." Sheila, as she told me, suppressed the temptation to tell her that her novel, published just two years earlier, had come into the world "paper-backed."

When I recall events of those weeks, I recall those events in which Sheila figured, and what I took to be our mutual responses to them. But I also recall her silences, the remoteness that came over her like a veil, when she became absorbed by a picture or a memory, or in some thought or imagining. I had seen this often before.

Sheila had arranged to see Sir John Rothenstein, then curator of the Tate Gallery and sometime friend of Lewis. She hoped to consult him in this capacity, at the same time she hoped to see the Tate's holdings of Lewis. She had found, as she noted later, that "all the Lewis works in the Tate collection which [she] wanted to see had been taken from the public galleries and stored in the basement as the result of pressure" brought on Rothenstein by Lewis's enemies. She had asked me to go along with her, so that I might have the opportunity to see Lewises that were not often available to the public. A guard did take us to the basement to see these.

The Tate had just opened a large retrospective exhibition of Picasso's career. The press had made much of the scale of the exhibition, and of the fact that nothing as yet mounted in France—or anywhere else, for that matter—could match it. While we chatted with Sir John before he and Sheila settled down to talk of Lewis, I had made some comment about the media's accounts of the Queen opening the exhibition. Sir John nodded, and then went on to tell us that on the day of the opening, after the ceremonies had taken place and the royal party had departed, he had received a telephone call from Buckingham Palace requesting that Her Majesty be allowed to return to the Tate that evening after it had closed, in order to view the pictures—unhindered by crowds and ceremony.

Sir John agreed to this, of course, and welcomed her when she arrived, attended only by a driver. He was prepared to accompany her through the galleries, but Her Majesty signaled her wish to be left alone. And so he retired to his office. And when what seemed to him an appropriate length of time had elapsed, he made his way in search of his Sovereign Lady.

He found her, seated with her back to him, absorbed by Picasso's jagged, pained, and painful *Weeping Woman*. He withdrew to his office.

The encounter of Elizabeth II with Picasso's epitome of female grief touched Sheila, and although she left no account of it, traces of her response might be found in Wilfred's number-grid poem "re elizabeth the second of england as leader of the peoples of the commonwealth," in an ex-patriot Englishman's reluctant admission:

4 I

was 5 haunted

by   6 the

sad 7 face

of   8 this

9 woman

who 1 is

   my 2 sovereign

mistress 3 and

my 9 king

Two times in particular remain with me from those weeks. One Saturday Sheila wanted to walk in the Notting Hill area, which had been a haunt of Lewis and of many of his colleagues. We checked out where Eliot and Pound had met, in Kensington Close, where Ford Madox Ford had lived on Campden Hill Road, and north of Kensington Gardens where Lewis had had his studio. It was a very warm day, and when time came for lunch we stopped at a pub—on Moscow Street I think it was. With our lunch we had a couple of gins and tonics, and continued then to walk along the northern perimeter of the Gardens—walking and talking—so oblivious to the passing of time and unaccustomed to the deceptiveness of London's long June days that we discovered ourselves still in the Gardens after they had been closed and the gates locked. When we had found a gatekeeper to release us, we continued along Bayswater to Marble Arch where I knew there was a Lyons Corner House. It was evening already and we hadn't eaten since lunch and we were still light-headed from the warmth of the day, from the aftermath of the gin, and from a slightly dizzy sense of the occasion, which included the pleasure of playing truant from our separate responsibilities. No sooner were we seated in Lyons than Sheila said that she felt faint and began to look about desperately for the Ladies. I spotted it, helped her up and propelled her in its direction. To my horror I saw her tilt into the path of a waitress, who, absorbed by the task of carrying a tray filled with glasses of orange squash, did not see her.

So single-minded was her pursuit of the Ladies that I don't think Sheila had any sense of what she had occasioned. She was still there long after the squash and the broken glass had been mopped up and so I asked the hostess to check on her. She found her in a dead faint, stretched out on the tile floor. When she had recovered sufficiently and declined offers of food or any further assistance, I took her by cab back to Marchmont Street.

The episode, I suppose, is no more significant than the lemon peel in her handbag. Sheila was given to fainting spells, and she had a fairly low tolerance for alcohol. But these are metabolic matters, for the doctor or the geneticist to speculate about. As in any shared experience in which the roles of witnessed and witness are as clearly defined as they were here, Sheila wanted to be reminded of the episode— as much for the sake of that time in London—as it became for her an example of how humiliating and unfunny pratfalls are. A banana peel on Bloor Street—her fantasy cause for an indecorous death—really signified for her a mortifying end and not a comic one.

Sheila was as much a witness as I to the other time that remains so vividly with me. It involved Marchmont Street and its circle. It was an evening, a buffet supper in honour of the Vice-President of Bolivia, who was stopping in London on his way home from an official visit to China. It was 1961, and Mao's China was already as mysterious and inaccessible as eastern Europe was fast becoming. There had been changes in Bolivia as well. The political party with which Raoul had been associated had returned to power, and most amiable relations had been established between the Bolivian Embassy in Eaton Square and Marchmont Street. Hence this particular evening.

The party included, as well as the Vice-President, the Bolivian Ambassador and his wife, the two second secretaries from the American Embassy, Eva Mae and Bea, Stephen and Raoul, of course, and Sheila and me. It was the curiosity of all of us about China that started the evening's conversation, that and the Peony brand cigarettes the Vice-President had brought from China and which many of us (including Sheila) happily smoked. He told us of an offer the Chinese government had made to build a tin refinery in Bolivia, a country which so far had no facilities for processing its main natural resource. Jobs that should have been available locally were taken by workers in England and the United States, where the tin was shipped to be refined. He spoke also of the shrewdness of the Chinese in not stamping his passport; stamping instead a slip of paper which he could remove when he passed through New York, whose customs officers would have taken a dim view of any traveller—even a diplomatic traveller—who had visited China. Then there was talk of

Stephen's portrait of the Ambassador's wife, which was soon to be unveiled at a reception at the Embassy, and of his hopes that a small drawing by Picasso which he had consigned to Sotheby's would profit from the interest in the painter that had gripped London and that its sale would help him pay the hotel's bills. (It didn't.) There was talk of the times and of the interests of the guests, and Sheila, as was always true of her, chameleon-like assumed the colour and moved with the rhythm of each new turn in the conversation.

When we had finished dining and the table had been cleared and folded, Raoul brought out some recordings of Andean music. The Ambassador's wife and the Vice-President moved to the centre of the lounge with handkerchiefs in their hands and started to dance a dance of flirtation in which the only contact between the dancers was provided by the handkerchiefs, which linked them, at first tentatively and modestly, but as the dance proceeded, with increasing wryness and elegance and suggestiveness. There was something remote yet casual about their absorption in the dance: they were dancing for their own pleasure, but also for the pleasure of all of us. It seemed to me then, as it seems to me still, that in those moments roots were struck that would attach all of us to that place and to that time.

We were aliens—all save Stephen, of course, our host. At about the time that Sheila was preparing to return to Toronto, a situation developed involving one of the maids who cared for the flat and the hotel. There were two maids, both Portuguese. The older of the two, Marie Esperanza, had lived for some years in England. She was either a widow or separated from her husband—I'm not certain which—and she had a married son who worked at the Nuffield Works in Oxford. Her English was halting but accurate. The other, Angelina, was much younger. She was one of those refugees who seemed mysteriously to find their way to Coram House and to Stephen's protection. She had come within the year from Portugal as an au pair to a family who then abused her. She spoke no English but, forced to her limits by hunger and humiliation, she left them without notice and, like some Dickensian waif, wandered the streets of London until, providentially, she found herself at the door of Coram House Hotel. Stephen took her in and gave her food and board and a job. When her former employers tracked her down, he went to court on her behalf and secured her release from whatever contract she had with them.

Angelina had a husband in Portugal and a young child. She had hoped that once she had established herself in England she could then sponsor her family to join her. It was not an unusual situation at that time. Her husband and child were living with his parents. Only a day or two before Sheila's departure, Angelina appeared one morning in the flat, red-eyed and distraught. Marie Esperanza explained to us that Angelina had received a letter from her husband advising her that their bed, which he had taken with him to his parents' home, was about to be sold. His parents insisted upon it. The bed had come from Angelina's family as a legacy not as a gift. She had no choice but to return to Portugal to save their bed, despite the fact that such a move would surely jeopardize their attempts to settle in England.

If my memory serves me correctly, Angelina and Sheila left London on the same day. But that was forty years ago, and time like distance has a way of allowing events and people to appear more closely related than they might actually have been at the time.

⌐

During Sheila's stay in London—on 15 June to be precise—Wilfred read a paper to the Humanities Association of Canada at its annual meeting, held that year in Montreal. Its title was "Interstructuralization in Drama and the Other Arts." Among those who heard it was Marshall McLuhan, who also gave a paper, on "The Humanities in the Electric Age," at the same meeting. McLuhan was very taken with Wilfred's paper, and published a version of it in *Explorations*. Wilfred recalled

*Sheila in London in June 1961 with—
on the left—Stephen Heathcote, the owner
of the Coram House Hotel.*

Marshall's presentation as "dazzling—instant theatre, in Hamlet's sense . . . it gave to the age its 'form and pressure.'" He came to believe that their papers that June "were a sort of blueprint for *From Cliché to Archetype*," their joint work that was to preoccupy Wilfred throughout much of this decade.

This was not their first meeting. There had been their chance meeting in the forties, after attending a play at Hart House. And Wilfred had spent the summer of 1959 in Toronto with Sheila, when they had dined with the McLuhans on at least one occasion.

Their meeting in 1961 in Montreal was repeated during that summer, as

Wilfred was en route to Toronto, where he stayed in Sheila's flat until her return from London. They then vacated the flat and spent the rest of the summer—until their departure for Edmonton—in the house of Norman and Betty Endicott, who were spending their summer in Vancouver. It was a resting place before the journey west, providing Sheila with the opportunity to finish "the first complete draft of the thesis," and providing them both presumably with time to try to recover what had not been irreparably damaged by years of pains inflicted and pains suffered.

~ XIII ~

IN ANTICIPATION OF SHEILA'S RETURN TO EDMONTON, WILFRED had rented a house on 117th Street, which belonged to colleagues who were on leave for the year. It was within walking distance of the University, a condition which Sheila—a non-driver—had set: "to leave you completely free of me as a daily chore." The previous Christmas, on a visit to Edmonton, she had met with the then Head of the English Department, Professor J. T. Jones, who had offered her a one-year renewable appointment with the Department at the rank of Assistant Professor. She was pleased by the offer, and even by its provisional nature. In accepting it, as she confided to Anne Angus, "I told the President . . . that I would not want to stay in the Dept if my being there created any sort of tension." What Sheila had in mind was the so-called "nepotism rule," according to which married couples were not permitted to hold full-time appointments in the same department at the same time, a rule which was then widely observed in Canadian universities. Sheila and Wilfred were to be the exceptions in their Department. It was not because she came as the author of a notable novel or as a teacher of some experience and distinction that Sheila found herself a pioneer in challenging the nepotism rule. It was because, at fifty-one, she was judged to be past child-bearing. Whatever the nuances of the situation, Sheila and Wilfred were the first married couple to hold full-time as distinct from part-time appointments in the Department of English at the University of Alberta. They—and especially Sheila—took this status seriously. They co-existed in the Department as two professionals, not as a couple. Colleagues thought twice before speaking of "the Watsons" or addressing a letter or card to them as "Dr. and Mrs. Wilfred Watson." Sheila would not think of picking up Wilfred's mail at the Department, nor he, hers.

Sheila was no stranger to the city when she moved to Edmonton in the late summer of 1961. She and Wilfred had lived there during the academic year 1954–55, after Wilfred had moved from Calgary College to the main campus of the University. Sheila had returned occasionally at Christmas to Edmonton during her years in Toronto. On one such occasion, in a letter to Anne Angus dated 23 December 1958, she described her trip west by train with characteristic precision and vividness:

> The train was almost empty except for a handful of southern
> Alberta farmers and their wives. They had gone on a package tour
> to the Winter Fair [The Royal Winter Fair held annually in
> Toronto]. The men talked about toad flax and saw thistle—about

the government and the Hutterites. One complained that 30,000 bushels of stored wheat stood between him and his son. "I can't give him the farm," he said, "and leave my grain laying there."

I must have come just after a thaw because the prairie was like a limoges plate—white and polished and etched with the yellow of cut grain. Between Tako and Unity [towns in Saskatchewan]—blue frozen ponds. Across the whole stretch of land pits of willows burning to purple at the tips of the branches.

Winter arrived early in Edmonton in 1961. Their sublet came with a large garden, and Sheila described herself "peering into other people's gardens to see which flowers are annuals, which perennials," so that she would know which bulbs to pull and which to bed against the cold. And cold it was! "The snow rises like a flood," she wrote in her journal that February. "It seems to pile up from under . . . 20 below this morning." And a few days later: "Still 20 below and the wind twisting the snow into Alpine shapes." Her first winter back in Edmonton was the coldest the city had known since 1885. Her schedule required her to teach six days a week, and although the closeness of their house to the campus reduced the strain of "coming & going," it could not altogether remove it.

Sheila entered full time into the English Department at a time of great change; her own presence, a symptom of that change. There was the new Chairman, Henry Kreisel, whom she knew from previous experience to be "amiable and flexible." And Kreisel had to deal with two former Chairs still active in the department and attending meetings. He had also to deal with the planned introduction of a full-scale graduate program and with the presence of half a dozen new appointments, including Sheila, of course. The sixties were to be an enormously important decade in the history of English studies at the University of Alberta, and Sheila had a part to play in this history.

When term began that first year, Sheila was assigned two freshman courses and the poetry section of a course in modern British literature. The prose section of this last course was taught by Kreisel. Her first year was a busy one. "I have been entertaining all our old friends and some of the young people," she wrote to Anne Angus: "—usually dinner. It's a chore in a way but I concentrate on simplicity." In the second term, when the University's Studio Theatre was preparing a production of Wilfred's *Cockcrow and the Gulls*, rehearsals, which Wilfred always attended, often ended with wine and coffee and food in Sheila and Wilfred's living room.

As a part of the sublet, "an amiable German girl called Irma" came in every second week to clean for them. Irma Sommerfeld was only one of the people who entered their lives in the course of this year who was to remain a part of their lives. Young and intelligent, she had fled to the west from eastern Europe, and had ended up sewing zippers into blue jeans in a factory in Edmonton before she turned to housework. Perhaps because of his own history, Wilfred felt that Irma deserved an opportunity for further education. He proposed that she attend the University at his expense. She appreciated the generosity of the offer, and the spirit in which it was made, but increasing obligations and her own uncertainty about her command of English led her to refuse it. Wilfred's response was startling, although not entirely uncharacteristic. The next time she came, he gave her a small piece of pottery, saying simply, "This—like you—is useless."

Sheila had sent Anne Angus a small pot at Christmas, "made," as she wrote, "by Pauline Boote who is we think one of the simplest yet most exciting 'potters' whose work we've seen." Boote, whose husband taught in the Economics Department at the University, became a close friend to both Sheila and Wilfred. It was in a pot of her making that the third of Sheila's remains given over to the Fraser River would be contained.

Another of Sheila's new friends from that year was the young woman with whom she shared an office and the "honour" of together constituting the second female appointment in the history of the department. Diane Lane joined it in this same year. A graduate of the University of Western Ontario and a doctoral candidate at the University of London, she was starting her teaching career as Sheila was returning full time to hers. Along their corridor was the office of a young man who had come to Edmonton a year earlier, whom Sheila had known as a graduate student in Toronto. They had been together in Harold Wilson's Chaucer course. Frank Bessai, a mediaevalist, had grown up on a farm in Saskatchewan; "the bee-keeper from Saskatchewan," as Sheila fondly referred to him. During her first year, he haunted her office, less in search of her company and conversation, as it turned out, than of the company and attention of her office mate. Within two years, Diane Lane and Frank Bessai had married, and they and their family became an important part of Sheila's life in Edmonton and after.

Diane Bessai's memories of their—hers and Sheila's—early years in Edmonton include instances of Sheila's warmth and a strong sense of her protectiveness where Wilfred's work and privacy were concerned. With almost obsessive solicitousness, she adapted the routine of the house to his preferences and movements. Sheila sensed that in returning to Edmonton after a separation of five years she was trespassing upon what was essentially Wilfred's world. Years later, when they would move from Edmonton to Nanaimo, she would be drawn—reluctantly, as we shall see—into a world shaped by his memory, his imagination, and his will. Still she managed to make a space for herself wherever she found herself—in Dog Creek or Powell River or Paris, for example—or, perhaps more accurately, she found herself wherever circumstances placed her.

The extent to which this was Wilfred's world is not difficult to imagine. He had lived and taught in Edmonton for six years when Sheila joined him. At first even her status at the University existed by virtue of his position. This was a matter of social history, however, which reflected his world although not necessarily his views. Wilfred wrote and worked at home, and it was there that over the years he had met groups gathered for informal sessions on creative writing. Diane Bessai recalls in her first year joining one or two of these sessions held in Wilfred and Sheila's living room. The group in this instance consisted of some students and a handful of people from the community—all women as Diane remembers—who had come together under Wilfred's eye to consider and to experiment with poetry and drama. And then at rehearsal time, there were the comings and goings of the cast and crew of Wilfred's play. It would be a mistake to assume that Sheila was merely a victim of Wilfred's set ways or of his thoughtlessness. When occasionally she put herself in a self-sacrificing way, she was liable to discover that what she had assumed about his preferences was wrong. It was years before she realized that preparing meals was a task he coveted, not something he assumed to be her responsibility.

In the winter–spring of 1961, Wilfred's niece, Joan Dunning, the only daughter of his sister Doreen, had asked her uncle if she might come to live with them the next fall and attend university in Edmonton. She was just completing high school at a girls school, St. Margaret's, in Victoria. Joan had carried on lively correspondences with both Sheila in Toronto and Wilfred in Edmonton, and she was clearly intrigued by the prospect of living in a household very different from the one in which she had grown up. Sheila pointed out to Wilfred that British Columbia matriculation would not admit his niece to the University of Alberta, that she would have to repeat grade twelve in Edmonton before being eligible to enter the University there.

They discussed this matter at some length in letters written during the winter–spring of that year, while Sheila was still in Toronto. "Decide as you think best" was her advice. Although she was concerned about taking on such a responsibility when she and Wilfred would be adjusting to life together after a five-year separation, Sheila understood her niece's desires and was aware of benefits for her of such a move: "she will at least not move from one provinciality to another without a third term," she wrote. In this same letter Sheila commented on the recent death of her great-uncle, Henry Doyle, who with Aunt Fan had entertained her as a child at their home at Chewasin Beach, where she had enjoyed what she recalled as "careless days" of sun and water and "composing in the tree." "Perhaps Joan will find some pleasure in her aunts and uncles too," she reflected.

Joan did in fact come shortly after their arrival from Toronto, but her stay was short-lived. In December she returned to the coast.

By and large, the separateness Sheila and Wilfred observed and insisted upon in their professional lives marked their domestic lives as well. They had lived apart for five years, had managed their own spaces, and when they came together they did not pool their resources—except to purchase their house on Windsor Road, which they did in the second year after Sheila's return—so much as divide household duties and expenses with a kind of ritualized strictness and consistency. They respected each other's sphere of social as well as domestic responsibilities. Carl Bessai remembers as a boy calling on "Auntie" Sheila with one of his brothers, the door being answered by "Uncle" Wilfred, who would linger only very briefly before resigning the occasion to Sheila and disappearing into his own concerns. I recall being invited by Wilfred in the early seventies to act as external examiner for a doctoral thesis which he had supervised. I was there as his guest, a fact that was borne in upon me less at his insistence than by Sheila's all-but absence. I caught traces of her—a sound in the kitchen, a face in a doorway, a presence in a chair. She had become a part of his ground, as he on similar occasions became a part of hers.

While their routines acknowledged their separate spheres, at the same time they bound Sheila and Wilfred together in sustaining their household and making it workable. Like some latter-day Wordsworth, Sheila found in repeated acts and ordinary objects beauty and inner grace that familiarity and repetition too often obscure. Their insistence on making lunch when Irma came to clean—Wilfred, always the main course, and Sheila, the dessert—and on sharing the meal with her, made a ritual of routine, as younger friends who have sought to emulate them can testify. For each of their birthdays she baked and delivered chocolate cakes to Diane Bessai and her sons so long as she lived in Edmonton: "I'm coming across the park," was her familiar signal. A recipe provided an identity when years later a friend, Leslie Sanders, became, as if by a kind of baptism, forever Poppy Seed, for a cake she had baked for Sheila. Tea towels had histories and lineages: "They're from China" was as much a comment on their background as on their quality.

Despite Sheila's memory in Paris of "wanting to do the traditional family things" by painting Easter eggs during their time at UBC, she and Wilfred paid little attention to familiar cultural rituals: running up the flag, or decorating a Christmas tree, turkey dinners or Easter lilies or poppies. They could have respect for the occasions that gave rise to such rituals, but they had little patience with their reduction to what they—and especially Wilfred—deemed to be garish and inauthentic routine. Sheila's instincts in her daily life as in her art were to value facts and occasions, those impulses that lie behind cumbersome accretions that can too easily obscure what they are intended to memorialize. In *The Double Hook*, published just two years before her return to Edmonton, Felix Prosper savours a cup of coffee, "floating," as the narrator observes, "in content of being." The brewing of the coffee is described in some detail as is the "knobbed glass" cup he uses, but readers are warned not to see the occasion for what it is not. "The cup which Angel had put into his hand, her bitter going, he'd left untouched. Left standing. A something set down. No constraint to make him drink. No struggle against the drinking. No let-it-pass. No it-is-done. Simply redeemed. Claiming before death a share of his inheritance." Felix's way is not the way of Gethsemane and of Calvary. His is, as his name suggests, a more fortunate, a homelier way.

⌒

The world of "knobbed glass" cups of coffee seems closer to the world of tea towels and chocolate cakes than to the scripturally-charged world of cups of bitterness. But sometimes it is difficult to distinguish "earth rising to heaven" from "heaven descending"—or nature "doing her best" from a miracle. In Paris, five years before her return to Edmonton, Sheila had reflected on her marriage to Wilfred in a journal entry already quoted. She used the phrase "without more than natural grace" to describe the status of the vows they had exchanged that December day in 1941 in the Vancouver Court House. Because it had been a civil and not a religious ceremony, there had been no nuptial blessing, only the marriage contract. "There is marriage and there is a marriage contract," she wrote; "the contract is material and temporal—Marriage itself is an act of faith and consequently an act of perfect love—or inversely and perhaps more truly an act of perfect love consequently an act of faith." She continued: "The law does not make marriage—It protects or rather tries to protect often bunglingly and inadequately in a temporal world something which is not temporal, although rooted in beginning as human life. . . ."

Her second thoughts about the origins of marriage itself—that "perhaps more truly" it is love that precedes and begets faith and not the other way round—make of her phrase "without more than natural grace" an acknowledgment of the reality and the validity of their marriage rather than a sign of uncertainty or regret. As with Felix's cup of coffee, Sheila insisted on seeing marriage for what it is by demonstrating what it is not. It is not made by the law—and it is not made in heaven. The law would protect and the church acknowledge an event "rooted" (to use her word) in "human life." The absence of the church's acknowledgment—there being no "more than natural grace"—did not in her eyes invalidate or in any sense diminish the nature or extent of the commitment she had made to Wilfred: "This is for always" were her words.

Sheila with Sweet William in the backyard of their Edmonton home.

I have returned to these reflections by way of prologue to events that occurred in the sixties, but also because Sheila's attitude towards domestic life seems an appropriate context in which to be reminded of her views of her own marriage. It was during her first stay in Edmonton that her then new-found mentor, Frederick Salter, observed to her that one wrote a novel like one built a pig pen—with craft, and carefully. In a similar vein, I am tempted to unpack the phrase "recipe for a good marriage" and to consider Sheila's views in light of her ritual making of chocolate birthday cakes, as these engagements embodied her valuation of love and fidelity. But I shall leave this and turn to the bed that Wilfred made.

It was very late in the spring of 1962 that Sheila's sessional appointment was renewed. She had become anxious, confiding to Diane Lane that she would go elsewhere if necessary to find a teaching position. The renewal—for three years with the prospect of tenure—along with some degree of stability in their relationship, made more permanent plans possible. They bought a house in the Windsor Park area, just west of the campus. It was a three-bedroom bungalow with large windows and good wall space for their paintings—Sheila described it to Marshall as possessing "a Mondrianish puritanical quality." It was surrounded by trees and shrubs—"choke cherry, pin cherry, plum, current, crab apple. Spruces," according to Wilfred's cataloguing—and it was located across from a park, which provided a pleasant prospect. It was also within easy walking distance of the English Department offices. They had been married for more than twenty years now, and this was their first home. Wilfred's sense of the occasion took the form of reviving his skill as a carpenter to design and build their bed.

If Wilfred's bed—the bed he built for Sheila and himself—did not have the "ivory inlays, gold, and silver fittings" of the bed Odysseus built for Penelope and himself, it was at least as large—a thing of bolts and slats, though, and not of straps. It was described by one friend as a cross between a bed and a pen. Its place in Sheila's marriage had little in common with the place of Penelope's bed in her marriage. A property of this last bed becomes a means by which Penelope determines Odysseus' identity. When she proposes the bed be moved, knowing full well that it cannot be, Odysseus exclaims, in Robert Fagles's translation:

> "Woman—your words, they cut me to the core!
> Who could move my bed? Impossible task,
> even for some skilled craftsman—unless a god
> came down in person, quick to lend a hand,
> lifted it out with ease and moved it elsewhere.
> Not a man on earth, not even at peak strength,
> would find it easy to prise it up and shift it, no,
> a great sign, a hallmark lies in its construction."

That sign or hallmark was its fixity, its rootedness. The portability of Sheila and Wilfred's bed, like the portability of the bed of Angelina and her husband in Portugal, provides a kind of barometer reading of their marriage. It was not long before the Watson bed was removed to a basement study, and when they moved to Nanaimo in 1980 it occupied a similar book-bound location on the ground level of their house, where it was used upon occasion by visiting couples, but—at Wilfred's insistence—only if they were married.

If the allusion to the bed of Odysseus and Penelope seems contrived, it is well to bear in mind that Wilfred and Sheila were readers of Joyce as well as of Homer, and that their sense of mythic counterparts for even the homeliest of objects and pastimes makes unconsciousness very unlikely. It is difficult to imagine Wilfred not musing upon a heroic counterpart, and equally difficult to imagine Sheila ignoring the evidence of such musings.

Sheila had returned to Edmonton on the understanding that Wilfred would free himself from any relationship which might threaten their marriage, and presumably the bed was a sign of that understanding. Its being relocated as soon as it was signaled the persistence of Wilfred's ways and of Sheila's resolve not to tolerate these any longer. By 1965 there remained no need for a shared bed.

⏤

From early in their friendship, Sheila had confided in Diane Bessai her concern that Wilfred had not set aside other relationships when she returned to Edmonton, as he had agreed to do. Diane had assumed that the five years of their separation had represented a practical decision—unfortunate but necessary. What she sensed now was the repetition of a type of situation which had occasioned, or at least had contributed to, that separation. She recalls an evening in the fall of 1964, when she and Sheila had gone back to Diane's home on Whyte Avenue after some early evening event. Frank had been baby-sitting, and he had been joined by friends who had dropped by to keep him company. It was clear to Diane that Sheila was anxious to talk with her, and so they sought out privacy in the bathroom, where Sheila gave vent to her anger with Wilfred's treachery, with his betrayal of her and of their marriage. As had happened in Calgary some twelve years earlier, he had again become involved with a student.

Perhaps the strain of the final stages of her thesis contributed to her response to a situation with which she had already become familiar. Or perhaps she came across a letter the young woman had written to Wilfred, for this woman had made a habit of writing to him to Windsor Road. Among papers Sheila sent me near the end of her life was one of these letters, and in their copy of John Pearson's nineteenth-century *An Exposition of the Creed*, I found ten more (one of which had not been opened), as well as the draft of a letter in Wilfred's hand to his new young friend. Some years later, when she was helping Wilfred sort his papers for deposit with the Archives of the University of Alberta, Shirley Neuman came upon two letters from this same young woman. She suggested to him that he might not wish to include them, but for whatever reasons he chose otherwise.

Sheila had been teaching for almost thirty years when she returned to Edmonton in 1961. In country schools and city schools, in separate and private and public schools, at the Universities of British Columbia, Alberta, and Toronto as a sessional or as a teaching assistant—she had taught since 1933, the year she had received her MA. She taught what had to be taught, whenever or wherever she was wanted. "I didn't choose," she had said of Dog Creek, "it chose me."

As a teacher as in many other respects Sheila was methodical rather than systematic; methodical in Coleridge's sense of what is natural "to the mind which has been accustomed to contemplate not things only, or for their own sake alone, but likewise and chiefly the relations of things, either their relations to each other, or to the observer, or to the state and apprehension of the hearers." Her temperament—reinforced, I suspect, rather than shaped by her reading—was well suited to the classroom, cautious about overviews and generalizations, adept at pattern recognition, sensitive to those who heard her. Her relations with her students were marked by generosity and courtesy. Her office door was always open (in part, perhaps, because she thought and wrote and spoke smokingly), and she came, in the relatively short period of fourteen years that she taught in Edmonton, to supervise more theses than any of her colleagues then in the English department. This fact led to jealousy on the part of some and a belief that she was willing to work with just about anyone, that she was not sufficiently discriminating in selecting students with whom she spent time and whose work she supervised. Sheila was aware of such criticism and responded to those who questioned her about these matters that any student who had been accepted into the graduate program was entitled to a supervisor.

Sheila was supervising the work of graduate students while she was finishing her own thesis. One doctoral candidate, Elizabeth Brewster, who was working with her on Ezra Pound and Vorticism in 1965, anxiously awaited the completion of Sheila's thesis that she might consult and cite it in her own thesis. Sheila's correspondence with her students reveals her reading with them and reading ahead of them. Sections of her library recall particular supervisions: her collection of Black African writers, for example, Jonathan Peter's work on Achebe, Senghor, and Soyinka; her books on Confucianism and on Chinese history—including de Maille's very rare (Sheila believed there was only one other copy in Canada, and that in the Governor General's library) multi-volume, eighteenth-century history of China that is the basis of Pound's Chinese Cantos—provided foundation for Jamila Ismael's thesis on Pound and the Chinese. Sheila was fed by those she nurtured. An MA thesis on *The Waste Land* as a city poem written by Peter Montgomery led her in time to consider a volume of essays—by diverse hands—on the city in literature.

Sheila was as practical in her supervision of graduate students as in other areas of her life. I remember her counselling me that I should view the doctorate as a union card—as a means for getting on with my work, and not as my life's work. She saw herself as helping students to achieve such independence.

In freshman as in graduate courses, she could make of a class—any class—a community. She spoke often of a "community of scholars" as those involved in some common pursuit, a community which included instructor as well as students. With all her learning and her experience, there was nothing Olympian about Sheila's presence in the classroom. She remained more engaged by people's capacities to learn than by their ignorance. She was not one of those who threw wide her arms in horror at the prospect of a first-year student not knowing who Plato was or not having read *Pride and Prejudice*. And she did not join the colleague who relished carolling at marks meetings, "Flunk 'em flat!" She taught hard, as she used to say, and examined light. Still she was a demanding and not an easy marker. She treated students—as many have testified—assuming that they were "with" her, that they understood where she and they were going. She would occasionally pause in class midway through a sentence, not out of forgetfulness or as a sign of the inevitability of what came next, but more likely to give students a breathing space in which to find or to declare their own bearings. One former student and later colleague, Pat Clements, recalls the eloquence of such hesitations, which persuaded her that Sheila was "thinking every phrase." She recalled her style as interrogative rather than declarative, that she was probing rather than attempting to prove some point. She rarely took the shortest, the most direct route, and she rarely provided good—in the sense of systematic—notes. Shirley Neuman recalls a group of students who were studying early modern British literature with Sheila, attempting to diagram one of her lectures. A series of arcs traced the curves of her thoughts and examples, some intersecting, others floating like birds in the space of the page. It was a sympathetic, admiring exercise which illustrated the importance of what Pound called "luminous detail" in her reading of literature and cultural history. And Sheila was, in Shirley Neuman's phrase, "deeply embedded in history," in historical movements and connections, in those communities of thought and imagination and personality that lay at the heart of Vorticism and Cubism, for example, two movements in which she took particular interest.

Wilfred in the classroom, as in his own work, was more given to hobby horses than was Sheila. In the late fifties and early sixties, work he had done on word-play in Shakespeare—and especially on the importance of the word "pluck" in the history plays—led to his almost obsessive preoccupation with genetic word-play in other authors. In the mind of Pat Clements, who had been taught by both of them, Wilfred focused a class on whatever detail was uppermost in his own

Wilfred with Marshall McLuhan in the backyard of the Watsons's home in Edmonton.

thinking, "engineering" a text to illuminate that detail. Clements described Sheila, on the other hand, as "de-engineering" texts with gentleness and respectfulness. Increasingly in the sixties, Wilfred's work with McLuhan led to interviews with students, which he held when he returned their essays, becoming McLuhanesque "probes" that dazzled at the same time they could puzzle unwary students who only wanted to know how they had done in their most recent assignments. For many students and colleagues, Wilfred was the embodiment of the temperamental artist, a person of intense enthusiasms and deeply felt antagonisms. One former student, Caterina Edwards, has spoken to me of having been "frightened" by his volatility, by the combination of gentleness and fierceness that he could demonstrate in the classroom. A colleague, Alison White, coined the phrase "certified savages" to describe those who would take apart colleagues at public meetings. It was a group which was thought by many to include Wilfred.

Both Sheila and Wilfred were extraordinarily generous to students and friends in need of financial as well as academic or personal assistance. Sheila would give Pat Clements money towards studying at Oxford. A few years later, when Frank Bessai was seriously ill and at home, she provided for a night nurse on condition her gesture remain anonymous. These are only traces of kindnesses that were legion, that deserve to be acknowledged, but are best left unrecorded.

The year in which Sheila joined the Department as a sessional, 1961, was—as I have noted—the year in which Henry Kreisel succeeded J. T. Jones as Department Head. Jones had shown little interest in extending the English Literature program.

Beyond the BA, the Department offered an MA, which required of the student simply further senior courses and a thesis. There was not a graduate program as such, no separate courses shaped to the needs of graduate students, and there was no doctoral program. The situation was very much as it had been at the University of British Columbia thirty years earlier when Sheila was a student there. And little had changed since then. In the early sixties, responsibility for defining English studies in Canada, including the training of PhDs, remained the all but exclusive province of the University of Toronto.

Soon after assuming the Chairmanship of the Department, Kreisel set up a committee to bring in recommendations about a doctoral program. Like Sheila and Wilfred, and Kreisel himself, many of the members of his department had been—in part at least—Toronto trained, and there was among them little will to ape the Toronto fervor for comprehensiveness. The "whole of history" had in the eyes of many become, in Wilfred's witty turn of phrase, "the hole of history": chronology giving way to vortex as the topic of each student's research and thesis generated a rationale for his or her program and for the means by which each was to be examined. The University of Alberta program would represent a student-centred rather than a canon-centred approach, which sat comfortably with a department whose membership had come increasingly to reflect creative as well as critical and scholarly interests. Established poets like Wilfred and Dorothy Livesay and such novelists as Sheila and Rudy Wiebe and Henry Kreisel helped to provide a setting which such young, academically trained writers as Stephen Scobie, Margaret Atwood, and Douglas Barbour found sympathetic to their interests. Wilfred wrote and had his plays produced, and journals and broadsheets abounded with the work of undergraduate and graduate students and faculty. From across the country, writers came to read in Edmonton. It was during this period that Sheila met for the first time many young writers who knew her through *The Double Hook* and who were to enter her life as she had already entered theirs. bpNichol had read Sheila's novel as a teenager in the winter of 1962–63 in Winnipeg, and George Bowering had read and initially despaired of it at about the same time. Sheila was to meet them in Edmonton, where she was also to meet Roy Kiyooka and Michael Ondaatje, who had already sent her a copy of his first collection of poetry, *The Dainty Monsters*, signing himself an admirer of *The Double Hook*. The Department of English at the University of Alberta and Edmonton at large provided audiences and venues for readings at a time when a revolution was occurring in the literary arts—and especially among poets—in Canada. Stephen Scobie and Douglas Barbour have both spoken to me of the excitement of those times in that place, where clearly it was bliss to be alive then, especially for the young.

～

Shortly after they had moved into their Windsor Road house, in the late summer of 1962, Jack and Doris Shadbolt, friends from their teaching days at UBC, stayed with Sheila and Wilfred while Jack prepared a preliminary design for a mural commissioned by the federal government for the new international airport terminal in Edmonton. In the wake of the *Massey Report* of 1951, with its confirmation of Canadian "culture," and in a run-up to the euphoria of Canada's centennial in 1967, the government had adopted a policy of diverting one per cent of the costs of airports to the commissioning of works of art for their enhancement. "A city which plants autumn crocus and a country which commissions a Shadbolt," Sheila wrote to Doris Shadbolt later that fall, "can't be entirely without soul."

Because of its place in Canadian aviation history, Shadbolt chose bush pilots and what they saw as his theme for Edmonton. It was a year and a half before his mural was completed and unveiled, and during that time he was a frequent visitor at Windsor Road. Early on, he did drawings of both Sheila and Wilfred, drawings that especially fascinated Wilfred. Years later, when he happened upon these—two of himself and one of Sheila—he wrote to Shadbolt of experiencing "for a moment the joy of living the life after death, while still alive." Sheila left no comment about these, although it was she who had preserved the drawings. At the time they were done, Wilfred wrote to Shadbolt that his drawing of Sheila "flatters one of my favourite artistic theories": "I have the uncanny feeling that you somehow or other drew Sheila's face but informed it with your own soul-form. . . . The result is you have an external resemblance, but it is invigorated with the artist–copyist's own soul." The result was not altogether to his liking, however: "too much of a mixture of partridge and Brahma bull," he quipped.

～

Until 1965, and even as she supervised students' theses, as we have seen, Sheila's responsibilities included work on her own thesis. She had completed a first draft— begun in the spring of 1958—in the summer of 1961, after her return to Toronto from London, and before moving to Edmonton. Her journal accounts of her

researches and writing recall the long days, "tough and opaque as leather," the loneliness, "with only Lewis for company," the subject that "taxes every nerve," the frustrations, the sense of inadequacy, all made tolerable, though, by what in Lewis most
deeply engaged and finally sustained her. Lewis might have likened himself to "the
mason-bee or the woodpecker" in his need to work, but McLuhan likened his candidate's work to another form in nature: "M M's quip is that I work like a glacier."

Shortly after she had completed her first draft and had returned to Edmonton,
her supervisor wrote Sheila an uncharacteristically exhortatory letter:

> Look ye, a stern note:
> Get that thesis here with the headlines. Let Frye and me decide.
> Doesn't have to be an official submission. I can work that out. Don't
> rely on your judgement in this matter.
> Just send it on. Now!

The "headlines" he referred to were titles he proposed Sheila use to mark subdivi-
sions of her thesis. "[E]xpository writing is not my strength," she had complained to
him. "[A]pe [Lewis's] *Art of Being Ruled* layout," he advised her. It may be worth noting that at this same time, McLuhan was preparing for the press *The Gutenberg
Galaxy*, in which he was to practice what he now recommended to Sheila.

Marshall's reference to "Frye and me" suggests both the possibility of Northrop
Frye as an examiner of the thesis and the probability of a kind of co-operation
between them that might well have struck Sheila as unlikely. If Joyce acted as a facilitator in her relations with Marshall, Lewis fulfilled the opposite role in her relations
with Frye. "Lewis challenges all his presuppositions," she had written to Wilfred in
late 1960, when it seemed that Frye would be one of her examiners; "If I attacked
Lewis all would be plain sailing." Overstated as this might sound, Sheila was not
entirely wrong. Some years later, Frye observed to David Staines that he found it difficult to reconcile what he admired in Sheila and her work with her interest in Lewis.
As the recently published 'Third Book' of his *Notebooks* reveal, Frye judged Lewis's
Apes of God "the most boring book I ever read."

Sheila had come to see Frye as a force such as Lewis might have imagined. In
the spring of 1961, she had written to Wilfred of some of the consequences and, by
implication, some of the causes of larger classes at the University of Toronto: "No
one really cares what the student writes or reads provided he serves as a projection
screen for the new Tyros." She then named Frye as one of these "new Tyros": "Frye
lacks the virtue of civility," she continued; "He talks but does not listen." She found in

his critical position something blindly mechanistic that she felt deserved the Tennysonian epithet: "So careful of the type [he] seems / So careless of the single life." He was not her audience any more than she was his. It is as well, then, that when she came to defend her thesis, in February 1965, Frye was not one of her examiners.

∽

The impatience that McLuhan betrayed in his exhortation to Sheila—"Now!"—was hardly typical of his communications with her between the time she left Toronto and the time she defended her thesis. His letters echoed rather with words of reassurance: "Don't you have any worries. You are in happy position of knowing very much more than your advisors or examiners!"; "Have no qualms. Your thesis will be acceptable and sensational, both"; "Am having a grand time with the thesis. Who do you have in mind as a publisher?"; "The thesis looks superb."

During this time, another project appeared which had the effect of reversing their roles. McClelland & Stewart decided to place *The Double Hook* in their New Canadian Library series, where they had originally intended to publish it. Malcolm Ross as General Editor of the series approached Marshall to write a preface for this edition. "I would really very much like to do a preface for *The Double Hook*," Marshall wrote to Sheila. "Without some briefing from you, it would take me a great while to do a proper job, and I don't have very much time at all these days. The sort of briefing I have in mind concerns basic themes and structure. It could all be put on a page, though the more, the better. If you see your way fit to aid me, then I will say 'Yes' to Malcolm Ross." She did as he asked, sending him in September 1964 what he termed "wonderful notes," although they arrived just as Ross found someone else to write the preface: John Grube, then of the University of New Brunswick, whose sister, incidentally, Sheila had taught at Moulton College. "May I turn over your notes to John G.?" Marshall asked her. Sheila agreed to this. And so the matter ended. In August 1966, McLuhan noted in a letter to Sheila, "Have only just now read John Grube's preface. . . . Seems to me most useful."

Sheila always maintained that Marshall had never read her novel, and their letters in the mid-sixties appear to support this view. Still, at the time of its publication, he had sent a copy of *The Double Hook* to the distinguished American critic Cleanth Brooks, asking him for suggestions about where it might be published in the States. Like Michael Hamburger's response to the similar gesture of Barker Fairley, Brooks's was enthusiastic and he too attempted to be helpful, but to no avail. Among papers

Sheila sent me in the mid-nineties is further evidence that Marshall had indeed read her. This is the beginning of a draft in his hand of a preface to the novel. There are one hundred and eighty words (the count was his own and appears in the margin). The opening paragraph includes the following passage:

> *The Double Hook* contracts the Canadian vastness into immediate lived reality without any abstractions at all. Canadian literary strategy has perhaps been to encompass our magnitude by abstractions, especially the abstraction of panoramic scenery. Yeats noticed without surprise that "the grass blade carries the universe upon its point." Such is the procedure of *The Double Hook*. Instead of huge visual gestures or the social abstractions of the novel about the minister, the farmer, the teacher, the Indian, the Mennonite, or the French Canadian, the whole Canadian fabric is included in each moment of experience in this novel. This achievement is possible only to a poet who can control a novel as a unified poem, including the totality in every part.

The voice, like the handwriting, is unquestionably Marshall's. Still, Sheila had already referred to Yeats's "grass blade" as an emblem for her novel. In a journal entry dated 22 September 1958, when she was rereading his "The Celtic Element in Literature," she recorded the same phrase that Marshall cites, commenting, "The *D. H.*, I suppose, is an attempt to make the grass blade bear this weight."

❧

Sheila defended her doctoral thesis on 12 February 1965. Its length (two volumes), its many illustrations of Lewis's drawings and paintings, and what one of the examiners termed its "very individual" format, including "the series of brief headlined sections," led to last minute changes: a list of the illustrations to go with the table of contents, a brief preface explaining her method, a brief conclusion, a thorough proof-reading. There are thirteen examiners named on the program for her defense, including some with whom she had studied (McLuhan himself, Norman Endicott, Kenneth MacLean, and William Kennett), and some who had reviewed *The Double Hook* (including Hugo McPherson, Donald Theall, and Milton Wilson) and one—Frank Watt—who had reviewed "Antigone." Malcolm Ross, whom she continued to think of as her first publisher, was also an examiner. The committee was impressed by her "complete control of her material," and by what Ross termed "the depth and brilliance" of her exposition of Lewis. What was a source of contention in the thesis was, predictably, Lewis himself and not Sheila's account of him and his work.

⏤

Sheila had promised herself that once the thesis was successfully defended she would return to work on "Landscape," the novel she had begun in the early fifties. But McLuhan and others urged her to find a publisher for the thesis, and in June 1965 she wrote to the Edinburgh Publishers Oliver & Boyd, and at their invitation sent them a copy of it. In September, she received an encouraging letter from them accompanied by their reader's report. This last was a richly detailed appreciation of Sheila's work with shrewd and precise advice on how best to turn it into a book. "[T]he work is deep and imaginative," the anonymous reader wrote, "and the subject matter is necessary for anyone who wishes to understand more thoroughly than has before been possible the cross currents of literary and artistic and philosophical thought during the first half of this century." This was high praise indeed, and Sheila was advised to cut the text by about 20 per cent, to tone down the citational erudition that was, as Marshall observed, "for the benefit of the PhD committee" only, and not to permit her own critical voice and personality to remain, in the words of the reader, "buried under the name of other writers." She might well have undertaken these revisions had other circumstances not intervened.

⏤

One of the briefest entries in Sheila's journals is dated "Aug 7.*" 1965: "Received into the Church again—Father La Certe." A few weeks later, on 11 September, she wrote me:

> Perhaps the simplest way to tell you what has happened . . . is to begin like Gregory of Tours "Credo" and then perhaps to recall the parable of the prodigal son—and to record that I thought very little about "admitto te" when I heard the words "absolvo te" and could say Abba Father.
>
> Now that I've told you I don't want—that is I am not able—to say any more because I have a whole language to relearn.

Earlier that year, on 16 April which happened to be Good Friday, Marshall had written to her: "Apropos request . . . for a Missale Romanum, if you can wait a few weeks I'm told there will be lots for free. i.e. big current changes mean that all the extant ones must be replaced. Present ones will be available. So I'll try to get a really fine one for you."

Sheila's relationship to the church of her birth and her youth had, since her undergraduate days at the University of British Columbia, been at arm's length. In Paris in the mid-fifties, she had noted that she had attended mass for the first time in twenty years. She had married "without benefit of clergy," but the absence of priest and nuptial blessing in no way called into question in her mind the commitment she had made to Wilfred.

At some point, perhaps before 7 August, there was a meeting of Sheila, Wilfred, and his young friend. Who or what occasioned this meeting is unclear to me. The young woman was herself a Roman Catholic (she mentioned in a letter to Wilfred biking to mass), and the position she adopted at this meeting appears to have been dogmatic and naive. She insisted—and presumably with Wilfred's agreement—that he and Sheila were not really married because they had not married "in the church." For at least the second time since 29 December 1941, Sheila was being called upon to acknowledge the valuelessness of what they had promised on that day.

⤸

At this time Wilfred had two cars. He referred to one, a Karmann Ghia, as his mistress, and to the other, a Volvo, as his wife. His mistress remained nameless, but he named his wife Griselda.

⤸

In the wake of conversations with a priest, Sheila found herself with two options. Her marriage to Wilfred could be "regularized" in the church's eyes by having it blessed by a priest. This presupposed the incompleteness of the original exchange of vows—not its valuelessness, as Wilfred and his friend maintained, but its incompleteness. Events seemed to have moved beyond this solution, however. Furthermore, the solution itself presupposed reservations about the commitment to which Sheila had subscribed and continued to subscribe unqualifiedly. A second option was that they live as "brother and sister." This was the option Sheila chose—

not for Wilfred but for herself. It should not be thought of as a punitive act, but rather, as her attempt to regain some sort of control over her own life. At this time, too, she fully expected that they might soon separate. Sheila remained faithful to the choice she made for the rest of their lives.

In the same month in which Sheila was received back into the Catholic Church, a cousin, Brian Doherty, wrote to tell her that their aunt Agatha Myatt had died. Brian was a son of her father's brother, Manning, and he had achieved some success in the late thirties and early forties as the author of a very popular play, *Father Malachy's Miracle*. He would go on to establish the Shaw Festival, in Niagara-on-the-Lake, Ontario. Brian and his brother D'Arcy, a lawyer who lived with his family in Toronto, had remained in more regular contact with their aunt than had Sheila. When she died, a widow and childless, they were left with the task of determining the wishes of family members concerning Dr. Myatt's possessions. Sheila asked if she might have a crucifix of her aunt's, and she was sent this as well as her prayer books.

Just before she was formally received back into the church, which was shortly before classes began, Sheila spent a week with her mother in Vancouver. Late in September, and after her return to Edmonton, she wrote me of her prospects for the coming academic year: "I am lecturing only eight hours a week this year—instead of the ten of last year. . . . If I ever get another book written it should be on this kind of timetable . . . since it gives me a stretch of time if I can keep it reasonably free from time to time at least." "[A]nother book" sounds like a return to work on her novel rather than to revision of her thesis. She had not yet received the encouraging letter and reader's report from Oliver & Boyd.

⌢

Two months later, Marshall wrote to Sheila, care of her mother in Vancouver: "Sheila our darlin'! Just got word from Wilfred about your vacationing in Vancouver. Make the most of it. You've earned it. Lots of time for prayers!" Marshall's letter was dated 14 November 1965, and Sheila was on sick leave, not on vacation. Always susceptible to respiratory infections, she had contracted what would become pneumonia, and had gone back to Vancouver because of this and because of her domestic situation. With Wilfred's new infatuation, things had worsened on this latter front, and she intended, when she returned to Edmonton, to get an apartment of her own. In December, and still in Vancouver, she drafted a letter to Marshall which she did not send. The draft survives among her papers, and it shows Sheila as close to the edge as she was ever likely to have come. She began this letter by recalling a time when Marshall had been ill in Toronto. "My mind has less strength," she said, than his had had, and then she commented, "I discover too how I've brutalized my—perhaps the verb should simply be left intransitive—how I've brutalized." She then provided Marshall with a piece of information—the name of the founder of the Oblate order of priests—which he had asked for the previous summer. This is followed by an anecdote about an Oblate priest whom she knew of in her youth:

> Father Le Jeune . . . used a sort of shorthand to record the various dialects like the Thompson and the Shuswap. He edited an Indian newspaper called *The Kamloops Wawa*. He was an old man dying in the hospital in New Westminster when I was a high school student there.
>
> He and others of the old missionaries were thought of as saintly men because they had gone on foot in the mountains and through swamps until their shoes were filled with blood.
>
> They all wore thick black boots like the ones Pound sent to Joyce. They were usually too poor to have socks. I suppose to have one's shoes full of blood now would simply be a sign of incompetence.
>
> I beg you to pray. At the moment I am too weak to think very much. I must somehow get back and endure until spring—or perhaps just go back, resign and disappear. I was felled here a bit like an ox—I knew the line was taut but thought it would hold.
>
> Mother has been very good to me but she is very old and should not have the strain of me shaking about in bed—full of pain and short of breath.
>
> These weaknesses I try to assimilate. Actually I think I mend. I snort a little when I move too quickly—perhaps this is a rudimentary laugh.

What must it mean to reach a point where it is no longer possible or necessary to distinguish transitive from intransitive—object from subject—abused from abuser—or where saintliness has become merely another name for incompetence, and only a matter of footwear. In a postscript, Sheila asked Marshall for "the history of the word 'background,'" and ended the draft on a note of dreadful premonition:

The backgrounds about to cave in on X—
Fall of the House of Usher
Pit and Pendulum
Jonah etc.

It is one thing to speak disparagingly, as Jonah did, of a people who did not know their left hand from their right, and quite another thing to find that there is no longer any difference between left and right. And who or what is X? Was it herself Sheila was referring to, or was she, as is more likely, using a traditional short form for the name of Christ? However one would read this unsent letter, it appears that for Sheila, in Vancouver, in November/December 1965, some equivalent to London Bridge was falling down—and the sky with it.

The casualness of letters from Wilfred and from Marshall at this time seems callous. "You're better surely!" Marshall began a letter written in mid-November, and then proceeded: "Just back from a long harangue by Earle Birney on the university and the poet. . . ." In this same month Wilfred began a letter, "I hope you have some relief from the germ by the time this arrives," and ended, "Must go. I hope the germ retreats decisively." Between opening and closing, Wilfred did write of the concerns for her health of various of their colleagues and friends in Edmonton. And we must bear in mind that he and Marshall had not read what we have read. Once she referred to her journals as letters to herself, for it was not in her nature to engross others in dark spaces in which upon occasion she found herself. What she had drafted became in a letter sent to Marshall in December 1965 simply, "Indeed, sir, you should pray for me. I am not at all sure how much longer I can remain sensible or useful." Such a draft letter—like her journals—has survived because she intended it to be read—after the fact, so to speak, when the dark space had been traversed.

Not long after writing it, Sheila returned to Edmonton and to Windsor Road.

∼ XIV ∼

WHEN T. S. ELIOT PROPOSED THAT ART DOES NOT IMPROVE, BUT THAT the subjects of art are never the same, he was challenging, as many of his contemporaries were, the nineteenth-century reverencing of Progress, Development, and Evolution; at the same time he was proposing that the western artistic tradition was whole cloth, not a remnant, not a thread. It is at any moment whole, even when it is not complete. So too with a life. Perhaps this is what the autobiographer recognizes, that his or her life can be whole without being complete.

"I am sending you my life," Sheila had said to me as she sent me banker's box after banker's box of her papers and her books. The books she sent were carefully chosen; seven thousand two hundred and eighty remained on their shelves after her death and Wilfred's. What papers remained did not add significantly to what she had already sent. Lacunae I had hoped would be filled—the journals she had kept during her two years in Dog Creek, which she claimed to have burned—remained empty. Her life could not, would not, be complete. But its wholeness remains obvious in any moment of it.

Leo Frobenius, an anthropologist in whose work Ezra Pound took a particular interest, and whose study of Africa was among Sheila and Wilfred's books, maintained that from the merest shard, a fragment of a pot for instance, it is possible to recover the culture that produced it. My way of going about things presupposes this view of evidence—as an alternative to the idol of completeness.

∽

From the time they had heard the papers given by one another in Montreal in the late spring of 1961, Wilfred and Marshall discussed and worked towards what was to become *From Cliché to Archetype*. Their correspondence during the next six or seven years was incessant and lively. The planned book was to be a real collaboration. "We must do this together," Marshall wrote to Wilfred in the summer of 1964. "A team is better than any solo effort if only because it permits dialogue and development, and also manifests those qualities to the public." This was to be the busiest and the most productive decade in McLuhan's career. It saw the publication of *The Gutenberg Galaxy* (1962) and *Understanding Media* (1964) and of at least six other books. Most of the latter, like "C/A" (as they came to refer to it), were to some degree collaborative.

During the early years of their work together, Wilfred and Marshall spent only brief times in one another's company: McLuhan made quick visits to Edmonton on two occasions, and Wilfred stayed with the McLuhans for about a week in the spring of 1963, when he was in Toronto for performances of his play *The Trial of Corporal Adam*. By the summer of 1964, the years of exchanging ideas and book lists, of playing off one another's insights, led to an attempt to establish a more formal arrangement between them that would result in their book. "I want direction about how you think we cd. do the cliche/arch book," Wilfred wrote to Marshall in July 1963. "My own idea," he continued, "is that I shd. do write up—I and you should take my draft and modify it by addition and subtraction into write up II and then I could get this put into final typescript." In his ebullient response, Marshall apparently—but only apparently—agreed with Wilfred's plan. "Hurrah! Yep. You do the first draft. I'll do no II, not in the nursery sense."

Sheila could not but have been delighted by Wilfred's involvement with McLuhan. It would be futile to speculate about her contributions to their ongoing dialogue, however. That her own concerns with Lewis and about her thesis overlapped with their interests is not surprising given her years of dialogue with each of them. At the same time that she had fixed Northrop Frye as one of Lewis's "apes," for instance, and was worried about his possible response to her thesis, Marshall and Wilfred were plotting his overthrow. There is indeed something of the "nursery" about Marshall's enthusiasm for this plan. "I agree with you entirely about the strategy of taking over the Frye world of literary genres via media as metaphors," he wrote to his cohort. "However, in terms of capture, the Frye audience as opposed to the Frye field, the concept and title 'C/A' may prove very effective. Actually we are not really engaged in the conquest of the Frigian empire so much as in the discovery of a totally new empire." It was in this context that Marshall had insisted to Wilfred, "We must do this together."

Perhaps "nursery" is not the analogy—or the setting—to be evoked here. Perhaps "nintendo" more accurately recalls their plotting and their playfulness—that or *Star Wars*. They remained children of their times, of the years "l'entre deux guerres," and their language would recur later in Wilfred's title for a proposed volume of essays on Marshall's influence, *Reconnaisance*, and in Sheila's occasional war-room vocabulary in defense of McLuhan.

These were the glory days for Wilfred, collaborating with, being continually stimulated by "the only person at Toronto I ever got an idea from." His sense of himself and others' sense of him soared by virtue of his association with McLuhan. He let it be known that the phrase "cliché to archetype" was coined by him, that he was nurturing and working with, as well as following, the world's new bell-wether. Even after things cooled between them and correspondence all but ceased, Marshall remained present to Wilfred, and only partly because of Sheila's continuing contact with him and with his family. He had experienced with Marshall something of what others have observed in his relationship with Sheila—an interaction of minds and imaginations which stimulated at the same time it edified Wilfred, bringing out in him what was best in a human as well as in an intellectual sense. Marshall had written of the friendship between "a dependent and uncertain" young Tennyson and "the vigorous and clear-headed" Arthur Henry Hallam in an essay entitled "Tennyson and Picturesque Poetry." Tennyson had described their glory days in terms that, without too great a stretch of the imagination, might be applied to the early correspondence between Wilfred and Marshall:

> When each by turns was guide to each,
> And Fancy light from Fancy caught,
> And Thought leapt out to wed with Thought
> Ere Thought could wed itself with Speech. . . .

But Wilfred did not suffer "the loss of his poetic insight and his critical judgement" that Marshall argued Tennyson had experienced with the death of Hallam, when their relationship foundered. The prospect of separation from Sheila, however, filled Wilfred with fears such as Tennyson felt, including the fear of separation from his better self.

〜

Shortly before her return to Edmonton in 1961, when she was beginning to see beyond her thesis, Sheila wrote to Wilfred: "I lay plans for completing the *Landscape* after the Passionate Image has taken wind." At about this same time, she confided to Wilfred her fear that her third novel's time had passed: "I feel the 'landscape'—if I can ever finish it will fall pat—It was in its inception prophetic—and should have been finished long ago." Hers were the fears of the satirist whose desire to expose certain possibilities in her world had been overtaken by the eagerness with which the world had realized those same possibilities. Her long admiration for Swift, Sterne and Chaucer, as well as her work on Lewis, together with her recent toying with a matter which would form the basis for her most recognizably satiric work, "The

Rumble Seat," provided a kind of intellectual and temperamental setting for the work that she now realized had been too slow in coming. Within ten years, she would find herself embroiled in an academic situation which now she could hardly have imagined. When this situation, which will be described shortly, had ended and after she had retired, she wrote to Marshall of her disappointment with what the academic world had become. It may be as close as we shall come both to what had provoked her to begin the "Landscape" twenty years earlier and what prevented her from finishing it:

> Perhaps I feel discouraged because the whole system with its emphasis on change-no-matter-what and security for the already recently entrenched, many of whom earlier fought for the destruction of tenure which they now enjoy, is resulting in a system which offers little promise for the graduates looking for meaningful work, or anything but a kind of freelance para-academic existence.

⤴

Work on revising her thesis was transformed rather than completed or abandoned. In October 1966, a newly appointed editor of *arts/canada*, Barry Lord, wrote Sheila at the suggestion of Doris Shadbolt to propose that she do "a major piece of up to 12,000 words with perhaps 20 photographs on Lewis." This was to constitute an entire issue, and it would be published in a year's time, in November 1967. Sheila accepted the invitation, and she produced in "The Great War, Wyndham Lewis and the Underground Press," what Lord's successor described as a "beautifully organized and provocative piece of work." The cover and a centrefold, reproductions in colour of two major oils in Canadian collections, were particularly arresting: a detail from "A Canadian Gunpit" from the National Gallery appeared on the cover, and "The Armada" from the Vancouver Art Gallery formed the centrefold. Sheila's essay continued the method proposed by McLuhan for her thesis. Its sections have headlines and look rather like articles in a newspaper, but the arrangement of these sections, including the interplay of words and pictures, has more in common with a carefully designed mosaic.

At the same time that she was preparing her number of *arts/canada*, George Woodcock, in his capacity as editor of *Canadian Literature*, wrote asking if she were interested in contributing an essay to an issue devoted to Lewis in Canada. At first he gave her free rein, but when she suggested writing on Lewis's "Toronto" novel, *Self-Condemned,* Woodcock replied that both Hugh Kenner and the editor of Lewis's letters, W. K. Rose, wanted to deal with aspects of it, and he preferred she pursue one of her other suggestions. Ultimately, neither Kenner nor Rose contributed to the issue, but, in the meantime, Sheila had been persuaded to write on Lewis and painting. Because of the impending publication of her number of *arts/canada,* she was hesitant about undertaking this, but "Canada and Wyndham Lewis the Artist," which appeared in the 1968 winter issue of *Canadian Literature,* provides a companion piece to the longer essay. It locates Lewis in relation to artists and artistic movements in Canada or, more accurately, it accounts for his isolation among Canadian painters, and his greater affinity with Canadian "neo-Thomists and . . . students of contemporary literature." In referring to Lewis's portrait of Mrs. Martin, she honoured the promise she had made to Paul Martin to vouch publicly for the authenticity of this painting.

⌐

Early in 1967, before she had been approached by George Woodcock, Sheila was invited by two undergraduates at St. Michael's College, Virginia Smith and David Staines, to come to Toronto to talk with students. "Unaccommodated Man" was the title of her talk, and it was as subversive as Edgar's use of nakedness as disguise in *King Lear.* The American critic Robert Brustein had recently spoken at the College, and Sheila used his *The Theatre of Revolt* as a point of departure for examining his and other critics' secular chic. With the support of Lewis, she questioned the wisdom of Brustein replacing one kind of dogma (what he had identified as "the values of Christian civilization") with what she termed "a dogmatic return to inaccessible primitive ritual." The talk was rich and heady, shaped for its audience: a corollary, if you will, to the "Credo" she had repeated in August 1965.

On this visit to Toronto, she saw the McLuhans. She was concerned by what she took to be the toll that Marshall's activities were taking on him. She felt that he was, in Wilfred's phrase, "desperately in need of relief from the pressures" that were being placed on him. The pressures became even greater when that fall he took up the Albert Schweitzer Chair at Fordham University in New York City. At the urging of Marshall and Corinne, both Watsons had agreed to visit the McLuhans in December 1967 at their temporary home in Bronxville. Marshall hoped that he and Wilfred would have a chance to continue the dialogue that was to result in *From Cliché to*

Archetype. The trip had to be cancelled, however, because early in December Marshall underwent twenty-two hours of surgery for the removal of a massive, though benign, tumor adjacent to his brain.

Plans were already underway for Sheila and Wilfred to spend the academic year 1968–69 in Toronto, as Research Associates in Marshall's Centre for Culture and Technology. In April they received official notice of their appointments, which were to take effect on July first. Recovery from his surgery, and his and his family's return to Toronto after a year in New York, made the prospect of friends at hand especially pleasing to Marshall. He was determined to finish the "C/A" project ("Enough C/A in my files for 10 volumes," he had boasted to them), that had been promised to Viking Press since 1963. Other projects also loomed; in particular a culling from Ezra Pound's letters of his advice to young writers. "Would not this be a natural for us at the Centre?" he asked Sheila; "it would be a natural project for us as a team."

After sub-letting their house in Edmonton and taking an apartment only a block from St. Michael's College, they settled in for what was to be a very unsettling year in Toronto. Philip Marchand has written of McLuhan's state of mind during the period after his surgery and his return to Toronto. He has described his "loss of memory and the tormented state of his nervous system" that inevitably affected his ongoing work with Wilfred. Marchand has provided a compelling account of the reversion of the years-long dialogue between Wilfred and himself into what he terms "two monologues," with Wilfred not certain whether Marshall had forgotten or simply chose to ignore what they had for so long discussed. Wilfred has left his own account of their exchanges in an essay which was published in 1974, entitled "Marshall McLuhan and multi-consciousness: The Place Marie Dialogues." Place Marie was the name of the apartment building where he and Sheila were living,

Sheila with Corrine and Marshall McLuhan in Toronto in the late seventies.

and the dialogues took place there over lunches Sheila prepared for these regular meetings. Wilfred was careful to distinguish these dialogues from those held in Marshall's Centre, that were recorded and transcribed by his secretary, and that became the matter of *From Cliché to Archetype.* "Here Marshall McLuhan ruled as a director," Wilfred wrote. By his account, the conversations held in their apartment were directed by Wilfred himself, and his essay should be read as an addendum to a book in which he believed his voice had eventually been lost.

One witness to some of the Place Marie dialogues was Jack Shadbolt, who had come to stay for a few days but was felled by pneumonia and was ministered to by Sheila (whom he termed "Nursie") and Wilfred (whom he dubbed "Kindly Bed-pan Boy") for longer than any of them had anticipated. In a letter of thanks to them, Shadbolt repeated something of what he had heard:

> While I sat in a state of wracked torpor listening to Marshall being so sure about his gloomy predictions for a complete collapse of American society within five years etc. I was getting a terrible sense of gloom but I felt convinced that he was engaging in intoxicated doom-saying.
>
> In spite of all the piece-meal evidence I didn't think he was making enough allowance for the organic reaction patterns of society that tend to restore a certain balance—though I was in no state and, in any case, am not qualified to produce the counter argumentation.

What Shadbolt heard sounds more like a monologue than a dialogue or conversation. There is no mention of Wilfred's interventions. These perhaps required a kind of distance and the spans of time that Edmonton and letters could provide, but which were not available in Toronto, the Centre, or even in Place Marie.

Sheila's role during the Toronto year was less clear than Wilfred's, but it was also more varied and demanding. Aside from making lunches, and mediating those of the "C/A" dialogues that took place over them, she assisted Marshall in the classroom. This became her major responsibility—simply to be there. She was once again a teaching assistant as she had been during her graduate days in the fifties, but her "demotion"—thankless and painful as it might have been, and upon occasion was— was of benefit to his students as well as to Marshall. She assisted him in a senior undergraduate course in twentieth-century poetry in English, which numbered Philip Marchand among its students. The trauma and the pain of Marshall's marathon surgery had not entirely subsided, leaving him often forgetful and irascible. She was present as his memory, tactfully providing the passage from Yeats or from Eliot that he knew only too well but which at present eluded him. It was a role she would return to later, when she would provide Marshall with a word he could remember but which he could no longer speak.

⌒

One project in which Sheila became engaged during this year was the commissioning and collecting of essays that were intended to be published under the title *The City and Literature.* The book was to be one of a series published jointly by the universities of Toronto and Chicago under the general editorship of McLuhan and two of his Toronto colleagues, Richard Schoeck and Ernest Sirluck. Sheila was to be both editor and a contributor to this volume, whose subject she had proposed to Marshall in the first instance. From notes she has left, it appears that the essays would have been arranged according to three historical periods: ancient, industrial, and contemporary. It seems that the overall organization of the book would have proceeded from a consideration of city as container to a consideration of city as consciousness. Within these broad terms, there were a series of topics—twenty-five in all—which included city as process, city as newspaper, city as clothing, as dictionary, as theatre, as clock, as midden—which presumably she was planning to include in the volume. The literary range was also to be very broad: at least from Aristophanes' city comedies to Joyce and Eliot. At this same time, in the autumn of 1968, Toronto was embroiled in a controversy about the building of an expressway to connect the northern perimeter of the city with the lakeshore at its southern limit. The opponents to this Spadina Expressway—one of whose feeder roads would have divided the campus of St. Michael's College—ultimately achieved a victory of sorts, and were encouraged by the presence and support of Jane Jacobs, the distinguished urbanologist, who had only recently moved to Toronto.

Another presence, whose stay in Toronto coincided with Sheila and Wilfred's and who became drawn into Sheila's work on the city, was the American scholar of renaissance matters, Rosalie Colie. Though she and Sheila met only a few times, a deep rapport developed between them. Colie was a poet as well as a scholar and teacher. Her presence in the classroom was recalled for me years later when Sheila commented that it was well that she, Sheila, had retired when she had, because the times would no longer tolerate her habit of touching—physically touching—those to whom she spoke. She might have been labelled a harasser, as Rosalie Colie might have been, wandering about a seminar room, unwinding and winding up her own great mass of hair as she talked, touching students—as Sheila too was wont to do.

Colie was very excited by Sheila's planned volume. She was interested in what she termed "urban pastoral" in the renaissance, and had written an essay on Castiglione's *The Book of the Courtier* in light of this paradox. This essay had been published, but she wished to re-work parts of it, and did so for inclusion in Sheila's volume. It is the only completed essay for this project that survives among Sheila's papers.

Old Toronto friends saw very little of Sheila and of Wilfred during this year. Sheila's solicitousness about Marshall and the demands of work she undertook for him, as much as Wilfred's social aloofness, kept them pretty much isolated. The extent of her preoccupations that year is reflected in the absence of any journal entries. Wilfred did continue with his own creative writing. The earlier plans about how "C/A" was to be written were, according to Philip Marchand, replaced by Marshall's secretary collating the notes she took of these "contrapuntal monologues" and handing them to his son Eric to revise. The teamwork so enthusiastically anticipated by all—and which Sheila continued to encourage—had disintegrated when the team became reconfigured.

In the spring of 1969, Wilfred went off to Wolfville, Nova Scotia, to participate in Acadia University's Summer School of Theatre. He was spurred on to this by Sheila, and it provided him with a welcome relief from the pressures of Toronto. His reference in a letter to "a gorgeous view of an intensely green world" from the window of his university digs summed up his pleasure in the place; in the directors, technicians, and actors; in a production of *King Lear* with a wonderfully good Gloucester and a Cordelia who, as he wrote Sheila, "moves with the grace of a she-bear"; and in seeing one of his own plays prepared for production. He remained at intervals in Wolfville for most of the summer.

During Wilfred's absences, Sheila was freed up to see friends and to enjoy something of the Toronto that had become her home in the late fifties and early sixties. But tragedy had struck the Bessai family in Edmonton. Frank had been diagnosed with brain cancer. Since their marriage in 1963, he and Diane had had three sons—the third, Thomas, a godchild of Sheila and Wilfred—and they were expecting their fourth child. In the late spring of 1969, Frank was brought to Toronto for further consultations and possible treatment. Sheila visited him in hospital during this time, and she visited with Diane, who had come to be with him. When further treatment proved futile, late in the summer they returned to Edmonton to await the birth of their fourth son in September and Frank's death in November.

The year in Toronto had been an odd, mixed thing for Sheila and for Wilfred. McLuhan's condition following his surgery made Sheila's presence of greater value to him than she or anyone might have anticipated. This was reward enough. Wilfred's extended contact with him, on the other hand, brought an end to the comraderie of the dialoguing days. He found the restless, multi-notional nature of Marshall's interests and of his mind—stimulating and suggestive as these were for providing contexts for focused considerations of "C/A" in letters and in short, infrequent meetings—revealed their ongoing dialogue to be but a single facet of Marshall's prismatic enterprise. He had discovered, too, that teamwork and dialogue were for Marshall always a beginning of exploration, but seldom its end. "A curious honeymoon," was the way he summed up his experience in a letter to Jack Shadbolt: "each moment taken up with furious debate about the marriage contract—and let Freud keep his old butt-fashioned nose out of this observation."

Despite the pressures of this year, Sheila returned somewhat reluctantly to Edmonton. At Marshall's insistence, attempts had been made to secure for both of them permanent appointments at the University of Toronto, but these attempts were not successful. Sheila had shown greater interest in the possibility of remaining than Wilfred had, perhaps because the University had shown greater interest in keeping her.

⌒

The department to which they returned in Edmonton in the autumn of 1969 had, under the continuing chairmanship of Henry Kreisel, remained committed to curricular experimentation and the encouragement of creative activity by its members. Stephen Scobie and Douglas Barbour had joined the Department in the year Sheila and Wilfred had been away, as had Margaret Atwood (for one year only), and within a year Dorothy Livesay had become its writer-in-residence. Paul Tiessen recalls being in a seminar on Canadian poetry taught by Livesay, with Atwood as a participant.

Frank Bessai's illness that autumn, and his determination to spend what time was left to him in his own home, called upon another strength of the department. Colleagues old and new came to sit and talk with Frank, or saw to it that the boys got to school or pre-school or whatever activities they were involved in. The Bessais had moved to the Windsor Park area a few years earlier, and their house was across the park and on a block or so from Windsor Road. With their customary tact, Sheila and Wilfred were present or not as occasions required.

In the same month that Frank died, November, the Studio Theatre at the University performed Wilfred's *let's murder Clytemnestra according to the principles of Marshall McLuhan*. It was produced as the final event in a conference originally intended to celebrate Dorothy Livesay's forty years as a poet, but had become more ambitious and, in the eyes of some, more pretentious. The conference's final title, *POET and CRITIC '69 POÈTE et CRITIQUE*, led Wilfred to propose an anti-conference, and his play might be read in part in that context. It is absurdist, recalling his and Marshall's consideration of theatrical absurdity at the beginning of *From Cliché to Archetype*, but it is set in a post-McLuhan world in which technology has been replaced by biology (recall if you will *Under the Rabbit's Paw*) as a source of new extensions of man—and woman: Wilfred's Electra has nineteen heads that are later replaced by nineteen vaginas. Patterns and preoccupations are discernible, which suggest that this might have been an exercise in exorcism, or a turning of his dialogues with Marshall on their head, or both. The fact that he drew from the same mythic materials that hover close to the surface of the opening of *The Double Hook*—the son who is prompted to the murder of their mother by his sister—also implicates Sheila in Wilfred's farrago.

One of those who attended the *POET and CRITIC* conference was Philip Stratford of the University of Montreal. He had hoped to meet Sheila that fall in Edmonton in order to discuss with her the possibility of a French translation of her novel. Stratford had done much to make Quebecois literature available to English readers, through translations he had made or had commissioned. As he indicated in a letter, he was not proposing to undertake such a translation himself, but would gladly act as a facilitator in order to make *The Double Hook* available to French readers. When such a translation was finally published, in 1976 by Les Editions La Presse of Montreal, it was the work of Arlette Franciere and bore the title *Sous l'Oeil de Coyote*.

Stratford persuaded Sheila to try her own hand at translation. She was to all intents and purposes bilingual. She had studied French authors in school and at university, and she had spent the year in Paris. Stratford was preparing translations of a group of contemporary Quebecois short stories for "the first book of its kind," as he described *Stories from Quebec* when it appeared in 1974. Sheila translated two stories by Madeleine Ferron, from her collection *Coeur de Sucre*: the title story, that she rendered as "Sugar Heart," and a story entitled "Le peuplement de la terre," which she renamed "Be Fruitful and Multiply." This last especially represented a remarkable wedding of author and translator. With "savage economy," Ferron told of a woman's life in three pages, from the morning after her wedding as a young girl to the final confusions of her old age. Sheila told me she would have given all she had written to have written it.

⌐

As early as 1963, Sheila had written to Marshall of a move by a new member of the department to establish a quarterly journal. "I have no time & no desire to join such a venture," she reported saying when asked to be on the editorial board. "I can think of a mag. only in y'r [i.e., McLuhan's] terms and Lewis's . . . a publication of limited and pressing objectives." The academic journal remained only an idea, but a magazine "of limited and pressing objectives" after the fashion of Lewis's *Blast* and McLuhan and Edmund Carpenter's *Explorations* was born in 1970–71, with Sheila as midwife. *White Pelican*, as the magazine was named, appeared as "A Quarterly Review of the Arts" for four years, from 1971 to 1974, with one issue published also in each of 1975 and 1976. There were then eighteen issues in all, and two volumes of poetry published by the magazine. These latter were Wilfred's *the sorrowful canadians*, published in 1972, and *Lions at her face* by Miriam Mandel, which was published—and won the Governor General's Award for poetry in English—in 1973.

Sheila was first among its six editors, whom she described in a prefatory note ("About Pelicans") in the first issue as "drawn together by proximity not by policy, by concern not by consensus." "Person by person or person with person," she wrote, the editors assumed full responsibility for choosing materials and preparing an issue for the printer, including typing camera-ready copy and mailing the subscriptions. Each editor or editorial team was left completely free of any kind of interference from the other editors. In this way they hoped to avoid the type of "neutered voice" that policy or consensus can lead to. The rotating of editorial responsibilities also ensured that no one need be burdened with these more than once in a year.

At the heart of *White Pelican* lay Sheila's sense of community and the nature of the English department at Edmonton as it had developed through the sixties. This "little magazine" had been hatched in the living room at Windsor Road one evening in 1970. Those who were to become its editors were present, and Sheila and Wilfred proposed to underwrite the cost of the venture. In light of this offer, one bit of policy was agreed upon: the magazine would accept no government grants and no advertising. The editors wished to remain accountable only to their contributors, to their subscribers, and to themselves.

It was a daring and, by any standard, a remarkably successful venture. Reviews and essays, fiction and documentary prose and photographs and drawings mixed with what was its mainstay—poetry. Edmonton poets, such as Wilfred, Miriam Mandel, Ted Blodgett, Stephen Scobie, and Douglas Barbour, were well represented, as were poets from other parts of the country, such as bpNichol and Michael Ondaatje. There were new voices (the first pages of the first issue were devoted to poems by Elizabeth McLuhan) and there were voices in French as well as in English. Some issues had a specific focus: one edited by Dorothy Livesay and Rudy Wiebe, on the North; another on Gertrude Stein, edited by Sheila, for example. Sheila contributed an essay to this last, one of three she wrote for different numbers of *White Pelican*. She took particular interest in their publication of excerpts from the diary Henry Kreisel had kept while he was interned in Canada as an enemy alien during the Second World War, and in an illustrated article by the Alberta architect Douglas Cardinal.

Sheila edited four (including the first) of the eighteen numbers and co-edited (with the painter Norman Yates) a fifth. There was a printing of 500 copies for each issue: between 150 and 200 going to subscribers, and the remainder to bookstores across the country and beyond. The subscription list reads like a catalogue constructed to please any writer: public and university libraries in Canada are there, along with the Board of Education for the Borough of Etobicoke in Ontario, and the town of St. Albert in Alberta and Cowichan Senior Secondary School on Vancouver Island. The library of University College in the University of London is there, and so too are the libraries of Georgia State University, Michigan State, and the universities of Hawaii, Wyoming, Harvard, and Yale. The Asphodel bookstore in Cleveland, Ohio, is there and the library of the University of Sydney in Australia, and so too are the New York Public Library and a bookseller in Dawson City and two subscribers in Inuvik.

The design of the cover remained the same, although its colour varied from issue to issue. Norman Yates had drawn an elegantly stylized pelican, and it was he who varied the colours of its ground. Sheila chose the name, and in a note "About Pelicans" which prefaced its first number she adduced ornithological, etymological, and mythological information such as to make the name seem inevitable and not merely artful. Yates was the only one of the group of six editors who was not a member of the English department. Aside from Sheila and from him, the editors were Stephen Scobie, Douglas Barbour, John Orrell, and Dorothy Livesay. Livesay was in the second year of a two-year appointment as writer-in-residence when the *Pelican* began publication, and so she retired after one year and was replaced by Wilfred.

To a striking degree, the magazine shared with the bird whose name it bore a quality which Sheila observed in her prefatory note to the first number. The white pelican "nests and breeds in southwestern Canada," she tells us, and according to the *Alberta Atlas* there are uplands and mountains, a river, a lake, and a portage in this province which are named for it. But, she observes, "its range . . . is more extensive." The little magazine named for the bird never lost its sense of place even when it ranged most widely.

White Pelican ceased publication shortly after Sheila's retirement in 1975. It posed something of a financial strain and it had served its purpose, and she was no more sentimental about it than she had been at the outset about the reputation of its namesake. "It may be necessary to state," she had quoted the first professor of zoology and comparative anatomy at Cambridge, "that there is no foundation for the venerable legend of the pelican feeding her young with blood from her own breast." What is more, the other side of that legend requires "pelican daughters," and their equivalents were waiting in the wings.

⌒

Alberta's English department, like others in the country, had grown enormously during the sixties. By 1971 it had more than sixty full-time members. In common with other universities in Canada, Alberta had to look abroad in hiring new faculty. The sixties saw American academics streaming into Canadian universities. There had always been an American presence in the department at Edmonton, but in the past this had been overshadowed by a British presence, or at least by the presence of faculty trained in British universities. Increasingly, Canadian students were going to the United States rather than to England to do graduate work. And increasingly, young American academics were looking to Canada for jobs. There were social and political, as well as practical, reasons for this.

Canadians still tend to look back upon that time through sociological and political lenses and with a certain smugness: in the United States, the Vietnam War, political assassinations, student dissent, race riots; in Canada, the euphoria of Expo '67, of a Prime Minister awarded the Nobel Peace Prize, and, by the end of the decade, the advent of Trudeaumania. The causes of the American hegira are not difficult to find. They were its consequences that concerned Sheila.

She remained deeply suspicious of colonialism of any sort, especially of inadvertent colonialism. The inadvertent colonialist can embrace a new world while—unintentionally—squeezing the life out of it. Since her childhood in New Westminster, she had been accustomed to living among traces of empire, those names and rituals and customs that retain their power by not being assimilated, by not becoming naturalized. The phrase "crown colony" was familiar to her from her youth, as were maypoles and may queens and the fact of "the old country" that provided the rule by which a people expected to be measured. Her sense of the genius of a place made her very sensitive to any attempts to transform it—into a bit of "olde England" in the case of New Westminster or into an American university in the case of Alberta and other English-speaking universities in Canada. When she was asked at this time if her own eschewing of regionalism in her fiction meant that she had become an internationalist, Sheila replied:

> Internationalism means the nationalism of the predominant culture, and if you've lived in western Canada you've suffered through several imperialisms. You've suffered through British imperialism, when nothing was valid unless it had come from Oxford or Cambridge or London. Then you suffered through domestic imperialism, which said nothing was important unless it had roots in eastern Canada. And so for me American imperialism, the new internationalism, is simply a third wave.

One of the new appointments to the department during the year that she and Wilfred were in Toronto was Morton ("Mort") Ross, a native of Iowa who came to Edmonton as a part of this third wave. In a group of essays about his life at the University of Alberta, which form part of a collection of his writings entitled *An American Critic in Canada*, he has left lively accounts—sometimes wry, sometimes sentimental—of an expatriate—and as the collection's title suggests, an unreconstructed—American academic in Canada. He ends an essay entitled "Where I Was Coming From" recalling his own bravado when he first came to Edmonton. "And I remember secretly, in my heart of hearts, whispering defiantly to my long string of benefactors, 'I'll show these Canadians a thing or two.'"

Henry Kreisel had been succeeded by George Baldwin as Chair of English, and in the academic year 1970–71, Baldwin's successor was to be chosen by the department. The department had been divided and had become polarized around two candidates, E. J. Rose, an American who had come to Edmonton by way of the

University of Toronto, where Northrop Frye had supervised his doctoral thesis, and John Orrell, one of the editors of the newly founded *White Pelican*. To the end, Sheila and Wilfred had supported Orrell's candidacy.

This is by way of prologue to an episode which was to cast a shadow over Sheila's last years in the department. Like Sheila and Wilfred, Rose and his wife, Shirley, were full members of the department. They had come to Edmonton in the late fifties, at a time when Shirley Rose did not yet have a doctorate and held only a part-time position. With her own position confirmed in 1962, Sheila felt strongly that—like others in her position—Mrs. Rose was being exploited by the University, so that when in the late sixties Shirley Rose completed work on her own degree, Sheila shared the department's pleasure in her becoming tenured. The now Dr. Rose had done her thesis for the University of London on the early-twentieth-century British novelist, and contemporary of Wyndham Lewis, Dorothy Richardson.

Because Sheila and Shirley Rose worked and taught in the early modern period, they had students in common. One of these students had taken Sheila's graduate course on Wyndham Lewis and had done an MA thesis under her supervision before she had gone to Toronto. After Sheila's return to Edmonton, he discussed with her possible subjects for a doctoral thesis. When Sheila raised the question of the makeup of the committee that would advise and ultimately examine him, the student proposed Shirley Rose as a member of the committee. Sheila responded that one or the other, but not both Rose and herself, should be on the committee. This represented a prudential decision. Sheila was aware of intellectual and temperamental differences between them, and she was concerned that what problems Rose had with her might interfere with the student's progress. As things developed, the near-undoing of all involved was a consequence of her decision.

When he submitted his thesis for defense late in the summer of 1973, the student had modified its title to reflect the sharper focus it had acquired during its writing. As well, at the suggestion of Sheila and his committee, he had included a bibliography of "works cited" rather than of "works consulted." At the time this represented a perfectly acceptable decision.

Notice of the impending defense of the thesis was posted in the English department under its revised title. Shirley Rose wrote to the Dean of the Faculty of Graduate Studies and Research noting the change in title and insisting that the supervisory committee was "not expert in vital areas of research relating to the work" of one of its subjects, and was, therefore, incapable both of advising him and of evaluating his thesis. Her measure of expertness was publication, and, unlike herself, no one of the committee members had published on this person. Shirley Rose sent copies of this letter to the Chair of the Department, E. J. Rose, and to the Chair of the graduate section of the Department, although not to Sheila or to any member of the student's advisory committee. On the same day, the Chair of the Department wrote to the Dean of the Graduate Faculty, requesting that the thesis defense be postponed pending an investigation of these charges. The Dean rejected the notion that the members of the committee lacked the expertise necessary to examine the thesis, and insisted that the defense proceed as scheduled. The candidate successfully defended his thesis.

If Sheila's refusal to include Shirley Rose on the committee occasioned the Roses's responses, these in turn provided evidence of what Sheila was attempting to avoid. The situation was, of course, complicated by the fact that the complainant was the Chair's wife, and that the Chair did not excuse himself from acting on a complaint lodged by his wife. So far the matter involved the competence of Sheila and the committee and not the competence of the candidate or the quality of the thesis.

A month after its successful defense, Shirley Rose wrote to the graduate committee of the department stating that she had found further evidence of the incompetence of the student's advisory committee. The graduate committee responded that the complaint should be sent to the committee, which, in a letter dated 21 November 1973, Professor Rose refused to do. When she failed to respond to a second letter from the graduate committee, they referred the matter to the Department Chair.

The following spring, Professor E. J. Rose wrote to Sheila. It was the first time she had been addressed directly by any of those involved in this matter, which had, after all, been under consideration since the previous autumn. Sheila was sixty-four years old, and in her second-last year of teaching before her retirement. It is well also to remember that the candidate had already successfully defended his thesis, and had received his degree; when the convocation list had been presented to the Council of the Faculty of Graduate Studies and Research (of which E. J. Rose was a member) for its necessary approval, no objection had been raised to his name being on it.

Rose's letter to Sheila was the first of two he wrote in the space of a week. He upbraided her for refusing to "re-examine" the thesis. Sheila replied that any initiative to re-examine must come from the Faculty of Graduate Studies, "whose advice and instruction," she wrote, "I will be pleased to accept." She then declared, "I do not intend to dignify the allegations made against me and the supervisory committee with a reply." In his second letter, Professor Rose responded to this declaration: "If you wish to read my letter as an allegation against or a judgment upon you and your committee, there is little I can do about that."

Six weeks after Rose's letter to Sheila, the Council of the Faculty of Graduate Studies and Research met and "rejected the attempt . . . to require [the former student] to alter his PhD thesis." The Council then retired into a committee-of-the-whole, and the Dean, Professor John McGregor of the Department of Mathematics, denounced as "disgusting" the attempts of the Chair of English, who was present, to blacken the reputation of a senior and respected member of the department. According to one who attended this meeting, the Dean's words were "most dramatic and damaging," and the Dean himself "very, very good." The body whose judgement Sheila trusted had vindicated her committee and her and, most important of all, her one-time student. Still, she drew little consolation from the outcome of what in a letter to McLuhan she wrote more than a year later she termed "the miserable affair."

The decision of the Graduate Council did not end the affair. Rose wrote to the University's Vice-President Academic, who happened to be a predecessor as Chair of English, Henry Kreisel, in order to state his case "for the record." The letter moves between ad hominem judgements and denunciations of "this University's parochial disregard of accepted standards," appealing again and again to "accepted international standards," to "an established international standard for research and scholarship," to "'universally-accepted' methods." But these he defined only in personal terms. "I have," he wrote, "an established and well-known international reputation." It is small wonder that Sheila did not complete her satire of academic life when a fiction which in its inception was intended to be prophetic had become a part of her own story.

It was an episode which she could not easily put out of her mind, or behind her. It is not difficult to see how certain decisions she made, or consented to, contributed to a situation whose origins were, however, elsewhere. For the appeal of academic colonialism is no longer to some distant place that occupies another time zone, an "old country." It is to a person, the Expert; in the words of the Chair, "the expert opinion of the resident specialist." All that was most tentative and unsystematic, although methodical and probing in Sheila's mind—qualities that made possible a sense of community in her classes, in her supervision of graduate students, and in the founding of the *White Pelican*—was challenged by what, finally, an ad hoc committee of the English department judged to be unacceptable. In rejecting the definition of an expert as "someone who has published on a subject," and the claim "that such an expert's opinion has the status of fact," this committee was also challenging a growing sense of territoriality, of scholarly turf, which threatened the kind of breadth that characterized Sheila's work. It was a victory of sorts, although not one that brought her any pleasure.

Wilfred had been a member of the student's advisory committee and he was unflagging in his support of Sheila and of the cause that had been laid on her. The arm's length nature of their professional relationship seems less contrived when seen in light of this situation. It may be worth noting that, shortly before this matter had erupted, Wilfred had placed himself in a situation similar to the one that Shirley Rose came to occupy. He had taken exception to the composition of an examination committee of which he thought he should be a member. The thesis in question was on *Tristram Shandy*, the subject of his own doctoral thesis. He had taught the candidate and had had disagreements with him. He insisted upon being included on the committee and was at his most unbending during the thesis defense. But that was an end to it, and the candidate was successful in defending his thesis.

Sheila's final year of teaching, 1974–75, was overshadowed by consequences of the events of 1973–74. The fact that the Roses were on leave provided some lessening of tension, but decisions had been made that prevented her from teaching a graduate course in her last year, and that made it very unlikely she would be permitted after her retirement to supervise the doctoral work of students who had already signaled a wish to work with her. Shirley Neuman had been one such student and recalls that when she defended her thesis, Sheila was present without status at the examination, and was ushered out of the room along with the candidate when the committee began its deliberations. Shirley remembers the ease and the grace Sheila brought to a graceless situation.

⌐

No one knew better than Sheila that darkness can be a companion of glory, and that glory can walk with darkness. At the same time that she was reclaiming herself from charges of incompetence, Frank Davey and Coach House Press published *A Collection* of her creative and critical writing in the *Open Letter* series (Winter, 1974–75). The collection published her story "The Rumble Seat" for the first time, as well as "Unaccommodated Man," the paper she had read to the students at St. Michael's College some years earlier. It also included three stories and nine essays already published, and concluded with an as-yet unpublished excerpt from remarks she had made in 1973, at her first public reading from *The Double Hook*, and with "A Semi-Bibliographical Note Concerning *The Double Hook*" by Douglas Barbour. The cover was by way of an allusion to Norman Yates's cover for *White Pelican*. There was no mention of "And the Four Animals" or of *Deep Hollow Creek*, which had yet to be recovered, or of her earliest publications.

A companion volume of sorts appeared in 1978. I say "of sorts" because it was never intended as a companion to *Sheila Watson: A Collection*, but it is a testimonial to the influence of her writing and her person on students, colleagues, and friends, and it does bear at least one trace of being a sequel. Its title, *Figures in a Ground*, is a phrase she had used to describe the writing of *The Double Hook* in remarks published in the *Open Letter* volume: "I would say that what I was concerned with was figures in a ground, from which they could not be separated." "Canadian Essays on Modern Literature Collected in Honour of Sheila Watson" is its subtitle. This Festschrift was edited by Diane Bessai and a colleague, David Jackel. Collected under the headings of Discovery, Explorations, and Identities are twenty essays as varied in form and content and authorship as Sheila's interests were and the subtitle admits. McLuhan contributed an essay on *Four Quartets*, and Michael Ondaatje one on *One Hundred Years of Solitude*. There were essays by Paul Tiessen and Douglas Barbour, by Eli Mandel and Rudy Wiebe, essays on Wyndham Lewis and Alice Munro and Daphne Marlatt's *Steveston*, essays on Imagisme and "little magazines" and African fiction and Vladimir Nabokov. There was a note with drawings by Norman Yates entitled "Figures in Space." Henry Kreisel wrote a brief and affectionate essay on "Sheila Watson in Edmonton." And her colleague Rowland McMaster did a series of photo portraits of Sheila, one of which forms the book's frontispiece. The book is indeed a celebration, as it was intended to be. The collecting and celebrating of her work, however, was not a sign that the work had ended.

Since the early seventies, Sheila had become increasingly involved in the work of the Canada Council—reading manuscripts under consideration for grants in aid of publication; acting on juries responsible for naming Governor General Award English-language winners in fiction (in 1979 and 1980) and in poetry (in 1973 and 1974); as a member of its Advisory Arts Panel (for three years, beginning September 1979); and as a participant in its public readings program. Her often onerous responsibilities answered to her sense of other writers—and especially of young writers—and of the community at large. They also brought her into contact with those who administered funding of the arts in Canada. Her correspondence reveals the respect and, occasionally, the real affection that developed between the bureaucrats and her over the years.

During this same period, she had become associated with *The Chesterton Review*, the journal of an organization which had been founded by a former student, Ian Boyd, now Father Ian Boyd. It was based in Saskatoon, where he taught at St. Thomas More College in the University of Saskatchewan. Sheila was listed on the journal's masthead as one of three advisory editors, the other two being Marshall and Hugh Kenner. She remained in this capacity—and actively so—until she and Wilfred left Edmonton for Vancouver Island in 1980.

Closer to home, at about the time of her retirement, Sheila was also approached by Athabasca University to prepare a study manual for Joyce's *Ulysses*. Athabasca is an open university whose campus is located an hour's drive or more north of Edmonton. As an "open" university, it depended less on students' closeness to the campus than on their access to such technology as telephone, television, and computers to link them to a resource centre. A classroom without walls—like the museum without walls of Andre Malraux (i.e., photography) and the concert hall without walls of Glenn Gould (i.e., recording)—it is an example of how technology has transformed our notions of ground and the relationship of figures to it. It is a McLuhan world, not in the sense of his having discovered or approved of it, but in the sense of his having helped us to understand and to cultivate it.

A former student of Sheila, Mary Hamilton, was a member of the team responsible for preparing and supervising a course entitled "Modern Consciousness: Habits and Hang-ups." The team had chosen *Ulysses* as "the main laboratory" because, as the course's introduction claimed, "habits usually appropriate to the reading of novels are likely to act as hang-ups when applied" to them. Sheila's contribution was an essay—over one hundred pages in length—whose title accurately describes its nature and contents: "How to read *Ulysses*." It is in no sense a reading of the novel: its kinship is with Ezra Pound's "How to Read" and his *ABC of Reading*. She continued—and intensified—the method she had used in her Lewis issue for *arts/canada*, and earlier in her thesis, the method of mosaic encouraged by McLuhan. She created a space from what at first glance appear to be randomly chosen and unrelated references and pictures and quotations. Only very gradually does the reader begin to see the extent to which philosophers and scientists, poets, novelists, and painters of the past and present cast light upon the novel and, at the same time, the extent to which the novel illuminates the reader's world. What she wrote of Joyce's method is as true of her own method here and elsewhere: "You will find that the elements you expect to find in a novel are not missing, but that you are being asked by the novelist to assemble the pieces of the mosaic yourself."

However else "How to read *Ulysses*" is read, it stands as a homage to McLuhan, published a year before a stroke left him speechless and two years before his death. Sheila was dissatisfied with what she had written, but Marshall assured her that the essay was "full of interest, certainly not a failure!"

Sheila and I met only occasionally during these Edmonton years. During the year they spent in Toronto, I saw as little of them as their other friends did, even though I was teaching in the College where she was teaching; otherwise, Sheila's visits were rare. She had come to Toronto to defend her thesis, in February 1965, and I saw her then, at a dinner which Norman and Betty Endicott hosted on the evening of her defense. She came back in the summer of 1967 for the baptism of her and my godson, Peter Brückmann. There were other visits, but I don't remember what occasioned them. I do recall certain episodes, one in particular that took place in the late seventies. Sheila was staying with me, and she asked if I would take her to confession. As we were walking to St. Basil's Church at St. Michael's College, she spoke playfully of the grace that must come to one who facilitates another's confession. Then, in a confessing mood, and as if examining her conscience aloud, she spoke of the corporal works of mercy— which range from feeding the hungry and visiting the sick, to burying the dead—and she confessed to a failure with respect to one of these. She had never ransomed a captive. And it was not, as she believed, that she hadn't had the opportunity to do so. As she went on to say, not long after her return to Edmonton, she and Wilfred had paid a young Native man to do the occasional odd job for them. Once, when Wilfred was out of town, this young man had telephoned from a police station. He had been arrested for some minor infraction that involved alcohol and a fracas, and he wanted Sheila to bail him out. Ransoming surely seems banal when cast in terms of bailing out, and "prisoner" is far less suggestive than "captive," [In a journal entry dated 22 February 1957, Sheila had written, "I remember wanting 'to ransom the captive'—like the word *longsuffering* the phrase seemed nobly vestured."] but, regardless of its guise, the opportunity had presented itself. Sheila hesitated. Wilfred was away and she was alone in the house. She imagined the young man appearing at the door. What had started as a light-hearted examination of conscience had led to a more serious admission of a victory for prudence—and a failure of imagination.

It must have been a Saturday afternoon—between four and six in those days— because a priest was on duty in one of the confessionals at St. Basil's. Otherwise, as I recall, the church was empty. It was summer, the late afternoon, and I remember the space being filled with a mellow light. I thought my thoughts and said my prayers, and when Sheila appeared from the confessional, and "said" her penance, we left. Going down the steps to the Church, I tripped, and, as luck would have it, I sprained an ankle. Later that evening, as she was preparing to leave for her scheduled flight back to Edmonton, and I wobbled on crutches with a bound ankle, she found herself once again assailing herself for abandoning someone in need. But prudence prevailed, as it usually—although by no means always—did with Sheila (a cat named Sweet William was an exception), and she went by taxi, leaving me to consider my new-found bond with an unransomed captive whom I would likely never meet.

Otherwise, we exchanged letters and occasional phone calls during these years. Sheila asked me to contribute an essay to *White Pelican*, which I did. And at Diane Bessai's request, I also contributed an essay to *Figures in a Ground*. It is difficult for me now to recover a sense of the two decades she and Wilfred spent in Edmonton. She remained present to me—often as a silent confidante and an intended reader—rather, I should think, as Marshall remained present to her.

⤳

In 1978 George Melnyk of NeWest Press of Edmonton published Wilfred's collection of poems entitled *I begin with counting*. Sheila had continued her entrepreneurial activities on her husband's behalf, and had charmed Melnyk into publishing a book about which he was somewhat skeptical. The poems represented a departure for Wilfred. They were prefaced by a brief "Note" in which he introduced the term "number grid verse" (NGV) to describe his latest metrical experiment. He stated simply that his use of number grids together with words was "like the haiku and other poetic metres, a device of counting." In 1981, after their move to Vancouver Island, he wrote a fuller account of his NG method, and used it to preface *Mass on Cow Back* in 1982. "NG as notation" showed Wilfred moving against certain tendencies of the poetic modernism with which he had been associated, published as he had been by its high priest, and with his early poetry tagged Eliotic. This preface was by way of being his declaration of independence, from Sheila perhaps as well as from Eliot:

> It is the union of numerals and words that provides NG verse with
> its radical novelty. . . . NG verse re-opens the experiment with met-
> rics which traditional verse began hundreds of years ago, an exper-
> iment which modernist verse put an end to. Some would argue that
> this experiment died long ago—but I'm not sure of that. Secondly,
> because its numerals establish its identity as verse, NG verse can
> approximate to prose, can avail itself of prose techniques, can act as
> an analysis of prose structures and rhythms, in a way not possible to
> modernist verse with its identity problem. Because NG verse doesn't

have to be hysterical or compulsive in order to distinguish itself from prose, it can celebrate the experiment in that calm reason which prose is best at. In short, NGV combines an extension of traditional verse with a respectful, distant friendship to traditional (standard?) prose, and is dissatisfied with that modernism which (in theory at least) confuses verse and prose, form and content, creation and performance, life and art.

Sheila rejected the label "poetic prose" when it was applied to *The Double Hook*—or to any of her writing for that matter. ("It always upset me," she had said, "because poetic prose means—to me—purple passages. I often think of Virginia Woolf in that way.") Her attempts to bring to prose narrative the economy of drama, however, did involve her in techniques of compression more commonly found in poetry.

A more radical feature of Wilfred's challenge to modernism arose out of his populist instincts. Even his banal, sometimes cruel reworkings of *The Double Hook* represented attempts to bring Sheila's novel and its concerns into the realm of popular culture. Incongruous though it might appear, Coyote found a counterpart in Harvey, the giant-but-invisible rabbit of Mary Chase's popular play of the forties, and Lenchen rocked. Shortly before their departure for Paris in 1955, when he was in Edmonton and she in Vancouver working on "Brother Oedipus" while being tended to by family and friends, Wilfred wrote about the discussions she had been having with her sister about her story:

> Your talks with Norah about "B. Oedipus" I think are vital to successful writing. It all lies in the engagement of the reader who is sheer incomprehensible "X." All technique must cross this point of engagement. The modern solution has been to make capital of difficulty. Personally, I think the "I've got a good story I must tell you" attitude is best.

His were the more populist instincts of the two. This was reflected in his work for theatre and in the performative nature of his number grid verse. NGV represented his attempt to democratize poetry. He claimed to have left "an enormous amount of freedom" to performers of this verse, to those who took his words off the page, transforming them from visual into auditory space. He also believed that his grid system of composition, rather like painting with numbers, made it possible for anyone to write poetry.

⌒

Sheila in one of a series of portraits done by her friend and colleague Rowland McMaster in the seventies

The next year, 1979, saw the disabling of Marshall, and early 1980, the death of Sheila's mother. Earlier in this decade there had been other deaths. In October 1974 her brother Bill had died in Vancouver, and two weeks later her cousin Brian Doherty had also died. Bill had eventually returned to the west from Toronto, and had gone into the Veterans Hospital in Vancouver. When he died, Sheila went from Edmonton to arrange his funeral, and in a letter to Marshall she referred rather cryptically to that event. "Sometime, perhaps," she wrote, "I will be able to tell you about the manifestation of God's loving kindness at this particular point in time."

The story of Bill's funeral was one that Sheila cherished. Because Norah had long before left the church, and her husband and children were not Catholic, and because her mother was in her nineties, it fell to Sheila to see that Bill was properly buried. This meant a Catholic funeral. Because he had never really lived in Vancouver, and was known to no priests and affiliated with no parish there, Sheila approached her mother's pastor to see what arrangements might be made. As it turned out, he was that old adversary who in the thirties had claimed that Sheila cut her hair with hammer and sickle. She did not identify herself as the youthful radical, and Monsignor Nicol seemed not to remember her earlier reputation—or even her. He assured her that the funeral would take place at an agreed upon time.

Bill's funeral was attended only by members of his family. Monsignor Nicol saw to it that there were altar boys—servers and acolytes—candles and incense and some music. There were no cut corners, and certainly no maimed rites. The solemnity was there, and the impersonality, and "God's loving kindness" in the form of an old antagonist's blessed forgetfulness.

Sheila's mother was to be buried from the same church almost six years later, in February 1980. Ween would have been ninety-seven on her next birthday, and she had been a widow for fifty-nine of those years. She had lived alone in her own house (the one that she and Norah had bought in the forties) well into her nineties, under the watchful eyes of Norah and her family. Sheila telephoned her each Sunday, and they maintained—at least on Ween's part—an Austenesque kind of chatty correspondence. Her world was Vancouver's Kerrisdale district, whose changes she observed—more often than not deploring them—and from which she viewed the rotation of the larger world—again, not altogether sympathetically. In one of the last letters she wrote to Sheila, dated 20 March 1977, when she was ninety-five years of age, she mused about this world in what was for her a familiar fashion:

> What an H. of a world, we are living in now! I feel so sorry for the poor old Pope—the changes they are trying to make in our Church, imagine women priests! The Anglicans have two here & they cant fill the pews! Oh, these woman libs.

She pulled herself up short—"Enough of that!"—in order to relish the pleasure of recollection.

> The reason I am writing (or trying to) is to send you this clipping from yesterday's paper about Emily Carr's paintings—hope you still have yours. I remember her so well—two of her nieces were great friends of mine. My mind goes back to those good old days in Victoria, better than it does [to] things of today.

She was an Islander born, and space as well as time separated her from the pleasures of her youth.

The real reason for writing this particular letter, as she stated at the outset, was more immediate: "Just a line to thank you so much for inviting me to live with you—but I live such a queer life—no one could live with me; and besides, this has been my home for so long, I'd hate to leave it—all my old things etc.—so forth, nearly everything has a memory." The move Sheila had proposed to her mother, to live with them in Edmonton, came at a time when there was increasing pressure on the family—and from within the family—to place Ween where there would be round-the-clock care. Sheila sympathized with her mother's desire to remain in her own home, and to those who felt that such an attitude was unrealistic or irresponsible, she responded that if there were an accident which left her mother unable to call for help, what she might then suffer would be a small price to pay for the years of independence that life in her own home had afforded her. When Sheila visited her after she had been moved into an extended care facility, she felt what absent children so often feel under such circumstances—guilt at not having been able to do more for her mother in her final days; guilt, too, at not having been in the position of those whose lot it was to act on her mother's behalf. At the same time she recognized the folly of thinking that she could stand between any person and her purgatory.

Ween Doherty died on the 24 February 1980. Her funeral was from the same church as her son Bill's had been five years earlier. They were both buried with Charlie in the cemetery high up on the hill in New Westminster that overlooks the Fraser River.

⌐

Some months earlier than this, Sheila had received news of the death of Mrs. Lewis. Word came in a cablegram dated 12 April 1979 and signed "Omar Pound." The message read simply, "Froanna died peacefully today."

A year earlier, Ezra Pound's son had written to thank Sheila for her financial assistance to Froanna, who had recently been placed in a home. Her circumstances were precarious, as was her health. When Pound wrote to Sheila, he had no idea who she was, only that as Mrs. Lewis's financial guardian he had received a cheque for two hundred pounds from her for Froanna. "Quite frankly, I don't know who you are," he wrote, "although I've seen your name many times in correspondence. . . . Do write (identifying yourself more!). . . ." Since their meeting in 1961, Sheila had tried to remain in contact with Mrs. Lewis. Marshall goaded her to write, to send her copies of anything she had done on Lewis. This was not always easy because for a time after she had negotiated the sale of Lewis's papers, Froanna went to live in the Canary Islands. When she returned to England, her financial and physical resources had been depleted, and Omar Pound had assumed responsibility for arranging for her care. Less than a week before her death, he had written another letter to Sheila and to Shirley Neuman to thank them for money they had sent to assist Froanna. He spoke of having seen her recently: "She's looking marvellously well, eating well, her room is a delight," and then he described an incident which seems to be about the end of a time as much as about the toll time had demanded of one who had been a witness to it:

> apparently I had said something, or shown her a WL painting that
> had suddenly reminded her of WL and she was upset because she

wasn't sure whether he was looked after properly, etc. Obviously something had clicked somewhere . . . but it had also upset her somewhat. . . . It's so difficult to know what the best thing to do is!! . . . She knows me, and can usually get close to my name . . . sometimes she even remembers it. . . .

~ XV ~

BEFORE SHE MOVED TO NANAIMO IN 1980, SHEILA HAD LIVED

in Edmonton from 1961 to 1980

in Toronto from 1956 to 1961

in Paris from 1955 to 1956

in Edmonton from 1954 to 1955

in Calgary from 1952 to 1954

in Powell River from 1951 to 1952

in Vancouver from 1949 to 1951

in Toronto from 1945 to 1949

in Mission City from 1941 to 1945

in Duncan from 1940 to 1941

in Murrayville from 1937 to 1941

in Langley Prairie from 1936 to 1937

in Dog Creek from 1934 to 1936

in Vancouver and New Westminster from 1927 to 1934

in New Westminster: on Merrivale Street from 1921 to 1927

on 5th Avenue from 1920 to 1921

in The Tower of the Provincial Hospital for the
Insane from her birth in 1909 to 1920

Wilfred was responsible for their move from Edmonton to Nanaimo, on Vancouver Island, in 1980. There are some who believe that his desire to leave Edmonton after their retirements was a consequence of Sheila's continuing preoccupation—some liken it to an ancient mariner's obsession—with the Rose affair. Others maintain that Wilfred had always intended to return to the Island, to be close to the world where he grew up. Sheila believed this, and spoke of him as one whose life moved in circles, inevitably returning to where he began. It was partly at least in response to a homing instinct which drew him back to the area where he had come as a fourteen-year-old with his family from England in 1925. By 1980, the one surviving member of his immediate family, his sister Doreen, and her husband, John Dunning, lived just north of the city proper, on a water-front property near Piper's Lagoon. It was close by them, and on the lagoon itself, that Wilfred found the property and the house that suited him.

Sheila was no stranger to the Island. She had worked for two summers at a crippled children's camp north of Victoria in the thirties, when she was a student at UBC, and she had taught for a year in Duncan. But she remained a mainlander who believed that the distance between any island and its mainland had little to do with mileage. That Norah and her family lived in Vancouver, only 40 miles as the crow flies from Nanaimo, would, she believed, make them if anything more distant than they had been from Edmonton. Sheila was not inclined to act upon nostalgic impulses. The here and now of Edmonton after almost twenty years had become if not her place at least her home. Friends and colleagues aplenty were there—lives that had impinged upon hers as hers had upon theirs. The University was there with its library, and within easy walking distance for Sheila, who didn't drive. The amenities of a large city were there, including an airport which could see her easily to the west or—and more to her taste—to the east. A move at this point in their lives made no sense to her.

Her most recent experience of the part of Vancouver Island to which Wilfred would return had come from reading Jack Hodgins's early fictions, in particular *Spit Delaney's Island,* and his novel *The Resurrection of Joseph Bourne.* She had been a member of the jury that had awarded the latter the Governor General's Award for fiction in English. She had delighted in the vividness and the documentary extravagance of his anecdotes, and she had seen him doing for and with Nanaimo and its environs something akin to what Marquez was doing for remote regions of Columbia and Peter Carey for the Australian outback—also what Sheila in her own first-written, although still unpublished, *Deep Hollow Creek* had done for the Cariboo country of British Columbia. One compensation for their move then was the prospect of living near the likes of Hodgins, even if the prospect of living in his world provided little inducement for moving there.

Hodgins proved to be a part of the world of his own making. He was an Islander born with an Islander's suspicion of mainlanders, and especially of mainlanders' intentions concerning the Island. The Watsons and the Hodgins did meet and socialized in their modest and tentative ways, and Sheila was pleased that Jack and Wilfred got along as well as they appeared to do. Then in 1981, Hodgins published a book of connected stories, *The Barclay Family Theatre,* and in a story entitled "Mr. Pernouski's Dream," Sheila found herself, or at least enough of herself to be recognizable. The story concerns the meeting of an Island real estate agent and an elderly couple from Saskatchewan on a ferry travelling from the mainland to the Island. The agent is determined to sell the couple a property (his "dream") even though they are merely visiting with no intention of moving there. It is as much the complacency of the agent about the attractions of the Island that is being scrutinized here as the hostility and self-importance of the prairie wife. As if in a distorting mirror, Sheila found in this wife reflections of her position and person. Her smoking and the ways in which she sat and held her body appear to have intrigued Hodgins as much as his prairie wife does his real estate agent. According to her docile husband, at home on the prairies, she is wise and saintly and beloved, a respected professor. On the Island she is merely a bitch.

Sheila was not so much hurt by this use of her as she was puzzled by it. She was confronted by her own hostility to the Island in a remarkably crude form, a form calculated to confirm rather than to modify her prejudices. To be "put on" by a writer was hardly new in her experience of her own or others' writings. Catherine Hansen's response to Miriam and to *Deep Hollow Creek* as "our story," after all, suggests this. It wasn't their story any more than Sheila was the Doris Eckhart of Hodgins's story, but, like her friend of Dog Creek days, Sheila now knew the helplessness of being possessed and anatomized by another's gaze. She knew also—or rather, she had confirmed—that the Island was not her place, just as years before there came a time when she had to accept that she had no place in the Cariboo.

It was symptomatic of Wilfred's different relationship to this place that Hodgins's Mr. Eckhart was altogether more gently rendered than his wife. Wilfred was determined to repeat his father's journey from the "old country" to the coast of British Columbia, moved now, however, by a different necessity. "Nothing in all my comings and goings to match it," he wrote to Jack Shadbolt: "The point here— lagoon point—at the end of a long spit, is just like the point at Chemainus, which I had to myself the thirteen years I worked at the mill there, but even more picturesque."

When early in 1980 Wilfred found the property that so satisfied him, understandably he wanted Sheila to see and approve of it. In a response which in its maddening clarity reached back through years of refusing to divorce Wilfred while agreeing to be divorced by him, back at least to Chaucer's Griselda (after whom, of course, Wilfred had named his wifely Volvo), Sheila refused to see and approve the property, at the same time agreeing that she would move there if Wilfred insisted. His telling her that he needed her savings as well as his own to close the deal was a way of ensuring her involvement, if not her wholehearted participation in this venture.

Although Wilfred had lived and taught in Edmonton five years longer than Sheila, he clearly had less to lose in moving than she. Despite his involvement in theatre in Edmonton, the kind of life he envisaged for his retirement was not so dependent on the resources of the city as was the case with Sheila. Not for the first time in their life together, Wilfred sensed, I think, that the only resource he needed to carry with him in order to strike roots and continue with his writing, aside, of course, from his own wits, was Sheila.

His return to the land near Chemainus—and Nanaimo is only a few miles north of the mill where he and his father had worked—saw Wilfred engaging with the place and with his own past with a kind of energy and in a variety of forms and media which suggest that his "complete and consuming passion [for] poetry," which Sheila had described years before to T. S. Eliot, had been well served by this move. The configurations and the shifting light of lagoon, spit, and outcroppings recur in his drawings and water colours, and driftwood he picked up on walks revealed faces he painted into life. But the most striking and at the same time the most significant legacy of his return to the Island is a volume of poems published in 1982, entitled *Mass on Cow Back*.

The title plays off the title of Wyndham Lewis's 1941 chalk drawing *Witch on Cow Back* as it memorializes an event which, Wilfred told me, had actually taken place in a patch of meadow on the outcropping across the lagoon from their living room window. An open-air mass was celebrated, and the touching incongruousness of the event provided him with the structure and certain ritual touchstones for his second collection of number-grid poems.

It combines Wilfred's poems with his drawings. These last are strange and powerful and frequently as startling as flattened collages. The poems are filled with names, some well known and others familiar only to those who knew Wilfred and Sheila's circle of friends and acquaintances. Jack Shadbolt, for one, was later puzzled to find his own name linked in a short story by Wilfred with a name which meant nothing to him. It was as if Wilfred had brought with him to his new/old home many of those whom Sheila had left with regret, at the same time recovering some— his father and mother, for example—who still haunted the place for him.

The poems are arranged in six groups: Kyrie, Gloria, Credo, Sanctus, Benedictus, and Agnus Dei, parts familiar to one who listened as often as Wilfred did to the masses of Bach and Mozart and Haydn.

Wilfred's interest in the mass, however, did not extend to enabling Sheila to attend mass. In Edmonton she had been within easy walking distance of the chapel

Sheila on the spit in Nanaimo.

at St. Joseph's College on the campus, where, after returning to the church, she attended Sunday mass. From Place Road nothing was so accessible. Sheila remained reluctant to ask Wilfred to drive her to church, and he did not offer to do so. This was another fact of their life together, and of her isolation.

Between his poetry and his painted heads—between words and wood—Wilfred appears to have recovered something of the life he had once led there. In the same letter in which she had spoken to Eliot of his "consuming passion" for poetry, Sheila described the young Wilfred indulging that passion "while he stripped bark from the great logs." The distance between his poetry and his work with wood was narrower now, as he populated their house with his painted driftwood totemic presences—some witty and playful, some pensive or doleful or menacing—which Sheila referred to, ambiguously, as their children.

There was another presence in the house on Place Road, one which had accompanied them from Edmonton. His name was Sweet William, a cat of mythic although unknown genetic lineage. He was one of two cats who had been part of their lives in Edmonton. The other, whose name was Jerome, did not make it to the coast, for he was given to fits of hysteria. He had a heart attack and died one Edmonton summer night in their chokecherry tree. Sweet William—and his initials, like those of Simone

Weil, are important, for like her he had, or perhaps was, an alter ego—Sweet William had been protective of Jerome. He had come into their lives under circumstances that are revealing of an important aspect of Sheila's temperament.

An acquaintance appeared at their door in Edmonton one day asking for Sheila's support for an organization of women who were protesting the proliferation of nuclear weapons. Sheila hesitated, not because she approved of weapons of mass destruction, but because being a daughter of Swift, she eschewed possibilities in favour of particulars. As she was fond of saying, she could respond to someone knocking on her door for help when she found it difficult to be engaged by issues that were removed from her present or were merely hypothetical. Making a virtue of this unexpected necessity, the caller asked if Sheila would be prepared to take in a kitten, a stray which a friend had brought home only to discover that her young daughter was allergic to it. This was how Sweet William had come into their house— name and all—for a little later, the caller's friend's young daughter herself appeared, bearing the kitten in a basket, and announced that his name was Sweet William because that was what he answered to.

This then was the household that became rooted, or in Wilfred's case rerooted, in this suburb of Nanaimo. It is difficult to know what was left behind, or disposed of, in Edmonton. Wilfred had complained that Sheila had thrown things away with an easy abandon when she was packing up the house there. He asked Diane Bessai to store a trunk containing letters from Sheila to him which he had led her to believe he had destroyed. Rather uneasily, Diane agreed to this. Years later, when Shirley Neuman was helping him sort and pack his papers for the University of Alberta, he told her of these letters, which were still in Edmonton, and said that he wanted them included with his papers. Shirley insisted that Wilfred tell Sheila of their existence, and when he reluctantly did so, Sheila agreed that they should be included in his archives.

⌒

Sheila's response to their new place was more palpable and reflective than it was overtly creative. In the landscape she found a new ground rather than new subject matter. She came quickly to love walks out along the spit, the climb over a steep promontory, which she always negotiated with sure-footedness, and then the path that circled the northern hump of land, along cliffs that look east to Georgia Strait, through a mini-forest of evergreens and oak trees, and meadows carpeted in spring and summer with wild flowers; and below, scavenging sea birds and otters and a blue heron, which she adopted as a kind of guardian of the place, and the tides. A small archipelago, reachable at low tide by foot, separated the Straits from the lagoon. Before the Second World War it had been used by Japanese Canadian fishermen as a base of sorts, and huts they had built then still stand. There were spots where Sheila would sit and smoke and talk—with a visitor or with Wilfred—endlessly intrigued by the beauty and the challenges to her eye. The place was without perspective, she would say, like memory in her earliest publication, a cubist landscape, and she often wished that Marshall had been able to see and to immerse himself in it.

〜

During 1980, ongoing work on behalf of the Canada Council brought Sheila east to meetings in Ottawa and stopovers in Toronto. This provided her with the opportunity to visit with the McLuhan family, to sit or walk with Marshall, who had been stricken in the previous autumn, to rest a hand—as one of his daughters observed—on his, to sustain a silent dialogue. Sheila told me that she had said to him, "It must be hell, Marshall," and he nodded, perhaps relieved at hearing the word that he could no longer speak.

Sheila possessed a sense of silence as well as of words. During this same year, on one of her brief visits to Toronto, I had the opportunity to witness the effects of her presence and of her silence on my father. He was living with me when she came to stay for a day or two. My father—now in his late eighties—had been a widower for seven years, and time had resolved itself for him now into a kind of incessant present. He believed that a bus or a train could take him to the time and place of his youth, and that he could reach my dead mother by telephone.

It was late spring, and on the day Sheila arrived a friend stayed with my father while I met her at the airport. When we reached my place, I saw my father, dressed in his best suit, looking down from an upper porch, expectant. I knew then that he thought I was bringing my mother back.

It was no ordinary scene, as they were no ordinary people. My father's gentle courtesy enabled him to maintain his poise in the midst of a dreadful disappointment. Sheila—to whom I had said nothing of what I had seen—grasped the situation immediately and sat with him in easy silence, holding his hand for what seemed hours.

That September my father died, and I took him home to Vancouver to be buried. Sheila came from Nanaimo for the funeral, in the Jesuit church beside the

Convent of the Sacred Heart. The next day I returned with her for my first visit to Place Road, the lagoon and the spit. Three images, or rather, two sensations and an image, remain with me in particular from that brief visit: the gentleness of Wilfred, his very great gentleness; the undemanding attentiveness of Sweet William; and on an evening walk with Sheila and Wilfred along the spit, the huge full moon of September resting in the branches of an oak tree.

It was on the radio, early on New Year's morning 1981, that I heard of Marshall McLuhan's death. I had just returned to Toronto from Christmas on the west coast. It must have been the eight o'clock news because I remember waiting a couple of hours before phoning the spit. Wilfred answered and said nothing in response to my news but, "I'll get Sheila." Her voice was dry and she was matter-of-fact. I said that I thought she should come, and she did.

The day of Marshall's funeral was a grey and bitterly cold day, too cold even to snow. There was much snow already, and the streets were icy. I remember standing outside Holy Rosary Church on St. Clair Avenue after the mass with Sheila, David Staines, Pat Brückmann, and Leslie Sanders, shivering while Marshall's coffin was being piped into its hearse. The interment was to be in a cemetery north of the city, and with David driving we set out to find our way independent of the funeral cortège. As luck would have it we lost our way, and by the time we found the gates to the cemetery, the grave side rituals had ended and the cars and limousines were departing.

It was not difficult to find the grave site. It was on a small rise and the coffin lay uncovered on ground too thoroughly frozen to be opened. "We can't leave Marshall," Sheila said. The earth was not yet ready to receive her honoured guest, and so for a time we were his only company.

⌐

It was not long before this that Sheila, Wilfred, and I had first talked of a volume of essays on McLuhan. I had believed that his importance as a teacher of literature, his contribution to literary studies as a critic, and his influence on students had been so overshadowed by his role as media guru as to have been lost sight of. I felt, too, as others have, that his own study of literature had prepared him for his more famous work. Because of Marshall's stroke, there was a certain urgency if we were to produce a celebratory rather than a memorial volume.

It was likely in December 1980—when I had returned to the west for Christmas—that we had first brain stormed around their kitchen table, with coffee and cigarettes and Irish whiskey. Sheila and Wilfred were so deeply committed emotionally as well as intellectually to McLuhan and his world, that they picked up and ran with the idea. Sheila in particular became excited by the prospect of broadening the concerns of such a volume to include Marshall's influence on the practical as well as the fine arts, on painting, poetry, music, and cinema, certainly, but also on book design and architecture, on city planning and historiography. My own quite modest proposal soon gave way before these headier possibilities.

Then we thought of possible contributors: Chris Chapman on film, Glenn Gould and Murray Schafer on music, bpNichol on poetry, Jane Jacobs on the city, Carl Berger on Marshall and Harold Innis, Donald Theall on Marshall's influence on communication studies in Canada, Pat Brückmann on his influence on eighteenth-century literary studies. Even the then Prime Minister, Pierre Trudeau, was to be invited to write about McLuhan's impact on government. It was Wilfred who came up with a title for the volume—*Reconnaissance.*

With Marshall's death, celebration necessarily became regret, even though we were determined not to produce a memorial volume. It was his living legacy that concerned us, but his death meant that another kind of work was also there to be done. This included a listing of his library—already begun by Steve McCaffery—and a corrected and expanded checklist of his publications.

By now, and I am referring to the year after Marshall's death, the simple impulse with which all this began had given way to an agenda which saw a companion volume of documents which would include bibliographies and other materials useful for future biographers. But there was also a change in tone, traceable in part to the title Wilfred had proposed and Sheila's taste for meanings and etymologies, and to her very great defensiveness on behalf of Marshall and his work. In a draft of a letter to Shirley Neuman, who with David Staines had been drawn into the planning of this project, Sheila mused:

> We like the title and have again been considering all the implications of the word *reconnaissance* including its use by the military—"an examination of a territory to gain information of enemy troops, of the terrain, or of the resources." The enemy or the "offensive" . . . declared themselves in the late sixties and early seventies. . . .

She then listed the occupants of the "enemy" camp, and continued:

> There have been, of course, the crossing of many swords (s/words) in the battle, but the "offensive" identified itself clearly and the echo

of its cries have continued to reverberate in academic circles at least. In one sense it has had its say. Its words are on record and can be retrieved by anyone interested in the history of such skirmishing.

A note of Joan of Arc had crept in, on the battlements and prepared to go to the stake, the spit transformed into a kind of war room. Sheila ended this account of news from the front with—for me at least—a rather wistful reminder: "We had thought of something else when the project was first considered."

By this time I had withdrawn from the project. My last act had been, in consultation with Shirley and David, to draw up a proposal for a two-volume work on McLuhan, which we submitted to Coach House Press. Shirley and David had been invited by us to join Sheila, Wilfred, and me to form an editorial board for this project. Sheila herself had a growing sense of her own difficulties in remaining part of it all. In a letter to David Staines written in November 1984, she commented on her own growing sense of isolation: "I had begun to realize that it would probably not be possible for me to leave the spit again, that I was cut off by the location and the passage of time from necessary sources of information including adequate library facilities." I, on the other hand, had found myself with responsibilities I had not anticipated, and with a sense that the project had gone beyond what had originally engaged me. Sheila blamed her own intransigence for my withdrawal. This was only partly true. She was right to think that it was the time to document McLuhan's impact on artists, scholars, and other public figures, and I regret that the project was never realized.

Sheila was correct when she observed to David Staines that it was unlikely she would have the chance to leave the spit again. This was in November 1984. In this same letter, she recalled an episode which had occurred the previous spring on what was to be her last visit to Toronto. She had come to accept from the Royal Society of Canada the Lorne Pierce Medal for her contributions to Canadian literature. This took place at the annual meeting of the Society, held that year on 29 May at the University of Guelph.

The occasion dove-tailed with plans to visit Smith College in Hatfield, Massachusetts, where David had been teaching and where he had asked her to give a reading. David drove her from Hatfield to Toronto, and then they and Leslie Sanders and I drove to Guelph where Sheila and David attended what she described as a "tedious and platitudinous dinner." She could not but have been pleased to be so honoured, but pleasure did not sit comfortably with her skepticism about the meaning of such honours. In her letter to David, she described her participation as "a culpable act of compromise," which was partially redeemed in her eyes by "a transforming act of grace" in the form of a comic return from Guelph to Toronto, which saw countless sacred cows—including herself—prodded and roasted. But our efforts were not wholly successful. Subsequent events led Sheila to connect the beginning of her final isolation on the spit to her willingness to compromise her own stern values.

I had arranged a dinner in Sheila's honour for the next evening, to which I had invited as many of her Toronto friends as I knew of and could contact. We cooked a salmon to fête the creator of old Mrs. Potter and Felix Prosper—despite Sheila's dislike of fish; Pat Brückmann arrived with a papier-mâché coyote's head; and grace was said by a Jesuit whose devotion to recordings of opera had led Sheila to rename him Vinyl. Writer friends were there and academic friends and simply friends.

It is a blur to me now as I suspect it was even then—until the telephone rang. It was Wilfred from the spit wanting to speak to Sheila. He told her he was having a stroke, and that already his right arm and hand had been affected. He spoke not in pain but with wonder and excitement. It was only a more extreme and public form of what had become a familiar situation. Earlier in this same year, he had complained in a letter to Jack Shadbolt of a "pinched elbow nerve," which might well have been the cause of this melodramatic complaint.

Sheila cut short her stay and prepared to return to Nanaimo, but before leaving she asked to read an introduction to *The Double Hook* I had recently written. Malcolm Ross, the General Editor of the New Canadian Library, had asked me to write it and I had hesitated, uneasy at the prospect of writing about the work of a friend without first consulting her, uneasy too that I had nothing to add to what had already been written. She encouraged me, and in response to my concern that a new introduction made no sense unless it added something to our understanding of the novel, she offered me hitherto unseen materials, including drafts of the novel and her correspondence with Salter and the essays that both he and she had written when he was attempting to find a publisher for it.

The materials gave me access to the development of the novel. Sheila had spoken often of its origins although not of the choices she had made in the process of writing and revising it. I was satisfied that I might be able to take the author's pulse without usurping the reader's role.

The night before she returned to the west, I left a copy of what I had written beside her bed. She emerged in the morning like thunder, and what is worse, silent thunder. Already assailed by Wilfred's needs, she seemed now to feel betrayed by my account of her revising *The Double Hook*. I took her by taxi to the airport, a silent journey. I felt miserable and angry: miserable at the prospect of having disappointed a friend, and angry, I suppose, because I found her response puzzling and excessive. Perhaps what I had written was simply bad, or perhaps, as a mutual friend later suggested to me, I had unwittingly come too close to some matters that Sheila found difficult to consider.

It was now—in 1984—twenty-five years since its publication, and Sheila's sense of her then only published novel had become so entangled with her sense of herself that it was difficult for her to take certain responses to it other than personally. I don't mean that Sheila was thin-skinned, but *The Double Hook* had become— like her name—an extension of herself, a way in which she was perceived and in which she had come to think of herself. She was protective as one might be protective of one's "good" name, or of a child. These are relationships that an outsider— regardless of how good a friend—probes and demystifies at his peril.

Her protectiveness extended to the book's cover. She thought that a cover should provide ground for a title. This was why she had ultimately been so pleased with Frank Newfeld's design for the first cover. She measured its successors—and there were a number once it had gone into the New Canadian Library series—by this, and found them all wanting: a drawing of herself, a design in colours, but, most offensive of all, a photograph from the Glenbow Museum in Calgary of a pioneer woman feeding chickens. When this cover appeared, she asked me to see someone at McClelland & Stewart about having it replaced. Not only did the picture have nothing to do with the title, it embodied precisely the kind of regionalism that Sheila was attempting to free herself from when she wrote the novel. It was soon replaced by a simple, stylized drawing of a double hook.

When David Staines succeeded Malcolm Ross as editor of the series, and set about to enhance its appearance by using Canadian paintings and sculpture on its covers, aware of Sheila's concerns, he asked me to help him find a picture fit for *The Double Hook*. The ferocious image that now greets the reader, Jean Dallaire's *Chien Apocalyptique*, was the result of this search. Sheila was not happy with it. It pictured a dog, not a coyote, and what was worse, a dog described as apocalyptic when she saw herself as the least apocalyptic of writers. Moreover, the "chien" had no "genitaux," the price undoubtedly of being "apocalyptique." In time, she accepted the memberless dog, even as she did my introduction.

Sheila's creative work in this decade—as throughout her life—was largely done in support of the creativity of others. She remained a teacher long after her retirement because she remained a reader, an audience for all, and a passionate champion for those in whom she came to believe. Many deplored the time she spent on the work of others—understandable though such efforts might be when those others were Daphne Marlatt or George Bowering or Michael Ondaatje or Roy Kiyooka; much less understandable when names were less familiar. Naysayers insisted upon distinguishing between the value of her own and others' work, between her creative and critical activities, distinctions that Sheila simply refused to admit. She entered as wholly and as unobtrusively into the aims and aspirations of others as she did into characters and situations she had herself created.

Sheila had published seven of Miriam Mandel's poems in the first issue of *White Pelican*, in the winter of 1971, and another poem a year later. In 1973, *White Pelican* published her first collection of poems, *Lion at her face*, which won that year's Governor General's Award for poetry in English. Her second and third volumes, *Station 14* and *Where Have You Been?*, were published by Longspoon Press in Edmonton after *White Pelican* had ceased to publish.

In June 1980, in what was to be one of a series of testamentary declarations, Mandel wrote at the beginning of a notebook: "To be edited by Sheila Watson, Nanaimo, BC if I pre-deceas (sic) her." This note was written during one of her many periods in hospitals, this time at Station 14 in the University Hospital in Edmonton. In the next month, in the midst of a sea of words in the same notebook, there is a cry: "Hey Sheila—come back." In the next month, August 1980, she wrote to Sheila and Wilfred: "Edmonton seems to have shrunk to half its size. Your absence is a sigh through the whole city."

Mandel came late to poetry even though she had lived with it for most of her life—as a student of literature at the University of Saskatchewan and as wife to the poet and critic Eli Mandel. Her poetry was to become her means of transforming chaos and vulnerability into words that are as spare as her feelings were often diffuse.

In 1982, on 13 February, Miriam Mandel finally achieved what over the years she had attempted many times: she died as the result of an overdose. In October 1980, she had written another testament, although again not her last: "If there is any part of me that is of use to the U of A Hospital, my body is totally theirs. Cremation with no service. Ashes not to be kept but flushed."

Mandel began to write poetry in the wake of her divorce from Eli Mandel, in 1968. Or rather, she began to write, for she insisted later that she was not consciously writing poetry. At this time, she was more frequently in than out of hospitals and, according to her obituary in the *Edmonton Journal*, she was visited weekly by Sheila, who brought "binders, notebooks, and advice." It was Sheila who persuaded her of the nature and of the worth of what she was writing.

After Mandel's death, when Sheila set about to collect her poetry, she used as the basis for her intended edition the contents of the three already published volumes. She did not, however, merely reprint these collections. She omitted some poems that had originally been included and included others that Mandel herself had chosen not to include. This is the heart of the collection, and it was supplemented by unpublished poems that Sheila had gleaned from her journals and from sequences-in-progress at the time of Mandel's death.

In the opening to her introduction, Sheila called into question the title she chose for the volume, *The Collected poems of Miriam Mandel*: "What we have here is not really a collection of poetry, but something now frequently called a long or serial poem. . . ." In the case of either title, the role of the editor is of central importance. As collector the editor brings her taste and judgement to bear in selecting what is to be collected. As editor of a single poem disguising itself as many poems, she uncovers what has not been obvious, and her powers to select and to arrange poems are at the service of her sense of the author's design. Although she did not entitle the volume "The Miriamiad," the poems Sheila collected in effect form a kind of lyrical epic, in the tradition of Whitman's *Song of Myself* or the poems of Emily Dickinson. Although Sylvia Plath and Anne Sexton might seem more obvious models for her work, Sheila made another distinction in her introduction which in effect removes Mandel from the company of these so-called confessional poets. "The poem," she wrote, referring to the volume as a whole, "is not a confession. It is a disclosure, the necessary deconstruction of any comforting evasion."

In her distinction between disclosure and confession, Sheila moved to the heart of Mandel's poetry. Mandel had admitted she was inclined to "choose more personal subjects" than many other poets, but to draw upon personal experience and to confess can answer to very different needs, and Mandel had been aware of this. For her, poetry was an alternative to confession, not a form of it:

> Not for me
> the luxury
> of holy water, priests, choir boys
> and
> greatest of all

confession.
I must find
other means
for dispersing the guilt.

And her poetry provided the "other means."

Kenneth Burke wrote that:

> once a man has perfected a technique of complaint, he is more at
> home with sorrow than he would be without it. He has developed
> an equipment, and the integrity of his character is best upheld by
> situations that enable him to use it. Otherwise, he would have to
> become either disintegrated or reborn.

As a Jew, Miriam Mandel found herself attracted to the rituals, the iconography and
modes of consolation of Christianity, and especially of Roman Catholicism. But elements in her own nature and in her tradition kept her from any but an imaginative
interest in these. She wanted, as she said in a late poem, "no saviors haloing about
my head": she sought no forgiveness, "unasked for, unwanted." "My longing to be a
book overcame me," she had written early in her career, and Sheila as her editor
helped her to realize that longing.

The year in which Mandel's collected poems were published, 1985, also saw the publication of *Seventy-One Poems for People* by George Bowering. The volume contains
a brief note by way of an afterward by Sheila, a note whose presence is unnoted anywhere in the book but where it appears, at the end. It was solicited by the book's editor, Dennis Johnson of Red Deer College Press. In a letter to Bowering's wife, Angela,
Sheila recalled her uneasiness about her presence in a book whose author seemed
not to have anticipated or invited it. "I have always felt uncomfortable about that
afterword," she wrote, "because I told Dennis Johnson that I did not want him to use
it unless George agreed to have his book encumbered with it." Her next comment,
"So much for reassurances," suggests that the decision to include it was the editor's
rather than Bowering's. This was, in fact, the case. Because Sheila had already written a preface for his 1982 selected poems, *West Window*, Bowering claims that he
would have hesitated to ask her to write a second preface, and for a collection he did
not especially value. Her presence—even if uninvited—was tactful. "I tried to let

him speak for himself," she continued to Angela Bowering, sensitive to the invasive possibilities of what she described as "binding oneself into or between the covers of someone else's textual space." For Sheila knew what it was to be an outsider, a coastal dweller in the Cariboo, a mainlander on the Island.

It is ironic that she should have felt herself an intruder in a book by George Bowering. She had no more enthusiastic and affectionate champion than he—enthusiasm and affection that Sheila reciprocated. She had been a member of the jury that in 1980 awarded his *Burning Water* the Governor General's Award for fiction in English, and he had been delighted with her 1982 preface to *West Window*, especially as she saw his work "in an international setting" of developments in literature and painting on the continent and in New York as well as in Canada. "I could just kiss you," was his final comment in a note of thanks to her, adding, "and likely will."

In 1985, aside from *Seventy-One Poems*, he edited and published a collection of essays on *The Double Hook*, including one by himself in which he hailed the novel as "the watershed of contemporary Canadian fiction." And in *Bowering's B.C.*, he speaks of *The Double Hook* as "the best novel to come out of the province," concluding the section he devotes to her with the claim that "more than any other Canadian novel, it is loved and referred to by the innovative poets and fiction writers who have arrived on the Canadian scene since 1959." "I call the interesting stuff written since 1959 the 'Sheila Watson canon,'" he wrote in *Craft Slices*. He includes Robert Kroetsch among those who, in his words, "have followed on Watson's breakthrough," along with the Leonard Cohen of *Beautiful Losers*, "Michael Ondaatje, bpNichol, Victor Levy-Beaulieu, Nicole Brossard, and Louky Bersianik." Bowering was even more succinct at the close of a letter he had written to her in 1982:

> On Thursday I got a phone call from Coach House Press, talked
> with Frank Davey, Michael [Ondaatje], and bp[Nichol]. Wonderful
> age we're in.

> & it's yrs

Bowering had first met Sheila in Edmonton in 1963. He had already read *The Double Hook*, which had been published four years earlier, although his first response to it had hardly prepared him for his later respect for it. "When I finished it," he told me, "I threw it across the room," in a gesture not of exhilaration or of homage, but of frustration: "I hadn't understood a word of it." In 1987 he published his own Cariboo novel. *Caprice* is a loose reworking of the film classic *Shane*, with the setting now the valleys of the Cariboo, and with a mysterious hero transformed into an almost equally mysterious heroine, the Caprice of the title. Bowering's judgement about the presence of Sheila's novel in the work of "innovative poets and fiction writers" can here be illustrated in his own playing with certain of her characters. In the town to which James Potter flees in the fourth section of *The Double Hook*, the town that is home to the beer-guzzling parrot, he is taken in hand by a blond-haired man named Traff, who with the help of a prostitute named Lilly finally relieves him of his wallet. In another town—still in the Cariboo country—although at a time before the motor cars that are present in the town of Sheila's novel, in a tale told some thirty years after Sheila's, a doctor speaks of "delivering a baby for one of Gert's girls," whose name is Lilly Traff. Like Sheila's Traff, Bowering's baby has a "cap of hair, straight and thick and yellow." Like the hair that reminded James Potter of the young woman Lenchen, who was carrying his child, the baby's hair reminds Bowering's doctor "of an old Shuswap story I heard"—the story perhaps of the yellow-haired Tay John of Howard O'Hagan's 1939 tale of the Shuswap.

It is a larky reference, an anachronistic homage, in a sequel to *The Double Hook* whose action predates the action it presumes to complete. With equal shrewdness and delicacy, the reference encompasses and implies a relationship between Sheila's and O'Hagan's novel.

In August 1983, George and Angela Bowering and their daughter, Thea, drove to Dog Creek from Vancouver. Bowering sent a card to Sheila when they returned, noting that his wish that they would see a coyote there was answered when "a big lanky one, crossed the road in front of us, went up the hill and watched us." It was in the following spring, in May 1984, that Angela Bowering, with a recollected sense of immediacy, wrote to Sheila at greater length of this same trip. She, too, described the coyote, as well as a little moose and a fool hen. The appearance of the coyote did not so much gratify a wish of hers as make her feel, as she said, "an intruder a desecrator." It was for her "like visiting a shrine," this pilgrimage to "a sacred place," and when they found themselves "off the map and also the topographical map," they went, she said, by "your book":

> & when we came to a place where 3 roads meet . . . I said James
> descends, it must be the leftmost branches down (the others were
> level & up a little), & we took it & came to a little tree fallen across
> the road & because signs had been torn off & we were on reserva-
> tion territory & weren't supposed to be I thought it was to keep peo-
> ple out & George said it was beaver teeth marked, so we went on &
> coyote appeared. . . .

The Double Hook provided Angela Bowering with a map for her own imagination as well as for Dog Creek and its environs. It was also, as she stated repeatedly in letters to Sheila, a life-line. She spoke of it as having saved her life—perhaps because it provided a focal point, a resting place for her own restless imagination, memory and intelligence. She called Sheila "mother of my imagination," "the other half of a dialogue between self & soul," "shamanka." She was one of those daughters of Sheila whom Sheila's sense of literalness left her uneasy about acknowledging as such.

Angela Bowering's celebration of *The Double Hook* in *Figures Cut in Sacred Ground* was published in 1988. In an introduction, Shirley Neuman described Angela's method as "Sheila Watson's own": "she enters the text as might a devout phenomenologist, immersing herself and us in it, following the preoccupations in its own spirit and as far as they will take us, never imposing herself." Still, one can imagine Bowering reading *The Double Hook* aloud as if the words had formed in her own mouth. "It is the dynamic response of your mind to a textual ground," Sheila wrote to her, "that fascinates me when I read your book."

What we have in Angela Bowering is a person possessed by a book and by its author. But this possession—and it is a word which she used to describe the effect of her first reading of Sheila's novel—did not isolate or distort her critical judgement. She remained sensitive to the significance of *The Double Hook* beyond its importance for herself. In a letter to Sheila written in July 1991, she recalled an episode which occurred in the context of a rumour circulating that the Coach House Press was planning to bring out an edition of the Ur-text of Sheila's novel:

> I was talking to Frank Davey at Fred Wah and Pauline Butling's con-
> ference in Calgary in early May about whether or not Coach House
> was going to do your book—Sharon Thesen had heard from
> Michael Ondaatje that they were—and Frank said he thought DH
> was a dangerous book, and I said I thought it was too, but what did
> he mean? He said he thought it was essentially conservative and
> Roman Catholic in its vision, that it suffered from the problems of
> modernism. I remarked that that was what we all had to contend
> with, and that conservatism didn't automatically = WRONG; if it is
> conservative, it does not minimize the complexity of the bafflement
> we endure as human creatures. It focuses it, I said, pointing out
> what is obvious about formal innovation, pointing out also that b.p.
> learned a great deal from it; he seemed to think DH was something
> b.p. had to struggle to get beyond, which may well have been true,

in a complicated way, but I said how do you know that he would have got anywhere important without it?

She ended this anecdote by turning back to familiar territory: "I get impatient with the murder of the mothers, fathers that inevitably goes on when it gets excessively ungrateful to what after all gave birth to it, and this is true of our literary parents as well as of our actual ones."

⤻

Frank Davey and Angela Bowering were both correct about bpNichol's relationship to Sheila's novel. The matter of his indebtedness to or captivation by it is a part of Canadian literary history. Some thirty years earlier than this exchange in Calgary, in the winter of 1962–63, an eighteen-year-old Nichol picked up a used copy of *The Double Hook* in a Salvation Army store in Winnipeg. In 1974, in response to a question of Daphne Marlatt about his early love of prose over poetry, Nichol recalled that incident:

> when I found Sheila Watson's *The Double Hook* I thought, right, there's everything that I could conceive of doing at that point in time done. So, I still wanted to write, and I thought, well, I think I'll just start writing. So I stopped worrying about it and started working mostly on poetry.

If Chapman's translation of Homer begot Keats's sonnet, by his own admission, Sheila's novel begot Nichol as poet. And when he came to write prose fiction, he did so under the eye of *The Double Hook*.

Sheila's own aspirations in writing her second novel in reaction to her first— her desire to create voices rather than a voice—echo in Nichol's response to Marlatt's question: "what is it about prose that holds you?"

> There's more possibility for playing around with characters and all those things. I think—this is purely personal—I've tended to use poetry as a medium of self-expression. And traditionally in prose you can write "fictions." So that's probably why I got interested in prose, writing about things other than self, you know (even though you're always writing about self anyways).

In the interview in which this exchange occurred, Nichol spoke at length of a work of his which at that time had appeared only in parts. *Journal* was not published in its entirety until 1978. In this earlier interview, he referred to it as "a novel," and his account of it sounds both familiar and strange to a reader of Sheila's novel:

> Well the state that is happening . . . is one in which external reality just gets subsumed into internal reality. And really all the incidents that happen, even when they start off as suddenly super-objective moments for me, like you'll meet someone or he'll do something, then it just gets consumed into the confusion, until finally he just has to shove all that aside and in a way just go back to his own beginning, which in that case is his relationship to his mother. You know, literally, he finds a grammar for memory in a sense. And then he can proceed from there. . . . And then it's just a long string of very clear memories that all sort of circle around a couple of incidents and the way he felt. But it's like just incident after incident of him feeling his way in this relationship to that woman. . . .

At this point, Daphne Marlatt interjected:

> Well she never does get outside him. That's why I keep balking at "character," because I can't think of it as character. It's simply a consciousness in which all these things orbit. And she never gets outside that container, she is always contained by it.

Nichol responded, "Right. It's entirely his view." *Journal*, when it appeared in volume form, bore the dedication "for Sheila Watson."

The prospect of a son's consciousness containing his mother—as her belly had once contained him—took another turn in Nichol's account of a dream which he sent to Sheila a few months after the publication of *Journal*. It is dated 31 March 1979:

> from *Six Questions After Michael Anthin*
> by Sheila Watson

> "I start out with the idea of place to fix you there Mommy. Interwoven—interspecies."

> dreamed March 79: commentary

> in the dream Sheila offers to read to me from a new story she has written called *Bear* after the character of Kallisto in her story

Antigone. . . . but before that she proposes to read to me from a little piece she had written called *Six Questions After Michael Anthin*,
in order to show me how she is using language to hinge from reference to reference in a dream oriented way. she cites as an example
the shift from Georgina to garage in which the buried associative
hinge is Gene's garage which is near where she lives. she starts to
read to me as above from a hand-written notebook & then stops &
says "no, this is an earlier draft. I'll read to you from the latest draft,"
and begins to look for it.

associatively the day before i had been having a long talk with
Michael Ondaatje and when she read me the title of her piece i
heard it as *Michael's Anthem* i.e. the animals that appear in his
poems (hence "Interspecies"). i had also been reading Fred Wah's
second draft of *Breathin' My Name With A Sigh* in which the
notions of place & family are interwoven & in which in the poem
which begins with the single word "mother" he ends with the lines
"mother somewhere I remember you flying over me / remembering
me in your tummy mummy out side a moist loss / caress & float."
hence, perhaps the other references. in the notebook as i looked at
it i saw the interpolated word "unanswered" between "six" & "questions" & thus the final dream title of the piece should read *Six
Unanswered Questions After Michael's Anthem.*

Like the character in his novel, bp as dreamer contains in his consciousness the
mother of his art. This is not so much simplistic or reductive as obvious. The same
issue of *The Capilano Review* that contained the interview with Nichol that I have
quoted from, also contains an interview with Sheila, which ends with her reflections
on influence:

You can't escape influence. It starts at the beginning of your life. . . .
You're never innocent. You're compromised the minute you are
born. Then there is the terrible responsibility for something like
language which you can't destroy—the utterances which are going
around you if you pay attention to them—the responsibility for taking something into your consciousness.

If you can't avoid influence, it is clearly best to celebrate it, and that is what bpNichol did in his own wild and graceful way in his homages to Sheila.

When we were planning the collection of essays about McLuhan's influence that Wilfred had named *Reconnaissance*, Sheila believed that bp would be the best person to write of Marshall's importance for the poets of his generation. She was delighted with his brief, what he called his "idiosyncratic essay": "[McLuhan] showed us," bp concluded, "a way to reenergize the language, the word world." And in his title—"The Medium Was The Message"—he combined his own taste for punning with a delicate elegiac touch. Nichol was thirty-eight years old at this time, and within six years he too would be dead, the medium and his Sheila-appointed messenger gone in the same decade.

~

The all-but-final question that Wilfred posed to her—"Why did we have no children?"—echoes eerily back through the evidence of Sheila's progeny. The role of matriarch or den-mother was not a role she invited or easily accepted. Her distance upon herself and her sense of fact saved her from falling prey to that particular form of veneration. The strength and the rootedness of her own sense of self made her very sensitive to the separateness of others, at the same time preserving her from the efforts of others to remake her according to their wants and needs. Her parenthood was a status bestowed upon her by her progeny—a case of the "child" being parent to the woman—and not the other way round. Sheila's sense of influence, as we have seen, is a sense not of something bestowed but of something inherited, of an inevitable condition of compromise, a kind of original sin.

Though very different in its consequences, Sheila's influence on Angela Bowering and bpNichol recalls George Bowering's judgement that the publication of *The Double Hook* had left "the innovative poets and fiction writers who . . . arrived on the Canadian scene since 1959" necessarily in her debt. And the debt was not solely to this novel but to her other writings as well as to her interaction with writers. Together with the real isolation of life on the spit there existed what was only an apparent isolation from writers and writing in the country. In the early eighties her continuing work with and for the Canada Council kept her in touch with new talent. And until 1984, her public readings continued, readings that had taken her as far east as Quebec. But they were her contacts with places and the people associated with those places that kept her in touch with the literary life of the country. Toronto remained central in her life even after her last visit in 1984, because of friends, because of the Bob Miller Book Room, that kept her stocked with reading, because of Father Leland at St. Michael's College ready to offer mass for whatever intentions she entrusted to him. I remember on one of her last visits—in the summer of 1983—she read at Harbourfront in connection with the publication of an anthology of Canadian literature edited by Donna Bennett and Russell Brown. It was an afternoon reading followed by a reception, and I remember that Sheila read "Antigone," and P. K. Page, who also read, said to Sheila that she would have given all her own work to have written "Antigone." After the readings, as we drank wine and ate cheese among large cardboard advertisements for the anthology, Elizabeth Smart, accompanied by an Antigone-like granddaughter, made her determined way to Sheila—they had never met—and attempted to kneel in homage before her. Sheila was startled and perplexed, as were bpNichol and Philip Marchand who were talking with her at the time. bp fell back, taking one of the advertisements with him. I remember Sheila and I remember Elizabeth Smart's determination and her granddaughter's poise in the midst of this slapstick and strangely moving scene.

Vancouver's Simon Fraser University and Capilano College also provided locations where she read and where she found kinds of literary activity that drew together, in the case of SFU, the Bowerings, Roy Miki, and Roy Kiyooka, and in the case of Capilano College, Daphne Marlatt, Pierre Coupey, and Gladys Hindmarch. And Nanaimo was not without its venues and its writers. Malaspina College was a mecca for local as for visiting writers. Michael Ondaatje stayed with Sheila and Wilfred at Place Road on at least one occasion when he read there. And among the poets and writers of fiction who lived in the area, none intrigued Sheila more than the man she first knew as her window washer, Jim Breingan, whose business card read, *Jack of Hearts / Window Washing Service*. His post-Laurentian vitality and his courtliness enchanted her, as did the exuberance and disingenuousness of his poetry and prose vignettes. Sheila's real lifeline in Nanaimo, however, was the Bookstore on Bastion Street and its owner, Thora Howell.

A paragraph from a letter she wrote me in the early nineties gives a sense of the various channels by which she kept in touch with a wider world of letters:

> Thank you for sending *Good Bones* as well as the Meissner *Loyola* and Daryl Hine's *Postscripts*. Perhaps because I picked up a copy of *The Carnal and the Crane* when it was published I have always associated his [Hine's] emergence as "a BC poet at a rather early age"—though I knew he had disappeared across the border and that he had edited *Poetry* for a decade. W[ilfred] was or is particularly

pleased at the moment to have the Hine. You might try to pick up a copy of Helen Humphreys *Nuns Looking Anxious* (Brick) for yourself. Pat Barclay, my Sisters of St. Anne (sic) connection, sent a copy of it to Wilfred after she was here. Wilfred had been much impressed by her first volume *Gods & Other Mortals* which he had recommended for a publishing grant when Kathy Benzekri sent it to him from The Canada Council for "evaluation"—or better for an "opinion." I managed to pick up a copy of Sylvia Fraser's *The Book of Strange* at The Bastion Book Store here for him. Michael sent us a copy of *The English Patient*. So much for living on the fringe; so I was, in all truth, grateful for the books you sent for a birthday which by coincidence established me, you may shiver to hear, as "a Nanaimo writer."

Her central literary relationship remained her relationship with Wilfred. When she was asked in the early eighties if he had been an influence on her work, she replied simply, "Any mind with which you are seriously in contact is an influence." And their minds did remain "seriously in contact." Those who were fortunate enough to participate in what Wilfred liked to call "the seminars" will know what I mean. These were highlights for many who visited them on Place Road; intense and demanding as their seminar room equivalents—still warm, personal, and congenial. They inevitably began in the morning at the kitchen table over early breakfast with Wilfred—the visitor made a special effort to be at the kitchen table early because Wilfred would be waiting. They continued through lunch and into walks out the spit and on to Cow Back and about the outcropping, and often into evenings by the fire—expertly laid and stoked by Sheila.

Courtesy marked these occasions, both as they proceeded and in their inevitable concern with matters of particular interest to their guest(s). It was Wilfred—early riser that he was—who introduced a subject, usually, although not always, literary in nature. Something out of Shakespeare, perhaps, or Robert Lowell or McLuhan. Something to do with perspective or architecture or language or the identity of Tristram Shandy's father, or some political folly such as the Gulf War. The seminars then proceeded in two stages: up to the appearance of Sheila (late to bed and late to rise) and after. Whatever problems existed in their marriage, whatever their differences about life at the spit, whatever the consequences of Wilfred's self-absorption or his uncertainties, or of Sheila's anguish, respect marked and shaped these occasions. One came to know that a subject had not been exhausted until Sheila had considered it. She did not fancy herself a *dea ex machina* emerging to sum up and conclude, but Wilfred could not conceive of anything reaching a final formulation without her contribution. This was as true in the case of his own writing as of the seminars.

Letters written during periods of separation see Wilfred again and again sending Sheila drafts of works, and Sheila responding with generosity and shrewdness that often belied the anger and pain that her journals of the same period recorded. She remained loyal to her sense of his gifts even when he was most obviously disloyal. Her supportiveness was unflagging. In one letter she questioned with great tact his reworking of the opening of a poem, at the same time admitting that her reaction might have excluded "the subtlety of the variations—or the 'texture' of your will," and that she might have "missed the centre of your meaning." She ended, "As far as I'm concerned I'd take the poem which ever way you gave it to me—though you will come yourself as you always do to the absolute rightness."

Wilfred could also be generous in praising Sheila's accomplishments and in acknowledging his indebtedness to her. Before she rejoined him in Edmonton, in 1961, he used to refer to her to his students as the best writer of short stories in Canada. To her he wrote of the opening of "Antigone," ". . . it is one of the most wonderful passages of prose I know." And he continued, "like Swift's, it abjures poetry and is of the very essence of poetry." "As I explored Yeats," he wrote during her Toronto years, "I realized how much you'd taught me, in the last two years, about modern poetry." He had encouraged her to keep and record her occasional poems and proposed to buy her "a plain, smooth-paged manual (intended I think for botany sketches)—for your other talent of drawing." He spoke in a more ambiguous vein of his own short story "The Lice" illuminating "the art of the *Double Hook*." Like Angela Bowering after him, at moments he seemed determined to "put on" Sheila's consciousness and imagination. His "put ons," however, and especially those involving *The Double Hook,* were often parodic, where Bowering's were always reverential. Sheila, on the other hand, maintained a judicious distance on Wilfred's work.

In the early seventies, George Melnyk had questioned Sheila about the practical problems posed by "two writers [living] under one roof as equals." "Is it possible for two people to live as equals!" she had exclaimed. "Artists are no different," she continued:

Of course it's difficult with two people banging away on typewriters or two people wanting intellectual space but you learn to stay out, to respect one another's space. As a writer I don't want to be parasitic on other lives. Maybe this is just a reticence or perhaps it comes out of two writers living together where you can become mutual victims. In my writing, experience had to be totally transmuted.

～

The eighties remained a very productive time for Wilfred, a time of new work and of shoring up. *Mass on Cow Back* was followed in 1983 by the publication of his tripartite play in number-grid verse *Gramsci X 3*, which was given a remarkable production at the University of Alberta in the spring of 1986, directed by Tom Peacocke. In that same year, 1986, Wilfred's *POEMS: collected / unpublished / new* was published. This was the first of three volumes, followed by a collection of his plays in 1989 and of his stories in 1993, that saw his canon established. It was Sheila with the help of Shirley Neuman and NeWest and Longspoon Presses in Edmonton who realized this project. When Shirley had asked her what she might do to help her in her unhappiness on the Island, Sheila responded, "Publish Wilfred." This represented simply the final stage in a role Sheila had assumed from the beginning of their relationship. She was his audience and his teacher, but she was also his editor and his agent. It was she who gathered together Wilfred's poetry, who examined drafts and established the text for his collected *POEMS*. She refused to be acknowledged as editor of the volume when it appeared, but it is as much a testimony to her taste and scrupulousness as her edition of Miriam Mandel's poems. Like all she had done on behalf of Wilfred and his work, this was an act of conviction, which was as much rooted in her feelings for him as in her sense of herself and of her own critical judgement.

In his archives there survive two versions of a dedication which Wilfred considered affixing to his collected *POEMS*. The fuller of these reads as follows: "for Sheila who taught me (following the praxis and theorem(?) of Hannah Arendt) the 3 kinds of love. Love past, the love of god. Love future, sexual love, and love present, the hatred of ecological and political injustice." The shorter version merely omits the parenthetical reference to his source. Neither, and indeed no dedication, appeared.

In the same folder in his archives that contains this would-be dedication, there is a draft declaration that reveals a sense of artistic purpose not taught him by Sheila. "My special interest has been the development of uniquely Canadian verse and dramatic forms," he wrote—"If the form is foreign, then the poem or play w'd fall short of being genuinely Canadian. Take care of the form and the content will take care of itself. As for nationalism, I see it as a passion to write the peoples of a country—it is dramatically opposed to racism." Such a statement suggests the distance between his sense of the narrowness and fragility of a Canadian identity and McLuhan's sense, and indeed Sheila's, of its transformative potential.

～

One consequence of Wilfred's activities, which was also an acknowledgment of his importance to Canadian letters, was an invitation to read in 1989 in the International Festival of Authors at Harbourfront in Toronto. He had over the years denounced such readings as "whoredom," but with Sheila's encouragement he relented on this occasion. However, a combination of his shyness and the nature of his more recent number-grid poetry, which really required a choral performance, led him to ask me if I would gather a group of students from a modern poetry course I was teaching to work through his poems and read a selection in his stead at the festival. Greg Gatenby, the event's impresario, agreed to the students reading only if Wilfred agreed to appear on the platform with them to introduce the selections. This was fine with Wilfred. I had no trouble finding volunteers. Five undergraduates, two young women and three young men, who came to call themselves "The Number Grids," worked for weeks to transform poems on the page into performance.

Wilfred arrived the day before the reading, to be interviewed by *The Globe and Mail* and to stay with me. It was, as it happened, Ash Wednesday. With Wilfred's consent, I had invited the students to supper that evening, to meet him and to let him hear what they had prepared. For most of them—perhaps for all of them—this was their first "acquaintance" with a senior poet. They were not disappointed. As I observed him with the students, I was reminded of Tom Peacocke's comments in his introduction to Wilfred's collected *POEMS*: "He has never lost his youth nor his innate capacity to relate to the young—indeed it is from that perspective that he approaches ideas, problems, and situations with a mind free of preconceptions. In fact, the child within seems a dynamic of his creative process." When they read, however, the child within him became somewhat peevish. Fortunately, the students seemed not to have noticed that he was disappointed with what we had done by way of preparation. His suggestions were few but they made clear to me the depth of his disapproval. I felt as I had when Sheila first responded to my introduction to *The Double Hook.*

The next morning, the *Globe and Mail* interview with Wilfred appeared, giving him pride of place among that evening's readings. He had something of the reputation of a Garbo, eccentric and reclusive, and the fact of his appearance was hailed as an event. Former students and admirers were gathering. But the event was not to be. Wilfred emerged that same morning complaining of flu-like symptoms. He said that it would be impossible for him to attend, much less participate in the reading. Between classes that day I contacted Gatenby's office, to find—through his secretary— that he was as intractable as Wilfred. He insisted that segment of the program should be dropped as the festival worked on the premise that writers read their own work and did not have them read for them. Thinking of the time the students had given to this project and of the depth of their commitment to Wilfred and to his poetry, I argued that they must be allowed to read. He agreed reluctantly—and through his secretary—that they could read, but first, not last as originally scheduled.

We had arranged on the previous evening that Wilfred, Leslie Sanders, and I would meet the students for supper before the reading. They were saddened by his absence, but their concern was with his well-being rather than with their own disappointment. In the best tradition of backstage courage they went on for him—and they triumphed. A few days later, the headline in the *Globe and Mail* for an article reviewing the festival read "Students Get A+." By the time I got home from the reading that evening, Wilfred had already risen from his sick bed, had arranged for a flight back to the west the next morning rather than some days later as originally planned, and waited eagerly for news of the evening. We never spoke of this episode again, although without a doubt it put a strain on our friendship. I think, like Sheila in the matter of my introduction, Wilfred had assumed that I would act as he would have, and in neither case did I meet their expectations.

A passage in a letter Wilfred wrote to Jack Shadbolt in the following November will play epilogue to this episode. Shadbolt had recently been honoured by the province of British Columbia on the occasion of a significant birthday. Wilfred wrote to congratulate him, and in the course of doing so he recalled the honour done him the previous spring in Toronto:

> As an event, compared to your birthday celebration, it was a very slender one. I persuaded the Festival of Poetry to let me have my multi-voice poetry read by a group of students from St. Michael's College, U. of T. They did me proud, under the direction of Fred Flahiff. They and he made the selections they chose come alive. They had barely enough rehearsal time. And *chez moi* poetry is an

art of rehearsal. But the number grids worked for them, just as Brecht's alienation-effect worked for Brecht's actors.

⤖

Among those who died in the eighties, aside from Ween Doherty, Marshall, and bp, was Sweet William, and according to a Vancouver newspaper, Sheila herself. "Ann[e] Angus called," she recorded in her journal on 9 January 1983, "to say that my death was reported in Van[couver] Prov[ince] Book section. . . ." Many years before, her maternal grandfather had travelled abroad in the company of a more famous subject of such an announcement, who dismissed it as "premature."

The dying of Sweet William was a source of particular anguish. As he grew older he became blind and crippled. His patience had become stoicism and his gentleness a kind of resignation. Wilfred and Sheila agonized over his condition, reluctant to have him "put down," but reluctant also to have his suffering prolonged. Having taken him in, in the first instance, as an alternative to a remote cause, Sheila was confronted in his final days by the prospect of deciding whether he would live or die—or rather, when he would die. To be put out of one's misery represented a type of intervention which she recoiled from. She understood a wish to end one's own life, and spoke occasionally of putting stones in her pockets as Virginia Woolf had done, and of walking into the lagoon. But the lagoon was shallow and such a gesture would have been futile and absurd and she knew it. William's plight was not hypothetical, however. Sheila telephoned me during this time and said that if she were near a church she would have a mass said for Sweet William in his suffering.

I thought of William's attentiveness when I visited the spit after my father's death. I thought, too, of those in the Roman Catholic tradition—that had been enunciated for me by John Brückmann—who would see animals in heaven—the dog of the Seven Holy Sleepers of Ephesus, for example, and the Queen of Sheba's ass, and Thomas More's dog. I hesitated to ask Father Leland for fear of the quandary it might place him in. I went instead to my parish church and asked simply that a mass be said for William Watson. On the next Sunday, he was among those commended to the prayers of the faithful.

⤖

The decade and a good deal of what Sheila equated with independence ended with a fall which occurred on 16 March 1989. Philip Marchand, whose biography of

McLuhan had just been published, was coming for a short visit and Sheila was determined to brush away cobwebs and clean a bit of the living room ceiling which had
become yellow with the smoke of Wilfred's and her cigarettes. Because Wilfred
would not tolerate the interruption that more extensive cleaning or painting would
occasion, Sheila was driven to domestic "ad hocery," cleaning what caught her eye.
Contrary to her own persistent admonitions to friends on behalf of those who
worked for them, that those who clean must have proper equipment—and in particular a sturdy stepladder—she placed a chair upon a table in order to reach the
offending patch of ceiling. She fell and broke her right heel, the first of a series of falls
which over the next few years made walking increasingly difficult and walks out
along the spit eventually impossible.

One of those who visited Sheila while she was in hospital at this time was the
poet, painter, and photographer Roy Kiyooka, who came from Vancouver, camera in
hand, to photograph the foot of his fallen friend. Later he sent her copies of a colour
picture—one of them mounted—along with a poem entitled "portrait of a foot."
Behind his expedition and his poem's references to the bird-like qualities of Sheila
lay events of another time, in the early seventies, when Sheila had published in *White
Pelican* a series of his photographs of old and abandoned footwear, a counterpart to
his more famous poems about and photographs of "stoned gloves." In its playfulness, sombreness, and precision, Kiyooka's poetic commentary on his photograph of
Sheila provides an appropriate conclusion to the decade of the eighties, an appropriate a prologue to what was to be her own and his last decade.

    portrait of a foot

        or how Bird found herself with
    an idyll on her hands and time-to-kill, all
    because of her (unbecoming) prat-fall—
    flaying cob webs off the ceiling from a pre-
    carious perch. or it's the bitter pill a
    house wife has to swallow if she doesn't dust
    her lintels routinely: only the fastid-
    ious friend coming for a weekend drove her to
    such a hazardous clean-up . . .

        looming: the fractured foot, with
    its tidily arranged toes, and black ellipsoid
        sole, is, nonetheless her, undivined
    sight-line. ah! see how a small tensile tuft of
        her grey hair hooks, the redolent air—
    like a diminutive, shaman's obsidian horn: full

301

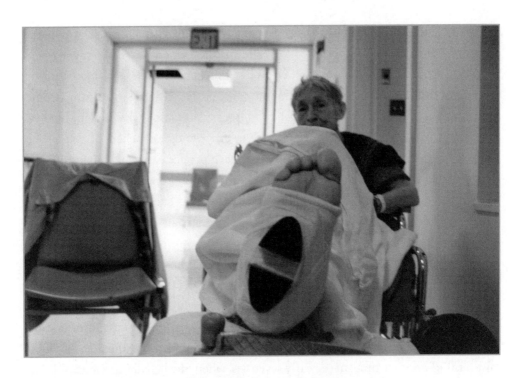

of cantankerous nouns and hibernaculum
syntax. some satyrs dance best when they're a bit
      hobbled. others flap their waxen wings
to take the weight off their fallen arches. still
      others have been known to fake a blessed—
ness by taking it on the chin. 'anonymity' ain't a
      fractured foot's best friend
              "grim & bear it".

    - - - just where the crease of your mouth
    would appear to, rehearse, a withering curse: the
    heapt-up blankets tossed on her midriff,
    hides, a small, calamitous pain . . . the frailties
    of old age, some gulf, to rage against . . .

        as if 'it' belonged utterly to
the rites of a convalescent and a compliant guest:
the chrome chair with the red seat,
the plaid-lined jacket casually draped over its back,
presides over the hospital corridor.
the familiar jacket belongs to a more frequent guest—
who moments before sauntered 'neath
the exit and 'round the corner behind the patient head,
to light up a cigarette. meanwhile:
the enamoured photographer got down on his knees close

to the fractured foot; sighting 'her'
discretely, horned head above her toes; all bathed in
a numinous, moment of repose; he clickt
the shutter, twice . . .

      that stalwart chrome chair with curved red lips
wedged in between its vinyl seat and back-rest: and that
big foot's cloven pad, furnish a biped's syntactical –
closet. 'elysium' is an unconfined state of mind, an un-
imaginable place, to have to hobble through. voila!

dear sparrow:

keep your petite feet, firmly grounded;
and let your wiley head do all the sumersaults, and
yes, let's bless even, the prat-falls . . .

p/s what I like about this photograph
is how every single thing in it counts: light switches,
exit lintels, white i.d. band, the light-struck
twin of that chair beside you, at the far end of the
corridor, the intricate-folds of the blanket,
swaddling you, together, with the shiney metallic parts
of your wheel chair and all the small rectilinear
things attached to the ceiling and the walls;
everything, including the substantive presence of, your
fractured foot, its white enshroudment, beside a
substantial chair: all framed by, lintels, cornices,
entrances, and exits, a co-presence bathed in a
                      plinth of light . . .
would you believe me if i said that—
the single node of disturbance in the whole photo
consists of that intricately curved-thing
perched on the edge of the blanket to the right of
your hidden shoulder . . . its prescience,
Part of the photograph's exacting, anomaly . . .

sheila:

let the spiritus
of your learned ness
leaven the pain
in your small abode:
"holler out" if
it smothers you. mother
lode.
  big goad.

～ XVI ～

I HAVE A COUSIN WHOSE NAME IS TERESA. TERESA HAS DOWN'S syndrome—"has," in the sense that she has blue eyes and fair hair. At another time or with different parents, she might have become one of those moody and stubborn charges "delivered bound into the hands" of the father-king in Sheila's "Antigone." So long as I can remember, her response to my question "What's new?" has been "Everything is new." If I could see with her eyes, as the narrator of "Antigone" muses about his father's bearish subject,

> If I could see with Kallisto's eyes I wouldn't be afraid of death, or
> punishment, or the penitentiary guards. I wouldn't be afraid of my
> father's belt or his honing strap or his bedroom slipper. I wouldn't
> be afraid of falling through a knot-hole in the bridge.

Sheila and Teresa were friends. Teresa was thirty-three years old when Sheila died. They had known one another for most of those years and only partly because of me; Sheila and Teresa's mother had been students at the Convent of the Sacred Heart in Vancouver in the late twenties, when Teresa's mother was only a beginner.

Sheila and Teresa enjoyed a friendship whose nature was known to them alone. They had been in one another's company a few times in Toronto, and once Teresa and her parents had visited Sheila and Wilfred for an afternoon at the spit. Sheila took to sending her packages containing things she thought Teresa might like and that she clearly wanted to share with her: small shells and small pleasing stones she had picked up on her walks, or objects from her own youth, trinkets and pieces of fabric, or a pair of moccasins. These packages sometimes came care of me, but more often they went directly to Teresa, who never spoke of them after they had arrived.

About two months before her death, Sheila asked me if I thought Teresa would like to have a small Inuit sculpture which stood on their mantle. It is a carving in soapstone of an old woman, hunched and patient. Later, she said that Wilfred would not agree to her giving it away. After Wilfred went into hospital, ten days or so before her own last fall, Sheila called to tell me that she was determined to send the carving to Teresa. A week after her death, the last of the boxes of papers she had been sending me arrived, addressed by Sheila and shipped on the day on which she had visited Wilfred in hospital and had later fallen while talking with me on the telephone.

When I opened the box, on top of the papers was a package addressed to Teresa. With it was an envelope, also addressed to Teresa. I delivered these to her.

The next time I called at my cousins' home, knowing I was coming, Teresa met me at the door. She had the envelope from Sheila and she handed it to me. I said I would read and return it to her. "No," she said, "it's for you." Sheila's final letter is brief and undated:

> Dear Teresa
> I am sending you this little Inuit carving of a woman which has spoken to me in its silence for many years.
> I want you to have her now, because there are things I think we both understand.
>
> > With all my love
> > Sheila

And then there is a postscript.

> The pot-holders I'm using for packing may be useful in the kitchen. The design fascinates me.

⌒

The principal event in Sheila's life in the nineties was her death. Very early in our friendship she had joked about the prospect of this event, persuaded that when the time came she would go indecorously. A banana peel on Bloor Street, as I recall, was her usual image for the efficient cause of the final, and inevitably embarrassing attitude she was convinced she would strike. By the nineties, however, such self-deprecating whimsy had given way to darker thoughts, occasioned by her own and Wilfred's frailties and by the deaths of friends. Two events in the late eighties in particular cast shadows over this final decade: the death of bpNichol at a shockingly early age and her own fall in 1989. A journal entry, written in August 1991, recalled these two events: "A half-moon shining in the middle of the spit and folding back on itself in the lagoon. I think of [bp]. . . . The damp air sheer torture."

The combination of enveloping beauty and torture was evidence of a more elusive, because more ambiguous, shadow cast over Sheila's last years. This was the shadow of the place to which they had moved in 1980. With a view which extended from a tidal lagoon at the foot of their property to the Coast Range of mountains on the east side of the Straits of Georgia, the place continued to engage her senses, her mind, and her imagination at the same time it became increasingly a place of pain and isolation. As in Paris and in Toronto, her journals became the confidante of her pain as well as of what sustained her.

These journals, which she had begun in 1955 at a perilous time in her relationship with Wilfred, end in November 1995, two years and three months before her death. Her entry on New Year's Day 1995 combines premonition with sympathy and memory and finally with the experience of a revelatory present. "*Timor mortis conturbat me,*" she began. "Always at this time I think of Corinne and the children particularly Elizabeth. . . . As always now before I go to bed I stand on the balcony for a few minutes looking down on the lagoon until my eyes adjust to the light hidden in the darkness and silence." "*Memento, homo quia pulveris es, et in pulveren reverteris,*" ["Remember, man, that dust you are, and to dust you will return"]

Sheila's sister, Norah Mitchell, and Norah's daughter, Sheila and Wilfred's "B. J." / "O Moon"—Barbara Mitchell—at Barb's graduation from UBC, shortly after Sheila and Wilfred's move to Nanaimo.

she wrote in the wake of that year's Ash Wednesday. ". . . a day of distracting pain," she wrote a few weeks later. And later still, "Very close to the edge—though perhaps not quite close enough—intuition or calculation? It is difficult to say—always so much left undone." No self-pity, no nostalgia, only what she termed "an almost intolerable sense of finitude." This last phrase, typically, did not occur in the context of her own pain but of painful political events: the Referendum vote in Quebec in November 1995 and the assassination of the Israeli Prime Minister Yitzhak Rabin.

Sheila's commenting on what had been left undone was typical of her. "*Ars longa,*" she would chant. And what was left undone? "I wish to God I could write about the nightmare of it all," she exclaimed to herself in 1993 when she and Wilfred were being drawn into "the home care system." "A book to be written 'Notes on the Home Care industry as a reduplicating series of employment.' To be thought about at least." She would have written her biography of Wyndham Lewis. She would have revised her will. She would have settled her possessions. She would have washed the kitchen ceiling.

What she had left unfinished—the collection of essays on cities in literature, and the essays on McLuhan's influence; her story of Orpheus and Oedipus and "Landscape of the Moon"—did not concern her in the nineties. It was the weight of possessions or, to be more precise, the responsibility for possessions that she returned to again and again in her letters and journal. "What responsibility has one for the books one mistakenly thinks one owns?" she mused in a letter in 1993. "I feel exactly the same way about the pictures, the masks, etc. although the masks are really not my concern"; these last referred to a number of West Coast Indian masks collected by Wilfred. The pictures included sixteen oils and watercolours by Jack Shadbolt, an Emily Carr, the A. Y. Jackson that Wilfred had bought for her in Calgary, a Henry Moore Sheila had bought in Toronto, as well as the Lewis drawings she had bought in London, and paintings and drawings by Michael Ayerton, Molly Bobak, and Norman Yates. Hers was clearly a custodial rather than a proprietary sense where these and other objects were concerned. Still there remained a sense of separate spheres of responsibility if not of ownership in this matter of Wilfred's and her possessions.

~

One of her literary remains—with which we are already familiar—came to engage her own and others' attention during this decade. I had first heard of *Deep Hollow Creek* about the time of the publication of *The Double Hook*, in 1959. Sheila had spoken of an earlier novel, which had also drawn on her experiences of the Cariboo, and that had created problems she had hoped to resolve in writing her second novel. I had assumed that it was lost or destroyed. In the early seventies, in her conversation with George Melnyk, she had referred to it as having "some good things," while she continued to deplore the presence and nature of its narrator. Whatever the circumstances of her recovery and re-reading of her first-written novel, after the move from Edmonton some of her earlier concerns about it appear to have been answered. She allowed others to read it. Sherrill Grace was the first. Grace was working on a study of literary expressionism in North America which was to include a consideration of *The Double Hook*. She mentions the earlier novel in her

Regression and Apocalypse, published in 1989, but only to note that it bears the local name of Dog Creek. The novel was also read by Shirley Neuman. When Sheila spoke to me of their reactions, I detected a new note of defensiveness, as of a parent on behalf of an undervalued child.

I asked to read the novel. What I had assumed about it was necessarily backwards out of *The Double Hook*. She had mentioned the name Stella—that I did remember—and a copy of the *Manchester Guardian* propped against the flank of a cow. What else she had mentioned over the years is no longer separable in my mind from her reminiscences of Dog Creek. Backwards out of *The Double Hook:* it is not easy to imagine a problem when all you have is its solution.

Sheila sent me the typescript of *Deep Hollow Creek* in July 1988. The next month I wrote her, not of its problems but of my excitement. Nothing she had said over the years prepared me for it. She was made uneasy by my enthusiasm, however, and she soon asked me to return the typescript.

Two years later, in the fall of 1990, I visited the spit. Increasingly preoccupied with the fates of her possessions and of her papers, Sheila spoke with grim humour of piling everything—herself included—on a barge, setting it alight, and being borne into the Straits of Georgia and oblivion. In the same grim vein I agreed with her that this would be a solution of sorts, but asked that she leave the typescript of *Deep Hollow Creek* behind.

"Whatever you do, don't destroy it," I said.

She stood at the door as I was leaving.

"You bastard," I remember her saying as she handed me the typescript. "You've got what you wanted."

What I wanted was quite simply that Sheila want what I wanted, and that she accept the publication of *Deep Hollow Creek*. Back in Toronto, and before approaching McClelland & Stewart, I went through the typescript, and in a letter to Sheila raised questions and even presumed to make suggestions. Her replies revealed her sense of the integrity of what she had written. There was no trace of her earlier defensiveness. And there was an interesting edge in her response to my suggestion that she had anticipated by thirty or forty years Gabriel Marquez's fiction, especially in her shaping and use of anecdote. "Since time has caught up with my concerns," she commented, "I am not at all sure that a mere flicker that finds its achievement in Marquez, Llosa, and I would add Carey is worth excavating." The comment was self-effacing at the same time it quite determinedly located her novel with relation to these later writers.

Her use of the word "excavating" to describe the recovery and possible publication of *Deep Hollow Creek* is worth noting. It was excavation of a domestic sort that she feared she might be accused of; emptying out drawers in search of something publishable. While she remained self-conscious about the small body of her work, she also remained very protective of what she had written and published—especially of *The Double Hook*. Perhaps because of her conviction that her first-written novel had left unresolved what she believed she had realized in a work which had become synonymous with her name, she feared that the publication of *Deep Hollow Creek* might somehow diminish, or at least demystify, the achievement of *The Double Hook*. Her responses to the earliest readings of her first-written novel and to my questions seem to some degree to have allayed her fears and persuaded her that *Deep Hollow Creek* had—as it were—rounded to "a separate mind" from the mind of *The Double Hook*—that it need not be read only backwards and in its light.

When she found herself its reader rather than its author—and this almost sixty years after she had written it—Sheila seemed able to connect the present of her reading of *Deep Hollow Creek* with the present of its writing. I had questioned a pronoun reference early in the novel, when a local, Sam Flower, is explaining to Stella, the teacher newly arrived from the city who is the novel's central character, how it is that she is to stay with his family. In her response, Sheila pointed to passages that answered my question, and then she assured me that she knew now as she had known then just what she was doing. "Stella is here remembering the 'pronominal' confusion of her first encounter with Sam—perhaps her first encounter with pronominal animosity at this pitch of intensity in which the signified is immediately present to the speaker but without the possibility of gesture to [anybody] else."

The present in which Sheila came to discuss her first-written novel saw, then, her recovery of the present of its writing. Because McClelland & Stewart had published *The Double Hook*, and also because Sheila had at an earlier time written their name and address on the first page of her typescript, I approached them in the late autumn of 1990 with a copy of that typescript. In October 1991, their fiction editor, Ellen Seligman, wrote to assure Sheila that McClelland & Stewart wished to publish *Deep Hollow Creek*, and with questions and some suggestions, to which Sheila replied with clarity and confidence that denied the sixty years that had passed since its writing.

Anticipating the design mark up of the manuscript for the typesetters, Seligman highlighted the irregularly sized spaces Sheila had left between certain paragraphs, and checked with her if all of these were as she intended. Sheila responded by recalling the complex functions she saw the spaces serving, their temporal and spatial as well as visual significance. "These internal breaks (or these visual spaces)," she wrote, "were intended to indicate a juxtaposition of space and time—montage in the problematic sense endlessly explored by Sergei Eisenstein and others in the late twenties and early thirties." She then went on to suggest—and very much in the language of the nineties—how much a part of her narrative these spaces were:

> The divisions I II III etc. play with time in the same way, that is between a twelve month calendar year and Stella's ten month school year. She arrives in the fall and leaves before the "dry heat" set in. The space in which she lives this duration she experiences as an introverted and enclosed space in which those invested with assumed power and privilege, no matter how banal, genteel, or trivial, dominate and marginalize the lives of which they have become the centre. That the space in which she finds herself is simply a cul-de-sac of what Michel Foucault later called "the economy of power" she begins to realize, as she also begins to realize that there is an incipient and hopefully burgeoning politics of resistance.

The most interesting aspect of the dialogue between author and editor had to do with the novel's ending and demonstrates the respect that each had for the other's taste and judgement. Early on Ellen had suggested that a passage which came some thirty pages before the end, and like the novel's final moments involved only Stella and her dog, Juno, might provide what she believed was missing in the matter-of-factness of the original ending. Stella speaks aloud to her dog in the passage that Ellen would see transposed to the end:

> If I hadn't come here, she said, I doubt whether I should even have seen through the shroud of printers' ink, through to the embalmed essence. The word is a flame burning in a dark glass. (p. 112)

"The passage . . . is so beautiful, so embracing, and so utterly powerful as a recapitulation, I see it as a magnificent ending to the novel," Ellen wrote. "The current ending, though good, doesn't carry the same feeling of closure or leave us with such an enduring image as 'The word is a flame burning in a dark glass.'"

Sheila agreed with Ellen's suggestion. "In a very real sense," she wrote, "your comment has solved the problem for me." What problem is not entirely clear, but she was prepared to see the passage moved, even suggesting that the last two paragraphs of the novel be deleted, the better to accommodate it. Spurred on by Ellen's questions and suggestions, Sheila had moved beyond mere recovery of *Deep Hollow Creek* as far as to reconsider its ending. This is how the situation and the text stood, until rereading it in galleys, Ellen had second thoughts about her original suggestion. She had come to believe that the passage that so enthralled her extended its influence over the novel's conclusion without having to be moved, at the same time she appreciated more fully Sheila's instinct to end her novel firmly in a matter-of-fact world. When the novel was published, the "word" as "flame" is where it originally was, and the ending—including the paragraphs Sheila suggested deleting—is as it was initially written.

Persuaded finally of the completeness of her first novel, Sheila was reluctant to do anything that might turn it into "a fly in amber." She knew that it must stand on its own—without a suggested explanatory preface, for example—or not stand at all. Her wishes were respected by Ellen Seligman in this as in all matters—Ellen, who in their correspondence and their conversations, acted as facilitator in Sheila's repossession of her first-written novel.

⤳

Canadians are reluctant to acknowledge literary events if they have not been judged so elsewhere—especially in France or England or the United States. Alone among major writers in English-speaking Canada, Sheila has not been published in any of these countries, although *The Double Hook* and some of her stories have been translated into Swedish, Italian, Spanish, and Japanese, and, as we have seen, a French edition of *The Double Hook* has been published in Quebec. Hers has been a modest international reputation. While critical response to the publication of *Deep Hollow Creek* was in some quarters enthusiastic and everywhere respectful, it was not generally perceived to be a literary event of the first magnitude. Alone among early reviewers, Philip Marchand in the *Toronto Star* judged that its variety of form, tone, and texture and its greater accessibility made Sheila's first novel "even more rewarding" than her second. What she had taken to be flawed, Marchand considered ahead of its time; what had provoked her to find its resolution in writing *The Double Hook*, he found to be greater even than what it had occasioned.

Nonetheless, *Deep Hollow Creek* continued in the shadow, even of works in whose begetting Sheila had—directly or indirectly—some role. 1992 also saw the publication of Michael Ondaatje's *The English Patient*, a work which possessed all the qualities of a true literary event, and in the character of Kip an echo of Kip in *The Double Hook*. Sheila admired Ondaatje's novel, as she did all his work. His own affection, respect for, and indebtedness to her were reflected in a spread of Sheila's photos from her time in Dog Creek and extracts from *Deep Hollow Creek* that he had prepared at the time of its publication for *Brick*, the magazine with which he has long been associated. "I can't believe you hid this book away from us for so long," he wrote to her in June 1992. "The book is a wonder. Every sentence kept me on my toes, and swerved me all over the place with fresh verbs. I love the story and the people, and the landscape—which has never, I think, been drawn this way before—the land translated with a new way of drawing." The younger writer's excitement is palpable and kinetic. An older friend, and one who had himself discovered new ways of drawing, and, indeed, of painting, Jack Shadbolt was impressed by the interiority of the novel's landscape more than by its visual qualities. It "achieves a kind of reflective detachment," he wrote to Sheila. "It seems secretive; like a diary." He quoted his wife Doris's judgement that "it takes a quiet mind" to read *Deep Hollow Creek*.

Both Sheila's and Ondaatje's novels were nominated for that year's Governor General's Award for fiction in English. To no one's surprise, *The English Patient*, which had already been named co-winner of England's Booker Prize, won. It was a choice which Sheila approved of, and from which she derived some relief.

⤚

Her relief was from a sense of uneasiness which she had come to feel about the attention paid *Deep Hollow Creek*. The source of the uneasiness was Wilfred, a collection of whose short fiction was published shortly after Sheila's novel. "The critical moment I . . . think," she wrote me in September 1993, "was the publication of *DHC* before his vol. of stories *The Baie Comeau Angel*, . . . and what he believes to be the lack of recognition of that publication. As you know," she continued, "our life together has been extremely complicated—But enough said."

Sheila wrote this letter from the Nanaimo Regional General Hospital where she had gone some five weeks earlier as the result of a fall on the road near their home. Diane Bessai was visiting from Edmonton, and she and Wilfred and Sheila had walked to the foot of Place Road, then across the spit of land that leads to the rock outcroppings Wilfred had dubbed "Cow Back." There are speed bumps near the end of Place Road to discourage drag racers from using the parking lot that links the road with the spit as a launching pad or terminus for their races. Returning from their walk, Diane looked back to see Sheila teetering for a moment on one of these bumps and falling, doing such damage to her foot, knee, and hip as to require hospitalization for two months (7 August–7 October 1993). She had scarcely recovered from her fall of 1989 when this happened.

Earlier that year, in May 1993, I had been in Vancouver on my way to Nanaimo to visit Sheila and Wilfred when Sheila phoned to say that Wilfred was ill—a euphemism she used with increasing frequency when he did not wish to see someone. Shortly after Sheila's fall on 7 August, I telephoned Wilfred to inquire about her condition. Barbara Mitchell had gone over from Vancouver to see her aunt and to lend Wilfred some assistance. I asked Wilfred to convey my greetings to her and my love to Sheila. "No," he said. "Love to BJ and greetings to Sheila. Sheila doesn't like love from a thoughtful person."

In the letter in which she spoke of the "critical moment" in her present relations with Wilfred, she elaborated on the subject of his behaviour. "Don't feel badly about W," she wrote. "At the moment he is completely irrational (or as Dr. Goodall said to me wisely, trying to cope with his own sense of mortality). He has turned in the same irrational way against B. J. cutting me off as it were from my family."

At the end of August, two weeks before she wrote this letter, I went to Nanaimo. Sheila and I had agreed by telephone that I would not contact Wilfred. I checked into a hotel and went to the hospital at a time when she was satisfied Wilfred would not visit. Looking frail, and in considerable pain, she was nonetheless as always the embodiment of clarity. We talked of many things, of things chronic and of the fiction of closure. She told me that she had advised Dr. Goodall that she wanted no extraordinary measures taken in the event of a setback of any sort.

As luck would have it, Wilfred appeared. When he saw me, he turned tail and left the room. I followed him, determined that we would exchange some gesture to remind him of my fondness and regard for him. When I reached him I took his hand. He cringed and fled. (My choice of words is no more melodramatic than his actions were.) These were not the circumstances I would have chosen for our final meeting.

Before returning to Vancouver the next morning, I went again to the hospital. It was the last time I was to see Sheila—almost five years before her death.

The publication of *Deep Hollow Creek* was only one in a long series of critical moments in their relationship. Sheila was accurate in recognizing Wilfred's determination to cut her off from her "family," an impulse which appeared to grow in the isolation of Place Road. It must be admitted, though, that even if his jealousy was aroused by the attention paid Sheila's novel (relative at least to that paid his own collection of short stories), he did, as he had told me, share Philip Marchand's opinion that it was a finer work than *The Double Hook*. But that, as we have seen, is another story.

～

Sheila was eighty when the nineties began. Her own frailty—the effects of her falls, chronic arthritic pain, developing glaucoma, the indignity of dentures—was echoed in Wilfred's illnesses, in cataracts that limited his reading, writing, and driving—and in the mortality of friends and—seemingly—of the world. Nineteen ninety-one was especially devastating. Anne Angus died on 24 January, and her husband, Henry, the following September. "I have had a life long debt to both of them," she wrote at the time of Anne Angus's death. In this same letter—dated 26 January 1991—she reflected on the shadow cast by the Gulf War, or as she termed it, "the eagle-toed 'operation desert storm.'" "Here we see military ships plying the straits. In Alberta they test the cruise missile. The number three—I had never really thought of a trinity of global wars in my life time—or had I?" Sheila's musings were neither idle nor were they exaggerated. An American nuclear submarine station was (and continues to be) located one cove north of Piper's Lagoon, and submarines did (and do) ply the waters visible from their living room. A neighbouring street—on which Wilfred's sister and her husband live—is named Polaris Drive.

Sheila was not alone in her musings. Roy Kiyooka wrote her in June of that same year from his home in Vancouver of the "man-made 'hell'" of the "500 oilwells scouring the Persian sky," and of the prospect of "another, unredemptive, millenial Apocalypse." Like Sheila, he linked global and personal mortality: "Don't know what lies ahead for 'us,'" he wrote, "but the certitude of death with that amazing avalanche of love-and-hate sequestered in us."

Each, however, found solace in and was sustained by different types of experience. Kiyooka, like some errant Puck, turned to memory as to a dream: "'We' are of such ephemeral substance as all the memorable moments heart has stored up in us." And then he recalled their first meeting:

> I remember our "meeting" in a long ago Edmonton: call it the phenomenological intersection of a "stonedglove" and a "white pelican." Ah! that lovely occasion taught me (again) that "love" like its embodiment "art" is after all a calling, and when one is called, it's an astonishment.

Small wonder that Sheila delighted in the dance of his mind and of his person. Still, his was not her way. She ended the letter in which the death of an old friend had dissolved into the Gulf War firmly in the present: "This evening a full moon and a swirl of sandpipers circling to the edge of the lagoon."

A few months later, in April 1991, Sheila recorded in her journal hearing "a beast—alone and apparently disoriented—crying at the margin of the beach beyond the lagoon." The place had become haunted. "Everywhere," she wrote, "the faces of souls immobilized in a thousand gestures in the stones along the beach." A few days later she heard the voice, not of a disoriented animal but of an anguished friend. "All day I have heard the voice of Esther crying on the telephone—Henry dying in Edmonton." A few days later still, another message: "Shirley phoned early this morning to say that Henry died during the night."

A week before Henry Kreisel's death, a friend had telephoned from Edmonton to discuss with Sheila arrangements for his funeral. This call came just as she and Wilfred were going to walk by the beach. "I could think of nothing as the water curled in at the edge of the low tide and a flock of passenger gulls rose and circled and dropped to the water again," she wrote, "except the devastating edge of intentional concern."

The "edge of the low tide" become "the devastating edge," the inertness of "intentional concern" set against the curling, rising, circling, and dropping of the water and the gulls—an imagist poem occasioned by untimeliness.

The facts of any one life find echoes in other lives. So what is particular about Sheila's response to someone's anticipation of Henry Kreisel's death? Her clarity, for one thing: her rejection of any filter or veil of sentiment, of nostalgia, or even of irony that might deprive an event or a situation of its vividness or, in this case, of its sting. Whatever place she found herself in—Dog Creek, Paris, Toronto, or the spit—provided images by which she kept before herself—and her readers—the essence of what she had confronted, or, more frequently, of what had confronted her. Her turning to tides and to flowers and to animals for such images was not a mode of evasion or a searching out of consolation. For she saw with Kallisto's eyes, measuring a moment's presence by what is truly present. "It is the connection with the visible real," she had written to Wilfred many years earlier, commenting on her habit of mentioning the weather and other natural phenomena in letters to him. She had quoted Thoreau as providing a precedent and a reason for this: "In any weather, at any hour of the day or night, I have been anxious to improve the nick of time, and notch it on my stick too."

On the first of May of this same year, 1991, Wilfred turned eighty. Deteriorating eyesight and his age held out the prospect that, with annual examinations required to renew his driver's license, he would soon not be able to use either his Alfa Romeo (which had replaced the Karmann Ghia) or his Volvo. He experienced the anger and frustration of the totally deprived before testing the testing system itself, however. Although his fears proved premature, both he and Sheila had borne in upon them the problems of living in a place whose location required a car even to go to the nearest store—not a matter of blocks but of miles.

1991 was also the fiftieth anniversary of their marriage—in the Vancouver Courthouse on 29 December 1941: the fiftieth anniversary of Sheila's declaration to herself on the Courthouse steps, "This is for always," which cannot be separated from her subsequent gloss: "whatever I have thought since this thought has never been in question."

⤳

Place Road remained for Sheila an isolated place, and it became increasingly so as she and Wilfred became more dependent upon others—and especially upon Linda Shannon—to take them about and to do for them. But the place also continued to fill her need for vividness and clarity and precision. Its images provided her with a vocabulary of sensations with which in her letters and journals she would grasp and articulate situations, especially her own. She found here—in this suburbanized coastal setting—something of the unmediated experience of nature that sixty years earlier she had known in the Cariboo. That experience had resulted in her two novels. This experience prepared her for her death.

The spit and its outcroppings, the lagoon with its seabirds and animals and tides—even its human visitors—contained a kind of life whose rhythms had become familiar to Sheila, occasioned no fear or dread in her. "The spit . . . consoles—" she wrote to me in 1992: "the constantly shifting light and wind, the total absence of perspective, the chirping of the crickets in the eel grass, the arrival of the stellar jays, the heron fishing on the edge of the incoming tide, the small flocks of mallards and American widgeons fanning out over the water in the lagoon." A Dickensian anecdote followed:

The human beings (fauna?) who haunt the spit also continue to fascinate me—a brisk little man, who carries a small pug nosed long haired lapdog down to the spit in his arms, whose acquaintance I first made when he called out to me: "God's in his heaven—All's right with the world," then, as a scholarly footnote, "Browning: *Pippa Passes*." Later he told me, one day, that his wife had taken care of him when he was ill and unable to work during the depression and had had to pick up discarded vegetables and to buy dog bones to make soup so that they could survive and that now she was completely crippled, could neither walk nor sit—only lie or stand—he would never abandon her to the care of others—nor would he abandon the aged lapdog who had been committed to their care by a friend who could no longer take care of her. Now we call him Pippa when we allude to him.

She ends with a kind of send-up of her own quest for precision: "Sometimes I wonder whether he ever read *Pippa Passes* in its entirety, or only the much anthologized song: 'The year's at the spring.'"

After a long period of recovery from her first, 1989, fall, and before her fall in 1993, she wrote, "Walked round the spit for the first time in two y'rs—looked down on Shack Island—the heron where it always was—the light intense—an opaque intensity." The light was not, however, always so predictable as the heron. Sometimes it recalled the geometry of an expressionist painting: "Daybreak—indigo and orange lateral thrusts of light the vertical mountain masked." By 1995, the last year for which we have Sheila's journals, light had been largely displaced by darkness, or it had been absorbed by it. Glaucoma made seeing as well as reading and writing difficult. Trees and bushes which stood between their windows and the lagoon, and which had been allowed to flourish as a haven for birds, became a wall obscuring the landscape that had sustained her.

Sequestered in a spot on an island for which she retained a mainlander's distaste, Sheila nonetheless took comfort in this place, even in the fact of her confinement. Restricted by age, health, and location, she turned repeatedly to night—"an embracing and silent dark"—as to a lover. "Tonight," she wrote, "an embracing rush of wind and circling branches." "12:30 and enfolding grey darkness and total silence as I stand at the open door of the balcony." But she also wrote, "my eyes adjust to the light hidden in the darkness and silence."

⤸

The last project Sheila completed before her death was a foreword for *The Work of Justice*, written by a retired Edmonton lawyer, Jack Pecover. Pecover's book provides a meticulous reconstruction of the events that led to the 1960 execution—the last in Alberta—of a young man found guilty of "the largest mass murder in Alberta history." The setting of this act—a small prairie town—and its victims—a man, his wife, and their five children—recall Truman Capote's *In Cold Blood*. Pecover, however, was not a novelist, and the accused was thought to have acted alone, and he denied his guilt even on the scaffold, and more significant still, the victims were his father, his stepmother and his five step-siblings. The charge turned what in Capote's case was an act of awful-because-random violence into the stuff of tragedy, for it is not unusual in cases of multiple murder for an accused to be charged with only one of the crimes. In this case, the young man was charged with the murder of his father.

Although Sheila's interest in this project was not surprising, the extent and the intensity of her commitment to it did puzzle her family and friends. She finished reading Pecover's manuscript in August 1991. Having found her way through its reconstruction of events of thirty years earlier, as her extensive notes indicate, she savoured and tested the potency of its words and its details. Her notes recall the kind of method and the range she had demonstrated earlier in that same year responding to questions about *Deep Hollow Creek*. As a reader, her engagement and her expectations were no less than they had been as a writer. As we saw earlier, a dog's name—Selassie—in her first novel provided a window upon events of the time when the novel was written. We can observe Sheila testing a name in Pecover's book. The accused's stepmother's name is Daisy May and Pecover described her as, "like her name, honest, unpretentious, likable. . . ." Sheila made the association with the character in Al Capp's comic strip *L'il Abner*, Daisy Mae, perhaps sparked by Marshall McLuhan's commentary on this same strip in *The Mechanical Bride* (1951). She then set chronological details of the life of Pecover's protagonist and his family out on a page opposite details of the history of Capp's cartoon: the protagonist was born on 15 July 1937 and *L'il Abner* appeared for the first time on 13 August 1934; Capp's Daisy Mae and Abner were married in 1952, the protagonist's father and his Daisy May had married in 1949; the comic strip ended in 1979 and Pecover's protagonist was executed on 11 October 1960. She had finally to admit that an anticipated epiphany remained merely unrelated facts.

⌐

If Sheila had been told that her pursuit of Daisy May/e had been only "a wild goose chase," she would have known the source of the adage, or she would soon have found it. It was years before, at the time of the publication of *The Double Hook*, when she was asked in a questionnaire for authors if she had any hobbies, that Sheila had listed one: "Reading footnotes." Among the questions I had asked her about *Deep Hollow Creek* was one about her references to the community where the trains stopped, where goods and people arrived and departed, as the Rock. I asked if she had intended echoes of Alcatraz, or of T. S. Eliot's "Choruses from *The Rock*":

> The Rock is the railroad centre (Williams Lake) north of *DHC* through which all the merchandise comes from outside and from which all the cattle are shipped to market and to which they must be driven for the buyers' inspection [she wrote]. Eliot's *The Rock* was not published until 31 May 1934 (Faber) and by Harcourt Brace in New York in Aug. 1934. This is the same year that Alcatraz (that rocky island in San Francisco Bay) became the site of a top-security Federal penitentiary named according to some authorities (i.e., *The New Oxford* ref. dictionary) after the pelicans (alca-traces) which inhabited it. (The current Sp. word for pelicans now is, or seems to be, pelicanos)—Checking I find that an alcatrace is a gannet in Godfrey's *Birds of Canada*—*Le Fou de Bassan* (Lennaeus)—particular attention is given to the gannet sanctuary on Bon-aventure Island. The discussion of this . . . colony of gan-nets is particularly interesting and perhaps throws a good deal of light on the irony of the name as a maximum security prison. Because of the unpredictable flight habits of my brother I know and knew too much at that time—the late mid-thirties—about Alcatraz than I care to enumerate.

She continued:

> Perhaps at the time I was haunted as Eliot seems to have been by the refrain from Matthew: "*Tu es Petrus, et super hanc petram aedificabo Ecclesiam meam*" ["Thou art Peter, and upon this rock I shall build my Church"]. The digression about Alcatraz is here only because you raised the question. The Indian Mission school at Williams Lake, whether I thought of Alcatraz or not, seemed like a penal colony out of which children were released finally into a starving

and decimated community in which language and culture—religious and social—had been destroyed—but not obliterated—not completely. If you have been thinking about Eliot's "Choruses from *The Rock*" which I presume you have you may remember the passage "Here were decent godless people: Their only monument the asphalt road and a thousand lost golf balls."

Sheila then pointed to a passage in the novel in which Miriam, the protagonist's companion, spoke of her aunt and "a golf stick." She returned, however, to Alcatraz:

> Incidentally, yet again and as always, in Thomas E. Gaddis's *Birdman of Alcatraz* of which I have the Four Square Book edition published by Landsborough Publications Ltd. London, 1957 Alcatraz is referred to as the Rock (p. 6) and ends with the following sentences. "He (Robert F. Stroud—the 'birdman') does not know the real name of Alcatraz. It is the Isla de Los Alcatraces, or Island of Pelicans. They used to call it Bird Island." (p. 240) He also points out that "The rock island, a United States fortification since 1853, once held captive Indian chiefs." (p. 197) All this, of course, is factually irrelevant to my use of the name at the time, as is Eliot's use of his ambulant Rock in the Pageant Play he wrote on behalf of the Forty-five Churches Fund of the Diocese of London. I was much more probably thinking also of Aeschylus's π&τρα to which Prometheus was fettered by KρATOE (KIA BIA) Force and Might. After all the typescript is more than fifty years behind me.

The etymology of Alcatraz and the fact that it had been known as Bird Island were as "factually irrelevant" to the activities of its birdman—in Sheila's eyes, at least—as a nickname for Alcatraz or a synonym for the Christian Church was to her choice of designation for the town in her first novel. But as Thomas Gaddis recognized—and Sheila, too, in quoting him—what is "factually irrelevant" can be utterly appropriate, like the history of the building in which she and Wilfred had lived in Paris. Even when certain facts have no bearing on the choices some people make—to mend birds, for example, or in writing—they can still enjoy a kind of relevance, which is all the more mysterious for being unconsciously achieved.

Coleridge observed of the person of method, that however "irregular and desultory" his or her talk (or writing) might appear, "there is method in the fragments." Everything "is in its place." It is a quality, the most important quality of "the mind which has been accustomed to contemplate not things only, or for their own sake alone, but likewise and chiefly the relations of things, either their relations to each other, or to the observer, or to ... hearers." It was a quality Jane Austen saw in her most problematic heroine, Emma Woodhouse, of whom she wrote: "A mind lively and at ease, can do with seeing nothing, and can see nothing that does not answer." Like her wanderings among Rocks—literal and figurative—her responses to the cries or flights of birds, or her reading of Pecover's manuscript demonstrate, Sheila, too, saw "nothing that [did] not answer."

⌇

As I look through the folder in which she kept notes and clippings for her work on Pecover's book, I am aware that this project, like all that Sheila undertook, had its own life, its own roots and genealogy. There is a note—dated 21 April 1992—to the effect that San Quentin Penitentiary had recently had its first execution in twenty-five years. Attached to this note is a transcription from Omar Englebert's *Lives of the Saints* of the entry for Saint Quentin, which includes a story of his intercession being successfully sought on behalf of a thief condemned to death: "the rope of the gallows broke, the judges, seeing this as a sign from heaven, set the thief at liberty." There are notes from Foucault's *Surveiller et Punir*, and from an essay by Gilles Deleuze on "societies of control," newspaper clippings and citations from dictionaries of slang and underworld argot, and a note on St. Henri II (notable for "forgiveness of injuries") whose feast day—15 July—was the birthday of Pecover's protagonist (whose last words before a terminally interrupted Lord's Prayer were "Father forgive them"). There are also notes on four of Dickens's novels, traces of what she called her "courtesy reading." I had been thinking about *Little Dorrit* and, as was her custom, she reread the novel so that we could talk about it. But she did not stop with one novel. Clearly, her fascination with Dickens's descriptions of the trial and execution of Fagin in *Oliver Twist* became part of the setting for her reading Pecover's manuscript. Her rereading of Dickens's account of revisiting the site of the Marshalsea Prison—whose walls were by then down—in his Preface to *Little Dorrit* also prepared her to write her own account of the transformation of another prison in her foreword.

⌇

Pecover's book provided Sheila with a window upon her own past. "To one who lived during the ten years before 1920 in the provincial mental hospital (MHI or #9) because one's father was the medical superintendent at the time," she wrote in her foreword, "any reference to the federal penitentiary separated as it was from the mental institution only by its high walls with their armed guards and by a narrow ravine familiarly known as 'the dump,'" to such a one, Pecover's story "spoke with an evocative and strangely disturbing force." The Fort Saskatchewan Provincial Gaol northeast of Edmonton, where Pecover's protagonist was confined and finally hanged, recalled that other penitentiary, a part of the landscape of her own childhood.

In her mind, the two places were linked by more than personal coincidence or their functions. She observed changes—what she termed "a transformed economy of enclosure"—which saw a storage room for kitchen drygoods become an execution chamber at Fort Saskatchewan (thus enabling the first indoor hanging in Canadian penal history), and—in a startling variation on swords beaten into ploughshares—saw the New Westminster penitentiary become "an exclusive complex of garden apartment units." The developers in this last instance, Sheila noted, had assured prospective buyers of their taste for the picturesque and their respect for the history of the place: "Although the walls are down, the penitentiary gatehouse . . . will be retained," they promised.

A final transformation—what Sheila described as "a eucharistic gesture"—resulted from the convict donating his eyes to the eye bank and his body to the Anatomy Department of the University of Alberta. It was not with irony, but with a sense of the literalness—and the wit—of this act that she observed the young man returning his "youthful body" to the same community that had taken life from it.

Four of Sheila's five collected stories—those originally published as *Four Stories*—feature or recall the grand type of the crime for which Pecover's young man was tried, convicted, and hanged, the crime of patricide. Her eponymous Oedipus is a tender of roses and would-be protector of a willow tree in "Brother Oedipus," a witness to the tragic obsessions of his Uncle Daedalus in "The Black Farm," an unnamed father of a latter-day Antigone and Ismene caught in the fates of their names, and finally, a wry interviewee of Pierre Berton in "The Rumble Seat." For Sheila knew that the most intense concentration in literature is achieved in domestic situations; that the greatest casualness and the greatest pain come, to vary her phrase, with a transformed economy of family.

In the opening paragraphs of her foreword to Pecover's book, she reflected upon a sentence which the young man had written in a letter to the Solicitor-General of Canada after his last appeal for clemency had been dismissed. The sentence reads: "I respectfully put it, Sir, that when the facts replace the unanswerd questions and infernce, the err of this confiction will be proved." She observed what she termed the "devastating effect" of *v* become *f* in the fourth last word—as if an impish Joyce had taken possession of this "functionally illiterate defendant."

In her own stories, the crimes of Oedipus are present in his name only, not in his actions. The same is not true of James Potter in *The Double Hook*, however. His actions in murdering his mother, in blinding Kip, in whipping the girl who is carrying his child, are unquestionably his actions; and yet, without any questions, they do not lead to his trial, his conviction, his execution. *The Double Hook* was published only weeks before the crimes for which Pecover's protagonist was tried, convicted, and executed were committed (on 16 May and on 25–26 June 1959, respectively). Whether or not Pecover thought of this or of any other coincidence, he—and his young man—found in Sheila a witness especially sensitive to the grace that can rise out of ghastliness. She had found in his account of "the largest mass murder in the history of Alberta" and its aftermath untamed awfulness, ambiguities, the rituals of justice, and "a eucharistic gesture"—in short, the untransformed poetry of fact. "[T]he err of this confiction will be proved."

I know of nothing that Sheila wrote or said about the comparative fates of Pecover's protagonist and of James Potter. The community of *The Double Hook* seems insulated as well as isolated from the work of justice, as if the impulses that led James Potter to his vicious acts are balanced and somehow neutralized by the impulses that led to the birth of his child. It is not amnesty or absolution that I am talking about, but a world which by a kind of silent consensus has also empowered Coyote, and with an equally silent patience admitted another side to murderous violence and allowed it to reveal itself. The convict in Pecover's history, however, did not live in such a community, and his other side could only reveal itself in gestures that required his own death before they could be completed—making Fort Saskatchewan as far removed from "the folds" of Sheila's "hills" as Shakespeare's Courts were from his Forest of Arden or the woods outside Athens.

There is as great a danger in considering last works as in savouring last words: the danger of reading them as elegy or valedictory or legacy, of reading them as final. There is as little of "autumnal serenity" in her foreword to *The Work of Justice* as in her final mute gestures witnessed by her niece.

᎛

Sheila, as I have said, was not a nostalgic person, which does not mean that she took no pleasure in recalling her own past. She drew upon personal experience in her novels and short stories, certainly, and she retold with relish anecdotes about her childhood, her days at convent schools, and her days of teaching. She was not, however, a hostage to her memory—like those impressionable and unmethodical minds that Coleridge wrote of. If the past did not become more present to her than the present itself—and the opposite is so often the case as one grows older—a need to ensure that her own past would not be lost came increasingly to preoccupy her. Her agreeing to the publication of *Deep Hollow Creek* was a symptom of this need. In the eighties, her collecting and editing of Miriam Mandel's poems ensured their survival, as her collecting and editing Wilfred's poems did the same for his. The gathering of his works into three volumes, and the lodging of his papers at the University of Alberta, provided Sheila with a precedent and with space for shoring up her own papers. Wilfred had been taken care of.

Her own gathering up was a more private matter than Wilfred's had been—both because of her fear of disturbing him, and because she did not have a solicitous help-mate to encourage and to assist her. She developed a morbidly comic sense of her own isolation in this enterprise, and a growing sense of urgency. She persuaded herself that a yard sale would be her wake and that garbage bags of papers—like the remains of some Gatsbyesque orgy—would simply be trucked away. There was, of course, melodrama in this sense of her situation and comic self-pity, too—but there was also real concern that the books and paintings and her own written remains would disappear.

She was concerned in particular about the books and pictures, but any decisions about them depended upon agreement between Wilfred and herself. This was not easily achieved—especially in the case of the pictures. In fact, it was only achieved by others after their deaths. A journal entry written in the summer of 1991 gives a sense of the pressures and frustrations that Sheila felt:

> Nothing but interruptions—the experience of shattered and overlapping time limits. The confusion re—Shadbolt; Space between pillars & Figure in the Slash [two paintings by Shadbolt] Jack & Doris [Shadbolt] are coming on Friday for lunch—that may or may not solve the problem. Trying to sort out W's papers.

Over the years they had collected oils and watercolours by Shadbolt which represented an important cross-section of his career. Because Wilfred felt himself closer to Shadbolt and had continued to correspond with him, he assumed proprietorial rights where their collection was concerned; this despite Sheila's claim that it was she who had bought their first Shadbolt, during the two years they had taught at UBC. Questions of who bought what and when gave way to anger on Sheila's part when she discovered that Wilfred had given away two of their Shadbolt paintings.

The books were less a source of friction. Sheila had been the more methodical collector—of books by and about Wyndham Lewis and his contemporaries, including Joyce and Pound, Beckett and Eliot and Edith Sitwell and Roy Campbell; books and articles by and about Marshall McLuhan; works by Canadian writers, especially writers from western Canada. The summer before her death, she did engage a former student, Anne Blott, who had worked on Lewis with her in Edmonton, to catalogue her Lewis holdings.

The range of her reading—and of Wilfred's—was remarkable, and their library of some 8000 volumes reflected this. The checking and research that Sheila did to answer questions about *Deep Hollow Creek* or to write her foreword to Pecover's book, for example, were done without benefit of libraries or the Internet.

They were the books that she first mentioned to me, more specifically, her collection of Ezra Pound. With the help of Linda Shannon, who for some years now had been "doing" for Sheila and Wilfred, she packed this in five or six bankers boxes and sent it to me. This was the beginning of—for Sheila—a long, arduous, and costly process whereby she sent me about twenty-five boxes of books and seventy or eighty boxes of papers. The remaining books, 7280 to be precise, were brought to Toronto after their deaths, in a truck driven by two young women who had travelled west with me from Toronto for this purpose; one a graduate student, the other a journalist, the one from Kerala in south India and the other from the Punjab. Strangers to Sheila and Wilfred, they became witnesses to the end of their time at the spit.

〜

At the beginning of the saga of the boxes I had no sense of when or how it would end, or that the last of the boxes would arrive a week after Sheila's death. When she first spoke to me of her concerns about her papers, I suggested she deposit them with the National Library in Ottawa, where McLuhan's papers are. In fact, she had been approached in the summer of 1992 by the Curator of its Literary Manuscript Collection. She did not respond to this approach or to my suggestion. Her main concern then was that her papers not be where Wilfred's papers were, at the University of Alberta. She felt no hostility towards the institution or the city, only reluctance to be archivally proximate to Wilfred. She was confronted by many choices but she had no will to make a decision. In sending her papers to me she had, I think, the sense of doing something towards preserving them without actually having to decide what finally would be done with them. "I am sending you my life," she had said to me, and this could only be done by a personal gesture and not as the result of protracted business negotiations.

Whatever her motives in packing up and shipping her papers, one at least clearly had to do with the preservation of her own and others' pasts. Collecting her papers was not for Sheila, I think, an act of recollection so much as anticipatory to being recollected. She was not, as I have suggested, given to nostalgia: after all, she had "bin" there. As the boxes appeared and I began the task of cataloguing their contents, I discovered—randomly present throughout these boxes—a series of note-books—twenty-seven in all—which contained, aside from notes she made of her reading, journal entries spanning more than forty years. As I read and transcribed these entries I realized their importance, not only in gaining access to Sheila, to the times, places, and people when, where and among whom she lived and wrote, but also in their own right: painful and wise and luminous accounts of being here. I told her they must be published, but because her relationship with Wilfred so dom-inated these journals—literally, from first entry to last—their publication would not be possible until after his death. There was silence at the other end of the tele-phone line, and then: "I want my story told."

When I proposed to Sheila that her papers and books be housed in the library at St. Michael's College, University of Toronto, she was satisfied that she could live— and die—with that decision. It represented a kind of homecoming for her, to the place where she had studied with Marshall, and worked with him, and taught for him. It was associated with family as well as with friends—with cousins, the Mallons, who as priests had taught at the College, and with her father's sister, who in the twenties was nurse-in-residence there. From her earliest experience, she appreciated that an institution could contain a home.

Sheila's journals ended before she undertook the business of sending me her life. The last entry is dated 17 November 1995, and reads as follows: "It is quarter to two. I can't sleep. The whole affair of the 25th has been an incredible strain. On the 25th Elizabeth McLuhan called to ask me what she should say—an extremely diffi-cult task for both of us—It is not me but Elizabeth whose work the College should be recognizing." The "affair of the 25th" referred to a convocation held by the Faculty of Theology at St. Michael's, which honoured Sheila by bestowing on her a Doctorate of Sacred Letters. This was an honour which in the past had been granted only to ecclesiastics, to theologians and to benefactors. When the College decided it was time the arts were given their due, they accepted the recommendation of Sheila as an appropriate candidate. The President, Richard Alway, wrote to her in June 1995 asking if she would accept the honour. "There is nothing that could please me more," she replied, "than the formalizing of a relationship with the University of St. Michael's College to which I have owed so much over the years." She added, "there is now always the possibility that because of distance or illness in the family . . . it might not be possible for me to attend the convocation." President Alway assured her that the degree would be awarded even if she were unable to attend the ceremony.

I had a sense of the pleasure that this gesture would afford her, at the same time I realized the inevitable result of what in a letter she referred to as "the usual consternation evoked by such incidents." Like the publication of *Deep Hollow Creek* and its nomination for a Governor General's Award, the whole matter of the honourary degree exacerbated a chronic situation. My brother and his wife, who live in Vancouver, offered to fetch Sheila from Nanaimo, take her to the airport in Vancouver, and return her to Nanaimo. But the logistics of travel were not the problem. As he had in the past, Wilfred would inevitably fall ill at the prospect of Sheila leaving. This remained a probability she chose not to invite, a responsibility she chose not to assume.

As her final journal entry indicates, Sheila asked a friend in Toronto, Elizabeth McLuhan, to accept the degree on her behalf. It was a heartfelt gesture, recalling her work with Elizabeth's father, her affection for her mother and family, and her respect for Elizabeth and her achievements as a poet. And as this final entry reveals, the whole was a source of "incredible strain." I had hoped that the pleasure of a prospect would outweigh the impossibility of its being realized. Perhaps I was naive.

⤳

Many fewer visited Sheila and Wilfred during these last years than would have. Sheila's difficulties and Wilfred's unpredictability gave pause to any who knew of their situation. Sheila's love of the presence of people, however, did not diminish, although her sense of the strain of visitors on Wilfred became even more acute. She relished conversations with those who did come, but more and more confined herself to letters and phone calls, to excursions to town with Linda Shannon, which inevitably included a stop at a coffee shop and talk with any who happened to be there.

Linda Shannon, whose mother had been a student of Sheila's in Mission in the early forties, became in the last decade of her life sister-daughter-friend. Helpmate and confidante and life-line, after Sheila's death, Linda became her surrogate with Wilfred dying. Wilfred's sister, Doreen, lived close at hand, but he had so effectively prevented commerce between them, and had so misrepresented each to the other, that Sheila had come to believe Doreen capable of green-garbage bagging her papers and mounting a garage sale of their books and paintings. Doreen was saddened when she heard of this, as she had been surprised when she had learned that Sheila had harboured the mistaken notion that in 1980 she had encouraged Wilfred to move to Nanaimo. In truth, she had advised him against the kind of precipitous action he took then. She had almost broken through this impasse in her relationship with Sheila when once she had exclaimed to her, "You are a good old girl." Sheila responded—to me not to Doreen—with surprise and pleasure, but her taste for analogy and for sources caused her to lose hold of what for a moment she had savoured. "I felt like Mrs. Bagnet," she wrote to me, "although Woolwich, Quebec and Malta are non existent. Incidentally W's grandfather, his father's father, worked at Woolwich or Woolwich in the arsenal."

When Barbara Mitchell wrote to me only days after Sheila's death, enclosing her final letter to her aunt, she observed with characteristic thoughtfulness, "I wished you had been present and I'm glad you were not, for your sake." During the last years, she, Linda Shannon, Shirley Neuman, and Irma Sommerfeld were among those who were witness to Sheila's growing weakness, to contracting physical limits that prevented walks out along the spit and over Cow Back, that prevented the gathering of drift wood to build a fire in the fireplace, that all but prevented even reading. In the past, when Wilfred could drive and she could walk, there was always the possibility of time apart, but even that luxury—and it was a luxury for both of them—had disappeared. Physical frailty, and the fears of Wilfred himself, had to be served. She must give him his medication, even when it required her to attend him throughout the night. Their own frailty and their increasingly frail hold upon their world lent the double hook of unpredictability and inevitability to their final months. The strength of Sheila's voice, however, the clarity of her words, and of her actions in sending her books and papers, left me unprepared for the suddenness of her end.

By way of coda: Sheila Martin Doherty Watson one April evening in Toronto—

> Spring has come all of a hurtle—the tulips in the beds outside
> U[niversity] C[ollege] have bloomed on short stems—have opened
> just above the surface of the ground surprised by the heat—heat
> and sunshine—grey violent skies—cloudbursts—leaves uncurling
> and magnolia buds—luminous green in the steel light of the
> storm—The squirrels and the birds in a frenzy of housekeeping.
> Children with kites—children with marbles—houses overflowing
> into the streets—the storm window off so that I can lean out into
> the cool of the night—

Appendix A
Notes to Chapter IX

1) It was only later, when she was working on her doctoral thesis, that Sheila, who had years before described her memory of childhood as "a picture in the cubist mode," discovered that she and Wilfred had spent their Paris year in one of the shrines of cubism. A German art dealer, and author of *The Rise of Cubism* (published in Munich in 1920 as *Der Weg zum Kubismus*), Daniel-Henry Kahnweiler had, in the words of her thesis, "opened a gallery at 28 rue Vignon to become virtually the exclusive agent of Braque and Picasso before the first world war." "All the early cubist pictures were shown there," she had written to Wilfred, "—and there came . . . Gertrude and Leo Stein to look at them and buy some of them."

2) Sheila's earlier reference to 10 August—in the entry for 10 September 1955—also associates great pain with events of that day. If she is referring to the August-just-past, she and Wilfred might well already have arrived in New York. If she is referring to an earlier time, it is perhaps to what she cryptically termed "the squalor of the Stockdale cabin" in her journal entry of 6 April 1955.

3) At the time she refers to, late in 1953, Sheila wrote to Anne Angus from Calgary: "We have been reading Gabriel Marcel's *The Mystery of Being* (a publication series of Gifford Lectures in 1949–50). It throws a great deal of light on the problems of writing. I found it in the P[ublic] L[ibrary] there. It also is slow reading. I would recommend it to Henry if he doesn't know it. It rather sets one back on one's heels." A "Christian existentialist," as Sheila described him later to Anne Angus, and a playwright, Marcel in these lectures was primarily concerned with a notion of "intersubjectivity," which he described as "a sort of intercourse, which can take place both between distinct personalities and within what we call the same personality." The last of these, a kind of interior intercourse, led to reflections upon the impossibility of recognizing oneself in an act once it has been committed. His description of an "exceptional" as distinct from a "habitual" act as "a kind of inner vertigo" echoes in the murderous act of James Potter in *The Double Hook*, which she was working on. His thoughts on the individual's relationship to his or her own past are calculated to give pause to anyone who would re-present a life, one's own or another's: "this rebuilding of the past is really a new building, a fresh construction on an old site, modelled more or less on the former edifice there, but not identical with it." Marcel's

skepticism about "dialectical or systematic connections" must have appealed to Sheila's own suspicion of critical systems. How Marcel's lectures were used as the ground of her own destruction, and what Wilfred's interest in Marcel was, are not clear to me.

4) In November 1953, Sheila had written to Anne Angus from Calgary: "I would like you sometime to read Simone Weil's chapter on Affliction (Malheur) in the book *Waiting on God*—not just because the idea has an intellectual strength, but because of its relevance to so much in the human predicament. What she says at least re-assures me that intense emotional suffering is not simply a sign of immaturity or indigestion." Sheila's cherishing the pears for their own sake is consistent with Weil's "Beauty is to things what sanctity is to the soul." Weil on affliction provides a gloss on Sheila's "This is for always": "But always at the first onset of affliction there is a privation of beauty, and invasion of the soul by ugliness. And then, unless we keep our love oriented, in defiance of all common sense, in the same direction, although it has ceased to have an object, we lose all contact with the good, perhaps finally."

5) The precision of Sheila's description of Buffet's "Cirque" originates in jottings and a sketch she made while she viewed the exhibition. In a notebook devoted largely to sketches of Parisians and of Paris scenes, Sheila listed various of the figures who appeared, and of the colours that recurred in these paintings.

6) At about this same time, Sheila wrote to Roy Daniells: "I found a book of 'Contes' from the Alps in which there is a story called 'Le Roi Cachan.' When the husband is angry with his wife and betakes himself to the third part of his kingdom he says: 'If you wish to find me you will have to wear out seven pairs of wooden shoes and seven pairs of iron shoes.' This seems logical. It is the finality of divorce which seems illogical."

7) In England, Sheila stayed with a friend—Constance Dyson—whom she had met in Vancouver with Ruth Humphrey. Mrs. Dyson was head of a women's college, Hillcroft College, which was located in Surbitan, Surrey.

Appendix B
Published Writings of Sheila Watson

"Memories of Our Alma Mater." *St. Ann's Academy: 1865–1932.* New Westminster, BC (1932): 37. Under the name Sheila Doherty.

"The Barren Lands." *The Canadian Forum* 15, no. 169 (October 1934): 20. Under the name Theila Martin Doherty.

"Rough Answer." *The Canadian Forum* 18, no. 212 (September 1938): 178–180. Under the name Sheila Doherty.

"Remedial Reading." *The B.C. Teacher* (January 1945): 128, 141. Under the name S. W. Watson.

"Brother Oedipus (A Story)." *Queen's Quarterly* 61, no. 2 (Summer 1954): 220–228.

"The Black Farm (A Modern Allegory)." *Queen's Quarterly* 63, no. 2 (Summer 1956): 202–213.

"Antigone." *The Tamarack Review*, no. 11 (Spring 1959): 5–13.

The Double Hook. Toronto: McClelland & Stewart Limited, 1959.

"The Speaking Image: The Engravings of Guillermo Silva Santamaria." *Obros y Autores* 1, no. 1 (December 1961): 34–36.

"Antigone." Rpt. in *The First Five Years: A Selection from The Tamarack Review*, ed. Robert Weaver. Toronto: Oxford University Press, 1962.

Dubbelkroken. Swedish translation of *The Double Hook* by Artur Lundkvist. Stockholm: Tidens Förlag, 1963.

"Wyndham Lewis: A Question of Portraiture." *The Tamarack Review*, no. 29 (Autumn 1963): 90–98. A review of *The Letters of Wyndham Lewis*, by W. K. Rose.

"Artist Ape as Crowd-Master." *Explorations.* In *Varsity Graduate* 11, no. 2 (May 1964): 50–53.

"Power: Nude or Naked." *Explorations.* In *Varsity Graduate* 12, no. 1 (December 1965): 50–56.

The Double Hook. New Canadian Library No. 54. Introduction by John Grube. Toronto: McClelland & Stewart Limited, 1966.

"Swift and Ovid: The Development of Metasatire." *The Humanities Association Bulletin* 18, no. 1 (Spring 1967): 5–13.

"The Great War, Wyndham Lewis and the Underground Press." *arts/canada* 24, no. 11 (November 1967). The essay fills the entire issue.

"Canada and Wyndham Lewis the Artist." *Canadian Literature*, no. 35 (Winter 1968): 44–61.

"Canada and Wyndham Lewis the Artist." Rpt. in *Wyndham Lewis in Canada*, ed. George Woodcock. Vancouver: University of British Columbia Publications Centre, 1971.

"About Pelicans." *White Pelican* 1, no. 1 (Winter 1971): 2–4.

"The Black Farm." Rpt. in *Stories from Western Canada*, ed. Rudy Wiebe. Toronto: Macmillan of Canada, 1972.

"Michael Ondaatje: The Mechanization of Death." *White Pelican* 2, no. 4 (Fall 1972): 56–64.

"Gertrude Stein: The Style is the Machine." *White Pelican* 3, no. 4 (Fall 1973): 167–189.

"Sugar Heart" and "Be Fruitful and Multiply." Translations of stories by Madeleine Ferron, in *Stories from Québec*, selected by Philip Stratford. Toronto: Van Nostrand Reinhold Ltd., 1974.

"Myth and Counter-myth." *White Pelican* 4, no. 1 (Winter 1974): 7–19.

Sheila Watson: A Collection. Open Letter, Third Series, no. 1 (Winter 1974–75).

"The Rumble Seat." *Sheila Watson: A Collection*, cit.: 33–40.

"Unaccommodated Man." *Sheila Watson: A Collection*, cit.: 97–114.

"What I'm Going to Do." *Sheila Watson: A Collection*, cit.: 181–183.

Sous l'oeil de Coyote. French translation of *The Double Hook* by Arlette Franciere. Montréal: Les Éditions La Presse, Ltée, 1976.

"How to read *Ulysses*." *Modern Consciousness: Habits and Hang-ups*. Athabasca, Alberta: Athabasca University, 1978.

"Antigone." Rpt. in *Literature in Canada* 2, eds. Douglas Daymond and Leslie Monkman. Toronto: Gage Educational Publishing Limited, 1978.

Four Stories. Toronto: The Coach House Press, 1979.

"And the Four Animals." First draft. Toronto: The Coach House Press, MS Editions, May 1980.

"Antigone." Rpt. in *Fiction of Contemporary Canada*, ed. George Bowering. Toronto: The Coach House Press, 1980.

"Wyndham Lewis and G. K. Chesterton." *The Chesterton Review* 6, no. 2 (Spring–Summer 1980): 254–271.

"Brother Oedipus." Rpt. in *Modern Canadian Short Stories*, ed. Wayne Grady. Markham, Ontario: Penguin Books Canada Ltd., 1982.

"Preface." In George Bowering's *West Window*. Toronto: General Publishing Co. Limited, 1982.

"And the Four Animals." Rpt. in *Canadian Literature in English* 2, eds. Donna Bennett and Russell Brown. Toronto: Oxford University Press, 1983.

"Introduction." *The Collected Poems of Miriam Mandel*, ed. Sheila Watson. Edmonton, Alberta: Longspoon Press / NeWest Press, 1984.

"Antigone." Rpt. in *Stories by Canadian Women*, ed. Rosemary Sullivan. Toronto: Oxford University Press, 1984.

"Antigone," Rpt. in *Illuminations: The Days of Our Youth*, eds. Andrew Garrod and David Staines. Toronto: Gage Publishing Limited, 1984.

The Double Hook. New Canadian Library. Afterword by F. T. Flahiff. Toronto: McClelland & Stewart Limited, 1984.

Five Stories. Toronto: The Coach House Press, 1985.

"About Seventy-one Poems for People." Afterword, in George Bowering's *Seventy-One Poems For People*. Red Deer, Alberta: RDC Press, 1985.

"Michael Ondaatje: The Mechanization of Death." Rpt. in *Spider Blues: Essays on Michael Ondaatje*, ed. Sam Solecki. Montréal: Véhicule Press, 1985.

"Be Fruitful and Multiply." Trans. Sheila Watson of Madelaine Ferron's story. *Canadian Short Fiction: From Myth to Modern*, ed. W. H. New. Scarborough: Prentice-Hall Canada Inc., 1986.

"Antígona." Spanish translation of "Antigone" by Lake Sagaris. *La Reina Negra y Otras Historias: Antología de Cuentos Canadienses*, ed. Lake Sagaris. Santiago: Casa Canada, 1989.

"By the Time I Got to University." *Line*, no. 14 (Fall 1989): 98–102.

An excerpt from *Deep Hollow Creek* in *Brick*, no. 42/43 (Winter/Spring 1992): 24–29.

Deep Hollow Creek. Toronto: McClelland & Stewart Limited, 1992.

Il Doppio Amo. Italian translation of *The Double Hook* by Francesca Romana Paci. Marina di Patti: Pungitopo Editrice, 1992.

"And the Four Animals." Rpt. in *Likely Stories: A Postmodern Sampler*, eds. George Bowering and Linda Hutcheon. Toronto: Coach House Press, 1992.

"Antigone." Rpt. in *Reading Life Writing: An Anthology*, ed. Marlene Kadar. Toronto: Oxford University Press, 1993.

"Foreword." In J. Pecover's *The Work of Justice*. Edmonton, Alberta: Wolf Willow Press, 1996.

"Antigone." Italian translation by Carla Pezzini Plevano and Francesca Valente Gorjup. *Altre Terre: Racconti contemporanei del Canada anglofono*, ed. Branko Gorjup. Venezia Lido: Supernova Edizioni, 1996.

Deep Hollow Creek. New Canadian Library. Afterword by Jane Urquhart. Toronto: McClelland & Stewart Limited, 1999.

"And the Four Animals." Rpt. in *And Other Stories*, ed. George Bowering. Vancouver: Talonbooks, 2001.

Wyndham Lewis and Expressionism. Waterloo. ON: MLR Editions Canada, 2003. (Sheila Watson's doctoral thesis).

"Rough Answer." Japanese translation by William Kischuck. *Kawamura Review of English Studies*, no. 8 (2003): 17–24.

"From the Journals of Sheila Watson." *Brick*, no. 72 (Winter 2003): 82–92.

A Father's Kingdom: The Complete Short Fiction, New Canadian Library. Afterword by Glenn Willmott. Toronto: McClelland & Stewart Limited, 2004.

"Brother Oedipus – a story." Japanese translation by William Kischuck. *Kawamura Review of English Studies*, no. 9 (2004): 2–15.

"Antigone." Rpt. in *Elements of Fiction*, eds. Robert Scholes, Nancy R. Comley, Carl H. Klaus, and David Staines. Toronto: Oxford University Press, 2004.

"Antigone." Rpt. in *Canadian Short Stories*, eds. Russell Brown and Donna Bennett. Toronto: Pearson Longman, 2005.

"The Black Farm—A Modern Allegory," a Japanese translation by William Kischuck in *The Journal of Kawamura Gakuen Women's University*, Vol. 16, no. 1 (2005): 151-166.

Sources

Sources have for the most part been noted in the text and in my acknowledgements. What follows is a summary rather than a detailed account of my indebtedness.

My main sources have been, aside from my own memories of persons, places, and events, the papers Sheila Watson, sent to me during the last years of her life. These include letters to rather than by her, although there are some drafts of letters she wrote but did not necessarily send, and in one case a correspondent, Anne Angus, near the end of her own life, had returned to Sheila the letters that over the years Sheila had written to her. The papers also include the journals Sheila kept between 1955 and 1995, extensive notes she took of her truly prodigious reading, drafts of stories and poems and novels. They also include tax returns, bank statements, contracts, bills paid—the detritus of living.

Sheila's sister, Norah Mitchell, and her family have shared with me materials and accounts that bear upon family history and lore, and, in Norah's case, memories of the early years. These are included in a draft, "As I Recall," which she had written in 1995 for the benefit of her own family. Her daughter Susan has shared with me her exploration of the family's history. Her daughter Barbara has shared with me what is obvious from the beginning of Sheila's story. Information about the background of the Doherty family in Ontario has been kindly provided by Father Frank Mallon, CSB, their family historian.

Various libraries and archives have given me access to times and places that were parts of Sheila's life. I returned again and again to the Public Libraries of Vancouver and New Westminster. The archivist of the Sisters of Saint Ann in Victoria helped me to gain access to the schools in which Sheila, her sister, and her mother were educated.

The archives of the University of British Columbia—including the papers of Jack Shadbolt and of Roy Daniells—provided, aside from these, important documents pertaining to the Letters Club of UBC and a copy of Sheila's MA thesis. The archives of the University of Alberta at Edmonton are, as the young might once have put it, "far out;" they are located some eighty blocks from the campus, although they seem closer to their mandate than any other archives I have visited. Wilfred Watson's papers are deposited here, and, of course, the archives of the University's Department of English.

McMaster University's archives include the papers of Jack McClelland, and the Baptist Church of Canada has its archives on this same campus, which include the archives of Moulton College. In Ottawa, I consulted the National Archives, where Marshall McLuhan's papers are deposited.

Archives at the University of Toronto have assisted me in tracing Sheila's and Wilfred's studies there, and, earlier, the studies of her father, his sister, and his brother. Ellen Seligman has kindly made available to me her correspondence with Sheila during the preparation of *Deep Hollow Creek* for publication.

I have interviewed, and in many instances taped interviews with, former students of Sheila, with former colleagues, friends, family, fellow writers. Sheila's papers, including these interviews, will in time be available in the library of St. Michael's College at the University of Toronto.

I am indebted as well to published works: To Sheila's own published writings, of course (see Appendix B); to her comments at her first public reading from *The Double Hook*, printed as "What I'm Going To Do" in *Sheila Watson: A Collection, Open Letter* (Winter 1974–75); to her "By the Time I Got to University," in *Line*, Number 14, Fall 1989; her interview with Jim Adams in *Western Catholic Reporter*, 11 May 1975; her interview with George Melnyk, "A talk with Sheila Watson," *Quill & Quire* (September, 1975); her interview with Daphne Marlatt, Roy Kiyooka, and Pierre Coupey, in *Capilano Review* 8–9 (1976); her interview with Bruce Meyer and Brian O'Riordan, "It's What You Say," in their *In Their Words: Interviews with Fourteen Canadian Writers* (Toronto: Anansi, 1984).

For information about Dr. C. E. Doherty's career in New Westminster, I am particularly indebted to Dr. Richard G. Foulkes's essay, "British Columbia Mental Health Services: Historical Perspective to 1961," which was published in *The Canadian Medical Association Journal*, volume 85, 9 September 1961, and to M. E. Kelm's "A Life Apart: The Experience of Women and the Asylum Practice of Charles Doherty at British Columbia's Provincial Hospital for the Insane, 1905–15," published in *Canadian Bulletin of Medical History*, volume 11, number 2 (1994). In a more general sense, I have been grateful for Geoffrey Reaume's *Remembrance of Patients Past: Patient Life at the Toronto Hospital for the Insane, 1870–1940* (Oxford University Press, 2000).

The history of fish canneries on the Fraser River, including the role of members of Sheila's family in this history, has been brought into focus for me by Mitsou Yesaki's and Harold and Kathy Steves's *Steveston Cannery Row: An Illustrated History* (Richmond, BC: Lulu Island Printing Ltd., 1998). The early essays in the catalogue for the inaugural exhibition celebrating the opening of the new Vancouver Art Gallery at Robson Square in 1983, published under the title *Vancouver: Art and*

Artists 1931–1983, provided important insight into the history of the visual arts in Vancouver during Sheila Watson's formative years. Margaret Ormsby's *British Columbia: A History* (Toronto: Macmillan of Canada, 1971) provided details of the unrest that disrupted the province, and especially the city of Vancouver, during the early and mid-thirties. My visits to the Cariboo district of British Columbia, and to Dog Creek, and Sheila's accounts of her time there, have been secured for me by Robin Skelton's *They call it the CARIBOO* (Victoria: Sono Nis Press, 1980), and especially by Hilary Place's *Dog Creek: A Place in the Cariboo* (Surrey, BC: Heritage House, 1999). Edith Down's *A Century of Service: A History of the Sisters of Saint Ann and their Contribution to Education in British Columbia, the Yukon and Alaska* (Victoria: The Sisters of Saint Ann, 1966) furnished me with important information about Sheila's early education. Alfreda Hall's *Per Ardua: The Story of Moulton College, Toronto, 1888–1954* (The Moulton College Alumnae Association, 1987) provided valuable materials about the school where Sheila taught in the late forties. Philip Marchand's *Marshall McLuhan: The Medium and the Messenger* (Toronto: Random House, 1989) clarified for me aspects of Wilfred Watson's relationship with McLuhan.

The quotation from Flannery O'Connor on page 315 of the text is from an article in *The New Yorker*, 29 January 2001, page 87, by Hilton Als, entitled "This Lonesome Place."

It has not been my intention to provide an exhaustive bibliography for this book, for such a bibliography would include everything I have ever read. Because my concern has been with a "life" of Sheila Watson, I am little inclined to write the life of that "life."

Acknowledgements

My largest debt, and the one I most willingly and gratefully acknowledge, is to Sheila Watson's family—especially to her sister, Norah Mitchell, and to her nieces Barbara Mitchell and Susan Mitchell. Norah Mitchell has died since I started this work, but not before she had shared with me her memories of her sister and of their family, and not before she had adopted me into her family. To Barb I owe a friendship based upon our ties with Sheila—and, more recently, with her mother. She has been less a source for me than a witness to events that in her recountings have changed the colour of my mind. Susan has shared with me her researches into her family's history. Thanks to her diligence and to her kindness, I have been able to find my bearings in the tableland of 'begets' and 'begats' that produced Sheila Watson.

My debt to Wilfred Watson's sister, Doreen Dunning, and to her husband, John, may be less extensive, but it is no less real than my debt to Sheila's family. Their determination to satisfy the wishes of Wilfred and of Sheila resulted in a kind of generous co-operation which has made my task possible.

When one writes about someone who has been a part of one's life, the range of indebtedness is especially wide and deep and complex. To Diane Bessai and to Shirley Neuman I owe friendships that originated in, and will always in some sense remain inseparable from, our friendships with Sheila. They have become my mainstays as they had in their separate ways been hers. To Diane I am indebted for access to Sheila's Edmonton years—and, indeed, to her I owe a 'home' in Edmonton. She has generously and sympathetically read what I have written, and she has been responsible for my association with NeWest Press. To Shirley I owe such traces as are present here of the intense clarity of perception and of memory that mark her recallings of Sheila and of Wilfred, and more than I can say, I am indebted to her selflessness in sharing these with me. I recognize that what I have written is not what either of them might have chosen to write, but I also know that I could not have proceeded without their help and encouragement.

In Edmonton, I am grateful to those who shared with me their recollections of Sheila and of Wilfred, and to the archives of the University of Alberta. The archives contain Wilfred Watson's papers and the archives of the Department of English, and its staff has been wonderfully gracious and helpful. Friends, former students, and colleagues of Sheila and Wilfred who shared their reminiscences with me include Juliet and Rowland McMaster, Patricia Clements, Irma Sommerfeld, Caterina Edwards, Mary Hamilton, and Douglas Barbour.

In the Vancouver area, I am indebted to Sherrill and John Grace and to George Bowering for time, for hospitality, and for sharp memories. I am also indebted to the University of British Columbia's Special Collections Division, to the Vancouver Public Library, and to the New Westminster Public Library. A week spent at Green College in the University of British Columbia in the spring of 2004 provided me with the opportunity to 'float' some of my ideas about Sheila Watson and about writing her life. To Linda Morra, facilitator of this stay and indeed discoverer—for me, at least—of Sheila Watson's letter to Emily Carr, I shall always be grateful.

To the Sisters of St. Ann in Victoria I owe special thanks for the generosity with which, through their archivist-librarian, Margaret Cantwell, ssa, they have made available to me documents that bear upon Sheila's school days in New Westminster. To the late Edith Down, ssa, author of the history of their order in British Columbia and friend of Sheila Watson, I owe an afternoon of frank and lively talk. Also in Victoria, Stephen Scobie spoke to me of Sheila and of his years at the University of Alberta. In Nanaimo, Linda Shannon shared with me her memories of Sheila's and of Wilfred's last years.

In the village of Ashcroft, up country from the coast, at the entrance to the Cariboo, the curator of the local museum and archives generously and bemusedly answered my questions—and sent me information—about a parrot named Bob.

It is very difficult to know where to begin and where to end when it comes to acknowledging indebtedness to people and to resources associated with Toronto. To Ellen Seligman of McClelland & Stewart, I owe the first suggestion to undertake this project, and to her I owe as well access to her correspondence with Sheila Watson when *Deep Hollow Creek* was being prepared for publication. To Leslie Sanders and David Staines, I owe years of friendship, their memories of Sheila, their encourage-ment, and in David's case, a sympathetic although not entirely approving response to what I had first written. To Patricia Brückmann and to Donald Theall, who were here from the beginning, I owe talk of those times, and in Pat's case particularly, memo-ries of Sheila. Both read early versions of what I have written, and both confirmed—in their separate ways—my responsibility for what I have done. Father Frank Mallon, csb generously provided me with invaluable materials about the history of the Doherty family in Ontario. Professor William Blissett answered with wit and preci-sion my questions about his days at ubc with Wilfred Watson, and his contact with both Sheila and Wilfred during their time in Toronto in the forties. Margaret Morriss, one of the first commentators on *The Double Hook,* is an old friend who worked self-lessly with me cataloguing Sheila and Wilfred's books and discussing this project. To her I owe—among much else—a sense of the bond between Sheila's and Michael Ondaatje's Kips. Tessie Chakkalakal, together with Anne Bains, had helped to pack and had transported those books from Nanaimo to Toronto, and Tessie, along with Leslie Sanders and Mark Bronson, participated with me in the ritual I describe in the Epilogue/Prologue to this book. I am grateful to Paul Tiessen and to Hildi Froese Tiessen for their recollections of student days in Edmonton, and of life under Sheila's watchful eye. I am especially grateful to Paul for persisting with, and overseeing the long overdue publication of, Sheila's doctoral thesis.

I am indebted to those who have been of assistance to me at the archives of the University of Toronto and to the archivist, Evelyn Collins, of the University of St. Michael's College, to the archives of the Province of Ontario, and the National Archives of Canada in Ottawa. At McMaster University, I wish to thank Dr. C. Mark Steinacher, the curator of the archives of the Baptist Church of Canada, where the archives of Moulton Ladies College are housed, and those who assisted me when I examined Jack McClelland's papers, which are housed in McMaster's Special Collections.

At various times during the past several years, friends and family have shared in my work in practical as well as in subtler ways. My gratitude—like humility, as T. S. Eliot described it—is endless, and includes in its penumbra Sharon Davidson, Jeanne Gershater, Tony Burgess, and Glenn Willmott, as well as those students who over the years have read Sheila with me. It also includes Mark Bronson, who dug and drove and listened and knew what the ending was all about, and Matthew Bronson, who drew what he felt, and Dorothy and Brian Parker, who have been a part of all this since that autumn night when, with Pat and John Brückmann, we sang to Rapunzel to let down her golden hair. It includes Patricia and Gerald Neely, who have tended to me in Victoria. And it includes my family, who remain always generous and patient, always unquestioning. Thicker than water, indeed!

I have saved three names to the last. To Kathleen Martin-James I owe the gratitude one feels when someone sees what you are trying to do. To Bill Kischuck I owe hours of Tokyo–Toronto telephone conversations about Sheila's work, the pleasure of seeing that work translated into Japanese, the excitement of witnessing another artist's engagement with Sheila's legacy. And to my editor, Smaro Kamboureli, I owe, besides the customary debts one owes one's editor, the satisfaction of knowing that someone has read what I hoped was on the page.

Index

Davey, Frank, 287, 289–90

Davies, Robertson, 200, 207–8; *Love and Libel*, 208

Davis, Herbert, 177

Day Lewis, Cecil, 141, 196

de Beck, George, 23, 204

Deleuze, Gilles, 321

Dickens, Charles, 54; *Little Dorrit*, 321

Diefenbaker, John, 209

Djwa, Sandra, *Professing English at UBC*, 65

Dobbs, Kildare, 81, 142

Dog Creek, BC, 1, 2, 34–46, 48–49 52, 56, 61, 74, 78, 84, 89, 167, 188, 204, 225, 230–31, 244, 272, 274, 288–89, 307, 311, 315; photos, 35, 38

Doherty, Agatha, see Myatt, Agatha

Doherty, Bernard (great grandfather), 6, 7

Doherty, Brian (cousin), 241, 268; *Father Malachy's Miracle*, 241

Doherty, Charles Frederick (great uncle), 7

Doherty, Charles Edward (Charlie) (father), 6, 10–18, 27, 204, 270; photo, 6

Doherty, Charles Edward (Kelly) (brother), 6, 14, 17, 27, 45, 58; photo, 18

Doherty, D'Arcy, 241

Doherty, Frederick (uncle), 6, 7,

Doherty, Mary Ida Elwena (Ween) (née Martin) (mother), 6–8, 13, 16–21, 27–28, 32, 45, 54–55, 58, 72, 193, 207, 268–70, 300; photo, 8

Doherty, Marguerite (aunt), 7

Doherty, Maria (née Henley) (grandmother), 7

Doherty, Norah (sister) (later Mrs. Mitchell), 6, 10, 14–15, 18, 24, 27, 32, 39, 45, 54–55, 57, 58, 72, 192–93, 207, 267–69, 273; photo, 328

Doherty, William Charles (Bill) (brother), 6, 14, 17–18, 27, 45, 57, 192–93, 202, 268, 270; photo, 18

Doherty, William Frederick (grandfather), 7

Doherty, William Manning (uncle), 7

Dostoevsky, Feodor, 129–30

Doto (dog), 78, 86–87, 102–3, 113, 119, 142, 148, 162, 171–72

Doyle, Fan (great aunt), 16, 27, 226

Doyle, Henry (great uncle), 16, 27, 226

Ducros, Mr. and Mrs., 158

Duncan, BC, 51–55, 272–73

Duncan, Ronald, *This Way to the Tomb*, 114

Dunning, Doreen, *see* Watson, Doreen

Dunning, Joan (niece of Wilfred Watson), 225–26

Dunning, John, 272

Dyson, Constance (Connie), 155, 215, 331

Edmonton, AB, 34, 52, 69, 74, 76, 81, 86–8, 157, 161–2, 165, 170, 178, 181, 208, 211, 221–22, 272

Edwards, Caterina, 233, 242

Eliot, T. S., 2, 3, 25, 30, 52, 59, 63, 78, 85, 99, 142, 145, 155, 163, 169, 190, 194, 199, 205–6, 214–15, 217, 244, 266, 275–76, 318–19; *Four Quartets*, 63; "Prufrock", 206; "Choruses from *The Rock*," 318–19; *The Waste Land*, 63, 169

Elizabeth II, 216–17

Endicott, Betty, 64, 175, 221, 265

Endicott, Norman, 64, 76, 175–76, 185, 195, 212–13, 221, 238, 265

English, Anna Virginia (daughter of Marshall), 9

English, Marshall Martin (great uncle), 8, 9, 16

Faber & Faber, 52, 70, 81, 85, 99, 128, 145, 155–56, 163, 196, 215,

Fairley, Barker, 184, 196, 237

Ferron, Madeleine, 254; "Be Fruitful and Multiply" (English translation of "Le peuplement de la terre"), 254; *Coeur de Sucre*, 254; "Le peuplement de la terre", 254; "Sugar Heart" (English translation of "Coeur de Sucre"), 254

Faulkner, William 44, 108, 169, 200; *As I Lay Dying*, 200

Fiddle (horse), 39, 43, 45–46, 189; photo, 43

Fitzgerald, F. Scott, 180

Flahiff, Fred, 185–87, 204, 207–8, 211–13, 215, 217–20, 232, 255, 265, 278–82, 298–300, 307, 312–13

Flaubert, Gustave, 185

Ford, Ford Maddox, 217

Foucault, Michel, 310, 321; *Surveiller et Punir* (Discipline and Punish), 321

Franciere, Arlette, 254

Fraser, Sylvia, *Book of Strange*, 295

Frobenius, Leo, 244

Frye, Northrop, 76, 184, 186, 200, 236–37, 245, 259

Gaddis, Thomas, 319–20; *Birdman of Alcatraz*, 320

Gatenby, Greg, 298

Gibbons, Stella, *Cold Comfort Farm*, 81

Gilson, Etienne, 67, 68, 203–5

Globe and Mail, 199, 299

Goddard, Grace, 22, 204

Golding, William, *Inheritors*, 114, 116

Gould, Glenn, 264

Gouzien, Madame, 91, 94, 96, 98, 100–3, 106, 113–14, 116, 118, 123, 125, 127, 132–33, 142, 144, 153, 159–61

Grace, John, 1

Grace, Sherill, 1, 42, 307, *Regression and Apocalypse*, 307

Grant MacEwan College, 34

Greene, Graham, 136

Grube, John, 237

Hamburger, Michael, 196, 237

Hamilton, Mary, 264

Hammond, Agnes, 101

Harris, Lawren, 211

Hart-Davis, Rupert, 196

Heathcote, Stephen, 213–14, 219–20; photo, 220

Heuze, M., 122–23

Hindmarch, Gladys, 294

Hine, Daryl, 294; *Carnal and the Crane*, 294; *Postscripts*, 294

Hodgins, Jack, 273; *Barclay Family Theatre*, 273; "Mr. Pernouski's Dream", 273–74; *Resurrection of Joseph Bourne*, 273; *Spit Delaney's Island*, 273

Hogarth Press, 94, 114–15

Homer, 203, 230, 290

Homer, Ethel, 22

Hopkins, Gerard Manley, 30, 137, 191

Howell, Thora, 294

Hudson Review, 81, 101

Humphrey, Ruth, 68, 87, 115, 161, 331

Humphreys, Helen, 295; *Gods and Other Mortals*, 295; *Nuns Looking Anxious, Listening to Radios*, 295

Hutchinson, Sybil, 77, 198

Innis, Harold, 280

Ismael, Jamila, 231

Jackel, David, 263

Jackson, A. Y., 77, 307; "Cariboo Spring", 77

Jacobs, Jane, 251, 280

James, Henry, 186

John, Augustus, 210

Johnson, Dennis, 286

Jones, J. T., 157, 222, 233

Joyce, James, 29, 59, 80, 169, 177, 185–86, 189–90, 230, 236, 242, 324; "Dead", 79; *Dubliners*, 169; *Portrait of the Artist as a Young Man*, 169; *Ulysses*, 169, 200, 203, 264

Juno (dog), 39, 45, 78; photo, 41

Keary, Emma (later Mrs. de Beck), 23, 24, 204

Kearns, Eliza (great great grandmother), 8

Kenner, Hugh, 248, 264

Kennett, William, 177, 185–86, 238

Kiyooka, Roy, 40, 234, 284, 294, 301, 314; "portrait of a foot", 301–3

Klee, Paul, "Sacrifice barbare", 97, 104

Knopf, Alfred A., 106

Kraus, Greta, 184

Kriesel, Henry, 223, 233–34, 253, 256, 258, 261, 263, 314–15; "Sheila Watson in Edmonton", 263

Kroetsch, Robert, 287

La Certe, Father, 239

Laing, Mr., 206

Lamb, Charles, 206

Lane, Diane, *see* Bessai, Diane

Langley Prairie, BC, 45, 48–51, 272

Layton, Irving, *Red Carpet for the Sun*, 202

Le Jacq, Father J. M., 38

Le Jeune, Father, 242

Leland, Father Charles, 3, 294, 300

Le Pan, Douglas, 200

Letters Club, 30, 44

Levy-Beaulieu, Victor, 287

Lewis, Anne (Froanna), 211–12, 214–16, 270–71

Lewis, Hunter, 29, 31, 68

Lewis, Wyndham, 29, 64, 124–25, 166, 175–76, 179, 182, 187, 193–96, 205, 208–12, 214–17, 236–39, 245–48, 259, 263–64, 306–7, 324; *Apes of God*, 194–95, 127, 236; *Armada*, 247; *Art of Being Ruled*, 236; *Blast*, 255; *Blasting and Bombardiering*, 210; *Canadian Gunpit*, 247; *Darts Player*, 215; *Gun Pit*, 210; *Human Age*, 214; *Malign Fiesta*, 124–25; *Monstre Gai*, 124; *Nude Study*, 215; *Self-Condemned*, 212; *Study of a Girl*, 215; *Witch on Cow Back*, 275; *Woman seated on a couch*, 215

Livesay, Dorothy, 234, 252, 256–57

Tennyson, Alfred, 80, 237, 246

Theall, Donald, 238, 280

Thesen, Sharon, 289

Thomas, Dylan, 76, 149

Thoreau, Henry David, 28, 192, 315; *Walden*, 165

Tiessen, Paul, 64, 253, 263

Times Literary Supplement, 98, 114

Toronto, ON, 1–3, 60–64, 70, 72, 74, 76–77, 89, 162, 167, 169, 171, 175–96, 204–8, 211–12, 215, 219–22, 225–26, 231, 235, 245, 248–53, 259, 265, 272, 278, 281–82, 293–94, 299, 304, 306, 315, 326, 329

Trotter, Marjorie, 61

Trudeau, Pierre, 280

Turton, Conway, 198

Twain, Mark, 8

University of Alberta, 34–35, 64, 74, 76, 81, 163, 191, 222–25, 230, 234, 254, 258, 261, 273, 277, 297, 322, 324–25, 339, 342, 343

University of British Columbia (UBC), 22, 24–25, 27–33, 44–45, 48, 52–53, 55, 57, 60, 64–70, 76–77, 89, 98, 101, 124, 128, 148, 185–86, 200, 204, 227, 234–35, 240, 273, 325, 339, 343

University of Guelph, 281

University of London, 224

University of Manitoba, 65

University of New Brunswick, 237

University of Saskatchewan, 263, 284

University of Toronto, 2, 6, 7, 27, 53, 60, 64, 176–78, 184–85, 200, 206–7, 234, 236, 253, 259, 326, 340, 344

University of Western Ontario, 224

Utrillo, Maurice, v, 93, 101, 111, 120–21

Vancouver, BC, 22, 24, 28–31, 41, 54–55, 65, 67–70, 72, 77–78, 86–87, 95, 135, 149, 161–62, 170–72, 272

Vanderpant, John, 31

Varley, Frederick, 31

Victoria College, University of Toronto, 68, 76, 176, 184

Wadsworth, Edward, *Dazzle-Ships in Drydock at Liverpool*, 210

Wagner, Geoffrey, *Wyndham Lewis: Portrait of the Artist as The Enemy*, 211

Wah, Fred, 289; *Breathin' My Name With A Sigh*, 292

Wain, John, 215–16

Watson, Sheila, "About Pelicans", 255–56; "And the Four Animals", 48, 49, 262; "Antigone", 2, 3, 12, 16, 23, 24, 70, 71, 80, 128, 202–3, 238, 294, 296, 304; "Barren Lands", 43, 44, 50, 80; "Black Farm", 70, 80, 101, 114, 127, 148, 163, 203, 206, 322; "Brother Oedipus", 70, 71, 72, 80, 81, 203, 206, 267, 322; "Canada and Wyndham Lewis the Artist", 248; *City and Literature* (editor) (unpublished), 251–52; *Deep Hollow Creek*, 33, 38, 40, 41, 42, 46, 47, 48, 49, 50, 61, 62, 63, 77, 90, 169, 188–89, 198, 262, 273–74, 307–13, 318, 322, 325, 327; *Double Hook*, 13, 34, 39–41, 47–49, 59, 61–64, 66, 70, 76–77, 79–85, 89, 100, 114, 116, 124, 141–42, 145, 147, 150–51, 155–56, 158, 163, 164–69, 191, 195–201, 205–9, 227, 234, 237–38, 254, 263, 267, 282,

F. T. FLAHIFF first met Sheila Watson when they were both graduate students in Marshall McLuhan's graduate seminar at the University of Toronto. Toronto became Flahiff's permanent home where he taught at St. Michael's College in the University of Toronto until his retirement in 1999.